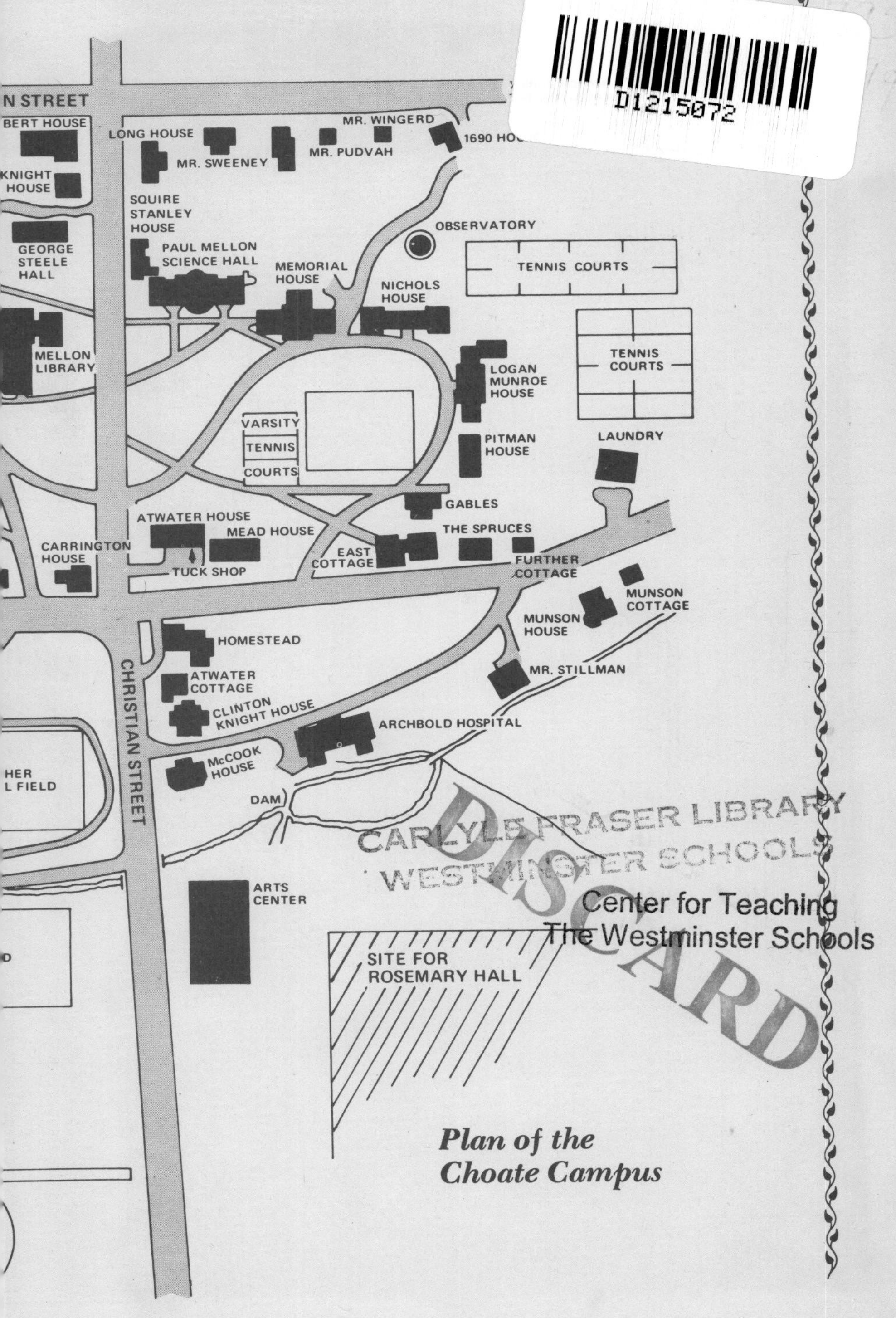

Plan of the Choate Campus

A WORLD OF OUR OWN

A World of Our Own

NOTES ON LIFE AND LEARNING IN A BOYS' PREPARATORY SCHOOL

by Peter S. Prescott

COWARD, McCANN & GEOGHEGAN, INC. / NEW YORK

Second Impression

Library of Congress Catalog Card Number: 75-104691

PRINTED IN THE UNITED STATES OF AMERICA

TO

My Parents

for many reasons,
but not least for
their concern that
their children
receive the best
possible education

Yet some men, friendly enough of nature but of small judgment in learning, do think I take too much pains and spend too much time in setting forth these children's affairs. But those good men were never brought up in Socrates' school, who saith plainly that no man goeth about a more godly purpose than he that is mindful of the good bringing-up both of his own and other men's children.

Therefore I trust good and wise men will think well of this my doing.

ROGER ASCHAM, *The Schoolmaster* (*1570*)

"The probability is, Adeimantus," I said, "that the direction given by education will determine the course of all that follows. Does not like always call like after it?"

Republic, 136

Our mission as concerns the native populations is one of civilizing and nationalizing. . . . We have a life which is the emanation of a spirit and the realization of a faith, to give to the peoples whom we wish to bring along with us.

J. M. R. NORTON DE MATOS,
a Portuguese official in Mozambique

You don't need anything outside. Everything is inside the School.

THE HEADMASTER OF CHOATE,
quoted by one of his youngest students

Contents

Preface

> None of us can tell it like it is. The best he can do is tell it as he sees it, tell it as it ought to be.
>
> SEYMOUR ST. JOHN

This is a book about a school, but it is only incidentally a book about education. Choate may properly claim that education is what the school is about; it does claim that it offers the best education available anywhere in America at the secondary level, and this may be true, too. I don't know. I have not studied any other schools, and because I distrust comparisons, I doubt whether such a claim is particularly useful or, indeed, verifiable. I wanted to look at Choate as a way of life. It seems that we Americans do not know as much about ourselves as we once thought we did. I wanted to see whether a detailed study of a single American institution—one not normally open to outside scrutiny—could tell us anything worth knowing about ourselves. I thought it would help if the institution I picked were one involved with training people to grow up and succeed in America.

I have not, of course, avoided education altogether. There is a chapter on classes in this book and, scattered about, a good deal of chatter about education—what it is and how it should be conducted. Most of it is not, however, my chatter; I am simply recording the views of men charged with educating a necessarily select number of boys of high school age. As I attended uncounted classes at Choate, I decided that Choate's particular kind of classroom education was not sufficiently different from what I knew of classroom education elsewhere to be responsible for Choate's special character as a school. One cannot find in Choate's classrooms much of what the headmaster calls "the Choate experience," which is the experience of living at Choate, pretty well cut off from the outside world, day and night, for years.

At the same time I decided I had no special interest in, or competence to talk about, theories of education. I have made no study of the subject. My sympathies, I suppose, are with John Holt and his perceptive observations of how schools and teachers can prevent children from learning, and with Martin Duberman, who writes: "The entire superstructure of authoritarian control in our schools must give way if we are to enable people to assume responsibility for and to take pleasure in their own lives. We cannot expect aliveness and involvement when we are busy inculcating docility and compliance."* On the other hand, I have no great confidence in students who wish to hire their own teachers or design their own curriculum. There are more exciting things to learn than students are aware of; more disciplines than they know, which, after tedium, break forth into delight; more good books to read than they have yet heard of; more of the past that is relevant than they suspect; and more use in "useless" knowledge than they, at their age, can possibly understand. In short, there are only dull teachers and dull students—no dull subjects. Those courses which the rabid adolescent finds particularly suffocating may, after he has pursued his interest down a narrow gopher hole, prove the saving of his soul.

And that is all the educational theory the reader will get from me. My interest is in people, in how they live, organize themselves into societies, and submit to rules and disciplines. I am interested in power: how it is obtained, consolidated, and used, and how people allow others to assume power over them. I am interested in private institutions that maintain positions of

* Sources of all materials quoted from other than Choate publications will be found in the "Notes" at the end of the book.

privilege and prestige in our supposedly open and democratic society; I am interested in the nature of autocracy because our American autocrats are such articulate explainers; they mean to be reasonable, even benign.

I am also interested in young people, not—as I indicated above—because I believe they have any special insights or powers, but because they are interesting people, because they are more mature now than they were when I was one of them, and most particularly, because in our country and in our time we are witnessing a massive rebellion against the young. Some of this strain is evident at Choate. The way a society teaches its children is, of course, a barometer indicating the health of that society, but throughout the country, grown people, usually with adolescent children of their own, are shrieking their fear and hatred of the young. We are only now, and very slowly, becoming aware of what is happening. It is a disturbing phenomenon —more frightening, I think, than our dwindling adventure in colonial warfare. What our attitudes toward adolescents will do to them when they in their turn become mature and powerful I cannot imagine, but any adult who has worked with teen-agers knows that they do not now see much in maturity to attract them. Because our government seems determined to encourage the tidal flood of feeling against youth, we may be in for bad days in the not too distant future—unless, of course, youth comes to its senses, dries up and goes away, or joins fraternities and twirls batons, singing "On, Wisconsin" as the marshmallows turn black upon the coals.

Finally, I am interested in language: in language used as a weapon, as a cloak thrown over truth, as an obstacle to understanding and an impediment to communication. Language is what we use to prop up beliefs we know no longer merit our belief. Language is what we use to confuse each other and ourselves. "What is real and what is not?" Mary Poppins asks. "Can you tell me or I tell you?" At Choate, everyone is engaged in explaining the truth, but their truths rarely coincide. Often the truth cannot be determined. What remains is what people *say* is the truth, and that is what they act upon. What people say, what they believe, I thought, was what I wanted to examine. I wanted to see why a few people with the best good will in the world seem to harm the institution they love and the extent to which the way they use language is responsible for the confusion. Why did it sometimes seem that the more people *said* they were doing a good job, the less able they were to *do* a good job?

None of these thoughts was in my mind when I went back to Choate to write my book about it. I had been a student there for three years, from 1950 to 1953. I had liked the school, pretty much, did not regret the time I spent there, had very much admired three or four teachers. I had come to think of the school as something permanent, unchanging, and, damn it, quite right in being just that. Outsiders disagreed, but what did *they* know? As is usually the case with country clubs, suburban homes, private schools or any piece of turf that people of means stake out for their own profit and enjoyment, Choate and its sister preparatory schools are regularly subject to irrational attack. In the spring of 1967 the brouhaha concerned reports that Ivy League colleges were spurning preparatory schools and openly courting public high schools. The affair made the papers, and Seymour St. John, headmaster of Choate, wrote an excellent reply to the New York *Times*. I had for some years thought of writing a book about Choate—a portrait of an institution—and St. John's letter provided the cue to action. Would St. John let me hang around the school for a few months to gather material for a book which would show Choate as it really was? St. John said yes.

As it happened, the year I watched Choate in action turned out to be the most unsettling that anyone could remember. I had thought I would complete my research by December, but in fact, I stayed on through June, to see how things would turn out. Things never do turn out, of course, and what I saw at Choate and have reported in this book are still very much in the process of development.

I began my research at Choate in September, 1967; I called a halt to it at the end of June, 1968. I remained in touch with a few masters and students at Choate, however, through December, 1969—many of these were kind enough to take the trouble to come to my house to talk to me at length about what had happened at the school since I left.

A few points: This book occasionally looks back into Choate's past and a year or two into the future, but its concern is with Choate's academic year of 1967 to 1968. When I say "that fall" I mean the fall of 1967, "that spring" the spring of 1968.

I have changed the names of all the students. The students are, of course, minors. They proved so remarkably candid and helpful to me, even in matters in which they broke the law, that they must be protected.

I have not changed the name of any adult at Choate, though I have occasionally concealed a master's name when it seemed appropriate to do so and, if necessary, changed other information about him—his age, for instance, or the number of children he has. The ages of faculty members, when given, are calculated as of February 1, 1968—roughly the midpoint of the academic year.

No dialogue in this book has been invented or in any way reconstructed. All of it was collected on a tape recorder, or in notes taken during an event, or, on a few rare occasions, jotted down within minutes of my hearing it. It is important to remember that most of what the boys and teachers say in this book does not represent their best judgments recollected in tranquillity, but what they actually said as an event developed, often when great emotion was involved. Heisenberg put a permanent crimp in my kind of research when he demonstrated that one cannot at the same time fix the position of a particle and the speed at which it moves. While I was at Choate, I tried to catch its motion; the book, by freezing that motion in a point of time as Choate goes on, perhaps fixes a position. The position is already slightly out of date, so it should also be understood that the opinions people expressed at school during that year may not be the views they hold today.

This book is in no way an official or institutional book. My presence at the school was authorized—had it not been, I could not have attended meals and faculty meetings, haunted dormitories and athletic fields. I made about one hundred trips to Choate that year, arriving at times before the rising bell and often staying to listen to bull sessions long after midnight. Everyone I met at Choate gave me freely of what he had least—his time—and nearly everyone was astonishingly candid. Until the end of the year, the question of the school's approval of my book did not arise. Understandably, after a difficult year ("The revolution toppled the high schools in 1968," Jerry Rubin wrote later), some at Choate developed doubts about the value of their candor and of a book that they could not control. Choate is accustomed to speaking of itself in the optative rather than in the indicative mood; it encourages others, as hard as it can, to do likewise. And so, for a few days in June I wallowed in a Sartrian confusion of *pour-soi* and *en-soi* because I was then told, in rather plain terms, that the way for me to write about Choate as it *is* was to describe it as it means to be, to describe what it is *for*. I was asked to submit my manuscript to the trustees; I declined to do so. No one at Choate has approved this book.

Perhaps the most important point is that Choate is an excellent school. I have promised to avoid comparisons, but I have no reason to believe that it is not one of the very best schools in the country. There are problems about Choate's kind of education, about the environment that Choate creates for its boys and teachers, but there can be no question—at least until we reconsider our entire concept of what education is—about Choate's viability. We need it, and therefore it is worth our support, our study, and our criticism. We need it to be better. A revolution, however, is under way at Choate, a revolution that began in the year I have described in this book. Some at Choate believe this revolution will destroy the school—a number of teachers have resigned for just that reason—and others believe the revolution will save the school.

Through no skill of mine, I was lucky enough to be present at the school as the revolution began. Choate's revolution was then, perhaps, not as spectacular as what was happening in colleges across the country, but it was an early sign of how disaffection in the colleges could seep down to younger students in much more rigorously controlled environments. Here, at Choate, one could see how such movements began. Moreover, I believe that crisis situations best show people as they really are. If we are strong, if we are good, we prove it when the bad news comes.

What I have tried to do, then, is to show, in the first part of this book, the kind of place Choate is—to introduce the scene and the cast—and then, in the second part, to show how Choate responded to a series of crises. Some of these problems Choate has faced since it began; others it encountered that year for the first time. Some at the school felt the succession of crises had accumulated a momentum of its own, that no answers had been reached by June, and that, for the first time, the school would open again in the fall not with its blackboards wiped clean, with everything to start from scratch again, but with these same crises unresolved, snorting and pawing in the classroom corridors and demanding everyone's attention.

My thanks are due first to Seymour St. John, headmaster of Choate, who allowed me unlimited access to whatever I needed to write this book. Without his cooperation, without his belief that "We never want anyone to see us except as we really are," I could not have begun. My thanks are due, too, to Choate's faculty and its wives, who allowed me to impose upon them remorselessly. I am particularly indebted to two men seldom mentioned in these pages. One is Porter Caesar, late of Choate and the most exciting teacher I ever encountered. Teachers like Caesar make learning worth the effort. I have not seen him for many years; he contributed nothing to the book, but he made it possible for me to write it. The other is Edward B. Ayres, Choate's alumni director, to whom I came with complaints and problems to be solved. I must also thank three former Choate masters—Jack Davison, John Lincoln, and John Geoffrey Wyatt—for their time, and Robert Atmore, a master on leave of absence that year. I am indebted to the late Dudley Fitts for giving me the title to the chapter on the two St. Johns. Two former masters at Choate, Jon van Leuven and Rodman Furnald, spent days poring over the manuscript, suggesting countless changes, never questioning the material that concerned them. I thank Choate's students who trusted me more than most adults would trust a reporter. They helped me obtain much of the more delicate information in this book; they made sure I met the proper people; they kept me informed of events at the school as they happened, or were about to happen. My especial thanks are due also to Helen Hudson, Eleanor Lake, David Barkhausen, James Ellison, and my parents for the professional skills they brought to the reading of the manuscript and the care they exercised in making suggestions. I am particularly indebted to my wife for her ideas, which I have pirated, and for her ability both to encourage and to challenge me on every point.

The faults are not theirs. They are mine.

March, 1970

PART ONE

SITUATION

Approaches and Arrivals

"Hurrah! hurrah! hurrah!" cried a young boy as he capered vigorously about, and clapped his hands. "I shall go to school." . . . "Well, Eric," said Fanny, raising her matter-of-fact quiet face from her endless work, "I doubt, dear, whether you will talk of it with quite as much joy a year hence."

F. W. FARRAR, *Eric, or, Little by Little* (1858)

It is no longer said—but sometimes thought—that teen-agers and middle-aged parents are so mutually destructive that it is better for both to be kept apart. The headmasters take over where the parents have failed and charge accordingly.

CYRIL CONNOLLY (1968)

New England *is* different, which is why they put the prep schools there. New England resists change, and when that is no longer possible it resists the fuss and foolishness of change that overcome the younger states, west of the Hudson River. New England rests upon its rocks, enduring. It is a good, sound place to go to school. In Connecticut, "The Gateway to New England," a senior Senator was recently shown to have diverted public funds to his private pocket. Censured by his colleagues, he announced that he is not only guiltless, but has somehow been vindicated—he ran for reelection. Why not? We in Connecticut change our opinions of our antique institutions slowly, if at all, so there was no hint of recalling this Senator when news of his guilt was splattered across newspapers in every state in the nation except Connecticut. Connecticut does things *its* way. It cherishes the death penalty, its punitive abortion and divorce laws. It maintains that a man may be deprived of property without due process of law—if someone sues you, the county sheriff arrives to confiscate your real property of equivalent value until, in future years, the case works its way through the courts.

But Connecticut cares about education and has done so since 1650 when, in the Code of the Connecticut General Court, the colony affirmed that "the good education of children is of singular behoof and benefit to any commonwealth." Some children, however, had not perceived this and cursed their parents ("they shall be put to death") and some parents were, clearly, "too indulgent and negligent of their duty" to instruct their children. Children who became "rude, stubborn and unruly" would be removed from their homes and placed with masters who "will strictly look unto and force them to submit unto government." Thus the beginning of Connecticut's first boarding schools.

Driving to Choate the usual way, which is up the Merritt Parkway, you can sense something of the character of the state, the heritage of the dour settlers who had fled repression in England and more repression in Massachusetts only to write Connecticut's Code of 1650. WELCOME TO CONNECTICUT, reads the sign posted at every border control point. DON'T SPEED. CONVICTION MEANS LOSS OF LICENSE. It does, too, although a girl once rather loosely connected to Yale said that *she* had always thought License Means Loss of Conviction. State Police Commissioner Leo Mulcahy, also known for his sense of humor, puts up little signs—HE WHO TAKES ONE FOR THE ROAD GETS A TROOPER FOR A CHASER—and puts out unmarked police cars.

Thus Connecticut. Over the Housatonic River and through the tunnel, bypassing New Haven, thank God, and on to Wallingford and Quinnipiac Street at Exit 64. There are signs for a summer theater, a Masonic Hospital, a Church of the Resurrection. The town announces itself with the Wallingford Steel Company belching smoke and glowing neon—STAINLESS STRIP TUBING SUPER METALS—an illuminated spoon handle on a billboard, and the sprawling, musty Victorian red brick plant of the Wallace Silversmiths.

This is Wallingford, population 29,920, the sign says, but more now. Altitude 100 feet. Connecticut is flat and ugly here and knows it. It is country to get *through* as quickly as possible, so exits from the parkway are infrequent. And yet, outside of Wallingford, a rural atmosphere unrolls quickly. Only a mile or two from Choate there are some real cows and cornfields, some very old barns. The farms here work, and one, at least, proclaims that it has worked since 1760. Few Choate boys have seen them. But if they are ignorant of the view from North Farms Road looking west to distant hills, they are well aware of the view from Wallingford where, from one particularly advantageous perspective, they can gaze at Vece's Pizza, the Pizza Plaza, and the Wallingford Pizza Center.

"Dating from 1760," says *The Handbook of Private Schools,* "Wallingford has long been known for its ancient homes, its peach orchards, and its manufacture of silver." According to a Choate myth current only a few years ago, the town is also famous for being, around the turn of the century, Vice Capital of the Nation. A separate house, so the rumor went, was maintained for each separate variety of pleasure. This peculiar rumor is due partly to the kinetic eroticism of schoolboys and partly to a corruption of fact. Choate is not, as the ignorant suppose, Wallingford's first secluded community devoted to the education, moral and otherwise, of its faithful. In 1851, a religious sect called the Christian Perfectionists, a branch of John Humphrey Noyes' Oneida Community, moved from New York State to establish a Wallingford Community. They dammed the Quinnipiac River, thus creating Community Lake; they dabbled in farming, and then manufactured silver. In 1890 an outraged citizenry drove the Wallingford Community out of town. George St. John, the headmaster who made Choate an important school, tiptoes around the incident in his autobiography, *Forty Years at School.* "What among the civilized and Christian portion of the world," he wrote, "are generally recognized as detestable crimes are not crimes as held by them, but are sanctioned by the law of love." This is obscure enough; what St.

John could not bring himself to say was that the Oneida Community entertained original ideas about marriage and what Noyes called "the business of breeding human beings." Noyes and his disciples abandoned conventional marriage in favor of "complex marriage": each member of the Community was married to every other, with a committee deciding which adults were fit to be parents of Oneida children. "Who can say," Noyes asked, "how much the present race of man in Connecticut owe to the numberless fornications and adulteries of Pierpont Edwards?" In any event, the Community practiced a kind of eugenics it sometimes called "rational procreation" and sometimes "stirpiculture"—until the good Wallingfordians rose in their wrath. It must have been the most exciting moment in the town's history since a mother and her daughter were convicted of witchcraft in 1700.

Today, according to a teacher of history at Choate, Wallingford is "a dump and deserves to be." There *are* a few splendors, like the Miss Wallingford Pageant, sponsored by the Wallingford Jaycees, and the Nehemiah Royce House, oldest in town, where George Washington, who had come to buy gunpowder in 1775, said farewell to local residents. Choate owns the house now and uses it to put up distinguished guests.

Business, however, is bad. Much of it has been siphoned off to shopping centers and discount houses outside of town. To buy an edible hamburger, you must drive a mile out of town; to buy a book, you must drive to New Haven. Many Spanish and Polish families living in Wallingford speak no English in their homes, and according to Choate's faculty wives, the Moses Y. Beach School, adjoining the Choate campus, is not the kind of place to send your bright child after the fifth or sixth grades. Many Choate wives organize car pools to run their children into New Haven's private schools and paperback books back from the Yale Co-op.

And so the visitor to Choate, finding no signs to guide him, stumbles off the parkway and into Wallingford. Several roads point temptingly astray, but to get to the school, you must go through the business district, turning left at the Walco Spa, and then up Center Street, the main drag of this tawdry town, past the eateries and acres of appliance stores where no one is ever seen buying anything, past the graveyard, decorously concealed by the wall at your right, and past the newspaper office and the boarded-up Wilkinson movie theater to your left. Left again on North Elm Street, past a greenhouse with a chimney that would do credit to a crematorium, and then, to the left, you see it: the spire of the Choate chapel.

When I drove up, on a September afternoon, and saw the spire, I knew I had not lost my way, not after fifteen years. I had come up five years before, to my tenth reunion, and had been given a funny hat and had not remembered names to attach to the faces of my classmates, and had been appalled by someone who told me he was now in the business of manufacturing brassieres. I did not come up again.

But now I had reached what is, for Choate, a magic number: I was the man who had been out of school for fifteen years. According to Choate legend, men who have been out for fifteen years fully appreciate what the school did for them—or so the boys at Choate are told when they complain about chapel or weekend restrictions. Any alumnus will tell you that even Stanley Pratt, the public speaking teacher who (we all thought) dedicated his life to making ours miserable, became a lovable guy after fifteen years. It must be true. At reunions, boys whom he had abused, excoriated, and condemned as utterly beyond redemption would, when they had drunk too much, stagger up to Stanley Pratt and (Good God!) pat him on the back. "Good ol' Stan," they'd mutter, the sodden men who, when sober boys, would have stuttered over "Mr. Pratt." And Stanley Pratt, supreme in his retirement, would smile like a tiger as he watched the fools drink, and grin like a crocodile to hear them call him Stan.

Lest the boys doubt that they will indeed come to love the school after fifteen years, alumni are brought back from time to time to tell them so. "It is indeed a truism," said one prominent alumnus to the Student Council, which had spent an hour trying to make him understand their criticisms of the school, "that after fifteen years you'll understand all this."

On a similarly balmy day—55 degrees and sunny on a December afternoon—Mrs. Walter Rush knows, when she too sees the chapel spire, that she has arrived at Choate. She has not been here before. Beside her, in the front seat of her Pontiac Suburban Wagon, vintage 1964, sits Joey, her oldest son, who she hopes will go to Choate. Mrs. Rush is here to examine the school and —she knows—to let the school examine Joey. Unfortunately, her husband, an impressive man, could not come because he has, that day, to deliver a report for IBM.

It is two in the afternoon, and Mrs. Rush is aware that the floor of her Wagon is covered with Froot Loops, white athletic socks, a can of Revlon hair spray, and sixteen Scotties two-ply tissues. This disarray is due, in part, to the necessity of changing into one's *good* clothes in the Wagon. She would not, after all, drive all the way from Eastwood in good clothes, but then neither would she arrive at a school like Choate (fourth in social desirability, according to a book she had just finished) in anything other than good clothes. Mrs. Rush is splendid in Ohrbach's basic black (school of Norman Norell) and a Bonwit emba stole. Joey wears last year's blazer, a little tight over a paunch surprising in a thirteen-year-old. His collar buttons down and creases his neck; his tie, black with orange Princeton stripes, hangs at a 30-degree incline. Eastwood High was never like this. Joey's hair stands up in back.

Only five weeks before, Mrs. Rush had read a letter in *Life* from a mother. "Sirs," the mother had written, "I'm frankly confused as to why parents pack their kids off to boarding schools and then lament over it. To me, a child is a priceless treasure, whose growing experiences must be savored daily for the time is brief. College is soon enough for parting." There was more to the letter, and Mrs. Rush had read it all very carefully, as she did most things in *Life*. She knew what the mother felt because Joey was, well, *some* of the time, a priceless treasure. But Walter, Mr. Rush, has firm ideas: "I approve of boarding schools," he announces at parties. "It may be good for the kids to get away from home, but it's lyrical for the parents." So here she is at Choate, as she had been at Deerfield and Hotchkiss, Exeter and Andover, Taft and Lawrenceville, doing what she knew was best for Joey, and yet still a little nervous now (*What if none of them take my boy?*), as she climbs the steps of George Steele Hall.

Choate's administration building, at that time only one year old, is made of bright new bricks, Georgian style. Clearly, this imposing structure is intended, some day, to mellow a bit, even sprout a vine or two. But before it can relax and crumble like the older, even more imposing buildings of Georgian brick around it, it must acquire self-confidence, the self-confidence of knowing not only that one is doing one's job as well as it possibly can be done, but that one has always done so. Such self-confidence exists at Choate, but—quite properly—the younger faculty members are not encouraged to express it.

Mrs. Rush is hardly aware of this. What has caught her attention in the reception hall is a bust of—Caligula? It looks like a picture she remembers from her own high school Latin grammar. No, it's Adlai Stevenson, Class of 1918. Underneath are the words: KNOWLEDGE ALONE IS NOT ENOUGH. IT MUST BE LEAVENED WITH MAGNANIMITY BEFORE IT BECOMES WISDOM. Statesmen tend to succumb to words better suited to chipping in stone than to speaking in public, but Stevenson would hardly have capitalized his nouns. Opposite Stevenson is another bust that presents no problems at all. Mrs. Rush recognizes both Modern Art and John F. Kennedy, Class of 1935, when she sees them, and this is clearly both. The clever sculptor, before he cast the head in something or other, left little pinches and hunks of clay sticking out everywhere—not, Mrs. Rush knows, to show that the sculpture is unfinished, but that Kennedy's life was. Beneath Kennedy's head is the "Ask not what your country can do for you" quotation, words that make Mrs. Rush uneasy because (though she won't admit it) she thinks it a perfectly reasonable question to ask.

Now Charles Pierce, director of admissions, arrives, rubbing his hands and talking chummily from the moment he enters the room. Parents, most of them, *like* Charles Pierce. "Friendly" is the word they most often use when speaking of him, and if friendliness is the key to what Choate is all about, Pierce supplies the first good-sized dose of it to prospective members of what Choate calls its "family." Pierce is fifty-six and without a doubt the best-dressed member of the faculty. His blazers and tweed jackets are impeccable, his foulard handkerchiefs arranged in devastating poufs, and his shoes—his shoes look as if a little leather-covered animal of inestimable price had died for each. A brush cut, horn-rimmed glasses, and a smile, but that is not the whole effect: Pierce's eyes are always fixed on *you*. You are what he is interested in. He remembers virtually everything he has ever heard that might relate to you, or to people whom you might possibly know, and he asks you rapid-fire questions: about you.

With the small talk finished, Pierce and Joey leave Mrs. Rush to fondle the antique furniture in the guest's salon, or to leaf through old copies of the school yearbook and newspaper, or to survey the books which line the wall and which, Mrs. Rush thinks, look as if they had been intercepted en route from somebody's attic to the Vassar Club Benefit Sale.

"Sit down right here, in my chair," Pierce says to Joey, astonishing the boy. "And in this little box just fill in the information that's asked for. Gee, this is a glorious day." Actually, the box solicits no information not already on the form Pierce is presently holding in his hand, the "Preliminary Application for Admission," which asks for both Joey's church affiliation and a $10 registration fee, but perhaps it is good to see what the kid himself knows. When Joey has finished, he is demoted; Pierce gestures to a wooden chair facing his desk and resumes his own seat. "Joey, why don't you sit over there."

The interview begins. Pierce knows that kids in Joey's position rarely volunteer information; it must be chiseled from them. He asks questions as fast as a machine gun firing carefully controlled bursts. Because kids respond slowly, it is Pierce's job to keep the pace snappy, so he often answers his own questions or makes statements that sound like questions, to which Joey replies by nodding. The result is that Pierce gets a lot of information that must be either correct or agreeable to him.

Pierce: You're going to stay on at Eastwood through the ninth grade? How many boys will be in your class next year? You want to stay on through the ninth grade, don't you?

Joey: Yessir.

Pierce: And I think that's fine. Actually, it's not a problem here anymore, three or four years. We're happy to have boys apply for three years. This wasn't true some years ago. In September we have eighty-two boys coming into the ninth grade. The important thing in your school is that there is a big enough group to make it competitive for you. There will be lots of competition, won't there?

Joey: Uhhhh.

Pierce: Now about sisters. No sisters? All men in the family.

And so it goes. Pierce probes to expose something that the boy likes. Soccer is one thing, tennis another, and Joey admits to having once given up guitar lessons.

Pierce: How about Glee Club?

Joey: Well.

Pierce: Well, it's something that you might. The important thing is to do something outside of the academic life. Any interest in drawing, dramatics, debating, painting? Are you interested in art at all?

Joey: Not that much, no.

Pierce: You don't feel you have the talent.

Nor is Joey much interested in reading. "You don't have much time, do you?" Pierce asks, always understanding. "This is an interest you can pick up again. You want to have fun, well, that's great."

Still, it is clear that Pierce likes the boy, who confesses an ambition to be a psychiatrist, "I used to think maybe a lawyer." "You've got a good set of marks here for your midyear," Pierce says. "Honor Roll. Great. Good SSAT. The top fifteen percent across the board. You're eighty-four verbal and eight-six quantitative. That suggests you certainly need a demanding, competitive school, Joey. What college do you want to go to? You're not left-handed, are you?" Pierce has detected Joey's virtually undetectable trace of a stammer. "Have you traveled outside the country?"

Without pausing for a reply, Pierce stands up. "I'm going to put you over here again, if you will, right here on the hot seat. I'm going to ask you to spell a few words for me." He gives Joey a pencil and a pad. "Neighbor. *Nay-bor.* Marriage. Take your time. Experience. Are you up with me? I'm sure they teach you how to spell at Eastwood, don't they? Ready for the next one? Library. Challenge. Bureau. Put your clothes in the *byur-oh* drawer. Existence. Wednesday. Parallel. All right, fine. Want to change one? You're going to make it wrong. Better be careful. All right. Now I want you to read a paragraph for me." He hands Joey a book. "Start here." There is a pause. "Do you want to read it aloud, Joey."

Joey (reading): "One of his steps doubled the area of the nation. Spain had long held the country west of the Mississippi with the port of New Orleans near its mouth. But soon after Jefferson came into office, Napoleon forced the weak Spanish government to cede the great tract called Louisiana back to France."

Pierce: What does the word "cede," c-e-d-e, mean?

Joey: To give back. (Reading) "The moment he did so, intelligent Americans trembled with apprehension and indignation."

Pierce: What does "apprehension" mean?

Joey: Sort of worry.

Pierce: Uncertainty. Yes. Are you this far in your American history? (Before the administration absorbed him, Pierce taught American history.) Do you know *why* the people trembled?

Finally, Pierce is through. "You didn't expect a workout, did you?" And he begins to talk about Choate: "We like to think it's a very friendly and warm atmosphere. How were you impressed with Lawrenceville? It's bigger. And it's different, isn't it? Did you get a feeling there of *friendliness?* Did you meet lots of the boys? It's just a *great* school, there's no question about it, Joey. A boy doesn't get to know as *many* boys there as he might at Choate. And maybe this is important. It depends on the boy. In the dining hall we change tables every two weeks and the forms are all mixed up. Living in a different house each year, you get to know more boys. Chapel, we have daily chapel. We do have substitutes for chapel—tonight we have a film showing the America's Cup race. That will be in place of chapel, that's starting at five thirty.

"The important thing," Pierce continues, "as you go around these schools is to try to get some feeling—do you know what I mean by conviction?—that this is right for *you*. Something *you* believe in. The right place for *you*. The place where you can develop best, and where you can *give* something, too—this is important. This is a two-way street. Each boy will give in his own way to make it a great school. That's what we're trying to do."

The Choate campus, which Joey and his mother will now inspect, extends over 800 acres. The intersection of two town roads divides it into four discrete parts, each with its own identity. Sometimes, on a sunny afternoon in June, a wedding photographer from Wallingford will halt a procession of Carey Cadillacs at this intersection so that the bride and her attendants may violate a few yards of Choate's eastern territory to pose before two splendid trees, a beech and a copper beech, with the imposing Georgian lines of Choate's infirmary behind them. Beyond the infirmary lies the nursery, principal glory of the Choate campus and a living memorial to John Ed Wilfong, the biology teacher who built it single-handed because he believed a man could pray as well when he planted a tree as when he sat in a chapel. Many Choate boys walk in the nursery when they can find a spare half hour; a few rise before dawn to do so. It is the only place where you can clear your head, escape the clutter of communal living, and be certain that, as long as you are there, no adult will loom up to talk at you. It is also the only safe place for a student to smoke. Soon the nursery may be leveled to make way for a girls' school, which is progress of a kind, the kind that makes both boys and men at Choate wonder whether, when it comes to the salving of the soul, girls or trees prove more reliable.

If the east quadrant belongs to the spirit, the south quadrant of the campus belongs to the body. Here are the athletic fields: the varsity football field at the intersection, the varsity baseball field to the south, the track field up on the hill, and the fields for league sports scattered here and there. Here is the gym, which the school has long outgrown, used now for the school's dramatic productions and as a locker room for visiting teams. Here is the Remsen Arena, where hockey is played on artificial ice. Biggest of all is the Winter Exercise Building, a cavernous, glass-roofed monstrosity with basketball courts, squash courts, locker rooms, and a huge central cage where once the Boston Braves worked out. In my day, when boys sought escape by climbing over the roofs of Choate's buildings at night, we trembled at the challenge this one presented us, and we stuck our feet through its glass roof, appalled to hear the panes shatter on the red clay surface eighty feet below.

The north quadrant is where the school began, and it remains the place where the school sleeps; three large dormitories and most of the smaller houses in which the boys live with the faculty are dotted around an open area devoted to tennis and touch football. At the top of the hill is the Memorial House, principal dormitory for the youngest students, containing its own study hall, dining room, and dean's office, which is known as the Hatch. Closer to the road stands the large science building, thirty years old and in need of $300,000 for renovation.

The west quadrant belongs to the mind of the school. Near the intersection stands the Lodge, the headmaster's house, a Charles Addams affair covered with thick, gray paint that has been mixed with sand. Margaret St. John, the headmaster's wife, does not know how many rooms her house contains, but she does remember that it has eleven bathrooms, and she has decorated those uncounted rooms with her own antique furniture, brought from her family home in Williamsburg. Farther south is the chapel, "the core of the school," as the headmaster occasionally observes, and then, up the hill behind the Lodge, an imposing complex of Georgian buildings. The library, with classrooms and a dormitory above it, is to the right; the new St. John Hall, with its classrooms and language laboratory, squats to the left; in the middle stands Hillhouse, the very center of the center of the school, with its wide front steps sweeping up to its wide front door, with offices to the right and a study hall to the left and dormitories on the floors above. Behind Hillhouse stretches the mammoth dining hall, with even more dormitories stacked on top. All buildings in this central complex are connected by subterranean passages, but, as one master often at odds with the administration points out, there is one important exception, one building with no communication tunnel to the core of the school, and that building, significantly, is the administration building, George Steele Hall.

Steele Hall is where the Gold Key tours begin, the official 45-minute tours of the campus conducted by Choate students for the benefit of prospective parents and students. Rich Mead, a fifth former and an affable extrovert, is good at his job, but he is also subject to uncontrollable fits of candor. "It's really very funny," Rich says. "The parents and the boy sometimes try to impress *me* when I don't have anything to do with getting the kid in. We're supposed to draw the boy out, find what interests him so we know what to show him, but what happens is the parents do all the talking and let the boy trail silently behind. The parents are always telling the boy to pull up his socks, button his coat, fix his collar. Those are the boys who feel they don't like the school. At the end of the tour, I ask the boy what impressed *him* most. Usually the mother gives him a dig, bam! right between the shoulder blades, and he says something like, 'What impressed me most was the small classrooms and the relation between boys and teachers.' You know, what he's been *primed* to say, and he hasn't even seen any relation between boys and teachers."

Rich takes Joey and Mrs. Rush on the tour. "What a lovely

library," Mrs. Rush says. "A very handsome-looking building, isn't it?"

"I've grown accustomed to it," Rich replies.

"Do the boys dine with the headmaster?" Mrs. Rush asks, but she doesn't want an answer. It's the school, now that she is in the library with its gigantic room for reading and admiring, that astounds her. "I'm sure," she says, "it's in the limelight, having had John Kennedy."

Rich looks at her. "This is the reading room. Boys can study. We have fiction along the walls."

"It's a very *formal* room," Mrs. Rush says.

"You should see it in the evening when everyone's lying around with his feet up," Rich says. He's right. There's an assistant librarian, a faculty wife, who scuttles around telling boys to take their feet off the chairs, their coats off the chairs, to open their eyes and put their hips *back* in the chairs.

The tour continues, through rooms for microfilm, records and tapes for foreign languages. "That's what I'm interested in, new developments," Mrs. Rush says, and then, suddenly, they have gone through a corridor and are opposite the dean's office.

"He takes care of all the discipline," Rich says. "Every day after lunch you'll see a small line or a large line here."

"It couldn't be large, could it?" Mrs. Rush says.

Rich reassures her: "If you do something wrong, like being late to class or drinking a quart of gin in your room, you get a little slip in your mailbox to see the dean."

Onward, past the study hall and dining hall. "This is the most beautiful school we've seen," Mrs. Rush says, "It's so classical."

But she is doubtful about entering a boy's bedroom. "Let me see if I can pick a neat one," Rich says. "Usually I'm pretty good." Rich knows, however, that he must *not* open the door of a sixth former's room; immune from inspection, they are invariably the messiest. "Sometimes," he says, "the mattress will be on the floor. That really shocks the mothers." He flings open a door.

"Isn't that cute," Mrs. Rush says.

"The carpet is provided," Rich says, launching into his spiel.

"The bed, the desk, the chair, the closet—everything else the boys bring according to what they want. All boys can have a radio and a record player. There's a ratio of one-third single rooms to two-thirds double rooms."

Mrs. Rush, looking at the room, says: "A double room would be nicer."

Rich says, "This *is* a double room."

They can hardly see the floor of this room for the clutter, but they *can* see the pictures on the walls. Mrs. Rush keeps her eyes averted; Joey stares: *women!* with nipples and buttocks and *everything* showing!

"It's a good, messy room," Rich says, "so you can't say I was trying to show you only the good ones."

"You were truthful," Mrs. Rush admits.

"It's about as messy as they come," Rich says. "I'm surprised the beds are made."

He pushes them on, through St. John Hall, with its one-way windows looking down into the Speech Room. "The dean can spot you," Rich says, "if you're asleep in lectures. Lecture courses are held here; they're supposed to prepare you for what you get in college."

Mrs. Rush, who recognizes that her role is to support Rich's monologue, says, "The transition should be a lot less, coming from here."

"The whole trend is different," Rich says, expansive now. "Now it's all for the public school and the boys who are not in the ivory tower. If you're different, they take you. If you come from a broken home, they want one of those. If you come from India, they'll take you. More than intellectual capacity. Even Princeton is changing!"

On they go, past the athletic fields to the Remsen Arena, where, amid much noise, Choate is beating West Haven High in hockey. "We never really get anyone hurt," Rich confides. "In football, an odd broken leg. About half the student body goes out for hockey."

"Have *you* had any trouble adjusting to boarding school?" Mrs. Rush asks.

"No problems," Rich replies. "I'm kind of an extrovert. It wasn't long before my mother called me on the phone and asked what happened. Was I still alive?"

They are at the chapel. "Is it represented by different faiths?" Mrs. Rush asks.

"Sometimes, like, they'll have a rabbi or a Catholic priest," Rich answers.

When they get to the infirmary he says, "It's surprisingly big, but it's never really crowded. Boys don't get hurt that often. I remember once they had to make Hillhouse another infirmary because three hundred boys had measles. Last year they threatened to call off Festivities—our dance—because of measles. They were afraid guys would give it to the girls."

By the time they reach the science hall, Mrs. Rush *wants* Choate. Joey has said nothing. "All third formers," Rich tells him, "take a basic science course, which is really physics."

"I've had it," Joey says.

"Don't say anything!" Rich says. "You'll be that much ahead of everyone else!"

During Christmas vacation the year before, Rodman Furnald, a senior at Princeton, sat at home and typed out on his Princeton letterhead thirteen copies of a very careful letter. "I am very interested in teaching at a boarding school next year," Furnald wrote. "I am most interested in teaching at a boys' prep school because I have had a number of worth-while experiences working with young people at mental hospitals and at camp," which shows that he had at least worked at the two extremes of what the prep school experience can involve. "I would like to teach English," Furnald went on, "although I could teach American history or some non-biblical course in religion," which, considering how difficult it is to get a teaching job in preparatory schools, shows a judiciously catholic competence. The tenth copy of the letter was addressed to the headmaster of Choate; the other twelve went to the headmasters of Groton, Exeter, Andover, Middlesex, Deerfield, Mount Hermon, Kent,

Hotchkiss, Pomfret, Taft, Loomis, and Hill, which just about covers the field from another angle as well.

Not everyone was impressed. Andover shot him down; Exeter muttered darkly about advanced degrees. Frank Boyden, then in the penultimate year of his reign at Deerfield, told Furnald that *he* had no room for him, but Deerfield's English faculty said not to worry, there *was* room, whereupon Boyden wired NO FACULTY CHANGES AT THE MOMENT, and the English faculty countered with a groan: dark as matters were at the moment, Deerfield might become "a particularly interesting place to be in the next few years." Eventually, Boyden offered Furnald a job.

Too late. Before this comedy was played out, Furnald had changed his mind: "I wanted to go to Taft if I couldn't go to Choate," he said later. Gordon Stillman, assistant headmaster and dean of faculty at Choate, wrote Furnald a polite variation of a form letter ("We are always glad to hear of promising young men like yourself who are considering entering the teaching profession") and then, with a peculiar twist, seemed to dash Furnald's hopes for employment while, at the same time, offering something rather more magnificent. "There is a slight chance," Stillman wrote, "that we could consider you for a regular appointment . . . a considerably better chance that we could consider you as an applicant for a Yale-Choate Teaching Fellowship."

Furnald didn't know that these teaching fellowships are tricky things. Schools sometimes find it useful to pay for a year of graduate study toward a Master of Arts in Teaching degree, thus obtaining a better-qualified teacher who is under considerable obligation to the school. It is also a nice way for a school to get a good, long look at a man it may want to hire. "Of course," as one of Choate's officers confided to a large group of alumni, "the teacher doesn't realize he's being tested." The device sounds handy, but Choate was not then particularly happy about it: Yale was turning down the candidates Choate recommended.

At the same time, Taft invited Furnald to apply for its Maillard Teaching Fellowship, which is even more canny: "A new teaching candidate . . . carries only half the usual instructional load and is assigned a veteran teacher for guidance and advice." Both "Fellowships" carried the same salary: $3,500. Furnald applied for both in February and Choate relaxed. "I think you know," Stillman wrote Furnald, "that Graduate Schools do not announce their decisions on admissions until April 1st. For that reason, I have to ask you to be patient with us . . . "

On March 1, however, Taft made its move. The headmaster, John C. Esty, Jr., called Furnald, told him he had won the Maillard Fellowship and, as Furnald remembers the conversation, told him he would need a decision "as soon as possible within the day." Now Furnald held the whip. "I called up Mr. Stillman and said, 'Look, the decision you're going to reach won't be reached for another month. I'm sort of pressured by Taft. I would be interested in Choate. What can you do about this?' Stillman said, 'Well, let me think it over and I'll call you back in an hour.' " Stillman then conferred with the head of the English Department, called Furnald back, and said, as Furnald reported later, "they wanted me and they would do for me everything that Taft was going to do. My salary was going to go up five hundred dollars, I would be able to coach squash and participate in Wallingford affairs. At the time he promised me the possibility of doing anything I wanted to do. So I said, great."

In less than a year, Furnald and Choate would stop saying "Great" to each other, but for the moment, they congratulated themselves. "With all modesty aside," Furnald wrote Stillman, "I feel we have both made good decisions." Then, in April, Yale played true to form by rejecting Furnald's candidacy for the Yale-Choate Teaching Fellowship. Furnald was nonplussed. "You take this Choate deal where there's not going to be a regular teaching position available—but you might try for the fellowship—and then try for the fellowship and don't make it and get accepted a month earlier for the teaching position!" In this way, Choate acquired a new teacher. "Regardless of the Yale decision," Stillman wrote, "we are—as I told you—happy to welcome you as a member of the Choate faculty this coming September."

On September 17, 1967, Rod Furnald meets with the other new masters and some of Choate's administration in the Masters' Room, just below the library, for indoctrination. Seymour St. John, the headmaster, speaks briefly, telling the new men that Mrs. St. John writes to the mother of every new boy at the beginning of the year and "she receives a flood of mail in return, believing in us." Some of his phrases seem to hang in the air, as if politely awaiting further amplification: "philosophy of education . . . values we hold for ourselves and our boys . . . the problem when the individual comes up against the community . . . the environment, the feel of the whole school, the morale . . . everyone derives benefit from this." Gordon Stillman follows him: "Not very much happens to a child that is worthwhile except through a good teacher. . . . We really expect great things of you. . . . We're not trying to indoctrinate you, not attempting to teach you your jobs."

There is some practical advice, much of it a matter of statistics: the average grade in school runs "about seventy-five. An honors class will run from seventy-eight to eighty-six." Seats in the dining room change every two weeks; 150 boys sit at each table every year. St. John intervenes: "The greatest thing a faculty member can give to a school is being around." Therefore, he suggests that new masters should "attend eighteen meals a week from the start. I suggest a structure first, and then drawing away from it."

Others talk—about discipline and housemastering—but they keep coming back to the same theme: "The real strength of the school," St. John says, "is the devotion of the masters. Being there shows that you are interested in the boys, and willing to share your life with them." Gordon Stillman has some words about "a sense of unity of shared purpose and endeavor. We hope you feel you belong to the Choate School, that every member of the faculty is interested in what the others are doing." St. John concludes: "We like to think every boy at Choate feels at home at school. We want every boy to be happy, to develop independence and his talents as far as he can, but always with regard to the ideas and needs of other people. We are interested in the boy's entire development."

The new masters listen in silence, and sit very still indeed.

Three days and many meetings later, the new boys arrive. It is one of those tricky September days, a touch of mist and a tang of autumn quickly disappearing, the tweed jackets some boys put on in the chilly Westchester morning a sweaty burden in Wallingford by noon. A few trees have turned to red and yellow; wasps still buzz in the air, and vast quantities of squirrels, for some reason best known to themselves, sprawl dead upon the highways.

The cars are pulling up to Hillhouse. Most are station wagons, some with zippy names like "Et Cetera Too" stenciled on the driver's door, but there is a sprinkling of Cadillacs and Mustangs as well. From the cars the trunks and suitcases tumble, and the tennis rackets, the sports jackets temporarily suspended from wire hangers, bookcases, barbells, and chest-pulls, chairs too big to squeeze through dormitory doors, guitars and radios, phonographs and rifles, fans, tape recorders, and mothers in tailored suits. Somewhere, out of sight, housemasters are flipping through mimeographed biographies—"Somewhat on the quiet side, Chip has considerable influence on those around him"—but Chip and all the others are here now, filing up the broad steps to be greeted by Mrs. St. John, to be affixed with a yellow cardboard name tag which they will wear, if they remember, until Thanksgiving, and to be sent to the study hall, where Alex MacFarlane, dean of students, gives each his chiseled grin, a card with the boy's room assignment, another with his course schedule, and a sealed envelope containing his mailbox combination.

Sixth formers, working in relays, escort the new boys to their dormitories. Leaving mothers to cope with cars and luggage, most of the boys walk across Christian Street to Memorial House, where they are welcomed by Lee Sylvester, as fair and gentle a faculty wife as the campus has to offer. Lee guides mother and son past the third-form study hall, with its mural of Gareth's First Vision of Camelot (a beautiful young man, his dirk in his belt, leans on an obliging limb, gazing at a cloud-wreathed castle while some Freudian swine mumble in the grass behind him), up to the second floor and past the St. Gaudens murals entitled *Penn's Vision,* or, more obscurely, *Penn Meets the Quaker Thought in the Field Preaching at Oxford.* The new boys hump the trunks. Sometimes a sixth former will help them up the stairs with a suitcase. One mother, watching this, turned on Lee. "Where's the *elevator?*" she demanded.

That afternoon, the new boys assemble in the Winter Exercise Building, strip to their jockey briefs, mount the scales, and turning to Colin McDougall, the master seated at the chart, sound forth with their particulars: "Johnson! Steven! Sixty-fourannahalf inches! One hundred nine pounds!" McDougall coaches fall crew and watches out for his kind of man. "Eighty-four pounds!" he exclaims, as a tiny tot of obvious coxwain talent bounces past him. *"You're* coming out for crew, aren't you?" This kind of recruiting infuriates Bill Pudvah, director of athletics and champion of football as the Only Fall Sport, who holds court at the opposite end of the building. *"Why* do you want to go out for crew in the *fall?"* Pudvah explodes. "Do you *want* crew? I like to see you get out there and play a real team sport, at your age. Did anyone try to convince you?" Pudvah has his suspicions as to who is manning the chart at the other end of the new talent assembly line, and he shakes his head, much as his predecessor, Ray Massie, used to shake his when he heard that a boy wanted to go out for fall *tennis.* "Only *fairies* go out for fall tennis," he would tell the new boys, most of whom thought fairies lived in the kind of books they hadn't read for years. "Are *you* a fairy?"

Pudvah, however, is stoical. "Do your physical fitness test," he says. "If you don't pass it, you can't go out for crew." Then, as the hapless child turns to leave, Pudvah has another thought: "You need a haircut. You better get a haircut. Where you from? Hartford? Don't they cut *hair* up there? Barbershop closed for the summer?" The next kid presents his card. "Ah, football! Good!"

The physical fitness test is adapted from the model devised by the President's Council on Youth Fitness; a boy who went to another kind of school would get a felt badge if he passed it. There is the shuttle run, a miserable ordeal requiring boys to run, pick up a block, reverse direction, and, skidding crabwise over a base line, set it down again. There are pull-ups, done the hard way, palms turned out; some boys manage twelve, others, their faces red and straining, just hang there, unable to rise an inch. Then comes the broad jump, and the squat thrusts, with much latitude allowed for awkward performances, and finally a 600-yard run, three and one-half times around the Winter Exercise track, with the best boy doing it in 1:51, which is not an "excellent" rating for fifteen-year-old boys, and the worst boy running one lap, slowly, before he fell out and vomited.

The Choate Master's Handbook takes a firm position on a number of subjects, but two regulations, in particular, apply to the opening of school, and even more particularly to new boys:

> As each boy in your House reports in the fall or returns from a vacation, collect from him any guns, large knives, other weapons, and ammunition, which are kept in the School armory . . . [and] collect from him any tobacco in his possession.

During the summer, each new boy had received a copy of the student handbook, ninety-six pages of information and instruction in decorum; he is expected to have read all this, but beyond the requirement that he memorize the school song, the school hymn, and the school prayer *before* the opening of school, no one expects him to have learned much about how

Choate works. The process of civilizing, Choate style, is a long haul and has its priorities. "Try not to overwhelm the new boys with details," warns the *Master's Handbook,* "which will only confuse and sadden them." Still, there is so much that a boy *must* understand at once, if everyone is to live safely and politely together, that housemasters, on the first night of school, call their new boys together for an indoctrination lecture.

Mark Tuttle, dean of the third form and senior housemaster in Memorial House, has much the largest audience. "I think you are well aware of the opportunity that you have here and that you're going to make the most of it," he says. "Not only the opportunities for learning, but also the opportunities for making friendships that will stay with you for the rest of your life. You put your best foot forward and do everything wholeheartedly and with a positive attitude, I think you will enjoy your life tremendously. You start negatively, not applying yourself, you're wasting your opportunities here, not fulfilling the promise your folks see in you when they sent you here, and it's no little sacrifice that they're putting up when they send you to a school such as Choate."

No little sacrifice: tuition that year was $3,300, plus about $1,000 for travel and clothes, books and hamburgers. And, of course, the sacrifice of these surprisingly small boys, with their unformed faces and their madras patch sports jackets, sitting cross-legged on the floor, blinking up at Tuttle.

"The sixth formers in the house—you will get to know them." Tuttle gestures vaguely toward the surprisingly *large* boys lounging on the stairways. Most of them are stocky and tall, and are, it is generally believed, chosen to take charge of the rough-and-tumble discipline in the Mem House *because* of their size. "They will inspect your rooms," Tuttle says, "see that you get places on time. They have a lot of privileges you don't have. Their main responsibility is running the school."

Tuttle runs down the roster of those who hold the building together: "Mr. Hester, I think it is, is the janitor for the building. Hester or Lester. Hester. One thing I want you to know right away is that these men are not working for you; they're working for the school. You'll show them the proper courtesies, of course, by not making work for them. Now the general rules in our house."

Tuttle clears his throat and looks at the boys. This is the time for them to take notes with the pencils and pads that they have been told to bring.

"Roughhousing we do not permit. You have a lot of animal spirits to get out of your system, and we hope that you all as growing boys *have* a lot of animal spirits, but you must use them out on the playing field. Sprinkler pipes you keep off of at all times." Tuttle pauses. Nobody is taking notes. In fact, the boys have not yet been taught *how* to take notes, so they sit and squirm a bit, punching their pencil points against their pads. "Do not *ever* put your weight on a sprinkler pipe," Tuttle continues—what the heck, they're not going to remember it all, anyway—"You break one of those, you can imagine the consequences." Laughter from his audience, for the first time. Tuttle perks up: "This happened a few years ago up above the dining hall in the West Wing. A boy was chinning himself or something from the sprinkler pipe. The total damage that that boy and his family suffered was rather high. There was quite a bit of flooding throughout the building."

After about ten minutes of talk about fire drills ("Slip on coat and trousers over pajamas; feel the temperature of your door; walk—don't rush—in absolute silence; answer 'Here, sir,' clearly"), Tuttle turns to "another thing of general information: no valuables in your room. We stress this and stress this, and it doesn't seem to do any good. Last year, every year, we have trouble in the house. It's pretty hard to trace money, you know. We do not lock our rooms, we don't want to be able to—our fire insurance would go way up—and we don't want that kind of school, don't want boys shutting themselves away. I don't think we can help you much if that's the kind of life you're going to be leading."

Each boy is still and serious now, to make it clear that *he* keeps his hands off other people's money and, for that matter, open doors are fine by *him*. There is an audible scuffle of relief when Tuttle tells them that the school once spent more than $3,000 clearning Scotch tape goo off the walls (and therefore there will be no Scotch tape on the walls), and that every nick in their room has been written down (so new nicks will be paid for: "Slash up your window shades, as a boy did last year, and you buy us new window shades") . Then there is the armaments problem. Guns will be collected; *dull* bayonets can be secured to the wall, but switchblades—no. "It should be obvious," Tuttle says, "but every year people come with them. Certainly not darts. One boy missed his dart board many times and paid thirty and some-odd dollars for new panels in his room."

Now there is only one matter of substance left: the child's duty to his parents. He must write home *every* Sunday. "Some of you may call home on Sundays," Tuttle tells them, "but that does *not* excuse you from writing a letter. Now let's not argue about this. Ninety-nine out of a hundred of you, if you said you called home, would call home, but there's always that one boy who doesn't want anything to do with his parents, that one guy who won't write home. That's probably why his parents sent him away. Couldn't stand to have him at home." For the first time, Tuttle has worked himself into a jam; he knows it, and he muddles through: "The rest of you, of course, were sent here because your parents wanted the best thing for you." He pauses; there is silence. "I'm just joking," he says.

The day is over. It is time to let the boys go to bed. Mark Tuttle has talked for an hour, and he hasn't covered everything, but he isn't winded. If he must play Mother Hen to the youngest children, and work from an office called the Hatch, he is also the varsity cross-country coach, and he began this fifteen-hour day, like most of his fifteen-hour days, with a six-mile run.

A la recherche du feu Saint-Jean

Concerning the government of the schoole . . . authoritie must be maintained, as in the Magistrate, by his so carrying himselfe as being a certaine living law, or rather in the place of God amongst them.

JOHN BRINSLEY THE ELDER,
The Grammar Schoole (1612)

Boys lack the experience and audacity to challenge him; masters lack the energy to engage; and parents have given hostages to fortune. As for that freer audience, the governors, a self-regarding instinct will not readily allow them to question the wisdom of their own choice. A headmaster who begins by dedicating himself wholly to this closed community may end in the placid admiration of his own image.

WILLIAM GOLDING, "Headmasters"

The Age of the Great Headmasters is over. The species is extinct, dead as the dinosaur and for much the same reason, and yet it lasted, virtually unchanged, for an unconscionable period of time. The first of them, Vittorino da Feltre, could have chatted chummily with the last, Frank Boyden. Their dialogue might easily be joined by the humanists who wrote books about theories of education in Elizabethan and Jacobean England, by Milton, and by Thomas Arnold, who in 1828 put the ideas in practice at Rugby, thereby establishing a tradition of schooling which, with many Yankee twists and modern variations, continues today in this country at private boarding schools like Choate. The schools go on, but the Great Headmasters are gone, killed off by a crisis of confidence in the two articles of faith that sustained them as they built their schools: a belief in the natural and stable order of society, and a belief in the truth of Christian Humanism.

I do not mean that the current generation of headmasters has necessarily abandoned these beliefs, but that a minority of their younger faculty and brighter students has. Except for the crumbling absolutism of their moral authority, headmasters today *seem* much the same as ever they did, and difficult they are to understand, too. The passion that consumes their lives is rarely visible except in situations in which they are telling others what to think and how to live; their awesome certainty of the correctness of their ideals and actions, and their force of personality that drives others to dance along in joyful deference, cannot easily be reduced to words. They are powerful men, and are therefore dangerous; they are men who feel *comfortable* with power, and are therefore to be distrusted. The man most at ease with his own power is the man who no longer questions his fundamental assumptions, who has so ordered his society that he hears no substantial criticism, who believes in his inmost heart that the power he exercises helps others to become the best that they can be. Perhaps to understand Seymour St. John, Choate's present headmaster, one must look to the tradition that he is determined to carry on: the Christian Humanist legacy of Vittorino.

Vittorino came to Mantua in 1428, at the request of Gianfresco Gonzaga. He was already famous as a teacher of the "New Learning" in Italy; his mission in Mantua was to educate the Gonzaga children to take their place as leaders of society. This he would do with a newfangled curriculum which combined principles of classical scholarship, exhortations to Christian faith and conduct, and a Grecian fondness for athletics. Vittorino's schoolhouse was a villa named the Pleasure House, a name he quickly changed to the Pleasant House. He allowed no heat in winter, "for cold was generally the result of idleness of mind or body." He lived with the children, sharing their food and lodgings, and, according to a Victorian biographer, "the power that went forth from him insensibly raised the tone of thought and motive in those around him." What was truly different in Vittorino's approach to education, however, was that he did not want to produce clever scholars or argumentative academics, but "to secure the harmonious development of mind, body and character" with the expectation that the boys he taught would then be able to serve church or state as the leaders their parents expected them to be. Vittorino's school was a tremendous success, drawing aristocratic children from all over northern Italy, and even some poor scholarship students who were treated exactly as were the rich.

This combination of concerns—learning, Christian conduct, the value of games, and Spartan living conditions, all made tolerable by the charisma of the headmaster—continues in this kind of school, though by Arnold's time at Rugby it had become something different. "That word, *gloom,*" wrote his son Matthew, "brings thee back, in the light of thy radiant vigour, again. . . ." Protestantism, particularly the cold, damp variety that blew off the Lake of Geneva, added to the necessity of coping less with the sons of aristocrats than with those of a burgeoning middle class, accounted for part of the change. Erasmus and Thomas More, who introduced Renaissance theories of education to England, were, like Arnold, elitist, moralistic, and preoccupied with virtuous conduct, but unlike Arnold, they treated their students with affection and enthusiasm more than with rules and rods; they cherished the individual child and gave him considerable freedom because they believed that though man was fallen, he was rational enough to arrive at truth if he were treated kindly. Arnold, however, stressed hardiness at the cost of coarsening his pupils' sensibilities. Intellect and emotion were dubious virtues; energy and integrity were extolled. One of Arnold's students wrote that the headmaster "used to attack offences, not as offences—the right view—against discipline, but as sins, heinous guilt, I don't know what beside! Why didn't he flog them and hold his tongue? Flog them he did, but why preach?" The flogging is gone today; the preaching remains. Gone, too, is much of the emphasis on future service to the state, the conviction that education inescapably leads to what Milton called "that which fits man to perform justly, skilfully and magnanimously all the offices both private and public of peace and war."

In 1946, John Kennedy, then running for Congress, returned to tell his school that "There is one field in which Choate and other private schools of this Country have not made a contribution, and that is in the field of politics. It's perhaps natural that this should be so. In America, politics are regarded with great contempt; and politicians themselves are looked down upon because of their free and easy compromises. . . . It is well for us to understand that politicians are dealing with human beings, with all their varied ambitions, desires and backgrounds, and many of these compromises cannot be avoided. . . . I believe that in the future, if Choate is really to survive, the men who teach at Choate must instill in its students an active interest in our politics and the National life around us."

Still, Choate has kept other ideas that Arnold cherished. One that it retains would have astonished Vittorino, Erasmus, and More: that of the school as a body possessing a life of its own, to which deference is due in the form of loyalty. Even when Choate proves itself wrong or incapable, loyalty inhibits criticism. It might be argued that, because education is concerned with opening doors and loyalty with closing them, the two are incompatible, but no Old Boy with an Old School Tie, from Arnold's day to ours, could even understand the argument. Loyalty is not only important to Choate, it is indispensable. If it is not drummed into the students, the students may not, in later years, express their loyalties with their checkbooks. And without contributions from loyal alumni, Choate would not survive. "Disloyal" and "nonsupportive" are the two strongest pejorative words in the administration's vocabulary, but they are words the administration uses with great frequency.

Choate has also kept the pessimistic view of the boy as a dubious ore which can, in the crucible of school, be forged into a precious metal, and then polished for as long as is required to produce a dull, rich luster. "There are so many basic fine qualities there," Seymour St. John wrote to a boy's mother, "that I can't help believing the superficial, foolish ones will in time rub off and the basic strengths will be what show." "Turn a bad thing into a good one," St. John's father was fond of saying. "We are hopeful that the young man will show his best side increasingly," says the assistant headmaster in a faculty meeting. Working with bright, mature kids who need no special help may be a satisfaction, but the greatest joy comes when the healing arts of a complete educational environment have done their patient work. Of one student, Seymour St. John wrote:

> A boy with test scores lower than we normally think we can succeed with, but who by incredible hard work has pulled himself up by his bootstraps and has been given the best of future educational opportunities. Beyond being proficient in a couple of sports, he has a humility and a desire to give to individuals or to institutions that are helping him in a way that will make him a needed man in his generation.

Choate, too, has brought back what Arnold lost: an interest in the individual that transcends professional concern to become affection. It is an extraordinary thing, when seen at work in Choate, and explains one of the many maxims that date from the early history of the school: "Choate was not *founded;* it was loved into life."

Of course, it *was* founded, in 1896 by Judge William Choate, whose more famous brother Joseph had been ambassador to England. Choate appointed his friend Mark Pitman as headmaster. Pitman lived with his three maiden daughters and the four boys who began the school; Pitman taught all the courses. "He died ere long," wrote George St. John, the second headmaster.

George St. John arrived in a horse-drawn buggy in 1908. He was thirty, had taught in other schools, had been hired to the headmastership of Choate by the Pitman daughters for a salary of $1,200. There were 51 boys in the school. I never knew the

Old Head, as my generation called him; for us he was only a figure who, from time to time, walked slowly across a corner of the campus. St. John wrote a poor book called *Forty Years at School;* he also wrote some altogether magnificent letters, uncounted thousands of them, all of which have been preserved. In his letters, the man comes across, snorting and groaning, breathing faith and fire; to read them for an hour is to understand the man and the force in him that created the school. "Oh, if we could only take these boys," he wrote to the father of one who was doing badly, "and show them things as they really are, so that they will really see! Tell Frederick we are going to." To another father, whose son had "been drinking rye whiskey about every other day," St. John wrote: "The boy's health and happiness and whole moral fibre are at stake. He has been drifting on a rather dangerous road." You can tell a lot about a man or a place when there is a crisis to be dealt with. Here is George St. John in January, 1917, writing first to a boy who had walked out of Choate and then to an erring alumnus:

> My dear Charles:
>
> I think you ought to be warned of the things in your own character which have made you discontented at Choate. There is nothing here at School to make a hard-working, wholesome man, with right ambitions for his college and life career, discontented—at least so far as we can possibly see. If there is anything, I am most awfully sorry for it, and wish sincerely to change it. I am awfully afraid that you may fall short of your best self under the conditions of a tutoring school, and yet I am going to pray that you won't. Prove to us, my dear fellow, that you can do fine work, and lead a splendid and idealized life, in the new surroundings. Make everybody have confidence in you and respect the earnestness of your character, as much as they now love you because you are friendly and young.

> My dear Sam:
>
> I have never heard news of one of our old boys which has distressed me as much as the news that has come to me of you in your first months at college. At first only rumors of your dissipation

came to me, and I refused to believe them. The rumors, however, have become more frequent, and I felt it my duty toward you to clear your name as I hoped of falsehoods. The further I have gone into looking things up, however, the more obvious it has been that the rumors were truthfully founded. You have been drunken, and it would seem that by your own words you have committed yourself to worse things than drunkenness. You have played the part of a young fool, bringing disgrace on yourself and your School and your family's name. Until you have cleared your own name and that of your School's by repentance that comes from your heart, by a splendid record in your studies, by a visibly new point of view and perception, and by a complete living-down of your cheap wrong-doings of the past, you are not fit to be counted as the boy and the man whom your friends and your School have cared for and loved and regarded as part of them.

I want you to come up and see me, Sam, at the earliest possible time. I don't want you to put this off; I want you to telephone me as soon as you can after you receive this letter, that I may know that you are coming up to talk with me frankly and honestly, as you owe it to the School and to me to do. Let us set things right, and take a clean new start, and beg forgiveness for the simple, wicked way in which you have abused your friendships and your privileges, and let us talk this whole thing through and out, my dear Sam, and believe that I am your friend always, whatever you have done. But we have got to get this straightened out. It all makes me sick at heart, and you have got to fix it, and do your duty toward yourself and your Father and Mother and us who care for you here at School.

Yours sincerely—and affectionately too,

"Turn a bad thing into a good one," St. John was fond of saying. "Forever pull up a briar and plant a rose." "The sight of a boy," he wrote in his book, extending the garden image, "for whom peradventure we might do something, and troubles vanished. The potential of youth—animal, vegetable, or boy—excited us. Somebody called us boy gardeners." Some of the alumni grasped the idea. "I realize," one wrote to St. John, "that Choate constitutes a spiritual experience which, like the warm rays of an April sun upon a garden, is in large measure responsible for whatever of beauty and productiveness my life may hold."

Occasionally, troublesome boys were not amusing. Once a fire cracker was exploded in a Hillhouse toilet. St. John summoned the entire school to the chapel and stalked down the aisle, clutching the fractured toilet seat in his hand. "Muckers!" he yelled, waving the seat around his head. "They shan't spit in our sea!" And he was quite capable of writing a parent these words about his son:

> I confess that I am amazed to find that Trumbull has so little perception, and that he is so self-willed in his relations with people and with duties. Under certain favorable conditions Trumbull is a gentleman, and an interesting gentleman; but if conditions do not favor, he is an uncontrolled, lawless boor. . . . It seems to me that the boy's point of view must at least be shiftless and I am afraid common. Our point of view is that our job is to change all this in so far as we are able.

"To be a schoolmaster," St. John told his faculty, "is next to being king." But among kings, there is always a Top King. "If you don't like the way I run my school," he said to one master who had ventured a protest, "perhaps you'd better find a school that you do like."

He died in January, 1966, at the age of eighty-eight. He had built a great school by the sheer force of his determination that the school *should* be great, that nothing as temporary as insolvency should be allowed to destroy great education. In 1921, when banks were refusing loans to Choate, the school nearly did die, but the suicide of a bank officer known to one of Choate's trustees resulted in the bank's promising to make good any obligation the officer had incurred. St. John hinted to the bank that a loan had been promised—by that officer—and he got his money.

Part of his genius lay in the building of buildings and the buying of land; more of it lay in the way he immersed himself in the life of the school, down to the most trivial detail. "I do not want to ask you for any rent," he wrote to one of his teachers, "but in a way you will be paying rent by keeping large areas clean and dusted—and above all, every toilet *clean and sweet all the time*. This last can only be done by hot water and soap and muscle." "The safety match," he advised the school's housekeeper, "which I recommend as infinitely better than the Vulcan Safety Match which we have been using, is called Gold-Medal Safety Match." And from such details, character can be built. Here he writes to a student in the infirmary:

> It takes a great deal of patience and thought for other people, and a genuine desire to make one's own self helpful instead of a nuisance, to have chickenpox in the right spirit. It is an art to have chickenpox well, just as it is to live at School well, and I pray that the spirit of Choate as you have seemed to conceive it, has so got into your life and your own spirit, that you can endure chickenpox, and could endure things a thousand times worse for that matter, in a helpful, thoughtful-of-others, generous way. . . . You know a great many people are called Christians, but only a few people really are.

Great teaching built great character. "I am sure," he wrote to a master having problems with a difficult boy,

> that when he sees that we Masters take our work more seriously than anything else on earth, he will see that we are not going to stand for any nonsense. I hope you will feel so earnestly about your teaching, that there will be something inside you, an atmosphere that will prevent anybody from taking the work of your classes with any lack of conception.

He urged his faculty to make time to give boys individual attention:

> It has always been axiomatic that idleness was the root of all evil. . . . They need to know intimately the Master who is teaching them; and to feel in their hearts that he is jealous of every minute of their study time and eager with all his being for their success. A boy's lack of interest—yes even his lack of character—will

> not hold out against this kind of personal interest and aid and drive. . . . The great teacher is the life-saver among boys; and the inspiring part of the whole matter is that we save a boy's soul at the same time we are saving his Algebra.

None could doubt that his love for his boys, rotters though some of them were, was genuine. Writing in 1916 to the father of a boy he had expelled, he concluded, as he often did on such occasions, by saying: "I would like him to know right now that I love him whether he likes it or not. Nobody can work for a boy sincerely and in the right way, unless in his heart he does love him."

"In general," says Semour St. John, "I would recommend that a son not follow his father in a job. You may go ahead with great strengths, with all the knowledge of the past and new ideas of the future—that's what you hope for—but if it turns into a watered-down version of what it was before, then you've made a horrible mistake."

Seymour St. John is fifty-five, a short man, but handsome and trim, looking still like the athlete and adventurer he once was. The man's vitality, his chemical attraction, is astonishing. His eyes sparkle; his gaze is steady, encouraging one to speak honestly, but briefly. It can be disconcerting. Few people argue with St. John, and those who do in public—say, at a masters' meeting—may be put down very quickly or ignored. What bothers a lot of people, what makes them feel that they should *rehearse* what they are going to say to him, is his intensity. "I think I push to fill the unforgiving minute, to get sixty seconds of accomplishment out of it," he says, and you know: it's *true;* in any given minute, he has lived a little bit longer than anyone around him, and, somewhere inside their skin, they know it. In the year I spent watching the headmaster, I heard many people say many true things about him behind his back, but I heard only one person criticize him truthfully to his face and get away with it. She was the wife of a prominent alumnus; they, with other prominent alumni, had returned to be briefed about the school for two days. "You have such a wonderful gift," the woman said to St. John. "It's hard to talk to you because you can twist any argument the other way." It takes students and new masters a term to figure that out. She said it nicely, so St. John smiled, but not much, and said nothing.

St. John was born into Choate, in 1912. He had two brothers, one of whom was called "Jimmy the Good" because he mopped up all the prizes. "When I was ten years old," Seymour says, "my father said to me, 'How does it happen that one of my faculty asked me why one of my sons was always building the school up and the other was always tearing it down?' I was just naïve enough, and a needle enough, to say, 'Well, which is which?' He wasn't particularly amused.

"Until I was sixteen," St. John went on, "I did very little that was effective. I was a student at Choate for about ten years. My father didn't like the little school I was in, so he brought me in while I was in the fifth grade." He took fewer subjects than most boys, crept along, was helped generously by the faculty. "I had a good time and was perhaps blessed with a sense of humor and was a thorn in my father's side."

At sixteen, he was sent to Le Rosey, a fashionable holding area for the sons of the rich in Switzerland. He had to learn Latin in French, but he played a lot of hockey and toured Europe with some Olympic players. "Nothing but French spoken," St. John remembers. "Our daily schedule in the winter at Gstaad was classes until about a quarter to eleven in the morning, and then hockey until lunch, one o'clock. And then skiing in the afternoon. There were those who did a little studying at night. Nobody cared whether you did the work or not. They really didn't. I'm sure my father thought it would teach me maturity, responsibility, to get completely away. And the plain fact was that biologically my mind, up until I was sixteen, was a scattered mind. It was like a searchlight that was turned down so that it had a very wide focus. By the end of that year abroad, I had learned to turn that focus down to a point. I was organized. I found that with a modicum of effort I could do better than the next guy. This was exciting to me.

"I came back more conservative. I don't mean politics; I mean adjusted to the older generation. I came back to Choate for two years." He was graduated in 1931, cum laude, and later with a Phi Beta Kappa key from Yale. In the summer he traveled in Europe: "I got in on the Hitler business in Germany. I had meetings with people like Himmler. I got a pass from him to get into the concentration camp at Dachau as a Yale reporter. That was 1934, the early days of Dachau." At Yale, he took honors in both French and German, which no one had done before. In the summer of 1935, he went to Japan —"just the time when Japan was getting pretty irritable about the West"—and, after a trip to Peking and Shanghai, returned to teach at Choate.

"It was a major decision," he says, "and yet an easy one. I was offered a job by my father. I almost went into medicine." He taught French for five years, coached JV baseball and football, and helped with debating. He was married in his third year.

Then came an important turning in his life. "During this time," he says, "I had the feeling that there were places that I had missed. When I say missed, I mean I was missing the boat. I felt incapable of coming to certain conclusions that I wanted to come to. I needed more background for them."

He had begun to meet people who he believed had reached important conclusions; they had been graduated from Virginia Theological Seminary. Still, St. John was doubtful. "I couldn't just take their answers because of what all of us, I suppose, in our egotistical way, think of as our intellectual integrity, which can be suspect. I couldn't accept a faith without its making rational sense to me." He took a year's leave of absence, went to the seminary, and for "six months down there I fought the old arguments just about as hard as I could." But he met a professor who breached his defenses, and he spent summers studying theology. He was ordained an Episcopal minister in 1942.

With the war, he wanted to go into the service. Although his wife's stepfather was an admiral, the chaplain corps would not have him, nor anyone who had not been a parish priest for two years. He enlisted in the Navy anyway, as an officer, and studied Malay because the Navy needed military government officers when they took over islands in the Pacific. He never used it; he was called to Europe, where in 1944 he was attached to SHAEF and got into planning for the invasion. He came into Utah Beach on D-Day plus one week. There was some fire; his commanding officer was killed. Then he went back to England, a lieutenant appointed assistant chief of staff for the Commander of Naval Forces in Germany. In 1946, he was back at Choate.

That was the year his father decided to retire. The trustees interviewed sixty candidates for the headmastership and, after much deliberation, mostly about the problem of a dynasty, elected Seymour St. John. Two members of the board resigned immediately, "in somewhat high dudgeon," St. John says. "They're great guys, too, and they became great friends of ours." He took over as headmaster in 1947. The trustees told his father that he must agree not to return to Choate for two years. "He was very much hurt by that," his son says. "My mother agreed with it fully, thought it absolutely right, but he had always pictured himself staying on as the patriarch, living in the Homestead and welcoming alumni—just a Frank Boyden kind of image. I always felt badly about it."

"We could," said Malcolm Manson, an influential member of the administration, "have been what Deerfield has become had George St. John stayed on. Very easily. George St. John and Frank Boyden had a great deal of respect for each other."

"For me," Manson said on another occasion, "the fascination of being a headmaster is 'seeing your garden grow.' " The horticultural image, apparently, is impossible to avoid. "Here's somebody doing *that,* and here's somebody doing *this,* and here we have to have *that*—and this, to me, is *really so exciting!* Just so great!"

Malcolm Manson left Choate in 1969 to become headmaster of a school in California.

"A beast, but a just beast," he said. "That's what a headmaster should be."

Making Good Husbands

> We stand by and hold to and insist on for our students the kind of values that I think you recognize I'm talking about.
>
> SEYMOUR ST. JOHN, speaking to the school's trustees

> What's in it for me?
>
> Recent Choate graduate, on being asked for an interview for this book

No one—visitor, student, or returning alumnus—can be at Choate for more than a few hours without hearing someone refer to the values for which the school stands. That is, he will hear people say that there are values for which the school stands. He may find it difficult to find someone who can tell him precisely what these values *are*. Values are comfortable commodities; like the faces in one's family, one lives with them for so long one forgets what they look like. Or, if the values are sharp in the mind, they are difficult to translate into words. Or, if words can be found, they seem strangely out of date. In the new boys' handbook, the headmaster says: "We shall reach our goals with success and joy." The broadside called "Goals for Each Choate Graduate" alarms students with its plethora of ill-defined terms: it yokes courage to responsibility (qualities the school often finds incompatible), and courtesy to honor. It exhorts the boy "to lead his life in accordance with enduring values," and it ends with the truth of religion.* Should anyone be so blunt as to ask: "Look here, what *are* the enduring values?"

* The complete "Goals" will be found in Appendix B, page 392.

he may get queer looks in reply: the assumption at Choate is that its values are not only universal, but universally understood. "I think most of us really want to be what the headmaster wants us to be," one senior said, "but he doesn't ever tell us directly what he wants." Most students at Choate *are* concerned with defining values by which they can shape and discipline their lives, but they are infuriated by what they believe to be a consistent confusion at Choate between values (honesty, courage) and manners (rising when a faculty member crosses your prow), between the values of the Sermon on the Mount and the values of the Westchester Country Club. Item from the *Choate News*, February 1, 1969:

> Speaking for the black students at Choate, Harold Ray asked the Headmaster whether his goal was for all black students to be assimilated into the "upper middle class values" of the School.
>
> Mr. St. John, "Will you define middle class values?"
>
> Ray: "The whole system of the school; mandatoryness—chapel, sports—"
>
> Mr. St. John, "The answer is yes."
>
> Later, Jack Buckler asked whether the School had the same goals for all students, Mr. St. John answered: "We aren't trying to mold anyone. . . . I was asked if what we consider normal standards of courtesy would be required of black students as well as white. My answer: 'yes'."

When someone at Choate is sure that he need not define his terms, he can talk for a long time about the school's values without touching upon anything of substance. St. John addresses his trustees on the values the school looks for in new boys:

> On values—we always look for values that we like, that we stand for, that we believe in; we do not go out of our way to find boys with very different values from ours. . . . If you don't have a certain type of environment, you don't train boys in the same way that you do if you do have one. If the values are so disparate that there is no general consensus, then you don't accomplish one of the things that you hope to accomplish. Not inculcation,

but rather a gradual understanding of a close relationship with other people who have the values that we have accepted as our values. . . .

Do we hold to standards? Do we say: these are our values? Or do we roll with the punch? Personally, I'm concerned enough about our standards and values in our country at large to feel that if we have to be, as we were twenty-five years ago, a last stronghold in the world, then we had better be the last stronghold. I don't want to be stuffy about that. And I don't feel that we have the only answer. I do feel that we must stick with certain basic values of Western civilization and the Judeo-Christian tradition and while we keep our minds open to all the ephemeral questions that arise, underneath we stand by and hold to and insist on for our students the kind of values that I think you recognize I'm talking about.

In admissions, we have looked for this kind of value in student background.

The trustees did not appear to be confused. Sometimes, however, the administration does try to find words to explain its values. Malcolm Manson, who is twenty-nine, very British, very buoyant, and chief idea man for the administration, explains what he means by values to a group of alumni:

Right now we are one of the very, very great institutions of this nation. This is a *wonderful* place! It is only going to remain wonderful if the same spirit of adventure, of innovation, of risk remains. . . . Among the intangibles that we are going to need for the future are the traditional strengths that are always in danger: friendliness, courtesy, respect, good humor, concern for each person, honesty, integrity, reverence for God and man. These are traditional, unfashionable, difficult concepts—but absolutely essential! You must never, never lose touch with them! I think there are other intangibles which are rarely stated, but are also of great importance. If I may use the metaphor here of a dry martini, it seems that you always have to have the correct sort of mix. And the mix depends upon the individual. But if you have nothing but gin, or nothing but vermouth, you have a horrible drink. I think we need a martini mix of loyalty on the one hand

> and constructive dissent on the other. Without both, the school is not going to progress as it should. One without the other—and I would call loyalty the gin here—is very poor. We need stability with our innovation.

"I knew when I stood up," Manson whispered to me, "that I was going to sound like a Jingo. And I did." It is impossible not to like Manson, not to be drawn to the thrust of his enthusiasm which occasionally misses its audience, if only because he speaks what he believes rather than what, in cooler moments, he knows will persuade. Once he stood up in chapel and said to the boys: "If I were a student at Choate, every morning when I got up, I'd shout 'Whoopee! I'm alive!' " For days, as he walked around the campus, shouts of "Whoopee!" drifted from windows, from behind the bushes.

Still, the problem of a workable rhetoric is acute. "There is no continual examination of what this school is all about," says one of the most concerned young masters; there is, instead, a tradition of moral homilies. Judge and Mrs. Choate began fuzzing the issue when asked what they were doing with their school: "We are making good husbands." Frail as it may seem, it served as the base for further fuzziness: If you teach them that, someone said years later, you will teach them everything else they need to know. It is impossible to hate such Pablum, and nobody does. The boys just wince and scratch. They don't disagree, but they can't take it seriously. "Reach for the stars," says the alumni director, "and you'll gather no mud." "The thing that makes Choate great," said a former head of Choate's Fathers' Association, "is what those who guide its destiny do over and above the line of duty." And, at the opening of school, the headmaster tells the boys, "I suggest the goal of being a contributor to your world and to your fellowmen. . . . We might put it into three words: Will It Help. W.I.H."

Scratch, scratch, wince, wince. It is vague, of course, but worthily vague. There is truth in it; it blocks thought, but it does not destroy it. This kind of language puts the necessary process of self-evaluation into deep freeze, but, somewhere in all that frost, there is something to thaw out. The headmaster wonders, though, why he has lost contact with the boys when he speaks to them in a group, though not his powers of persuading any single boy, when talking face to face. The answer is that he doesn't use that kind of rhetoric when he talks directly to a boy. Rhetoric of that sort will not endure many cracks and strains.

When Choate is explaining itself to the generality, it often discovers it must begin with first principles: a defense of its form of education. Private schools, say those who are opposed to them, cost too much; they attract immature children who require closer supervision than a vast, impersonal public school system provides; and, anyway, they are antidemocratic.

The first charge is hardly worth discussing: if a boy is ineligible for scholarship money, his family must either pony up $3,300 for the tuition or look elsewhere. Choate is quite correct when it insists that it is, in fact, *inexpensive*. It spends $1,000 per year per boy in excess of what it charges. A motel room in Wallingford, offering no more than a bed and a bath, costs $112 a week; a Choate education costs $100 a week.

There is some truth in the second charge. Choate, or any institution which provides close supervision and individual care, attracts those who need it. Many of the wealthy casualties of our affluent society are packed off to those quasi-military academies that advertise in the Sunday magazine section of the New York *Times,* and there, perhaps, they are yelled at and beaten by rods. Although Choate has quite a few boys from broken homes, sons of parents who travel a great deal, or of parents who have little time for their children, it also attracts top boys from all over the country, and takes no boy who is not intellectually adept, or potentially so.

The argument that schools like Choate are snobbish, elitist, and antidemocratic is particularly intriguing because it presupposes that they, or any school, should be otherwise. "I think the purpose of school is education, not the support of democracy," said one father who had put three children through preparatory schools. "I don't believe in public education beyond the point of necessary literacy," he went on. "How can you expect a government to teach anything but its own policy?" A cynical argument, perhaps, but there is truth in it. Private schools properly consider themselves a valuable alternative to public education. "They are," say the authors of a study on the nature of the private school:

> centers of innovation and educational reform, set a much-needed standard of academic excellence, serve as a model for public schools and provide salutary competition for them, diversify the educational system by the inclusion of schools with specialized goals, offer religious education, and represent free enterprise without which education would be a state monopoly.

Private schools, therefore, preserve our democratic freedom of choice.

"This type of independent school," says Seymour St. John, "is a specialized school; it goes all out to be a specialized school. It's a school for boys who are able to meet much higher than normal academic challenges. We don't—like the public schools which are nonspecialist schools—take students all the way down as well as all the way up. We like to go all the way up, but we only go partway down, on the ability scale. We're specialists for people who can do, and, we hope, can be motivated to do."

Still, the charge of snobbism rankles. Some time ago, the men who ran the private schools decided that, like undertakers and garbage collectors, they might be able to improve their image if they changed their name. Today, "private" is a word used only by the people; "independent" is the word the schools use. An administrator of an Oklahoma independent school explained the difference to me: "Private suggests exclusive, snobbish," he admitted. "But independent suggests that the school is free of outside, particularly government, control. The distinction is very important to us."

It is true, too, that the distinction between private and public schools is eroding. Public funds, one way or another, are making their way into private schools; all that is left is "autonomy of control," its "nonsystemic character." The word "independent," though it has some of the smarmy elegance of "Sanitary Engineer," is probably justified.

Lee A. DuBridge, speculating on whether independent schools could survive the competition of public education, cited "four essential advantages which the private school inherently possesses: 1. The freedom to select students. 2. The freedom to match the size of the student body to the size and capability of the teaching staff. 3. The greater freedom to select teachers unimpeded by frequently irrelevant state requirements. 4. The freedom to innovate and experiment in curriculum, in teaching methods, in student-teacher relationships. . . . In a single word, these freedoms add up to individuality. In the independent school the STUDENT is an individual with all of the complex of talents, abilities and inhibitions, problems, and ambitions which make him a UNIQUE person."

Administrators of independent schools are adept at demonstrating that their schools are indeed democratic. Most of them know that the issue is demonstrably false, that their schools are perfectly undemocratic, yet excellently qualified to teach boys to live in a democracy. They know that schools have no more business being democratic than has a family, or a corporation. There is, however, a myth abroad in the land that public schools are democratic—which, of course, they are, if you consider buckling before state and community bureaucracies democratic, toppling under pressure from an illiterate and bigoted citizenry democratic, requiring a child to raise his hand to apply for a slip which will allow him to walk past the hall guards on his way to the toilet democratic. A public school is the creation of an often indifferent community; it cannot be better than that community. A private school can be better, and often is. Still, people persist in confusing exposure to different kinds of people with democracy, and they want to *hear* that Choate is democratic.

"Boys who come to Choate," Gordon Stillman told a group of alumni, "have a more democratic experience than if they stay at home. They have an unusual opportunity for an enlargement of their experience. The privileged boys come to us from country day schools—they run into a greater range of humanity here. They would not be playing ball with boys on the Lower East Side if they stayed home.

"They will meet underprivileged boys and middle-privileged boys. They will meet all kinds of men of distinction and achievement in many fields." Stillman paused to discuss a militant black leader who would meet the boys when he came. (He didn't come, being detained in Harlem on a murder charge.) "Our boys wouldn't have met him if they stayed at home," Stillman said. "We have a deeper, broader experience in democracy than other schools can offer.

"I believe Choate's primary aim is to produce responsible citizens. We provide the opportunity"—here he hit the Calvinist strain again—"for the common man to become uncommon. We give them ideas they never considered before, in a way no school under political control can do. We are of service to society. . . . We try to create for the boys here as completely democratic a society as we can—within our own limits."

Parents like to echo the democracy theme. "Our school is reasonably narrowing," said one mother with a son in the high school in Darien, Connecticut. "You don't have an opportunity of meeting people from, you know, all over the lot. In Darien, you meet all kinds of people from one town."

Her husband was more concerned with the high school's laissez-faire attitude, another property often confused with democracy. "The education is excellent," he said, "*if* the individual is motivated. Equally, there's a sort of amorphous mass of kids to whom the education must be offered and they can take it or leave it. There is comparatively little insistence on level of performance, so the motivation to perform must come from within."

And then there is, well, the leadership question. "Why *hope* they're going to rise to the surface in the Darien High School when I can put them into Choate?" His son, age fourteen, agreed: "There has to be someone to lead all those hordes of people who just mill around."

Leadership is something Choate is always talking about, almost always in extremely vague terms. Leadership is, after all, very close to power, and therefore one of the three great pornographies: like sex and money, it is generally recognized as a Good Thing, but specific talk about it is bad form. "Our philosophy," said the school in a fund-raising brochure, "is that Choate is a station of service to the country." That's vague enough, modest enough. "We have very much in mind," the brochure continued, "our responsibility for educating those who, by their very position, will be leaders in some aspects of this country's life." Leadership in terms of government service, in politics, is, as John Kennedy pointed out, very rarely mentioned.

Others are not so restrained. "Where the hell do you think the country's leaders are going to come from?" a Choate mother asked me. "From the *public* schools? Ha!" More often, though, the leadership to which Choate's students are headed seems to be part of an invisible network. "There is no door in this entire country that cannot be opened by a Choate graduate," says John Lupton, who works for the school's development program. "I can go anywhere in this country and anywhere there's a man I want to see, who can be of some service to us, I can find a Choate man to open that door to him for me." G. William Domhoff, in his book *Who Rules America?* explains how this invisible web is woven at the preparatory school level: the schools educate the big-city rich from all over the country; they are the proving ground where new-rich–old-rich antagonisms are smoothed over and the children of the new rich gracefully assimilated; they permit upper-class children from smaller towns to become acquainted and the brightest members of other classes to be assimilated into the future power structure. All of this, says Domhoff, is important for society.

"Some people," says Donald Bullitt, a senior at Choate, "think this is a school for the privileged and we must open it up to the masses. Well, I *agree* it is a school for the privileged. I thought it was set up *for* the privileged. It was a way that the privileged could get a good education so they would want to do something for the whole."

Don is not entirely unsympathetic, and he is not stupid, but he gazes at the world with tunnel vision. He is Choate's most conservative student, the school's most noisy supporter. You can almost hear the tumbrils rolling after him, trying to catch up with him; when he speaks from a prepared text at an open session of the Afro-American Association, the black boys flash their white teeth at him, and if they had knives in their belts, they would be stroking them.

"I'm not saying we shouldn't have underprivileged boys," Don says, "but what exactly can these boys *do* when they get out? They don't have the power or the influence to get the jobs or positions where they really could be an active force in society, so therefore they have an education, but feel even more frustrated. They might turn into, say, radical leaders of a movement below."

Don, himself, has influence. His father got him a summer job with a Senator. A signed photograph of Lyndon Johnson hangs over his desk. "Look at the moral concern of the boys who are affluent," Don continues. "They are the ones who can do so much more than, say, Joe Rigney"—the leader of Choate's black students—"because Joe is never going to have the resources behind him to do anything. What *can* he do? He can't *force* moderation. He has to be radical to make himself heard. We don't."

Choate is a community: not just a community that occupies a certain area in space, but a community extending through time, looking before and after. "With her," wrote George St. John, "is the care of a great and preservable tradition." No public school thinks in such terms: its sense of continuity extends laterally, to other schools in its system. "She preserves," the Old Head wrote of Choate, "and hands on to each generation, an inner decency of thought and motivation, a haunting inner code, persistent compunctions which bring straighter thinking and truth's own expression."

"What we have to offer," says Robert Atmore, one of the most energetic teachers, and most admired by the boys, "is the diversity of the people and the way of life in a boarding school. It's a community and we should think that way. It lives according to certain ideas or customs or traditions. We have things we think are valuable and we can't always define them. But we know 'em and we do 'em and we change them and they develop. That is the point of the student coming."

It is indeed, but, strangely, it is the point most often missed by those who discuss the pros and cons of preparatory schools. A public high school may provide as good an education as Choate does, but it doesn't provide a different quality of life. Life at Choate is something like life in the Iroquois long huts; it cuts across the nuclear family structure—Mummy, Daddy, 2.6 children, and Spot the Faithful Dog—to create an environment where a boy must learn to know well people who share certain of his goals and assumptions, but who are not related to him.

"It's hard to put into words," says Seymour St. John, "because they have become hackneyed, but it's the atmosphere that people breathe. The atmosphere is made up of so many trite words, but very real words. First of all, the basic Christian ideal of love: caring deeply about each person. It's terribly hard to take care of five hundred and seventy people; in fact, for any one individual to *know* five hundred and seventy people is almost impossible. But if one boy in the school is lost, the school is too large by one. I deeply believe this. I must admit that twenty years ago, every single boy who walked out of the dining room for Thanksgiving vacation I could call by name. I even stood there on occasion, shook hands with every boy, and called him by name. Not just as a tour de force, although it became that to some degree, but to have them know that I *did* know them and that there was somebody who was at least *that* intimately involved. Who recognized them. It makes an astonishing difference. Today, I can't do it. That bothers me. But by the end of the year I know most.

"The atmosphere promotes a climate of warmth and support. This, like any good, can be pushed to an extreme and overdone. You can be overpaternalistic; you can hold a boy's hand so long that he isn't forced, or doesn't feel the need of thinking for himself to a strong enough degree. At the same time, it's more likely for a boy to feel that nobody really gives a darn and that he is on his own. Lack of support, lack of care in the atmosphere, breeds, I think, some of the most unfortunate results of group living. Group living, my father always used to say, coarsens. There's something in it, you know; it does! You get an individual boy in his family and he's the sweetest guy in the world; you put him with a dozen guys his own age and all of a sudden it's a coarser fiber—why? We know why: it's just the human animal.

"Then there are the disciplines of the community. Very hard to put your finger on. First of all, academic discipline; disciplines of action and conduct; personal disciplines of courtesy. I've been quoted as saying that Choate wasn't a happiness factory. At times the student body would like it to be a happiness factory. This is one of the things you hope people will learn: happiness is a by-product. It's another cliché, but one that fifteen-year-olds, and maybe fifty-six-year-olds, have to keep being reminded of.

"Love and discipline—in their broadest terms—this is what it comes down to; it is what everybody would say about every family and presumably about every school. But I think, from the point of view of the basis on which the school was founded, of Christian principles, that basically loving one's neighbor is something we just stand by. You have to go back to principles when you get into tough times, and you often do with an individual or with a group. What principle can you go back to? If it isn't love your neighbor, I don't know what it is.

"It's difficult for us to practice. It's difficult to teach the young."

As in any isolated community, one can see Choate's principles —some of them, anyway—at work in its funerary rites. Three memorial services were held during that year at Choate. The first is the speech the headmaster gives in chapel in memory of Choate's particular hero. The sermon varies little from year to year, and the boys listen to it with ill-disguised impatience because it signals the beginning of the fall holiday, a day without classes and therefore a day eagerly awaited by the school. The holiday, an ill-concealed surprise, is announced at breakfast by the headmaster, who grins into the microphone behind his table and says: "I will lift up mine eyes unto the hills." "Whoopee!" yell the boys, or at least they get as close to that particular word as they ever will; after breakfast they change into old clothes and file into the chapel as the steeple bells play "Yellow Submarine."

"Our fall holiday," says the headmaster, serious now, "for over thirty years, has been called Tom Curtin Day. In memory of a boy who died the year after he was graduated—maybe it was two years after. He was of the class of '32 at Choate, went on to Yale. I suppose those who knew him from afar would have known him best as an athlete. He was a small fellow, about five eight, weighed about a hundred and fifty pounds, but he was one of the greatest backs Yale ever had. He was a very unusual person, known most, I guess, for his modesty. He was quiet and dignified and friendly and the same to everyone. A rare kind of person.

"All of us need heroes to look toward and to try to emulate. Perhaps to look back over thirty years is hard, and Tom would be the first to say, 'Pick another that might be more fitting for you.' And I think that's fine, too."

Curtin went to Japan with the Yale baseball team, contracted leukemia, lived only a few months longer. St. John reads from an obituary printed in the New York *Herald Tribune:* " 'One of the tragedies of news gathering is here: integrity, simplicity and ability to face illness with calm courage are in their very nature hidden. . . . Here, unmistakably, was stuff of the rarest and finest. Integrity was the core of his being. Because of it, nothing went to his head. He was the college hero of the football field and all the glory of the headlines that goes therewith was his, but no one could have guessed that from the fact of his bearing or manner. An outstanding undergraduate of his time, looked up to by everyone, admired and loved, he was straightforward and simple when a boy at school. He did not know how to be a politician, or to be anyone but himself.' "

Those dirty politicians again! The *Tribune* undoubtedly had in mind those dogs of New Dealers who even then were hoisting the red flag over Washington, but the sentiment endures at Choate, John Kennedy's speech at the school notwithstanding. There is no school holiday for the dead President, nor any for Adlai Stevenson, '18.

St. John pauses at the end of the *Tribune*'s eulogy. All of the qualities that Choate admires in a man have been summed up in this piece of journalism, written thirty-odd years ago, and yet, there they are, alive as you and me. (Not the paper, of course; the paper died: it is the values that endure.) Integrity, courage, modesty, and silence, all wrapped up in shoulder pads, a jersey, and a helmet. It is impossible to calculate the effect of this presentation on boys who grew up watching Captain Nice and Super Chicken, Dudley Doright and Roger Ramjet, on the Saturday morning cartoons. Nobody has taken heroes seriously since, well, the *Tribune* ran into economic difficulty. To take Tom Curtin seriously is to revert to days of Superman and Captain Marvel, when a hero was super because of what he *was;* today's grass heads, the marijuana generation, know that to be super you have to take something—a pill, chicken sauce, whatever. The more serious among them know that it is the heroes of the thirties who screwed up today's world, that the heroic fathers of these heroes screwed up the entire twentieth century. The boys are in favor of humility, all right, but of a different kind, and since this guy Curtin sounds just the least bit *stupid,* can't we get a whole new lexicon of virtues while we're at it?

Unwittingly, the school itself encourages such subversiveness: just a few nights before, some English classes were required to watch a television broadcast of *Cat on a Hot Tin Roof,* a distinctly anti-Choate play in that everybody yells at the sodden, faggoty football hero: "Stop being a hero! Be a human being!"

"And it's for this reason," St. John concludes, "for the very reason that there is more than one kind of immortality, that we continue to have a day in Tom's memory. Our heroes, our saints of the past, men and women from the various ages of history, we look up to, and hope perhaps we can take a portion of their greatness and make it a part of ourselves."

That winter, one of Choate's masters died: Howard Preble, teacher of French, and a good and kind man. The boys were called to chapel, and St. John preached a moving eulogy—he is quite good at this, at least when the matter is close to hand, unimpeded by annual repetition. During the service, St. John read the tribute to great teachers that he reads every year at the opening faculty meeting:

> Great teachers have little external history to record. Their lives go over into other lives. God deals with them as we with candles do: not light them for themselves. These men are pillars in the intimate structure of this School. They are more essential than its stones or its beams; they will continue to be a kindling force and a revealing power: part of the necessary atmosphere men breathe.

Then, the headmaster announced there would be an unscheduled holiday in Preble's honor. The mood in the chapel changed; there was almost a cheer. Two third formers—the youngest boys—were so angry at this reaction that they turned to poetry, as many students did when reacting to other crises that developed during the year. One wrote:

> It warms my heart to see so many smiling faces.
> Happy in their blind greed.
> But in this holy place it's all right to do both.

To giggle inanely at death.
Death, which will soon be smiling at you
From its dark security.
Good old Mr. P., I had a rough tomorrow. . . .

And the other:

. . . so in memory of our dear departed
he'd want it that way
silence
tomorrow is a holiday for us all
sudden electricity
feetscrape pewcreak
headturn
static flash
toothshine
girlfriends vanish homework disappears
meaning
lost forever
suddenly I break out laughing with fatigue
the fools
I've been awake all
night

Spring brought the murder of Martin Luther King, Jr., and the third memorial service. It was a voluntary service arranged by the boys to coincide with the funeral on April 9. Mounir Sa'adah, the school's other ordained minister, was intrigued by the idea of a "voluntary" chapel service; he stood at the door with his pocket counter and clicked off 197 volunteers attending. Very good. Sa'adah has always maintained that if chapel were made voluntary, about a tenth of the school would attend; this was much better than that. Still, he was worried that some of the boys were just as glad that "another Negro agitator" was out of the way. Some students, according to a third former, "were hoping to get a free day. That's really all they cared about." Others protested that when Governor Lurleen Wallace died, she wasn't given "equal grief."

The boys conducted the service. Two Negroes read from the poetry of Langston Hughes. Two folk singers sang a song; the Maiyeros, elite members of the school's Glee Club, sang, too. Some boys performed a responsive reading that a senior had prepared:

Voice 1: Let us try to remember the sweet, fresh winds
Voice 2: of love
of reason
of respect for us because we are men.
Voice 1: Let us try to remember a man who worked for the understanding of men by fellowmen.
Voice 2: A man who worked for us all to be able
to feel the cool rich loam of our own land;
to work and smile the smile that comes with well-earned rest;
to cry in the cold wet a song of sorrow
for what we have done to other men.
Voice 1: In the lap of luxury this comes late:
Voice 2: A realization of others' pain comes hard.
But we are lessened in a real way by the death
of a great man.
We are here to honor him,
to pay respect to his words and work.

There was more, but Tom Curtin would hardly have understood it. Most of the boys who took the trouble to go agreed that it was the best chapel service of the year.

Spirit: God and Boy at Choate

Every clod feels a stir within it,
An instinct within it that reaches and towers.
GEORGE ST. JOHN, quoting James Russell Lowell

I suppose God is a good thing, you know, and when I came to Choate I really believed it. But after having it rammed down your throat for three years, I came away an atheist. I really think it's Choate's fault. It's a great big scene, you know, and religion should be a personal thing.
A sophomore at Yale

"If I can get to the house before the chapel bells begin to ring," says Seymour St. John, "I can still take a shower and dress and be in chapel in time." The bells begin to ring every evening at six; at six ten, after a solitary chime warns stragglers that the doors are closed and that they must report for five hours of work crews, the service begins. "One of my problems," St. John continues, "is that this year that has happened too often, to the point where my chapel talk just plain wasn't well enough prepared. It's been my fault, trying to keep too many balls in the air at one time."

The boys agree. "A lot of this stuff," says one of the third formers, "the chaplain or Mr. St. John have to make up two minutes before the service. The boys come in, they don't expect anything, they don't get anything. It's like you can't make a person like bananas if you keep on stuffing him with bananas. If they took time, had chapel services three or four times a week, and could prepare something important to say instead of something stupid, you could get a lot more effect out of it. I asked Mr. St. John about it. I said, 'You must have a very hard time preparing the sermons.' And he said, 'Oh, I'm afraid to say I have to ad lib a lot of it.' "

"Chapel," St. John tells the new boys their first evening at school, "is a central part of our school lives." He explains that the daily services, which last for twenty minutes, are for believers of all faiths. He says that the school has been "strengthened" (a favorite word of his) in the past by the presence of Moslems, Buddhists, and Hindus, but that a religious service must have some base, and here, in this chapel, that base is Episcopalian.* He hopes that each boy will be stronger in *his* faith for having attended these services, and he urges them to sing the hymns and take part in the responses and prayers.

"*Each boy,*" warns the *Student's Handbook,* "*by his acceptance of a place in School, puts himself under obligation to take an active part in these services.*" The italics are not mine; they indicate the nervousness with which the school approaches the problem of chapel. "After many months," the headmaster tells the new boys, "it may seem less than exciting. But, if you are like most alumni, you will look back and say this was something to treasure." It is a strange confession of weakness. His faculty, the more confident among them, would show more resolution in discussing the problems of memorizing geometrical theorems or irregular verbs. This burden, they would say, becomes a joy when one understands the discipline and the vocabulary.

Decorum is important, even in approaching the chapel. "Boys should be quiet as they approach the building," the *Handbook* says, "and carry on no conversation as they enter." Nor can one keep one's hands in his pockets; some of the faculty got quite exercised over this during the year. To maintain decorum, four members of the St. Andrew's Society, a self-perpetuating

* According to the school chaplain, there were at Choate that year 90 Catholic boys and 40 Jews—to cite only those whose faiths might make them feel uncomfortable at an Episcopalian service.

body of cleaner-looking kids charged with special chapel duties, stand outside the chapel doors, hands clasped solemnly before them. For some reason, Alex MacFarlane, dean of students, finds it necessary to stand outside as well. Inevitably clad in his double-breasted, belted, fur-inside greatcoat, he looks, as he stands against the building, like somebody's special agent (maybe even ours) holding up the Berlin Wall. "A cold duty, Mr. MacFarlane," I said one evening. "Ah, ha!" he replied. "It gets colder."

Inside there is a noise of shuffling and an impression of much brown wood and white plaster. The windows are long and narrow, and there is a balcony where many of the boys must sit with a view of nothing but brass and glass chandeliers suspended by scarlet cords, with scarlet tassels dangling below. On the altar are candles to be lighted ceremoniously and a cross to bow the head to; behind these hangs a dismal picture of a ship and some men in apostles' uniforms—one of them, presumably, is St. Andrew. "I have disliked the inside of the chapel quietly for a long time," Malcolm Manson says. "With the chance to change it, I was delighted. The idea of having it terribly simple, and a big black cross appeals to me tremendously. Life size, you know, where you could put somebody if you wanted to: a utilitarian cross." The seniors sit in the front pews and are the first to leave when the service is done. In every other pew, or thereabouts, masters may be seen taking attendance. One or two boys are sleeping; the masters, who can hardly reach them, look elsewhere. Very few boys look at the speaker. Once, when I sat nearly behind the headmaster, I realized how disconcerting this must be.

Nor is it easy to hear. The acoustics are dreadful, though acoustical speakers (installed, says one master, at a cost of $10,000) jut from every cranny. In February, the gasping organ wheezed its last, succumbing after burning its motor for a while. (A new one was ordered for $125,000. Then it was decided to knock out the south wall and add 250 seats at a cost of $350,000. Some masters grumbled that the money should be used to raise faculty salaries, unaware that although a donor can always be found for chapel organs and chapel seats, it is very difficult to find donors for faculty salaries. Communion was not served at Choate while the repairs were under way.)

That spring, hymn singing was led by the Glee Club alone. For a while, Duncan Phyfe, organist and choirmaster, forsook such unmanageable tunes as "Jesus Calls Us o'er the Tumult" for simple songs everyone knew: "Fairest Lord Jesus" and "My Country, 'Tis of Thee." The result, however, was not the same, and sometimes the choir was inattentive. One evening Phyfe threw a hymnbook at a boy whose eye roved toward the firmament. "We are lucky to have such a leader in our choir," St. John observed when order was restored, "and any time he wants to throw *two* hymnbooks, that's all right with me."

St. John rarely discusses chapel without mentioning the letters he gets from alumni who, late in life, discovered how much they loved the services. "One of my favorites," he says, "that I've quoted many times, came from a boy named Lawrence who wrote that Choate had planted time bombs in him that had been going off ever since. He would come on these thoughts and hark back to something that suddenly made sense in the light of new experience."

Another boy wrote: "I like to feel that I, as a product of the Choate school, am endowed with a special gift. An ability to endeavor to create a better world by giving of myself. . . . You have given me words to live by on 500 or 600 occasions in the Choate chapel. I tried to listen carefully then and to live up to the ideals you helped to form."

Sometimes St. John reads these letters to the boys in chapel. "You'd be astounded how many of these come back," he says. "When people kick and press against chapel, my reaction is, well, we've got to be better. A lot better, but we don't have to throw out chapel. There are ways, there have to be ways, to make this effective." He does not, however, believe that voluntary chapel is the answer. Choate's schedule for the boys is simply too tight, there is too much competing for their time, and if they were allowed not to come they wouldn't. "If you're lucky, you get a third." Other masters feel ten percent would be more likely. "You lose a large percentage," St. John says, "and you deprive them of something—if you believe in this at all—that is *perhaps* the most important thing of all the things we're trying to teach. Chapel isn't the only place to teach it. It should be taught in the houses, on the athletic field, in the classes, this thing should be taught right across the board. But there has to be a central clearinghouse, somehow, and the church has held it over the centuries."

When he became headmaster, the boys had two evenings free from chapel a week. St. John changed that. "It seemed to me that this was valuable and wise to hold on to as a regular, daily concern. The boys coming together, and the group participation, which we used to get better than we've got this year, in singing, in prayer—even that, without any talk, has value. It's been said that preaching is like squirting an eyedropper of medicine out of a third-story window and hoping that it hits somebody in the right place. If you've hit ten, you've done well. Then what have you got the other five hundred and sixty there for? Maybe for the community. Perhaps the feeling that this is one nation under God, one school under God, and here we are."

On Friday nights there is no sermon. Friday is music night, and on the first of these, Steve Wilder, a senior, played five pieces by Couperin on his cello, accompanied by Phyfe on the organ. There were no hymns and no prayers, and it was as ungodly a performance as you might wish unless (as would be unlikely in the Choate chapel) you happened to think of David dancing before the Lord. Steve played well and the boys dozed; heads heavy from football helmets in the afternoon dropped on their neighbors' shoulders. "I like chapel," Steve says, "I really pray there. Other boys do, too." "Whew," said one of the others when Steve had finished, "sort of sleepy music. But then some of the speakers are pretty sleepy too."

No one at Choate that year could agree whether God had a role to play in the chapel, and if He did, to what extent He should be present. A Jesuit priest who had visited St. Paul's School announced uneasily that religion seemed acceptable in the classroom, but not in the chapel. "I am suspicious," he wrote, "that some of the ineffectiveness of chapel services derives from lack of dogmatism. In other words, the attempt to offend no one by the preaching and praying of the sound theology of the Protestant Episcopal Church ends up by offending everyone. What often results is an indifferent naturalism bordering on humanism." Little sound theology of any kind is preached at Choate.

St. John himself seems to be of two minds. One Monday evening he concluded with a promise to return to a more God-oriented service; the following Monday he concluded by reading not the thirteenth chapter of First Corinthians, "which is right on the button of what I'm trying to say, you may know it well," but Leigh Hunt's "Abou Ben Adhem" about a man who, because he loved his fellowmen, was judged to love God. "It's a corny poem," St. John said, "but then some of my favorites are."

"Christianity for me," said Stephen Longley late one night, "means something about Christ. You generally learn about Christ from the Bible." Longley, one of a sizable minority of Choate's faculty educated in England, favors a return to the Prayer Book service.

Rod Furnald disagreed: "That's an assumption, Steve."

Longley: Where else are you going to learn about Christ from?

Furnald: Love.

Longley: You may learn about love, but you don't learn about Christ.

Furnald: I don't see how you can justify compulsory Christianity.

Longley: How can you justify compulsory English?

Furnald: These boys are probably going to have to read, they're probably going to have to write, they're probably going to have to express themselves later in life—therefore, English is relevant.

Longley: As someone who believes in religion, I would say: Probably these boys have souls, they would have to develop them . . .

Furnald: But this is a very Christian standpoint, Steve.

Longley: I agree.

Furnald: Your own personal faith.

Longley: Not my own personal faith. *Probably* they have souls, *probably* they have a potential to develop their souls or their spiritual capacity. One does not develop these by an academic analysis of what something is, but by a personal involvement in it.

Furnald: That's why I want to have chapel services for those boys who believe they have souls. I don't believe they have souls.

Longley: Okay.

Furnald: Then is chapel compulsory for those boys who don't believe they have souls?

Longley: I don't know. But for someone who believes entirely in the intellect and power of the mind, all of this sport jazz which he has to do in this school has no relevance at all. And yet he is forced to do sport. It is the structure of the school. Unless the school is to be structured with some sort of format which is compulsory, then the thing falls apart.

Furnald: I don't think that's fair, putting sport in the same category. You can measure the results of compulsory athletics on a boy. Can you do this with the soul?

Longley: No. No more can you with your English literature. Or whether a boy is really being appreciative of poetry. It's neither here nor there. You're *exposing* him because we believe that in the process of growing up he should be exposed to certain things we call disciplines, so that he gets an all-around development, so that we don't turn out a lot of crabs. We turn out people that can at least walk straight. I don't think boys appreciate the liberating realms of doubt until they have some sort of straw that they can hold on to if they happen to be drowning.

"Putting God back into the chapel would be the last suggestion of the students," said a student, but St. John is concerned with showing the students how God relates to more mundane matters. He looks forward to the new auditorium where, as he told the students, "we can address the whole school in a secular spot. A place for matters we occasionally speak of here: matters of discipline, of school policy, any matters except the directly God-connected matters." One of the reasons the boys resent chapel is that the headmaster uses it for harangues, for bringing the kids into line, stinging them into singing a little louder, being polite to visiting athletes, refraining from cutting obscenities into their desks in study hall. If anything in the school goes a bit out of joint, St. John tells his faculty or his Student Council, "I'll take a chapel evening on it soon."

St. John defends the practice. To the boys he said: "I must admit that for me all this is connected with our deepest beliefs, our beliefs of what is good and right and strong, which *is* religion—again, to me. For some, God-connected; for some, perhaps not yet, or not at all. I don't feel that talking about what might be called secular things in chapel is necessarily out of place." St. John believes, too, that everyone operates from a basis of faith whether he knows it or not. "It might be a faith in God," he told the boys. "It might be a faith in No God, which is also a faith. That faith might concern Me First, which is a faith that all of us, I think, are apt to go through at one time or another. Then there is the faith of Perhaps No God, or Perhaps God, which puts society, the community, first. The greatest good for the greatest number, and this is highly practical. It can be highly religious."

This last faith, which is not St. John's own, was the one he referred to most often that year: the rights of the community over the rights of the individual asserted, as often as not, in this place which lends an authority greater than that of any of the people assembled there. Many boys seem to share the religious fermentation of their times, when religion has become a dirty word to many believing Christians. Religion, some feel, *must* be more than what is "good and right and strong"; if it isn't, to hell with it. They share the deep anti-institutional feeling of many priests and laymen who have been trying to strip the dignity, the rightness, away from religion, to get rid of the fetid moralizing that permeates not only the Choate chapel, but destroys, there and elsewhere, the awareness of holiness. Ministers come to Choate to talk about civil rights, exhorting this body assembled before God to the same fervor it can get from hearing Walter Cronkite. The sense of the numinous is lost, to be found perhaps in drugs, and the boys feel the lack.

In the spring, three of Choate's ablest seniors prepared an exhaustive survey of student attitudes. Most of the student body took part, providing the researchers and, eventually, a horrified faculty, with so much inflammatory revelation and opinion about sex and cheating, drugs and smoking, that the replies to ten questions devoted to religion were almost overlooked. They were, however, the clearest word Choate has ever had on the effectiveness of its chapel services. "Of all the areas of school life about which the students had a chance to express their opinions," wrote the seniors in a report evaluating the results of their survey, "religion fared the worst."

Nearly 20 percent of the students professed agnosticism or atheism. Less than 16 percent felt that "Choate's chapel system successfully encourages the student to think about religion," and fewer than 20 percent felt that they had become more religious since being at Choate. "Of course," wrote the three seniors, "we are not passing through the most religious stage of our lives, and we may well appreciate the Chapel later on, but it seems odd that the most religious persons think that the Chapel system falls far short of its goal." Odd, indeed:

more than 90 percent of the students denounced chapel services as being anything from "dull" or "meaningless" to "boring *and* meaningless." Moreover, three-fourths of the students felt that Choate had no business encouraging "students to be thoughtful religious persons," and two-thirds of them felt that no prep school chapel could provide such encouragement if it *were* desirable. The students voted heavily for chapel services led by students and services directed more toward discussions of current events, but if chapel were ever to be made voluntary, only half the students indicated that they would go as often as twice a week and 28.3 percent said they would never go at all.

"How many faculty members go to chapel?" a third former asked. "Most of them don't. And yet they make the students go because this-is-the-whole-school-together."

Years ago, faculty members not assigned to taking attendance would still come to sit in the balcony of the chapel. They don't do that any longer; only those who are on duty attend. Very few schools require faculty attendance in chapel, and some of the masters resent ever being obliged to go. "It's the only time I can see my family," says one teacher. Another admits that he usually wishes he didn't have to go to chapel, but once he is there, he is glad he went. "The boys get something out of it," he says. As for the faculty, well, they should be in chapel "to back the regime."

"This is what boils my ass," a faculty member said. "Seymour wants compulsory chapel when nobody wants to go. Of course he says nobody would go if chapel weren't compulsory because it is the goddamn truth. A banality which defies elaboration. Seymour is a preacher, but a preacher without the air of real authority. He doesn't really want to bring the boys out. There is an intellectual reserve: he holds it back. And that is why he is ineffectual in chapel. He wants to be thought to lead the boys to make their own decisions. And yet he doesn't *really* want to. His father was so bombastic that Seymour holds back."

In a typical sermon, St. John will weigh one good against another, the ideal versus the realistic. "We think of a rule from the Sermon on the Mount," he tells the boys. "Be ye perfect as your Father in heaven is perfect. Everybody knows they can't be perfect. That's the *ideal*. Reality means some good and some evil, with an effort to be more good than evil." He may, at this point, be holding his hands before him in a gesture imitated cruelly by both boys and masters: his hands, like plates on a scale, move alternately up and down. He concludes by saying, "There have been those, of course, who avoided the struggle by not participating. These have not been the contributors."

Just before Christmas, when St. John had gone to Vietnam, Ralph Symonds, divinity student and teacher of speech and drama, gave the best sermon of the year. He talked about Guy Fawkes Day, already a month gone, and the nature of rebellion—"Barrels of gunpowder had been blowing up for years before 1605. Only these were barrels of words." "Speech is action," Symonds tells his public speaking classes, and here he uses the podium as a fulcrum on which to turn his small frame, sometimes speaking at right angles to his audience. He adopts various voices drawn from history and imagination and engages himself in debate—"Come ON, Jesus! That man Caiaphas is IN; that dirty Samaritan is OUT—like you, WAY OUT." Jesus then tells a story about a Samaritan who was neighbor to a Jew.

There is no sound anywhere in the chapel. Some of the boys know exactly what Symonds is doing, others are confused, but the theatricality has caught them all. It is a real Bishop Latimer-Lancelot Andrewes kind of sermon that grabs its listeners and bangs their ears with the unexpected immediacy of metaphor. The faculty, however, remains stony-faced, impassive.

Symonds moves quickly to the Friday before Passover when another protest was squashed, another political agitator done away with by the establishment. "So," Symonds concludes, "the lid on Guy Fawkes' barrel, the barrel that blows everything to heaven, that barrel lid keeps coming off just a bit, and all sorts of protests keep coming out. Words in Jerusalem, gunpowder in London—and now YOU in San Francisco. Listen. Listen to this hopeful and *gentle,* hopeful and *sad* protest. Perhaps for some people it is the way to pray. Perhaps the protest *is* the prayer. Listen!"

And then comes a burst, perfectly timed, from all the chapel's acoustical speakers: guitars whanging and NOISE to split the ears and Scott McKenzie wailing "San Francisco." Symonds whirls and strides down the aisle, unbuttoned clerical gown flapping. No hymn, no closing prayer. McKenzie *is.*

One of the faculty in the gallery leans over to a guest to apologize for having subjected her to such a performance.

"At least he prepared it well," says one of the boys. "And I'm grateful to him for that."

And the headmaster said, "Ralph Symonds is an interesting guy. He does something in chapel that conveys interest and liveliness, shock treatment. I've never been certain what else got conveyed."

Body: Mud in the Afternoon

> It is on the playing fields of Milton, and Groton, and maybe Choate, that the seeds will be sown that in later years, and on other fields, will cause you to turn into sick bay with a bad back or a football knee.
>
> Letter from John F. Kennedy to Robert F. Kennedy, November 14, 1943

> Remember, most people have to play in the outfield of life.
>
> Letter from a parent urging a child to learn team sports

On certain days in spring it is almost possible to believe that Choate can be leisurely, even calm, about its sports program. Somewhere, perhaps, boys are laying their lacrosse sticks against one another's ears, but the first varsity baseball game against New Haven College is a quiet affair. Spring has come early this year, the weather is good, and the long afternoon light lies cool against the white façade of the Winter Exercise Building. Faculty infants, still hobbled by their snowsuits, tug at their older sisters' hands, but the Choate boys, those few who have bothered to come, sprawl back in the bleachers and peel off their shirts, in hopes of an April tan.

Choate has an easy lead, 4–2 going into the sixth, when New Haven scores three times. This is a bit embarrassing because New Haven has only two men on its bench and has pulled its right fielder in as a relief pitcher, but then nothing bothers Tom Yankus, Choate's unflappable baseball coach. Choate counters with five runs in an inning of its own. As the balls pop softly into the hazy afternoon, Yankus sits quietly on the bench. There is nothing much to say: this early in the season the balls are always hitting the bats. Choate alone uses 160 pitches, and a great many of these finish with the ball being hit somewhere. Fortunately, New Haven's men are poor at base-running. One who safely crossed home plate is tagged out because he failed to touch third base. So is another, who has somehow managed to fall off second.

The game lasts three hours. The boys come and go, chat, punch each other's arms, and take bets on whether a master's four-year-old son will actually swallow a piece of used chewing gum that a student has thoughtfully put into his mouth. A few of these boys, including some of the baseball players, know that when Sunday comes the serious stuff will begin. It won't be *really* serious, of course, just sort of hacking around, tossing the football back and forth as Bob Williams, the kindly varsity football coach, just happens to be there looking on. And yet, and yet—there are only 75 places open in football camp next fall and 95 boys who want to come.

"We have to somehow winnow out the twenty boys who can't make it," Williams says. "I think it's important that you work on football all year round. I like to talk to boys all year round about football. It keeps them thinking. I'll have passers out in the spring on Sunday mornings—to fool around."

The opening day of football camp, twelve days before classes begin, finds Bob Williams very tense indeed. By September 30, when Choate plays its first game of the season, Williams is unapproachable—a short, stocky man darting nervously behind a protective screen of lesser coaches. This is Williams' fourth season. Last season was his first to show a winning record, and now he has to begin with Exeter, a school with half again as many boys as Choate. Exeter had beaten Choate 40–7 the year before and is definitely out of Choate's league, but playing Exeter is important for Choate's image of itself, if only to support the headmaster's belief that Choate is the best school in the country and Charles Pierce's contention that Choate competes with

Exeter in attracting the best students. "When we took them on," Bob Williams says, "we thought we might win three out of ten."

It is a glorious summer afternoon. Cheerleaders scramble into inept pyramids. The band bleats out of tune. One boy sits backward in the bleachers, memorizing a copy of *Mad* magazine, but the stands are crowded and an aged cop from Wallingford tries to restrain behind a sagging rope a few dozen Choaties and faculty toddlers who crawl over and under it as soon as his bent back is turned. Many masters and boys clutch transistor radios to their ears, listening to Boston and Minnesota fight it out in the American League's penultimate game. Cars are drawn up around the field, one demanding from its bumper sticker:

WHEN ARE WE GOING TO WIN IN VIETNAM?
AND WHY NOT?

Beyond the field and the mayhem, beyond the visting school's bleachers which are strategically placed so that the waning afternoon sun strikes the visiting audience in its eyes, there is a distant hillside, looking like a painted piece of scenery, where the sun also falls, and where cows are grazing.

From the bleachers a girl's voice, thin and clear, screams: *"Push 'em back!"* This is the marvel of a home game on a Saturday afternoon: girls. A new rule allows girls who have been properly invited to be on the grounds for such occasions, but there are pairs and foursomes of town girls with exotic hair who walk around looking over the Choate livestock as if they were still anticipating invitations, proper or otherwise. "Honey attracts the bees," says Ted Ayres, alumni director. The sight of so many obviously available teen-age girls would unleash the Humbert Humbert crouching inside any master. Those girls who are not from town, those who have managed to get away from Farmington or Rosemary Hall, wear horse-blanket-plaid suits and culottes, their hair (invariably lank and blond) hanging straight below their shoulders. Some of the older boys ostentatiously stroke their girls' long, aristocratic necks and take long drags on cigarettes; they are last year's graduating class, come back from Yale and Wesleyan to spook their horny schoolmates. By an unspoken tradition, boys who bring girls to Choate football games parade them, with much hand holding and leg rubbing, back and forth before the stands from which arises, just below the threshold of audible sound, a great and musky groan.

Bob Williams, in bow tie and seersucker jacket, sees none of this because Exeter has scored early and then, for two periods, there is no score. The first half is all Exeter's because Choate is playing a peculiar strategy: run ineffectively for three downs and make an incomplete pass on the fourth. Choate fumbles twice as it nears Exeter's goal line but, in the final quarter, intercepts Exeter's passes as it completes its own. All through the season it would be this way: a determined defense would keep the damage down until a late-starting offense could get itself in gear. Trailing 6–0 going into the final minutes of the game, Choate scores for the first time on a 34-yard pass play, then kicks the extra point.

The stands go wild: "We're Number *One!*" Seymour St. John, who sits with the team on the bench, waves for silence, afraid of a jinx in the remaining minutes of the game, but nobody pays any attention. "What a great way to end," says a boy when there are two minutes left on the clock. "Don't say that!" St. John shouts. "I'm superstitious!" Then he yells at the referees that Exeter has no right to the final time-out it has claimed.

Only Choate's coaches seem upset at the end. They feel the team has not played particularly well. They curse one boy—"He does *nothing* out there!"—worry about injuries, the lack of depth on the bench. "We just don't have any linebackers."

"The Exeter game was a surprise," Williams admitted when the season was over. "We should have been beaten. Their personnel was about forty to fifty percent better than ours. We beat them because we outsmarted them, essentially. We threw a play that's been around sixty years that they had never seen, see. We saved it right to the bitter end with two minutes left to go; we threw it and got away with it.

"It helps a lot to win the opener," he went on. "I don't care who you play. Exeter or the Little Sisters of the Poor, it doesn't make any difference as long as you win it. The kids pointed for this. They really wanted to win this game. They take a lot of gas from their friends at home who go to Exeter."

The season wore on. Choate beat Loomis, Tabor, Hotchkiss, and Mount Hermon. Theoretically, there is no scouting in Choate's league, but Williams manages to find out a great deal about the opposition. The week before the game he decorates the locker room with an enemy banner, press cuttings, taunting remarks made by the other school, and his own notes:

> Hotchkiss has a first rate football team and they hate our guts. These facts should combine to produce quite a game. . . . Their big offensive threat is their tailback, Lescault, who is a very good back. HE MUST BE STOPPED. Their wingback weighs 200 pounds and is a good blocker and pass receiver. HE MUST BE STOPPED. . . . Hotchkiss will be very high and will come down here looking for a win. We must be ready both mentally and physically to meet them. To do this we must start to prepare ourselves *now*.

Choate beat Lawrenceville, too, but it was a hard game partly because Lawrenceville, like Choate, uses a single-wing formation. "Single wing," Williams says, "is a much better offense. We can't play in this league with a T formation. We've tried it. The boys aren't big enough. This is the first big team we've had." One of his tackles stands six feet three and weighs 257 pounds. Ten boys on the team weigh 190 pounds or more. "We're in better shape than our opponents," Williams continues, "and we will wear you down. We'll just wear you out to the point where in the fourth quarter you can't move. The single wing helps to wear you out: two men always operate on one.

"I think more people would use it if they understood it. I'm a terrible T-formation coach because I don't understand a T formation. I just don't. I try. When I put single wing back in, we had terrible alumni trouble. The alumni were on our back, trying to get us fired.

"Two of them," Williams recalls, "are vociferous gentlemen. They didn't play football, but they're financially important to the school. They write nasty letters to the headmaster. It makes it very, very difficult to coach at this place. Because the headmaster pays attention to them. Also, he feels that *he's* an expert. There are two things in life people are experts on: politics and football. Everybody knows everything about both fields."

Williams estimates that he spends 1,200 hours a year on football. Even when football is not in season, he spends three hours a day studying it. In the spring he reads everything current that is published about football. "They have a coaching book club," he says. "They publish a book a month, so I get a book a month." During the season he studies each week the 800 feet of film that are taken of the varsity and JV games. This is less film than is expended by any of Choate's opponents, but it is all that the budget, which is supplied by alumni friends of the team, allows. Williams spends six to eight hours "grading" these films, preparing a critique of each game and each player which he delivers to the team the following day, Sunday morning. He prepares charts of four kinds of blocks and how many of each kind of block each member of the team contributed. To do this, Williams studies what every boy does in every play, sometimes rerunning his film eleven times. Then he exchanges films with the rival school and does the whole thing all over again, studying the skills and weaknesses of the opposing players who will return next year.

"So," says Williams, "we put in a lot of time on football, and most people who criticize us put in about six hours a year. They watch six games. But that's all right. Harry Truman's statement 'If you can't stand the heat get out of the kitchen' is a wonderful statement for coaches.

"I think coaching is great. I think the best relationships I've had—I've been here sixteen years—have been in coaching, not in teaching." Williams teaches math; the boys think he does it well.

"The kids who come back," Williams says, "and are really enthusiastic are the kids who played for you, not the kids you taught. They're noncommittal. The emotional qualities of football are such that people who go through that together don't forget it. The people who go through math class together—it makes very little difference. It's just the way it is."

Still, the teaching is important to him, even if only half of the coaches in the league teach anything but football. "My theory," Williams says, "is never coach if your livelihood depends on it. You're just asking for trouble. You're going to get fired."

After the Lawrenceville victory there was a tea dance in the library. All sixth formers, members of varsity and JV sports, and the band were entitled to import girls. "Meals," explained Alex MacFarlane, the dean of students, "are not a part of the picture. Girls should not arrive until after lunch." The first girl came at ten. "Girls must be gone after chapel in the evening," MacFarlane insisted, but he admitted that "the last will leave here about ten thirty." Under an El Greco sky, with great clumps of yellow leaves blowing from Choate's magnificent trees, the girls arrived, some in boots and raincoats, some in ponchos and patterned stockings, and some in cars of their own. Some wore acne, some wore arrogant expressions, some chewed gum, and others blew cigarette smoke in the faces of their tortured dates.

In the library, rugs, tables, and couches have been removed. An illuminated portrait of the Old Head's wife, Clara St. John, flanked by vases of white flowers, calmly surveys the scene. So do a few faculty members brought in as chaperones. The room is huge—one wonders why it was ever built so large—but it is not big enough to contain the electronic noise created by the Passengers, a rock group from New Haven. A horrible-looking flame-red punch is passed around by smaller students in white jackets. The girls, very pretty in miniskirts and bare feet, have parked their shoes against the walls. For the most part, each girl dances apart from her date, gyrating in frantic circles of her own.

They look very small, and all the varsity athletes look very large. When the music changes, just a little, everyone dances cheek to cheek, some of the girls virtually crawling up the boys.

"Only one girl out there knows how to dance," a student told me. He introduced me to her. Armed with my technical expertise, I said, "You're the best dancer out there."

"I know," she replied. She goes to ballet school in New York.

"Look out," said the boy, "you'll be a chapter in his book."

"I deserve a chapter," she said. Choate boys do not have such cool.

"Most of the girls," I said to Seymour St. John, "are very pretty."

"They have to be," he replied, "to wear the clothes they do." He looked, as we were all looking, at a girl in a striped and many-colored dress whose lithe movements edged her skirt above the tops of her stockings. "They look bored with each other half the time," St. John said, but I didn't think so.

Outside, a New York taxi waits. It has been on campus all afternoon. Briefly, I imagine a long-legged, mink-coated teenager stepping from her Sutton Place apartment, waving thin fingers at a passing taxi and telling the driver, "Take me to Wallingford, Connecticut. The Choate School." Actually, the cab belongs to Neal's Taxi Service, "In Business Over Ten Years. By Appointment DI-23769." "I specialize in this," Neal says. He brought three girls up from the city for a round-trip fare of $105, presumably less tip.

The next week, in faculty meeting, the entire school prepares to move in buses up to Deerfield for the Big Game. In the days of the Old Head, Choate went to Deerfield, in northern Massachusetts, in an eight-car private train; the masters had to know where each boy sat because the administration, sitting in private chambers, improved the journey by summoning students for discussions of their various delinquencies. But those were the old days; now the concern is with dress and deportment. No blue jeans will be allowed: "Housemasters will make a check," St. John says, "table masters will make a further check, bus masters will make a final check." "Boys admiring girls from bus windows," says Bill Pudvah, director of athletics, "may absorb what they see, but may not shout." "It's the first time we go as a student body away from the school," the headmaster observes. "We want to put our best foot forward. We don't train for it. We march as stragglers, but that's all right, too." His reference is to Deerfield, which *does* train for it: everyone is supposed to march in step behind the band, his coat folded over his left arm.

Lunch on Saturday, November 11, is held at ten thirty, then the school gets into eight buses. The teams have already left, each team to its own bus and following its own customs: the soccer squad, for instance, is not allowed to talk on the ride up, but may on the ride back. As the kids pile on, waving BEAT DEERFIELD banners, megaphones, and red plastic ram's horns, a master reads the roll: "Baldwin, Belluci, Bishop, Butterworth." One boy crouches in his seat with a copy of *The Atlantic,* another with *Reflections in a Golden Eye*. The buses leave at eleven, with a police escort, through red lights to Route 91 north. There is a NO SMOKING sign in the front of the bus, which is hardly necessary since only the driver smokes.

The ride north is quiet and dull. Shortly after the Massachusetts border, Route 91 inexplicably vanishes. The bus must jiggle onto Route 5 and make its way past the McDonaldburgers and the site for the soon-to-open electrically heated Loew's drive-in theater, Discount City, Donut Dip, and Castro Convertibles, past a graveyard, Vincent's Steakhouse, and Cyril's Motel, past a Triple-S Blue Stamp Redemption Center, some fur storage vaults, and the Church of the Holy Family, not to mention uncounted Shell and Esso stations, all of which is what America is really all about except that nobody is looking; in fact, one boy is reading poems by Andrei Vosnesensky.

The cheerleaders confer quietly, explaining that the headmaster gives them "a lot of grief" over their cheers, some of which he finds indelicate. To counter such stuffy opposition, and to avoid responsibility, they encourage their friends to start the prohibited cheers from the stands.

Cheerleader 1: I don't think he'll go for the new one.

Cheerleader 2: Which?

Cheerleader 1: "Rip-em-up, tear-em-up, give-em-hell, Choate!"

Cheerleader 2: It's a bit like "B-L-O-O-D, BLOOD!" He didn't go for that at all.

Cheerleader 3: My favorite is still what they shout at North Carolina when the other team scores: "Ahhhhhhhhhhhhhh, SHIT!"

Cheerleader 2 (wistfully): That's a bit out of our league.

For the past few days strange signs had appeared on walls at Choate: PUT THE PICKLE TO THEM. Everyone knows that pickles and Deerfield share a fondness for the color green, but beyond that, the message remained a mystery. Mounir Sa'adah, however, was so upset by it he berated the boys in chapel for their heartlessness. No one knew what he was talking about, but one boy thought it had to do with the French colonial army using pickles to torture Algerians' rectums, and, said the boy, since Sa'adah is Syrian, that explains that.

Coming into Deerfield, past the dull red brick main building and the handsomely preserved colonial houses that surround it, Jon van Leuven, bus master, reads the marching orders: Don't rush for seats. Don't throw anything under the stands. When we get to the stands, five things will happen in this order:

1. Deerfield cheers us.
2. We cheer Deerfield.
3. Deerfield cheers Mr. St. John.
4. Choate cheers Mr. Boyden.
5. Cheer captains face the flag at attention.

"Then," says a boy, "all hell breaks loose."

In the locker room for visitors, Bob Williams is talking to his team, getting them up for the game. It is one of the most subtle arts of coaching. "He tells us," says one of his players, "that we'll have very few times in life to prove we're really good and this game is one of them. I agree with that, basically. I think a few times in your life you ought to try something bigger than you are. Then," the player continues, "he kind of rocks us, talking softly about offense and defense, rising to a crescendo, then falling, then rising again, then he grabs his clipboard and shouts, 'Let's go!' and we all explode out of the gym."

"I talk to them for five minutes," says Williams, who always measures time precisely. "I don't think any more or any less is effective. I start by telling them what this game means in regard to the season. The last game is a great opportunity for these boys because they may never have such an opportunity again. Then I cover the specific assignments.

"You can't give this all at the same volume, you see. Different places have different resonances. For the Hotchkiss game I was in front of a blackboard, and for some reason the resonance was incredible. It was really wonderful; it sounded like the Voice of God. You start slowly and you build up, and then I think you gotta change your pace and slow down and then you gotta build again, and you really have to play this. You play this by ear—you can't preplan it. You gotta watch some boys—it seems to me the guys with less intelligence—who get hooked. They get this glassy stare the first half minute you talk. You know right away; these guys just quiver. Other boys don't get anything whatever. You can tell. You try to avoid the kid who gets hooked right away, you gotta lay off him, not look at him, because he can overdo it. He'll get so emotional he'll go out there and blow up.

"The final thing I say to them is: 'You can win this ball game.' "

Winter trees, distant hills, an overcast sky. Frank Boyden, the oldest headmaster, drives his miniature motorized surrey-with-the-fringe-on-top toward the football field: a royal electric progress as he waves gently to his admirers right and left. "I wonder," one boy asks, "whether Mr. Boyden has a Louis Quinze chair to watch the game in." The Deerfield band, in green blazers and white buck shoes, plays a tune for the rest of the school to march to, and the school *does* march in step, but more sloppily than in earlier years. Choate appreciates this regimentation and yells "What do we eat? *Green meat!*" Two students wave a gigantic banner which says AVE ATQUE VALE and shows a blue-and-gold-clad Salomé displaying on a platter the green-haired head of John the Baptist Deerfield.

The teams come out, Choate in blue and gold, and Deerfield in green jerseys with white stripes. Choate receives, begins a running game, and scores within minutes. The stands go wild. Deerfield clearly has an inferior team; it has been clobbered three times already this season, and Choate's undefeated record is assured. A minute later Deerfield scores on a passing play. Deerfield, in fact, is catching passes—straight projectiles that never waver—everywhere. Soon the score is 19–7, favoring Deerfield. Choate's star back is out of the game; the blood will not stop running from his nose. "We want *blue blood!*" Deerfield yells. There is something about prep school football that you cannot get at the Yale Bowl or Shea Stadium: you can *hear* the tackles and the curses, you can see the players' faces drawn tight in pain or concentration. Choate is penalized 15 yards for roughing the kicker and a photographer on the sidelines nearly weeps. Bob Williams, in blue windbreaker and bow tie, stalks before his benches, scratching at his crew cut. At half time, when both school bands come out to march, the score is 19–13.

"At half time," says Bob Williams, "if we're behind, I tell them we're going to start over. We've had a poor first half. The first thing to do is check the defense. You spend five minutes on that and then you talk to them for five minutes. You say, 'We're six points behind and we've got to come back, but we can score!' You've got to be very careful. I've lost a couple of games over the years by making the boys overconfident. It was a nothing-nothing game at the half, and they were so confident when they went back out that when their opponents scored they just fell apart. You can change the emotional tide in a ball game, but if you get excited, or really upset, as I did at Loomis this year, they try so hard to overcome their problems they just fall apart. You can get mad at the half, but you shouldn't do it while a team is out there operating."

"When he's mad," says one of his players, "he throws his clipboard on the ground. When he's *very* mad, he throws both his clipboard and his hat on the ground. I've only seen him do that once."

"You can use anger during the game," Williams says, "to obtain a special result. But you can't overdo it. You've got to be awful careful, but you can play it. You have to make some very subtle adjustments in your own thinking sometimes.

"I thought we could win that Deerfield game by a point. I thought we were still in the game."

Choate scored in the third quarter on an astonishing pass. But with Choate trailing 26–20, Deerfield put in its substitutes: its team grew visibly smaller as victory grew more certain. As Choate dropped another seven points, Williams managed to look composed, but the rage that came from the Choate stands was hot to the touch. "How much did they pay you, ref?" one boy screamed. "If we ever played Deerfield without referees," said another, "we'd win it. We've been robbed for three years now." At the end of the game two students, livid with rage, thought they saw a chance for retribution: "Put it in your book!" they demanded. "Put it in your book how we were cheated! Christ, how those referees cheated us!" "We got some bad calls," the co-captain of the team recalled later, "but we got some pretty good ones, too, that we should never have got. So it balanced out."

It was dark on the ride back, and most people slept. There was a flicker of excitement when it looked as if a police car were trying to arrest our bus and groans of disappointment when it passed us by. Later, outside Springfield, one of the buses was attacked by a flurry of rocks flung from a railroad bridge. Some windows were smashed, and one boy, struck over the ear, bled for a while. All the buses stopped and the police were called. Hilarious students began to rock our bus until it nearly tipped over. Angry, the driver started moving again and immediately got lost, circling aimlessly through the less scenic streets of Springfield.

"We've got a renegade bus!" came a cry from the back. "The driver's drunk!"

There was some talk, too, that the driver had plotted it out in advance, that he was heading for some hidden armor-plated garage where he would hold the boys for ransom. "God," said one boy, "think of the money he'd make! Forty-five Choaties with rich parents! We ought to be good for five thousand apiece."

We did get back, and as we stumbled from the bus a boy said to me: "If you think football's bloodthirsty, wait till you see hockey."

"I play on the faculty hockey team, called the Wobblies," one master said. "Once the headmaster bawled me out. I got checked and knocked down and he skated over to me and said, 'Come on, get up! Play the game!' I was getting up as quickly as I could. This school assumes you are a good loser and a good winner, but if you lose, you're a damned loser, and you have *failed! Wow!* You have failed badly, you're a loser, and don't you forget it, buster."

"It's a sin to lose here," his wife added. "Maybe this is true in most men's organizations. I don't mean just on the athletic fields: it's a *sin* to be a loser. In women's schools one of the finest attributes we have is the ability to lose gracefully.

"There's the idea, too," she continued, "that the coaches have to take this deadly seriously. You can't get any fun in the game! And not just in the varsity, but down through the leagues."

Her husband remembers a story about one of the hockey coaches. "We lost a wonderful hockey game. Both teams played beautifully. After the game was over, one boy skated around the rink with another of his teammates. They had their arms around each other, they were talking about the game. Then, as boys will, they began hipping each other, then chased each other, then one of them fell and laughed. This coach comes out on the ice and grabs one of the boys, and shakes him, and throws him over the boards and says: 'When you lose a game I don't want to see you smile on this rink or you'll never play hockey for me again!' "

"Games," writes Cyril Connolly, "are still the most efficacious escape from the tyranny of the Phallus," but many of the masters and more than a quarter of the students feel that Choate places far too much emphasis on its athletic programs. Nearly everyone at the school will speak out frankly on the subject—I once heard a Student Council member tell a gathering of alumni agents bluntly that athletics should either be made voluntary or be restructured to consume far less time—but few alumni believe it. Eighty-eight percent of the students believe that athletic *success* (not, it must be noted, athletic *activity*) is important to school morale, and the administration, with good reason, knows such success is important to draw money from alumni.

A typical Wednesday afternoon's athletic schedule will involve eight interschool matches with four rival schools. This is what was happening on October 11:

3:00 P.M.: Varsity soccer and JV soccer vs. Williston—here
3:00 P.M.: Soccer 3–4 vs. Williston at Easthampton
3:00 P.M.: Football A vs. Loomis—here
3:00 P.M.: Football B vs. Cheshire at Cheshire
3:30 P.M.: Football 3–4 vs. Notre Dame High—here
3:30 P.M.: JV Cross-Country vs. Williston—here
4:00 P.M.: Varsity Cross-Country vs. Williston—here

Class time is cut back on Wednesdays and Saturdays to allow for athletic schedules, but even so there are further incursions. "I can make a categorical statement," says Jon van Leuven, a young science master, "that athletics have continually interfered with my courses here. Even the least demanding of these courses. Nominally there are supposed to be five meetings of every class a week, but there are, on the average, substantially less than that—closer to four—because of the away games that drop students out of class. One can't give tests at the proper time, boys miss important classes."

The science department feuds with the athletic department over the problem of coordinating science laboratory work, which must take place in the afternoons, with athletics. The labs begin at two fifteen and should be finished by four fifteen, but sometimes the boys must—or choose to—stay until five to finish an experiment. Theoretically, each boy gets a "free day" from sports and that day becomes his lab day, but the head of the science department believes that boys have been told they will not be allowed to stay on varsity teams unless they cut their labs. Also, the free days vary as practices are called or canceled. "No one knows when their free days come," Van Leuven complains. "This is a source of tremendous hostility. You can't carry on a lab because you don't know who's going to be there. Masters coaching some sport come walking up to a science teacher and ask: 'Will there be a lab this week?' And you say, 'Of *course* there'll be a lab this week, there's a lab *every* week.' And he says, 'Well, I just figured I'd ask to see if my boys could get an extra day of practice.'

"There are many masters around here," Van Leuven says, "who value their courses far less than their athletics and who are poor teachers to begin with—unquestionably poor teachers by universal admission of their students. That they're carrying an educational position here is a joke, a formality. These are the people who schedule weird things like extra practice and say, 'Oh, well, I thought just this once it would be all right.' I can't conceive of Alcibiades and the boys wanting to walk out of the academy and start hitting each other." But one of the varsity football players says: "After sitting in class all day, I just have to get out on that field and hit someone."

Choate, like many schools, has a long history of finding a special mystique of moral worth in athletics. The basic premise is:

> *Team sports build character*

and the unspoken, but essential, corollary attached to it is:

> *Character is built in direct ratio to the degree of competitiveness and violence involved in team sports.*

It is an absolutely astonishing doctrine. Jesus and Gandhi—not to mention Buddha, who sat, seemingly inert, for so long under that tree—would gasp in disbelief, but except for a few scrawny or ancient masters who grumble ineffectively in private, it is a doctrine that goes absolutely unchallenged at Choate.

Many years ago, Jack Maher, who for twenty-seven years was head football coach at Choate, spelled out the basic premise this way: "It goes without saying that a boy who plays a cooperative team-sport has a better chance to develop an out-going personality than one who concentrates exclusively on an individual sport." Tennis players and golfers, presumably, emerge from their schooling as depraved introverts, but at least they can give a dark and interior chuckle at the thought that they have skills in sports which they can play when they leave school. No one can deny the grace and beauty that can be seen in a well-played game of football or hockey, but almost no one plays such games once he is out of school. The most popular sports at Choate—football, baseball, hockey, basketball, and lacrosse—are played with such competitive fervor, often with such violent and overcharged emotion, that the sheer physical, sensual joy of being alive within one's own body is entirely lost, and although the boys are trained, often at great cost to their egos and bone structures, to play these useless games extremely well, they are left, at the end of their schooling, with no expertise that they can use except in watching others play these games for money, with no skills in a usable game that they can play throughout their lives for pleasure and for exercise.

"For a boy the ferocity of athletic involvement often verges on the sacrificial." The sentence comes from a propaganda pamphlet Choate released in the summer of 1969. It is a dubious statement, reflecting more the way one wants to think about violent sports than the way they actually are. In spite of Jack Maher, games like football accentuate self-consciousness: with the camera grinding away and the coaches scrutinizing the action, each boy knows that what *he* does is of utmost importance. He mustn't miss a tackle; he must try to obtain for himself what Choate calls one of the "special niches in the gallery of boyhood saints." Never mind: what is curious about the statement is that Choate seldom acknowledges the value of ferocity, the need for violence that is the corollary to its philosophy of athletics. When I was at Choate, there was no violent spring sport. Baseball? Rarely. Crew? Tennis? Of course not. Since my day, the problem has been solved: lacrosse is very big at Choate. No one suggests, however, that violence, which of all spring sports lacrosse alone possesses, is the reason for lacrosse's sudden surge in popularity. Nobody says to a kid: "Go out and get your face pushed in!" The joys of having one's face pushed in are reserved for recollection. It is bad taste to talk openly about the pleasures of pain and bloodshed, except in a nostalgic way. The Old Head, George St. John, showed a zest for them when he wrote about the salutary effects of pain on a young football player:

> I walk with him over to the infirmary. His lower lip has a long cut and two teeth are hanging loose. He's trying not to show the pain. "It's too darn' bad, George," I am moved to say.
>
> "It's—all—right—Mr. St. John," he stutters, blood spattering from his mouth. "My mouth shouldn't have—been there."
>
> He had missed the signal.

One can bet young George learned his lesson; if not, he will, as he moves to take his place in executive life, have to criticize his subordinates through his dentures.

Then as now, decorum demanded that one talk only about the joy of participating in the game, of stretching young muscles in the golden afternoons. Major Peter Dawkins, a Rhodes scholar, Heisman Trophy winner, and captain of an undefeated Army football team, came to Choate that fall to talk at a sports dinner about the traditional values of team sports. They teach poise, he said, self-confidence, the value of teamwork, working for something other than yourself, and doing the best you can for something other than you. Then he said something extraordinary: "Team sports teach you who you are. You know when the big game arrives you will have to provide everything you can—and then you learn whether you can do it."

"That's a lot of crap," a boy near me remarked. Certainly there was a silence in the audience: most of the boys there knew that Dawkins had learned *he* could "do it" in any sport he ever tried, but most of *them,* of course, couldn't because sports are by their nature selective. Few boys have a chance to match great skill to a great occasion. Some of them, perhaps, hoped that there were other ways in which they could find out who *they* were.

Although the official talk concerns playing for the joy of playing, without regard for victory or scores, one-third of all Choate students insist that "Winning is all that counts." Two-thirds agree that it is important for Choate to play in the most competitive of interschool athletic leagues. Only a little more than half, however, are willing to say that they unqualifiedly enjoyed their experience in athletics at Choate. None of these statistics can please the headmaster, but some put the blame for distorted emphasis of athletics on him. "It isn't just the head of the athletic department," says one faculty wife. "It's all sanctioned by the school. Seymour, when he gets out there, wants to be all things to all people, which is laudable, but you can't be. He wants to be the good hard sportsman to the sportsman, but at the same time he's a Christian, and yet he doesn't want to be thought not a businessman."

"What's the point of playing if you don't win?" I was asked by a mother who had sent two sons through preparatory schools. "You don't really mean to tell me that you enjoy a game if you *lose?*" In fact, I had mumbled something along that line, and she stared at me in disbelief. "Then you lack the competitive spirit," she said, "which these games are designed to teach. I don't believe anyone plays for the fun of playing. Boys have to play rough sports, have to learn how to *hurt* each other. That's life. And"—because I had brought up another unpleasant subject—"it doesn't matter if the coaches cheat. *That's* life, too."

"Boys are fundamentally decent," intones the *Master's Handbook* in a section on sportsmanship. "Above all—and this is a solemn thought—they will follow your example." Perhaps the most solemn charge laid against Choate athletics is that some masters cheat on the field. It is not a new phenomenon. In 1920 George St. John wrote to one of his faculty:

> A matter has been troubling me during the Summer. . . . One of our boys was talking to us one day about a game which one of our Choate teams played with Loomis. The boy said so-and-so was not allowed by Loomis to play on our team, because Loomis found out that he was too old, or had played on our First Team. Then the boy added, "But they didn't get Vander Horst, anyhow."
>
> We inquired whether Vander Horst was in any way ineligible for our Team, according to the rules which both schools had agreed to follow in making up the team, and the boy said, "Why sure he was." We then inquired whether you knew this; and the boy said, "Why I suppose he must have known—I don't see how he could help it."
>
> I do not believe you did know it. I am so sure of your good sportsmanship that I am not worrying about that. The thing I am worrying about is that any boy in the School should think that any one of us Masters was willing to cheat in order to better our chances in a game.

This kind of behavior enrages the boys. "The worst thing I've ever seen a master do," said the head of the Honor Committee, describing a master's anything-but-honorable conduct on the field.

"A lot of masters cheat," said another. "When I was in B League my coach cheated. In fact, when I was in A League, my coach cheated. Making bad calls. The two coaches trade—one refs one half, and the other, from the opposing school, refs the other. They'll just *tend* to give their team the benefit of the doubt. I do not like that at all. I would rather play a fair game. I don't see any point to it—they're so trivial, those little games."

Two of the youngest boys were incensed by such cheating, and by bad sportsmanship on the part of masters who shout abuse at each other during the heat of the game. I had asked: "Do you learn by faculty example? Like on the athletic field?"

"Hooooo!" one of the new boys cried. "You should see our coach! Really terrible!"

"He used to fight with the other coaches," said the other boy, who told me how this master would bully Konthath Menon, an Indian teacher of impeccable dignity. "Mr. Menon wouldn't pay any attention, so he'd yell, *'Salaam, sahib!'* "

"Not only that," said the first third former, "he'd cheat for our team! He would actually cheat! He would nullify the other team's goals and call fouls right and left."

"It's inspiring to have him on the field," said the second boy.

Charges and countercharges of cheating can grow startlingly complex. One master insists that St. John dropped him as coach of a JV team because a Hotchkiss coach had complained of his tactics. "Actually," says this master," the Hotchkiss coach was the one who cheated. We were winning, but at the half one of our alumni overheard the Hotchkiss coach telling his boys, 'You can't play well enough; the only way you'll win is by playing dirty.' I remonstrated with him." But it was the Choate master who was dropped. "I wrote a two-page, single-spaced letter of explanation to the headmaster," the former coach says, "but there was no reply."

"The boys could do modern dance, for heaven's sake," says Dino Rice, a faculty wife. "That would shake up the troops. You get a tremendous amount of exercise through modern dance."

And Pauline Anderson, the only woman with faculty rank at Choate, has another solution: "I'd have everybody out for cross-country. Once a week the boys would choose which girls' school they want to run to, and they'd run there."

Mind: Old Wine in New Bottles

> Ruined by luxury, there sit the children—with a grown man, and what's worse, a trained and educated man, standing before them, pouring out his energies. He isn't hearing them their lessons out of a book . . . he is explaining with all the art of a Jesuit, enlivening with anecdotes, sprinkling about with apt questions. The children are all on the *qui vive,* and asking questions in their turn—why don't he knock 'em down for their impertinence?
>
> HENRY MORLEY, with Charles Dickens, *Mr. Bendigo Buster on Our National Defenses Against Education* (1850)

> We try not to make them think, because that's not taught here.
>
> A master at Choate

Ralph Symonds cannot believe what he sees on the paper in his hand. "Is this handwriting or footwriting?" he asks the boy before him. The boy stands silent, with marbled eyes and lips ajar. Symonds glares at the written copy of a speech the boy has just finished delivering: a report on his interview with his cleaning woman, who had told him: "Hippies are pigs. They should go live in the forest," all of which the boy has dully delivered in a voice which faded toward the end as he began to rub his eye.

"Well?" Symonds asks. *"Which?* I can't make the question simpler: it's monosyllabic now!" He peers at the boy—perhaps cretinism is his problem. "How do you get on in *exams?"* Symonds asks. "What's your *average?"* The boy mumbles. *"Eighty-two?"* Symonds shouts, all frozen incredulity. "How can you get an eighty-two with words spelled this way? Your trouble is your standards are so low you're satisfied with your atrocious monotone! Standards everywhere are going down." Symonds sighs; it is one of his mellower mornings.

Since anyone can remember, public speaking has been Choate's most flamboyant course. When Stanley Pratt taught it, it was a course to be feared. Pratt meant to be feared. Let some wretched child pull his nose as he stuttered over his plans for a forthcoming vacation and Pratt would bang on his chair, open and shut windows, hurl threats at inattentive boys in the audience. "You may be nervous speaking in public later on," Pratt would purr, "but you will be terrified speaking in public here."

Symonds maintains the tradition. "Are you sufficiently discouraged to begin?" he asks a boy who has been staring at his feet. "Yes, you, you lump"—the boy is undeniably fat—"what's-your-name, you Smith-thing, you!" Smith is holding a book of dramatic photographs. He will advance to the podium, breathe through his diaphragm—"You will push air through it: it's the bellows which pushes air through your larynx which makes *sound!*"—and will speak for exactly one and a half minutes on some idea that comes to him when Symonds directs his attention to a particular picture. Smith has ten seconds to prepare his speech and to come up with a title.

"Number two," Symonds snaps when the boy is in place. Number two shows a Negro child peering in fascination through a fence. Like all good photographs, it eliminates the need for words, an economy that Smith is now feeling acutely. "Right," says Symonds, "your ten seconds are up. Let's have a title."

Smith: Um.

Symonds: Um? *That's* the title? All right.

Smith: Um. "Amazement."

Symonds: Close your book. Go on, talk.

Smith: When I see this picture, I—

Symonds (shouting): No, no, *no! That's no good at all!*

Smith: This boy is looking at—

Symonds: No! You're not to describe the picture. It must remind you of something else.

Smith: Um.

Symonds (patiently): "Amazement" you were going to talk about.

Smith: Amazement. Um.

Symonds: Look at *us.* (A long pause, punctuated by "Um's.") No, we don't want a mime speech, where you look amazed for a minute and a half. You have to speak.

Smith (after long silence): Um. Um. We are in a jail. The boy is looking through.

Symonds: Well, come on.

Smith: The boy's father's been put in jail for, ah, beating this kid. And, er, the boy is surprised to see his father, er, with balls around his legs and, ah, shoveling coal. Er. (Pause.)

Symonds: Is that the *end?*

Smith: Yessir.

Symonds: Well, that was twenty-five seconds.

Smith (resuming): The father, er, er, naturally wanted to *see* his son, and is, ah, embarrassed.

Symonds (exasperated): All *right!* Sit down. Very poor, you know. You've got a bad case of the um-and-ers. May I point out to everybody that every word has an *action.* This is an exaggeration, but that's how you *speak,* with action. You can't just open and close your mouth like a fish, which is what most people do. Speech *is* action. The moment you begin to speak properly, you act.

It is an act, of course—or the boys believe it is. They love it. When Symonds shouts: "You're our cliché boy. You have a genius for saying nothing at all in the most ways possible. I congratulate you! It was very weak!" the cliché boy grins inside. It is the same in Symonds' drama class:

Student: Do you think—

Symonds: Oh, dear, that's a difficult question.

Student: Like in *Macbeth*—

Symonds: Do you mean *as* in *Macbeth?*

Student: I mean, it's supposed to look *true,* isn't it, this play?

Symonds: Stop saying "true!"

Student: I mean, it's *real*—

Symonds: A play is *real?* You mean Duncan is killed every night? A rather profligate art, isn't it? So many actors gone.

"Maybe it *is* acting," says Don Beaton, not talking about Symonds, but about teaching in general. "But maybe I *am* an actor underneath. A master must maintain control of his classroom. He has a lot of techniques for this."

"I'd rather call it role-playing," Tom Colvin says. "I think by insisting on small details, like keeping on one's coat and calling a master 'sir,' you can maintain a foundation of discipline which allows you to be completely informal elsewhere."

"It's role-playing," Jere Packard agrees. "It makes it easier to communicate with the boys. At that age they would rather cope with a role. It means they don't have to commit too much of themselves in response."

Mounir Sa'adah sees it as a temptation: "Either you play for the boys' applause," he says, "or, if it comes to you, you get to like it and then play for it." Still, he adds, "Masters fail generally through lack of imagination. They fall into comfortable ruts and do not find ways to renew themselves."

Malcolm Manson, however, disagrees with the idea of the teacher as actor: "No man," he says, "can be a teacher for very long and be anything but himself."

And that, say some of the boys, is precisely the problem: too many teachers are themselves dull people and they conduct dull classes. "I've been in classes where the boys fell asleep," one says, "but that's the first class I've seen where the teacher fell asleep." Boys object to middle-aged teachers who look constantly at the clock, and to older teachers who seem to have a glazed eye fixed on some invisible calendar. "He doesn't think in terms of classes anymore," one third former said, "but in terms of years. Counting the years till retirement, each year exactly the same as the year before." Some teachers are unaware that boys can tell when a lecture has been used before, when a joke has been repeated at the same time, with the same inflection, unchanged through generations. "In his class," a boy said, "he just asks you questions. He doesn't know anything about the subject to say himself. The outlines he puts on the board are outlines of the textbook. He has to *grab* at things to talk about in class. Several times we've had to stop a class short because he ran out of things to say."

Teachers are aware of the shortcomings in other teachers. Burr Johnson feels that many teachers are not properly informed about the fundamentals of their subjects. Mounir Sa'adah believes teachers cannot see themselves in action, as students do. "Some teachers," he says, "are so absorbed with themselves that they are not aware that we are in class to pull something out of others. Self-centeredness has no place in a class." Sa'adah believes department chairmen should try to help younger teachers. "One can point out that as much as a thing is exciting to him, it isn't exciting to the boys. Has he entered into their minds, into their desires, their abilities, their emotional conditions, to sell them the goods? A lot of us are not aware of these things.

"A little bit of imagination in the classroom would do a great deal of good, and some of us lack it. For instance, I have a man who is very loyal to the school, very conscientious, willing to learn, but he came straight from college to here, and I am very anxious for him to go for a year to study—not history, but the approach to history. The *teaching* of history is what I'm interested in. His method is becoming too 'learn this, take a test, get a grade for it.' It's too *mechanical.* I want him to make his classroom interesting, to make history exciting, so I want him to go for a year to study. But the school can't afford to pay him for that year. If he does not study, and if he stays with us another five or six years, it will be an embarrassment to get rid of him. At the same time, it will be an embarrassment to keep him."

The charge of dullness, however, can be made against the students, too. The boys themselves are not dull—"I am constantly amazed at how good they are," Sa'adah says—but many of them bring a dull approach to learning to the classroom. "A kid comes to class expecting to be *taught* something," Stephen

Longley says. "He comes to jot down a relevant fact or an important thing which he knows he's going to be tested on next day. In other words, he comes to shop at the counter of knowledge." Sa'adah once asked his students to write a paper on their reactions to Fascism: "Do you (a) approve; (b) disapprove; (c) have no opinion?" "The first thing they asked me," Sa'adah says, "was, 'Sir, what do *you* think?' " It is part of the students' determination to study their teachers, not their subjects. "By the middle of their third-form year," Malcolm Manson says, "most students have got the system beat. They know how to play their masters to get good grades."

In the most popular classes, the masters move fast, keep the boys off balance: "Did you know," Charles Twichell asks, "that the immemorial gesture of the extended middle finger dates back to the third century B.C.?" The kids relate to that. Twichell teaches Latin: "I can show it to you in Plautus, third century." *"Elephans, cum dormant, ad aborem se applicat,"* Twichell chants, sitting on his desk and sipping from a cup of coffee. None of this Julius Caesar stuff anymore. Boys learn Latin from the *Gesta Romanorum* because information about the sleeping habits of elephants is of more interest than where Caesar dug his trenches. With one hand Twichell indicates the boy who will translate the passage; with the other he sends a boy to the blackboard to draw the elephant; at the same time he explains that this bit of monkish science derives from Aristotle and no, the elephants did not have joints in their knees, that's why they had to sleep against trees. The way to catch an elephant is to chop the tree down. Bam, the elephant falls and you've got him. Evidently, Latin is great fun, which is an improvement because for 300 years it wasn't. "Latin," says one sixth former, "has the potential of being the most boring subject, but that guy elicits what verges on loyalty, absolute loyalty, from his students. The kids love him."

Richard Hunter takes his slow section of English 5 at an even brisker pace. The problem here is to bring the world of Art to the world of Boy and hope that the latter will be impressed. Hunter begins by reading a letter he has received citing all the big executives who have shot themselves, died penniless, or languished in a jail. Any impression? Hard to tell. "Robert Frost," Hunter tells them, "mocks his reader. He has his tongue in his cheek. He is a philosophical poet." Rustle, shuffle. "Fifteen years ago," Hunter continues, apparently working two themes at once, "a young man left Trinity College. He could have been at least a vice-president of General Motors."

The boys laugh. "That's *you,* Mr. Hunter!" The future vice-presidents let Hunter know they are with him.

"No," Hunter says, "just a man taken at random. I knew him well. Today he's leading young Americans through unexplored paths of knowledge."

Hoots, laughter.

"And that has made all the difference." Hunter is back to Frost again: "The Road Not Taken." "I doubt Princeton and Yale and Harvard will plead for your attendance," Hunter says, "but when you are accepted by all three, you will have to make a *decision,* probably on impulse: which is closer to Vassar or to Smith."

Ho-ho again, but are the boys catching on? Hunter moves on to a poem called "A White Rose" by John Boyle O'Reilly (1844–1890). Poetry, all teachers know, is difficult to teach. "They will read a novel," David Waters says, "with, in many cases, greater insight than I have, but when you get to poetry, they write about themselves."

"I don't know much about roses," a boy tells Hunter. Hunter manages not to wince at this idiotic egotism. It happens even in colleges. "O rose, thou art sick; the invisible worm . . . ," and the kids don't care about rose diseases in the eighteenth century. What the hell, they never *saw* that rose, and there are plenty of roses now. . . . Poetry is difficult to teach. Hunter takes it image by image.

"What's the connotation of 'dove'?"

"Peace," says a boy.

"That's the trouble with language," Hunter says. "You're opposed to the Vietnam War. A dove used to connote *white:* purity, innocence, a bride." Hunter pauses. Things are getting serious. He leers at his class. "I hate to mention ethnic groups. You know how to tell the bridegroom at an Italian wedding? He's the one wearing a clean T-shirt."

When the laughter subsides, Hunter is back to roses: "Who wrote 'My love is like a red, red rose'?"

"Shakespeare?"

Hunter glares at the offender. "No! He was the hero of his country."

"Lyndon Johnson."

"No!" Hunter bellows. "Stalin!"

"Stalin?" The kid believes him.

"Bobbie Burns." Sigh. ("These kids may not be bright," Hunter says later, "but they're happy.") "We're still talking about white rose—purity—and red rose—passion. True love can't be just the white kind of love; it also has to have some of the red stuff in it. What does a 'falcon' suggest?"

"High," says a boy.

Giggles, laughter.

Probably nothing can be done about John Boyle O'Reilly, but fifth-form English attempts to do a great deal with Robert Frost. "We spend five weeks on Frost," Burr Johnson says. "The kids get sick of it. They'll start saying by the end of January, 'Sir, when can we get off Frost?' "

Small wonder. Most of these boys have never thought of poetry at all, unless in grade school they read "The Raven" or "Evangeline," and here they are, looking intensely at poetry for the first time and what do they get? A poet who's queer for birds. What boy cares about birds? Johnson is lucky: he has such a boy. "What is special about this oven bird?" he asks his class. "It builds a domelike nest," the boy replies. "No other bird does that except an Eskimo bird." The ornithological school of criticism: Johnson's face wrinkles in pained horror. Frost is a doubly difficult poet to teach because, unlike most modern poets, he doesn't *seem* to be difficult on a first reading, and a first reading is more than some of these boys have given "The Oven Bird" or the other poems on that day's assignment.

"What, just basically, is Frost doing here?" Johnson asks, referring to "Neither Out Far Nor In Deep." He points to a boy in the first row who has spent the class reading *Giants in the Earth* and, apparently, writing an essay inside the front cover.

"Let me just review it," the boy replies, picking it out, obviously for the first time. This boy is smarter than the rest; when he has finished, he knows he's lost, raises a face of mock supplication: help! He laughs nervously. People out on the beach, looking at the sea, but then there's Frost asking a question at the end, the way he often does, when a poet should be *telling* us, shouldn't he?

"What are these men looking for?" Johnson asks.

"Nothing," the boy replies.

Johnson collapses: "You've just killed Frost!" The boy giggles. Johnson, recuperating, gives a little speech on what the sea has meant to man, to Herman Melville, to himself. Johnson himself would like to sit for a year in a house by the sea and watch the seasons change—"It would be really fulfilling"—but instead he is talking about the meaning Frost accuses men of looking for in water to boys who didn't bother to read the poem the night before.

Frost presents such problems! The poems begin easily and the boys can't detect the modulation to commentary on man's estate. The ironic kicks at the poems' ends elude them entirely. Boys, says Johnson, at this age cannot move back and forth adroitly between the concrete and the abstract, but that is what Frost is all about. They can't see the traps that Frost sets. If the teacher tells them, they can hear that part of Frost's voice which says, "Open wider, please. This may hurt a little." They are told not to underestimate Frost, that he can fool his reader, but they cannot grasp—and some of their teachers cannot grasp—that other part of Frost that mocks his critics. "Splitting symbols is harder than splitting logs," Frost might say. "Don't mind me. I'm just a country farmer. I like to clean the pasture spring," and so on.

The boys don't get it. Frost looks easy. He uses simple language, and, of course, Frost is *great*. All things considered,

Choate comes on strong for him, but of all poets he is the worst to use to introduce students to poetry. "Sir," the boys say again, "*when* can we get off Frost?" meaning: When can we get off poetry? They already have.

Audio-visual aids, a necessary teaching tool for a generation raised before a television screen, are big at Choate. Even Frost's poem "Come In" would be a snap to understand if, in some animated cartoon, the thrush in the shaded thicket wore jowls, a freckle, and Frost's peasant smile. Until then, the boys have Clifton Fadiman, an amiable Virgil who steers students on a technicolor tour of selected circles and pockets of the literary Inferno. Speaking above the clatter of the movie projector, in words that are not quite coordinated with the movements of his mouth, he explains that *Great Expectations* is "a horizontal novel," he would even say "a developmental novel," and "two major characters, Pip and Magwich, have been added to the population of our mind." As Fadiman talks, he moves slightly to reveal a set of Britannica's *Great Books* in the shelf behind him. Britannica produced the film. "Prison of the imagination," Fadiman is saying, "the terrifying brute and the terrified child." The word "deeper" keeps recurring in Fadiman's commentary, and of course, the room into which his two-dimensional discourse is projected has been darkened, and the teacher silenced, as if in deference to the death of learning. And then, oh, marvelous! Fadiman's image fades and real-life actors come on to act out some of the scenes from Dickens' novel for the amazement and education of the student. We see Pip meet Miss Havisham, with wedding cake, cobwebs, and all. As costume dramas go, it's easily a fifth-rate *Tom Jones,* or maybe even a sixth-rate *Great Expectations*—if anyone in the room ever caught that film on TV. No matter how bad a teacher may be, he *has* to be better than this. Fadiman robs the teacher of his own authority, his own showmanship, his own views—if he has any—of the novel. As the film rattles to its end and the lights come on, the teacher winds up with a discussion of Fadiman discussing Dickens.

Such trickery is put to much better use by the French Department. Some French is still taught in the old way at Choate, with older teachers lecturing in smooth and unpretentious French, *style américain,* and students responding in monosyllables if possible, or two words if pressed, but most French is taught in the new way, and the effect can be electric:

Clif Clerke (the teacher): Je suis Monsieur Saint-Jean?

Student: Non. Vous êtes Monsieur Clerke.

Clerke: Je suis professeur. Vous êtes élève. Je suis élève?

Student: Non, vous êtes professeur.

Clerke (pointing to another student): Il est professeur?

Student: Non.

Clerke (not letting him get away with that): Non?

Student: Il est le.

Clerke (nodding encouragement): Il est élève.

Good try. This is only the second day of French for these third-form boys who have been chosen specifically because they have never had any French before. It is the first day in which they have actually heard or spoken French because the opening class is devoted to Clerke's lecture on what is properly called "Voix et Images de France," but is always called the St. Cloud method, after the school in France where it was developed to teach French colonials, not proficient in French, how to speak the language like a Parisian. Choate was one of the first schools in America to experiment with this program, which requires extensive training of its teachers. The system works through a series of tape recordings by Frenchmen and filmstrips, together with some basic texts. Kids learn to read French late in this program—and some claim they never learn to read competently at all—but they learn everything else—accent, intonation, rhythm, grammar, and even gestures—from the second day, and they learn it exactly as French children learn it from infancy, by association of image and sound and not by the sight of the written word. In the beginning there is no homework; the class meets six days a week instead of five.

"You have to be very alert," Clif Clerke tells his boys—twelve of them, arranged in two parallel rows facing each other. "It's very difficult to be alert constantly for forty-five minutes. It's very *exhausting*. Near the end of the morning, as this is, you tend to get a little weary, to slacken off a little, but you mustn't. Because if you miss what's said, there's no place you can go to pick it up. It's gone. Gone."

He says this in the first lecture; they are the only English words ever permitted in a St. Cloud classroom. French culture, Clerke warns the boys, is not like American culture. "A window will be a French window, but it won't be an American window. If someone's making gestures, he's making French gestures, he's not making American gestures. A language is everything; it's a personality, all the gestures he makes, an environment; it's the way he eats the meals, eating with his left hand." All these points are to emerge in the filmstrips: a plate on the table, when a man has finished eating, has the knife and fork crossed upon it. *"Oui"* is always said as a man nods his head; *"non"* with a waggle of a finger; *"Je suis"* requires a man to point to himself. The point, says Clerke, is that to understand a language, a country, a literature, one must have a total understanding of what is going on. Grammar and vocabulary are not enough. More important, we must get rid of the idea that words have equivalent values across two languages: there is no such thing as a good translation. St. Cloud, it is said, will teach you to speak French like a Frenchman.

It doesn't. American boys will always mangle French sounds unless they have learned to speak French in the home. No Frenchman will be fooled. A Frenchman, like a hawk, has an extra lid over his eye; the hawk lowers his lid when he flies into the sun, the Frenchman lowers his when an American speaks French. Never mind. St. Cloud teaches Americans to speak better French than any other method, partly because it is taught from the start correctly. From the second day, Clerke talks at full conversational speed. Even if a kid can't get what is said, can't reproduce it—as the system requires him to do—Clerke won't let up. He beats the rhythm out on his desk with a pencil:

Vous habitez à Paris?	Dot-dot-dot dash, dot-dot dash.
	Voo-zah-bee tay ah-Pah ree.

It takes two years for the boys to get ready to read anything in French. "Kids don't have any idea whether *'Vous avez'* is one or ten words," Clerke says. "We have to make them so responsive to sounds that they will not be *able* to say *'mon voiture'*—it will always sound wrong." The system is so demanding it does not work for all; some boys will be recycled into the regular French program. "Boys are basically shy," Clerke says, "shyer than girls. A girl will say anything in class and say it loud. But the boys mumble into their collars. They can't take any kind of psychological pressure. But on the athletic field it is entirely different. There the boys are completely bold and can take anything."

"I SPEAK VERY LOUDLY," Clerke informs his boys the first day, "and I want everyone in the class to speak out!" He used much the same tone of voice to the boy who said, "Uh, sir, will we learn the grammar?" *"Certainly* the grammar!" Clerke shouted. "How do you think you learned *English* grammar?"

"From a book."

"You *did?* You're an unusual child. Where were you born? Here? How did you learn with a book? When your mother said, 'Did you wash your hands today?' what did you say? 'Yes, mother, I did wash my hands today.' You're conjugating the verb 'to wash' in the present tense. YOU LEARNED THE RULES! You want to put *terminology* on it, that's not grammar! What we want you to be able to do"—St. Cloud is the only program with a team spirit—"is to use the *language*. Not put categories on it. You can't do that in English, why should you do that in French? YOU DON'T NEED TO KNOW THAT RIGHT NOW!" Thump, thump, thump on the table. "Who *cares?"*

A St. Cloud method teacher has to be at least half actor, must know how to flap his arms and milk the proper answer from a student. It takes longer to teach this way because the instructor can never just point out an error and correct it. He must jump on the error in such a way—and with enough speed—that the student can pick it out for himself.

"Il est fini," said a student in a third-year St. Cloud class.

"Il est mort?" the teacher snapped.

The student takes time to figure that one out. Finally, it comes to him: "Il *a* fini."

"Ah, bon."

Some of this correction requires much rewinding of the tape machine and starting again just where the student made his error. Clerke has become so efficient that he can land on a kid at the precise syllable the boy is mispronouncing.

"C'est moi cravate," the boy says.

"Non," Clerke says.

"C'est moi—"

"Non! C'est votre clé?" He has jumped back now, to a phrase the boy got right a minute before.

"Oui, c'est ma clé."

"C'est votre cravate?"

"C'est *ma* cravate." The boy smiles.

Clerke smiles. He can make a boy see that he is wrong—and do it loudly—but he does not humiliate the boy because, just after he pounces, he seems to draw the mistake out as some kind of universal error.

By the third year, conversation moves quickly. One or two boys can make a joke in French, and the French acculturation part of the St. Cloud program becomes formidable. "Un repas sans fromage n'est pas un repas français," announces Lesson 28, called "Au restaurant." In a special language laboratory, which looks like a room from Cape Kennedy's Mission Control and which costs about $20,000 to equip, the kids sit in little isolation booths with green acoustical panels. They wear headphones and speak into microphones, repeating the lesson they hear on a master tape. An instructor sits at the control system, able to listen in on any boy without that boy's realizing it, and able to cut in to talk to that boy alone. It is here that St. Cloud students are examined. Each boy, wearing a headphone set, is asked a question and given five or six seconds to formulate the answer. The question is then asked again and immediately a tape recorder attached to each microphone is switched on for just as many seconds as it takes to say the correct answer at the correct speed. The boys all reply simultaneously and, since there is no time to listen to anyone else's responses, cheating is impossible.

Choate's other foray into space age education is its computer course, taught by the head of the math department, Robert Clements. St. John says that "the math department is our most conservative department," but there is nothing conservative about Clements' course. In the middle of the year, he had two sixth formers attending, boys who were taking second-year college mathematics. The course was held in the boys' free time and was not for credit; it met two days a week on the third floor of Steele Hall, where Clements introduced the boys to the mysteries of the IBM 26 Printing Card Punch, a machine Choate rents for $2 a day, and to the Fortran language for programming. Here the kids learn to punch out a program—"Don't write letters home," Clements tells them. "Don't punch out obscenities"—which will be fed to an 1130 machine in Wallingford, which can do 100,000 additions in a second and costs $25 an hour to employ. This machine, however, is only small potatoes. The following year, Choate would hook its teletype console to a 360 computer at Yale which charged $240 an hour to perform. "You can see," Clements says, "the necessity for avoiding infinite looping." Looping is what happens when statement A says refer to statement B and statement B says to refer to statement A—"forever at $240 an hour. The first thing that machine does when you plug into it is to check your account. Have you paid your bill?" Clements' life is mathematics. When he has a spare moment, he will pull out some papers on which he has worked out variations on magic squares.

Other teachers, lacking access to equipment that makes teaching exciting, must spin the excitement from their heads. Jean Pierre

Cosnard lectures an honors French section on French art—in French. Walking into his room, one thinks he is walking into a classroom at the Sorbonne. Cosnard's course has nothing to do with St. Cloud, but it requires an extension of the skills boys are taught there because no concession is made to any limited understanding the boys may have of French.

David Waters' lectures to his honors section of senior English are equally informed, very much like what the boys will get next year in college, and among the few classes an adult might enjoy. Still, this year the boys objected. Like Cosnard, Waters moves very rapidly and is sometimes dogmatic: "If, when you've finished *Zorba the Greek,* you've not been moved or excited by anything in it, you'll never enjoy reading novels. . . . If you can read Dylan Thomas' *Quite Early One Morning* and be completely unmoved by his control of words, you'll probably never be a writer." The boys grumble, lapse into silence, staring at their loafers, and, when alone, will say the course is a failure. Waters agrees. It happens sometimes. "In previous years we have developed a free and swinging banter between me and some of the students, but I can't do it with this particular class. I didn't try. It's never a thing one tries." Waters discusses Graham Greene's *Brighton Rock,* a book his boys don't like. "In the eyes of God," Waters says, "Pinky may have more of a chance than Ida." "In the eyes of Catholic Graham Greene," a boy replies. Waters is a Catholic. The class just didn't work.

Mounir Sa'adah makes first-year Arabic exciting by finding cartoons and composing captions in Arabic which he carefully cuts from Arabic newspapers because he does not have an Arabic typewriter and he wants the boys to see the writing as it should be done. "The elephant is not in the door of my neighbor's house": his boys learn how to say and write *that* in Arabic, and some more useful phrases, too, like "Thank God, I have beans in my mouth." "The Arab," Sa'adah tells his boys, "regards whatever comes to him as coming from God."

Rod Furnald opens each class with his "quote of the day." Boys may come into his classroom to find written on the blackboard:

The only kind of holiness
You get in a holy war
Are the holes you get through your head.
—a poem

A continuance of the bombing will save lives.
—LBJ

Furnald may read them James Reston's column or denounce a doctor who had delivered an atrocious lecture on drugs to the school the night before. His classes for fourth and fifth formers in English are rooted in immediate concerns. He will switch from Hawthorne's sense of evil to a sermon by Jonathan Edwards to a discussion of determinism. "The possibilities, at your age," he tells the boys, "are more real than the limitations." Furnald himself is about six years older than his students. He draws out their possibilities in graph form on the blackboard:

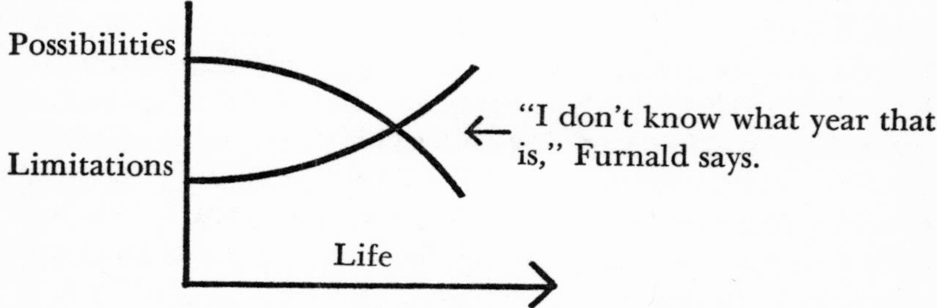

Like most English teachers everywhere, Furnald is burdened with a grossly inadequate textbook:

She was a ——— of delight
When first she gleamed upon my sight.

The students are supposed to choose the missing word: "Ghost, phantom, spectre, spook." The class chose "spectre" because it was "richest in meaning," and Furnald didn't seem to notice. How can you be *right* about this kind of thing? Education is not a matter of filling in missing words, and with that in mind, Furnald suggested to his class that they did not have time to cover in class what they had to cover, so why not meet all evening in his room? Kids could leave if they had other things to do. A voluntary thing, get a good discussion going, forget about bells and schedules. The dean of students told Furnald to cease and desist: the evening discussion would violate the study hour.

Like Robert Clements, Jim Spencer has a course of his own devising for boys who are working well into college level studies: Chemistry 2. Science at Choate is taught very differently from the way it was in my day, when dilettantes like me could doze through a required year of biology knowing we would have nothing more difficult to do than draw a lobster shell one afternoon in spring. The teaching of science is integrated now in a program called the Physical Science Study Curriculum set up by MIT and sponsored by the government. The new method began when the Russians put Sputnik up in 1957. Scientists realized then that the science they were teaching was thirty years out of date. There was, too, the problem of the geometrical increase in scientific knowledge: no teacher can keep abreast of his subject today. Harold Brown, head of the science department, figures that a good third of the biology he teaches is new since 1952. Masters now must spend summers going back to school; fortunately, the PSSC approach to science came to Choate when most of its science masters were ready to retire and new, young men could be hired to teach it.

PSSC recognizes that there are simply too many facts to learn. Kids want to learn facts that they can write down and repeat on an examination, but PSSC is not much interested in *what* happens in science; it cares about *why* things happen. It requires a lot more demonstration and imagination; it lacks the securities and certainties of the old science, and is therefore harder to teach. It works best when a rapport with a student can be established: "You're trying to get him to think along with you and you must think along with him," says Jim Spencer.

PSSC begins with a basic science course given to all third formers, a course that is, for the most part, physics. It is a course in how to approach experimental methods, in how to record data, in how to plot graphs. The teachers try to get the boys to utilize what math they have learned along with their science, but boys resist this: they like to keep what they learn in separate pockets of their minds, just as they keep the facts in separate sections of their notebooks. The teachers do not think this introductory course is a success. Peter Benson says, "The most useful material to present at this stage, which is absolutely *essential* to science, is also the driest, the most analytical. We must make it interesting. How to get in the rigor without destroying the excitement. Graphs and vector analysis are *not* exciting, even to a scientist; they're a *tool.* The kids are frightened, not enthusiastic." Larry Pond agrees. His section of Science 3 is a slow one and, he says, only about 15 percent of the boys "seem to catch on to the concept of logical thinking. They begin hard by memorizing all they can, hoping somehow that this will obviate the necessity of understanding the principles behind. *Thinking* is what's hard. Anything that's laid on to them they accept with audible relief."

"See," says one of Pond's third formers, pointing to a shaky graph he had drawn, "that's where it really slowed down." The line on the graph rises like a cat that has sat on the burner of a stove.

"Speeded up," Pond says quietly.

"Yeah," says the kid, "speeded up. That shows how confused I was."

Still, the boys who stick with science past Science 3 tend to stick with it through Choate. Ninety-five percent of the boys who took physics their fourth-form year signed up for chemistry their fifth-form year. "Nobody," says Brown, "would have been more surprised than they." Chemistry is taught by the Chemical Bond Approach, a new technique* which recognizes the vast growth of factual knowledge, that boys cannot memorize even the highlights of what is known, but must understand the general principles behind it. The CBA approach is for the bright boys: for boys able to visualize models and able to describe verbally what models are made of. It is not a "descriptive science" as was the old science everyone over thirty learned;

* A technique already out of date, some teachers say.

it is concerned with numbers, and with how matter is put together.

"Everything we do here is quantitative," says Jim Spencer. In the slow old days, students worried about the color of chlorine gas. How does it behave when mixed with hydrogen? What about its taste, color, odor, state, density, and solubility in various substances? "That just isn't chemistry today," Spencer says. "Chemistry is *numbers.* I show the boys how abstract science can be. You stick a liquid in a machine and then don't look at it again—you look at a meter. The student has got to know at what point he stops looking into a test tube and starts looking into his mind for an answer." The biggest problem, as Spencer sees it, is what to do with the new facts he continually encounters. "If a student comes across a new fact, how does he fit it into what he knows? We teach him how to make up theories." In fact, students work in what are called "discovery labs" where, literally, they don't know what they are looking for.

There are three boys in Spencer's Chem 2 class. They, too, are volunteers: he would not have chosen them himself because one had done quite badly the year before and there is no sign that any of them will go on with chemistry. Their textbook is considered outside reading for first-year chemistry in college. Spencer stands in the classroom in a dirty white jacket behind some blue, yellow, white, and red sponge balls of varying sizes, stuck together in various ways. On the blackboard is written:

$$E_o = \frac{h}{2\pi}\sqrt{\frac{k}{\mu}}\,(1/2)$$

$$KT = (1.38 \times 10^{-16})\ (298^{o}k)\ = 4.1 \times 10^{-14}\ \frac{\text{ergs}}{\text{molecule}}$$

The class is very quiet. A few questions are tossed back and forth, and there is a lot of silent scribbling. Spencer and the boys are working on some formula; they haven't found a missing factor. Assumptions have been made: that they are dealing with diatomic carbon monoxide molecules of certain size; that they are rotating, translating, and vibrating in space. "Prove to yourself," Spencer suggests, "that the vast majority of molecules will be vibrating at the minimal level required." Pause. "As usual, math gets in your way." After some more fumbling and scratching on the board, a student asks Spencer for the derivation of a formula. Spencer grins. "I can't go back and derive *that* formula," he admits. "I've forgotten the calculus. It's just one of the formulas I know."

Unlike many Choate teachers, Spencer believes that there are some very bright boys in the school, and that some of those have passed through his classes. These boys in Chem 2 will have a free term in the spring to concentrate on whatever interests them. "So," says Spencer, "I will actually be conducting three classes."

One of Choate's efforts to keep students interested was to make classes and cultural events to which the boys were exposed more "relevant." Relevance was a big word at Choate that year and caused strife among the faculty. Ralph Symonds, for instance, staged a presentation of Sheridan's *The Rivals,* undoubtedly one of the great plays of the English stage. Nobody showed much interest in it. Symonds protested, sending an angry letter to the headmaster and other teachers. One of them responded: "It is not a play for our time," he wrote, "and especially for students of these terrible times. The play is excessively mannered, wordy, insincere"—*sincere* is another big word on the education scene these days—"and essentially silly. Its conceits and verbal sallies might well have amused an audience in less exciting days. . . . Most of the characters in this play are either effeminate or embarrassingly coy and the trifling plot could hardly hold anyone's interest. . . . Sheridan has nothing to say to the ages." The teacher went on to say that Symonds would never catch the students' interest without relevant plays: *"relevance to life as the boys know it. Hamlet* is relevant because Hamlet is a young man in a poisoned kingdom exactly as many young men feel themselves in our country today. I honestly don't see how you can expect boys who may have to face enemy bullets in a year or two . . . to pay any attention to *The Rivals.*" Symonds fumed.

Sure, one can make relevant connections between, say, Coriolanus and Lyndon Johnson—both commanders had beans in their ears—but such connections are rarely made at Choate. In English 3, for instance, students read *The Odyssey* and *The Bridges at Toko-Ri* simultaneously, but no one attempts to show parallels of melancholia produced by war and separation, or even two methods of narration. You discuss one book, then you discuss the other. "You can't hit kids at this level with too much," Herbert Gutterson, chairman of the English Department, says. Gutterson, at the beginning of the year, had grave doubts about the usefulness of relevance. "We teach good books," he said when a cry was raised for more black literature. "Good books have no color. An English teacher cannot trumpet these concerns in his classroom. Our concern is with language and with literature. I want to have a perspective on this so we won't feel we must jolt our curriculum for whatever minority is before us this year. I *do* want to be relevant."

But, by the end of the year, he had changed his mind. With Gutterson's blessing, David Rice reorganized English 5. "The thought now," Rice said, "is we're not only involved with teaching English, but also preparing the kids to think about the issues of their nation." Rice planned to assign an anthology of short stories by black writers. "We'll be considering them as literature, but also as a manifestation of social pressure within the United States. They're pretty gripping stories. Each one of them is like a punch in the stomach."

In an attempt to be relevant, Gutterson and another teacher assigned John Sack's book *M* to their classes. *M* is Sack's report of the months he spent with an infantry company from basic training through its blooding in Vietnam. It is one of the better and truer books about war, but because Sack thinks war is lunacy, it is also a very funny book. None of the sixth-form boys liked it. Some thought Sack was showing off; others said they had had *enough* of the Vietnam War; all agreed that Sack's "tone" was inappropriate to such serious business as war. "It's all right for you to be funny," one boy told Gutterson, "or Sack to be funny, but *you* don't have to go there." Another said, "There was a lot of jokes in it I didn't understand. You know, they're Army jokes. I didn't expect what I read." A little-reported aspect of the generation gap is that adults often act like hippies and kids like squares. These boys were very square, ignorant of, and apparently unconcerned with the necessity of appreciating a variety of tones of voice, of points of view. Gutterson sympathizes. "How are you going to get seventeen-year-olds who are going to get draft cards in a year to take a detached view of this?"

Another approach to relevance in courses, to keeping boys interested in what they are learning, is to let them study what they want. Choate already lets boys do this to a certain extent. Many courses—particularly the honors sections of courses—let qualified boys knock off the spring term to study some special subject on their own, under the guidance of a knowledgeable teacher. A paper or some other evidence of serious intent is usually required. The program is called Independent Study and asks that boys file applications, outlining exactly what they hope to accomplish. "I plan to design an ocean racer," one boy wrote, "to one or maybe two of the present cruising boat rating rules, CCA or Storm Trysail rule. The bulk of the work will involve the use of math, as I will be trying to find the best formula to fit the existing rules." His design, the boy said, should be judged by David Vietor, his faculty advisor, Emil Mosbacher, who wins boat races, and O. Stephens, who builds boats. The head of the math department decided such a project should represent 75 hours of work and told the boy to save all his scratch papers and final drawings "as evidence of time spent on the project." Meanwhile, other boys in history were planning a movie of the history of the stock exchange and a musical program about the Depression (the exam would require a singing performance). The leader of Choate's black students spent the term investigating "The Nature and Impact of Slavery on the Black American, esp. in regard to self-image," and others wrote papers on such subjects as "The Red Scare After World War I," "New Deal: Panacea or National Disaster?" and "Vanderbilt, Rockefeller and Ford: Symbols of Their Age."

It seems to work. One boy, by no means Choate's brightest, spent the term "designing a project to put into use in the ghetto areas in the cities. I'm putting this project into effect in the Hill section of New Haven, from Spring Street through Congress Avenue, from Howard Avenue over to Union Avenue." To hear the boy talk, it is impossible to believe he is not actually *doing* this, that it exists only in his head and on paper. "I'm putting in housing, that's my first step. And I'm knocking down a lot of old tenements. . . . The second part of it is helping business. I'm knocking down a lot of small businesses on Washington Avenue. A lot of them aren't in use anymore. There are a few that are still alive, but they are just about ready to fold up. I'm forming a merger with four of them, getting two bakeries to join and two restaurants to join." And on he talks, ticking off plans—"After housing and business, you need employment, and after employment, you've got to educate 'em." He takes weekends off from Choate—"I don't speak to anybody. When I'm down there, I just plot out the area"—and does not come back until Wednesday. "I worked on it from nine in the morning until twelve at night, just eating right next to the work, and things like that. I guess for about two and a half weeks now I've worked on it from about seven to one every night. I couldn't put anywhere near this amount of time into something I'm not interested in."

Nothing is more perennially interesting and relevant than sex, and that fall St. John decided that Choate would launch a program of sex education, beginning with its oldest boys. First, however, the faculty had to be educated, and so, before school opened, the entire faculty convened with their wives to hear a minister, a psychologist, and some doctors from Yale present a program on sex education that, obviously, they had all given many times before.

The minister, from Yale's divinity school, looked over this

group of educators and their wives and said, "I wonder if we wouldn't have to say that there is much more to sex than reproduction." There was a shuffling of feet. As the minister continued to slide his well-oiled phrases into the middle distance—"It turns out to be plumbing education . . . the drama of what it is to be a man"—some of the faculty wondered if St. John and those who had worked with him hadn't made a dreadful mistake. The minister looked as if he had been sent from Central Casting. He was expert in the pregnant pause, the significant look, the forced colloquialism, the leaden lightness of touch. The psychologist was no improvement: "Let us learn together," he said. "Decision making may well be the theme of this course."

Later on, in other lectures, this same captive faculty would listen to a lecture entitled "Concerns of Contraception and Abortion" by the chairman of Yale's Obstetrical-Gynecological Department, and would attempt to follow a complex medical-school lecture on "female plumbing" (as Yale continued to call it). One afternoon a social worker from Yale's Psychiatric Institute was pulled in to mumble about "Adolescent Dating and Courtship," and by this time you could see one of the older masters reading *Punch* and another sifting through the pile of mail that had accumulated in his box over the summer. Worse still, there was compulsory attendance at a showing of a film called *Phoebe* which, haunted by the ghosts of Fellini and Antonioni, mixes realism and fantasy in depicting the state of mind of a girl who becomes pregnant before marriage. The kids dance; there is a frolic on the beach and sex in an old deserted house—it was nothing if not ambitious, but it provoked a rebellious brand of film criticism from Choate. "No house that looked like that on the outside would look so clean on the inside," said one faculty wife, and she was right. There was some symbolical criticism, too—"An empty house is pleasure without responsibility"—which is the kind of comment Choate's faculty is good at, but hardly apropos.

Most of the faculty education in sex, however, took place in small discussion groups, because, as one of the zombies from

Yale said, "we are to a certain extent talking about ourselves." The point of the discussion groups was to prepare the faculty for frank and informed discussion of sex with the boys. Immediately, one of the youngest wives protested: "My decision," she said, "was how intimate a discussion do I *want* with a teen-age boy? These boys are not much younger than I am."

"I'm hearing a tremendous amount of fear," said the Yale psychologist who presided. "How is it the anxiety level is so high? What does this say about our confidence in instructors?" It is amazing that the faculty did not throw their coffee cups and ashtrays at the man. He sat there smiling, his stubby fingers interlaced and his second chin propped plumply on his collar. One of the Choate directors of the course had prepared a paper defining homosexuality, and some phrases like "homosexual relations are inherently less fulfilling and tend to be less pleasurable than heterosexual coitus" had perplexed the faculty. "How do we know?" one asked. "I don't know what a confirmed homosexual *is,*" the psychologist said pleasantly, but it was clear that he was the only one in the room who didn't. "Psychodynamically," he added, "this is open to discussion."

"Since *you're* a psychologist," one master said, "why don't *you* present this?"

"All of us are learning together," said Choate's director of the program hastily.

"I think we are picking nits," said the master.

The psychologist sighed. "This is our last session," he said. "We haven't been speaking much of interpersonal relations on the boy-girl level. We must recognize that girls have sexual feelings, too." He smiled broadly as he went on to talk about "the snowball effect of sexual arousal." And so he continued—"It gets tougher if we allow ourselves to get sucked into normative judgments on adolescent sexuality. . . . Alcohol and sex go about as well together as alcohol and driving. If you need alcohol for sex, there is something wrong," etc. Finally, he rose at this, the end of the last session, for his valedictory: "I think your anxiety level is high enough so that you will go into this seriously."

Thus armed, Choate's faculty and wives launched the sex education program. There were formal speeches to entire forms: on masturbation, for instance, which began with a dictionary definition and modulated, much to the boys' amusement, through the traditional results of the practice: "genital cancer, pimples, insanity, even dark circles under the eyes." The boys cackled with laughter when they were told that "boys at boarding school are kept busy playing violent athletics to keep their minds off sex." Masturbation, they were told, "is a highly personal thing. Each person must decide for himself."

In the evening, after the lecture, boys meet in small classes for discussion. "I will try very hard to keep my attitude out of this," one master tells his boys. "I hope I won't have to keep talking all the time. That's really pretty much up to you." He mentions two problems that are bound to arise: "the tendency to press personal questions—'How many times do *you* do it?' Personal opinions about specific situations we will avoid. Furthermore, the problem that someone makes a fool of himself is almost inevitable. I hope you will treat each other charitably." The discussion does not exactly move. The master has to pry responses from his students with everything short of a crowbar—"What's *wrong* with masturbation?" "People sort of think it's sort of a weakness of character"—until the end, when, after a few jokes, he allows the class to loosen a bit. "You're thinking about your girlfriend or some girl you have known," the master says, confidential now, "this can be troubling—"

"My sister," a boy says, in an audible aside.

"How about a lacrosse game?" another asks. "Or whipping guys with belts, big black leather *boots!*"

There are giggles everywhere now.

"Sex is a very strange and a very broad thing," the master says, sensing it is time to conclude. "It has many ramifications we'll be discussing in some detail."

After the classes, there are "postmortem discussions." "*Can* you talk about masturbation out of context? It exists in a total picture of sexuality. Perhaps it should be a *third*-week topic?" Another was upset because in his class a boy had asked, "How often is *excessive* masturbation?" "Three and a half times a week," another master snaps. "There's a boy in *my* class," another master says, "I can see him now, going back to his priest and saying, 'Choate tells me to masturbate.' "

"Perhaps," suggests one of the older masters, "we should go back to the old way of having a whore teach these boys about sex."

"Nonsense," says another. "That's the age-old dream of the benevolent whore who devotes a part of her life to education."

Exciting as sex may be, good teaching is nothing more than what an individual teacher can provide, often quite unprepared, in response to a challenge from a boy. "There was an incident in class today," Mounir Sa'adah says, "which excited me very much. A student asked me, 'Would you kill a man that's coming to kill you?' And I said, 'Basically, the highest value for me is freedom. Freedom for everybody. If I killed that man, I would have deprived him of freedom of choice. If I allowed him to kill me, if there was no way for me to get out of it, then I have practiced *my* freedom of choice. Therefore, in the balance of values, I think I would rather have him kill me than me kill him.' Rather startling. It brought an interesting discussion with regard to Vietnam.

"They had learned their book, but this didn't make them thinkers; it made them rememberers. When you come into a discussion like this, it begins to enter their lives, their own choices, their own experience. It's not digression because if you can relate anything to a problem in their mind, you have so fixed it in time for them that the material they remember will be retained much longer than if they had taken it simply because it is in the book and might appear on the test.

"No teacher has the right to impose in any course his own idiosyncrasies at the expense of the core of the course."

Once, at a meeting, Jim Spencer heard a teacher say: "Kids aren't interested in molecular structure and bond lengths. They're interested in lipstick and deodorants: let's teach them chemistry in relation to deodorants." Spencer jumped up and said, "No! They'll care about anything *you* care about!"

"The point I like in teaching," Spencer says, "is when the boy stops asking me and starts asking himself. It's what I call 'the payoff.'

"What is teaching, anyway, but being enthusiastic and making others enthusiastic?"

An Intangible Institution

> We must seek out those craftsmen who have the happy gift of tracing out the nature of the fair and graceful, that our young men may dwell as in a health-giving region where all that surrounds them is beneficient.
>
> *Republic,* 104–5

> Another reason he hadn't accomplished anything in his field during the last few years was that he was continually plagued by meetings and paper work. There was political indoctrination every Monday and technical instruction every Friday; Party meetings twice a month; meetings of the Party Bureau for the Institute twice a month, too; and two or three times a month he was called to the ministry; once a month there was a special session on security and vigilance; every month he had to work up a plan for new scientific projects, and every three months he had to send in a report on its fulfillment; then, for some reason, every three months he had also to write individual reports on each prisoner. . . .
>
> ALEKSANDR SOLZHENITSYN, *The First Circle*

Some of Choate's faculty say that no more than half of their teaching is accomplished in the classroom. Richard Hunter, English master and varsity soccer coach, has taped to the mirror in his bedroom two stanzas of what must—though he does not know the author—be Victorian verse:

> And the lecture you deliver
> May be very fine and true,
> But I'd rather get my thinking
> By observing what you do.

For I may misunderstand you
And the high advice you give,
But there's no misunderstanding
How you act and how you live.

Next to care for the individual student, teaching by individual example is what Choate is all about. To teach a boy to be upright, just, and honorable, one must himself be upright, just, and honorable. It is an awesome task, but a flattering one as well. The older masters—particularly those hired by George St. John—are entirely dedicated to it, and some of them are quite bitter about younger men who may be amused by, or indifferent to, the assumptions and presumptions that are implied by a concept of Total Teaching. Younger men, the older ones protest, do not see Choate's kind of teaching as a profession, much less a vocation: they want to be wage earners, stalking as quickly as possible through a nine-to-five day, and then closing their doors on students and their problems. Choate just won't work if such a "non-supportive attitude" becomes prevalent, but Father Francis Moan, the English Jesuit observing the American St. Paul's, believes that nonsupportiveness is inevitable. "In our age of specialization," he writes, "I am suspicious that fewer and fewer teachers will be willing to take on all the burdens a master is expected to bear . . . such as teaching, coaching two sports, running one or more societies, being a housemaster and generally being on one or more faculty committees."

Still, some of the younger masters come to Choate because they are attracted by the long hours. "You're able to teach by example in your own personal life," said Tom Colvin, who is twenty-eight. "You're able to teach out on the soccer field, on the basketball court: everything you do is in essence a means of teaching, really. It's not teaching *material,* but teaching a style of living, I guess. I consider this fully as important as what goes on in a classroom.

"There is no evidence of the effect of this. No concrete evidence, certainly. This is one of the frustrations, I guess. It doesn't bother me particularly. Teaching by example is a continual act of faith—that's the best way of putting it. I'm convinced that it tells, because in my own life I have encountered a few people whose approach to life had tremendous impact on me. While these men probably don't know it, they have influenced me more than anything I have picked up in any classroom. I would assume that with the kind of commitment I make here, I may have that kind of influence on some people. The opportunity is greater here for this kind of impact than in any other kind of environment, simply because it's a total environment. I feel it very strongly; I guess it's the reason why I thrive in this kind of atmosphere, where I'm working twenty-four hours a day, and unhappy when vacation comes. I almost feel at loose ends in vacation."

Other young masters have doubts. How much of one's life can one give—and for how *long*—to this kind of teaching? One, who came to Choate to replace a man "who knew his field far better than I but had burned out intellectually," looked around at "the charred hulks still haunting the Choate campus." There were, he decided, fewer at Choate than elsewhere, but he was worried about burning out. "This happens, alas, to many good teachers when they reach fifty. I fear for myself fifteen years from now. Perhaps sooner."

Eleven years ago, in an introduction to the *Master's Handbook,* Seymour St. John defined the qualities he believes go into a great teacher. He sees no reason to change now what he said then:

> He is the man who in his deepest heart wants above all else to help boys grow to be men of fineness, character, integrity. His ideal lends him naturally all the qualities necessary to teaching greatness: in his individual work with boys, sensitivity and a well of understanding; in the face of apparent indifference, endless patience; in difficulties, optimism; in discouragement, faith. And then to that daily, weekly, yearly routine, to that life that could become repetitious drudgery, he brings personal dedication and self-discipline that demand higher standards of his boys than any number of words; he brings inspiration to his classroom; he

> brings a humor and a perspective that always see youth—its strengths and its weaknesses—as part of a life that one day will be a contributing force for good in our world. He recognizes, even in the daily round, that we are working on a small bit of mosaic in the large and universal pattern, that our work carries a deep and eternal significance.

Like an angelus, struck in the middle of the working day, a religious bell rings in the middle of any formal exposition of the school's aims and purposes. The scholars pause and bow their heads. St. John continues:

> But of most vital importance is the individual master—the dedicated teacher—helping, with all that in him lies, to work out each boy's salvation. The greatness of our School can never come solely from a set of rules; it must come primarily from great *individuals* who through sensitivity and devotion of heart and mind and spirit will see those ways in which our tasks can best be accomplished.

Speaking informally, the masters put it differently. "What we try to do," says one, "is a patch job on a kid. The parents do what they can and then hand them over to us. We put on the patches and present them to the colleges."

There were eighty masters at Choate that year, including one woman and the nonteaching administrative staff of executive rank. For each master, there were 6.8 boys. Eight new masters were hired for the fall term—a little more than average, but, I was told, the draft had been at work. To hire those eight masters, Choate considered three hundred applications and interviewed ninety men at length at Choate.

"The present generation of students," says Gordon Stillman, dean of faculty, "has been described as combining in itself a strange blend of personal hedonism, social idealism, action orientation, and uncompromisingly condemnatory moral emotionalism. Those are pretty big words. A pretty terrifying generation." Stillman was explaining to a group of alumni the qualities needed in teachers who must handle this generation.

"First of all, we want men who are interested in young people and optimistic about their future. They cannot in any way be cynical about youth, they cannot think of young people as barbarians, as sloppy, slovenly, disreputable characters." Teachers who want to work at Choate, Stillman continues, must possess ability in their fields and the desire to become more able; they must have "an imaginative and flexible approach to the subject matter," must communicate skillfully, must be vigorous, vital, yet filled "with the milk of human kindness." They must be capable of sympathy, compassionate "men who have emotional stability, balance, poise—emotional maturity, I suppose you could call it—and yet, at the same time, the capacity to explode every now and then in some kind of righteous indignation." The headmaster had, the day before, exploded with more indignation than anyone at school could remember, and most of the faculty thought it A Good Thing. Stillman skipped over *that*. The Choate teacher, he went on, should have breadth of interests, openness to new ideas, "a sense of proportion about his job" because "the school is not the center of the universe. . . . He should be humble about the task that is in front of him, but not so humble as to be scared. He has to have self-confidence. He has to *start*. He has to speak. The bell rings and he is on stage. He cannot at that point have stage fright."

A master should be a creature of habit—getting to breakfast each morning at seven fifteen—but "it's very nice for each one of them to have a little touch of eccentricity about him, something that sets him apart from the others, that in due course will make him a campus character." In this phrase, Stillman touched upon something that is almost gone from Choate, as from all the preparatory schools: the free soul, the unattached man so self-confident that he lives by his own rules, a man who may be crazy, a genius, or possibly a saint, a man who flouts the suffocating, standard-brand propriety of boarding schools, waving his long gray beard and flashing his glittering eye at students who are at first appalled and then mesmerized by a kind of man, a kind of life, they never knew existed.

"I suppose," Stillman says, "I should qualify that by saying that we don't really look for what might be called oddballs."

"Instead of fire drills," said John Joseph, "he staged Archie drills." John Joseph is fifty-six, a man with wispy silver hair and a dark complexion that brought him the nickname "Arab," which is invariably pronounced A'rab. Joseph is the last of the great independent campus characters, a man much milder now than once he was, and he was talking of the greatest of them all, Porter Dean Caesar. Caesar objected to fire drills as he objected to anything that stank of bureaucratic indignity and inconvenience. His Archie drills were everything fire drills were not.

"Early each year," Joseph recalled, "he'd bring his whole house together and explain that every so often, at irregular intervals, he would stage an Archie drill. They would know when the time came because he would fire a gun off from his room and then roll two large brass cannon balls down the front stairs. As soon as *that* happened, they would hear screaming. The boys were then supposed to run to their rooms, shove their bureaus in front of their doors so no one could get in, and then hide under their beds. Two sixth formers were designated as Archies and given the most gruesome masks I ever saw, God knows where he got them. The Archies would run around, trying to find a door not properly barricaded. If they did, they brought the boy to Caesar for sentencing—he had to eat a goldfish or some such thing.

"I remember when I first ran into this I was a new master. I hardly knew Caesar at all. One night I went over to his house to get some information of some kind. When I got to the front door, I heard a pistol shot, and of course I thought somebody had killed himself. I ran in the door and was nearly knocked over by two brass cannon balls bouncing down the front stairs. Pete Caesar came out of his front door and didn't look at all glad to see me. 'In there!' he said, pointing to his apartment. 'What happened?' I asked. 'I can't talk to you now. In there!' he said.

"Later I told him I thought those Archie masks would scare any boy to death. He said, 'Don't be silly. Boys are resourceful. Try it yourself, you'll see.' Well, the upshot was that I took one of those horrible masks to try on the boys in my own house. It was after lights when I got back, but I remembered that one boy on the ground floor always slept with his window open. I went around to his window, thinking I would stick my head in with the mask on to see what he would do. But, as fate would have it, that night he had the window closed. I had a nail file in my pocket and I started to work the window open, but I couldn't help tittering at the same time.

"Now, it's important to remember two things about this boy. He was the best shot, the deadliest marksman in the school. And he was very dim-witted. He must have heard my nail file and my tittering because as soon as I had the window open, he had a flashlight turned right on my mask. He must have slept with a flashlight by his pillow. I just turned and ran. I took the mask off and came in the front door and said to two of my sixth formers, 'I saw a horrible-looking man peering in Jed's window. Let's see if Jed saw him. So we went into Jed's room and there was Jed, standing with a rifle aimed out the window. 'What are you doing?' I asked. 'Well, uh,' he said, 'there was this ugly guy playing pranks out there, trying to scare me. If he, uh, comes back, I'm going to shoot him.' He was so stupid I didn't even dare tell him it was me because he might have shot me then."

Pete Caesar was a bachelor, a tall, nervous man who smoked incessantly—even in class—with his cigarettes tucked at a jaunty angle into a cigarette holder. In those days, no master was supposed to smoke in front of the boys, who then, as now, were not allowed to smoke. Caesar wore sneakers to meals, when no one was allowed to wear sneakers, and he wouldn't go to chapel, when everyone was required to go to chapel. The only sport he coached was tennis, and he did as little of that as possible. The rumor was that Caesar was immensely wealthy; Caesar encouraged the rumor, and he was.

"He had three automobiles," Joseph remembers. "He had a

big Buick convertible and on sunny days he would ride around in it with the top down. He had another Buick convertible and on rainy days he would drive around in it with the top up. For sporty occasions he had a little MG."

For some years, Joseph and Caesar, two bachelors, shared the same table in the dining hall. "At the table he would ask boys if they wanted any chocolate pudding," Joseph says. "He would then turn the dessert plates over and dollop out just a little bit in the rim on the back of the plate.

"Our table was the most popular table in the school. Boys would come every meal to see if there was an empty place. The reason it was so popular was that we kept a running story going about our adventures up the Orinoco. The times we escaped the headhunters and the crocodiles. It was all based, of course, on Evelyn Waugh's *The Man Who Read Dickens.*"

Caesar, it was said, had a set of Ming china in his room. Every week he would pick up a plate or a cup, open his door, and throw it down the stairs. When the boys, attracted to the sound of smashing, opened their doors, Caesar would say, "That'll teach you to respect material things."

"Caesar had a lovely Picasso on his wall," Joseph says. "One of the original drawings from Ovid's *Art of Love.* His parrot broke the glass in the frame and began to nibble at the picture. I said, 'For heaven's sake, put some new glass in the frame,' but Pete said, 'No, the parrot likes the picture.' Little by little, you could see the Picasso disappear until there was nothing left."

Caesar had a stuffed bear in his room, standing erect. The bear held a plate, and on the plate was a human skull. "My grandmother shot that bear," Caesar would tell anyone who asked and many who didn't, "and that's my grandmother's skull. It seemed appropriate."

John Joseph refused to ring bells in his house. He woke us all to the sound of harpsichord music played full blast on his phonograph. None of us had ever heard a harpsichord before. Joseph believed it was a civilizing influence.

There are no more such men at Choate. There will be no more: they are not safe. Arrogant; intolerant; divisive; disloyal; the weakest team man on the faculty—these are the words with which the headmaster recently chased one of his youngest teachers from his school, but the words apply equally to the great eccentric teachers of the past, who might have thought the words *compliments,* who transmitted exhilaration to their students in part because of their own symbiotic relation to the school. As often as not, these men rummaged among the boys to find the few that interested them. Superlatively sure of themselves, they flouted the rules, baffled their colleagues, and spoke sarcastically of anyone they pleased. They teased the boys, insulted them, left them hanging in a chasm of contempt, and made them think. "I *think* he has a soul," John Joseph said one night, waving a cigarette in my direction. His eyes narrowed; he was not smiling. I was seventeen. My roommate's soul had been acclaimed and admired without argument all evening, and I was hurt. A silence hung within the smoke as Christopher Veiel, another eccentric master who inherited a fortune and left Choate kicking up his heels, shook his head in disagreement. "But," said Joseph finally, spitting out his words, "he'd never admit to having one. He wouldn't be seen dead in the same ditch with his soul."

In place of such men, St. John imports quantities of teachers from Europe, particularly Englishmen, who provide a broad base of culture and enthusiasm, as well as great conviction in the worth of prep schools, and in law and order generally. St. John likes European teachers. Foreign affairs are a hobby of his, and foreign teachers, with strong, decisive personalities, can usually be relied on for their unswervingly loyal devotion, and for the quick, gut-conservative reaction that St. John often wants to hear expressed, but which might seem impolitic if it came from him. "None of us," said one of the Englishmen, "would dream of addressing Mr. St. John as anything but 'Headmaster,' or sometimes 'Sir.' " The Englishmen may also come a little cheaper than the home-grown variety, the new young American masters who, says Gordon Stillman, "need convincing of the rightness of our ideals and of our standards."

The boys, hardly knowing what they've missed, look desperately for a colorful master. Clif Clerke, they say, flew a fighter plane for France. His cousin was a German baron, flying for the Nazis. They fought aerial duels, like Snoopy and the Red Baron. Clerke, they say, is the only survivor of a plane crash in which he lost his hair. He wears three wigs of differing lengths, drives a Jaguar XKE with tumescent tailpipes, and so on. Clerke said nothing and finally left the school. It is hardly the same.

In the last five years Choate hired forty-five men and lost fifteen. "We do such an excellent job of choosing teachers," Stillman says, "that we rarely have to tell a man, 'You're no good for us.' And, of course, if we ever have to do that, it is usually a mutual decision. He is unhappy with us and we are unhappy with him." Seven of the eight new faculty members that Choate took on that fall, however, were gone within two years. In the spring of 1969, 25 percent of the faculty had agreed with Choate that they would not return; about the same number left a year later.

The hiring of faculty for Choate, says Stillman, is a complex affair. Universities, with more flexible budgets and a wider range of openings, can find a man who is brilliant in his field and offer him a job. Choate, however, has no need for men involved in research: they need teachers who can coach sports, run a house and a table in the dining hall, advise boys, and write endless reports to the families of boys. Such men, Stillman says, must be "really paragons of virtue and ability, with a loyalty and firmness that one doesn't always find, along with an ability to have close rapport with their students."

The lowest salary paid any master that year was $4,000. The top salary was $12,000—though some in the administration pulled down more—and the average salary was about $7,500. To these figures must be added the perquisites that Choate provides: free room and board in term time, laundry, infirmary care, a few small grants toward travel and educating faculty children in private schools. Choate's trustees believe that these perquisites are, for a single man, worth about $2,000 to $3,000 and, for a family man, between $4,000 and $6,000. St. John believes that it is easier to save money working at a place like Choate than it is to save when one works in business, or in public schools. Some of the faculty obviously enjoy outside incomes, and others, like Jean Pierre Cosnard, make handy profits by taking students abroad in the summer.

That year, Choate offered some insurance to its faculty. Stanley Trotman, insurance executive and Choate trustee, worked out a program with his own company and then came to sell it to the faculty in November. The school would pay for $1,000 worth of group life insurance, and offer an opportunity to masters to buy more. But there was a kicker—the kind of emotional blackmail insurance companies are so adept at devising—75 percent of those eligible to buy the additional insurance *had* to buy it, or no one could. "I'm overinsured already," said one master. "Sounds to me like a screw deal." But masters who didn't need the insurance would feel bad if, by not signing up, they made it impossible for masters who did need it to do so. There was much mumbling confusion as Trotman moved on to explain major medical insurance, which, though the faculty had not voted to accept it, had been in effect since 12:01 that morning. "We will pay the incision-excision fees for operating on a gum provided they don't remove a tooth at the same time," Trotman's assistant said, and the faculty let up a groan. At the end of the meeting, the faculty was as confused as their students would be at the end of a class on gerunds and gerundives. A vote would be taken later. "They're entitled to miss the boat," muttered one faculty member who supported the package. "They're human beings and they're entitled."

When a master arrives at Choate, he may be overcome by the work that is expected of him. That year, Jere Packard, who perhaps does more than most masters, taught three courses of history, coached three sports, ran a house where he was on duty half the time, coached the debating team, advised Choate's Political Union, acted as unofficial adviser to the Military History Club, attended faculty meetings on Monday night, policy committee meetings on sixth-form responsibilities on Tuesday and Wednesday nights, lectured on sex education on Thursday nights, worked part-time in the office of admissions and scholarships, and, in his spare time, corrected papers, prepared exams, wrote reports, talked to the boys, and took his turn in chapel and in the dining hall.

Jon van Leuven, who thinks he ought to be teaching in a college because he needs time to write poetry, plays, a novel, and a book on economics, says that he gets up at six thirty in the morning. "I don't go to breakfast. During my first year I never went to breakfast; luckily, nothing was ever said to me about it. I don't have *time* to go to breakfast. In order to do any writing at all, I have to stay up until two o'clock at night." Jim Spencer, who with another man is rewriting the basic textbook on the chemical bond approach to chemistry, can find only an hour a night to work on it and wonders whether it will ever be done. "There is too much petty shit!" another master yelled, but Mounir Sa'adah believes that overbusyness of masters at a school like Choate "is in the nature of a private boarding school. There are some teachers who don't know this; they don't belong in private schools. It *is* demanding. Teachers are with boys continuously. Some succumb to it completely and become kind of arrested adolescents. They become overbearing, didactic, expecting to be unquestioned.

"Every teacher has, I would say, two or three evenings a week when he can be on his own if he wants to be," Sa'adah says. "I am not short on time, I'm short on longer stretches of time. If I want to do any sustained intellectual work, I would not be able to do it. But in life it's a question of either-or. You can't have everything. One has to make a decision and find out where he wants to contribute his little lot. I do a great deal of reading and I enjoy it immensely. I have kept in touch with theological developments as much as I want to—the ethical aspect of it, which is what interests me—and I think I have kept within range of historical development. I'm not a scholar and I will not be a scholar teaching here or in any secondary school. Secondary schools are not for scholars."

A master's day begins at 6:30. He should be dressed by the rising bell, which rings at 6:50. From 7 to 7:10 he greets the boys—shaking hands in the morning is encouraged at Choate—and he must be at his table for breakfast by 7:15. Fifteen minutes later, he returns to his house, where, hopefully, his sixth formers have checked on the neatness of the boys' rooms. Classes run, in 45-minute segments, from 8:05 to 1 P.M. There are six of them, with a 15-minute break in the middle, and some masters are talking of the need for more classes in the afternoon. Lunch is at 1:10. "Encourage conversation," the masters are told. "Discourage sodden revictualing." Boys leave lunch early, running to sports, or to special conferences for boys who need extra help that begin at 1:40 and are over roughly 30 or 40 minutes later. Athletics are scheduled from 2:30 to 4, but in fact, they usually run far longer than that, from 2 to 5:30, or in hockey season, when time on the rink is carefully allotted, well into the evening. There is supposed to be a late afternoon study period in the houses—the hour or hour and a half when a master can take a shower and talk to his children—before chapel bells begin to ring at 6. Dinner is at 6:30; at 7, there is coffee in the master's room. From 7:30 to 8:30 there is something called "Sacred Hour," when the boys are supposed to study in absolute quiet. The master works correcting papers and quizzes. From 8:30 throughout the evening, the master is supposed to be available for boys who drop in to chat. Most masters, however, make it very clear that there are some evenings when they will entertain privately: when their doors are shut, boys may not knock. Lights go out on a staggered basis, depending on the age of the boys and the requests for "late light" permits. The master gets to bed by 11.

"When you coach a sport," says Richard Hunter, "time becomes very, very valuable. I get up at five in the morning—if I'm to get any work done. At night people are always walking in. I have a small house—only ten boys in it—but they want to talk. We don't have any bells. We have one bell, one all day, and that's the rising bell. I say good morning and from then on, it's automatic. We have to give these boys responsibility; I think boys realize that privileges come with responsibility. I tell them I have two systems of bells. One is one bell a day. The other is fifty-four bells a day. You ring a bell, the rising bell. A minute later, they're in the bathroom, then with a bell they start peeing, then with another bell they stop peeing. I offer them one or the other. They choose one bell a day."

All Choate teachers, for most of their careers at the school, will be required to run, or help to run, a house or dormitory hall. It is the most challenging task any of them face because it has nothing to do with the special skills teachers acquire in their subjects, but everything to do with their personalities and temperaments, with what kind of men they really are. The core of the school is not, as is often said, the chapel or the library. The core may be found in the classroom, but Choate's classes are not essentially different from classes elsewhere. Insofar as Choate has a core that it can call its own, it lies in the houses where the boys live, in the personal relationship between students and faculty that most masters find exhausting but extremely rewarding. A few, by virtue of longevity, leverage, and influence, have worked their way free of house responsibilities, but most teachers would probably admit that, lacking the brilliance or degree of training that a college requires of a teacher, they came to Choate for this experience of being a part of the lives of the boys, for this after-hour teaching by precept and example.

Boys at this age are perhaps more interesting than at any other. They have just passed into sexual maturity. They are beginning to learn empathy; they are beginning to learn how to think. Nearly all of them are entirely receptive to new ideas—as they may not be by the time they get to college. The younger boys, at least, are still open, still willing to tell an adult what their problems are. In the three or four years that a boy stays at Choate, one can see extraordinary changes take place. None of the boys presents any serious intellectual challenge to any adult on the campus. Each is at a time in his life when he needs advice on many subjects and he has no place to go for it but to the masters whom he finds sympathetic. The master acts as more than a surrogate parent: he is a priest. Why else would St. John tell him that the "salvation" of the boys is in his hands? The housemaster advises and confesses his small flock, dispenses grace and penance, acts as repository for a horde of trivial, sacred secrets, and intervenes on behalf of the sinning student before the Great Priest at the Lodge, the Reverend Dr. Seymour St. John.

The *Master's Handbook* makes it clear that "Upon the Housemaster depend the morale and discipline of the House groups, the personal and scholastic welfare of each boy, the training in leadership of the Sixth Formers, the tone of the Houses, and therefore of the School." Since no great responsibility comes unencumbered by Mickey Mouse impedimenta, the housemaster is required to submit to the headmaster rough drafts of his replies to letters from boys' parents; he is advised to mark with red dots the light bulbs in house common rooms so that, if stolen, they may be recovered; and he is told, too, where to pick up his supply of "attendance slips, inter-House permission slips, breakage slips, Chapel attendance slips, grade cards, conduct reports, and commendation reports"; he must also listen by the hour in faculty meetings to debates over towels that have been lost and refrigerators that boys may use in houses. "I don't think," one faculty wife insists, "that you can have the same person teaching you in English class and handing out your clean laundry," but, somehow, it is all worth it. The housemaster is invited, even required by the school, to become involved in the lives of the boys. "You will want to learn all you can about each boy in your House," the *Master's Handbook* says, "his problems, interests, hopes, uncertainties, and doubts; win his confidence, sense his weaknesses, and work with him to overcome them; know about his triumphs and praise him for them; be aware of his disappointments and help him bear them and turn them into victories."

The housemaster is told that he is the man primarily responsible for the health and scholastic success of his boys: he is their faculty adviser and he is expected to meet with them often to discuss their problems. "Speak of the tone of the House and of harmony and sweet reasonableness," the *Master's Handbook* urges. It's a way to begin, at least. And with new boys: "Break the icy reserve with which they greet you. Any gesture of friendly interest on your part will be pathetically welcome." The *Handbook,* written by a master now retired, is full of such witty comments, many of them reflecting a pessimistic view of boys: "You are not doing your job as his advisor unless you jolt him from his narrow, placid path. . . . It is up to you to sense the potentialities of each boy and to help him, by prodding if necessary, toward a full realization of them."

Choate has long lived by what it calls its "Open Door" policy. Masters, except when they are entertaining, are expected to keep their doors open so that any boy can come in at any time to talk about anything at all. The effectiveness of this policy, of course, varies. "You could knock on his door and he wouldn't open it," says one senior of his housemaster. "You could be dying of blood loss and he wouldn't care." Another complains that his house is the worst on the campus because his housemaster is "one of the most unpleasant people I've ever known. He's a real sadist, the cynic-type person. You can't be a cynic and a beautiful person at the same time." "The masters will leave you alone," another senior says of his house. "We could sit around and talk seriously, get to be pretty friendly, and live our own lives without the masters. It was really rather enjoyable. You weren't ashamed to claim it as your home." But a young master complained that his boys would not come to him with intimate details of their personal lives. That was what he was there *for,* a man almost as young as they, and why were they holding back?

Other masters make an art of the Open Door policy. "I live in the biggest dorm in the place," says one sixth former, "thirty-two people above the library—but Mr. Maillet makes it kind of homey, kind of clubby. I think it's the best place I've been in yet. I like Mr. Maillet very much. He's decided to confine his life as much as possible. As far as I know, he has two, maybe three, friends on the faculty. The others he barely tolerates or is extremely prejudiced against. The only people I think he's really interested in are the people in his classes and the people on his floor. He feeds them very well and lets them use his color TV." "I have no financial worries," says Maillet, a bachelor. He feeds his kids pancakes, hard candy, corn bread, salad, and bean suppers, plus day-old baked goods at a cost of $60 a month. "It's a kind of bribery," he admits, "but I have no trouble with boys keeping their rooms clean. My philosophy is that a housemaster should be an ear, and occasionally a tongue."

John Joseph, who lives in a clutter of Picasso drawings, Lautrec prints, books from Blackwells, and a shaggy dog, has always a cup of tea and an inexhaustible supply of interest waiting for any boy who drops by. Many do, including football players and reedy bookworms who may just sit and study, preferring to work in Joseph's quarters rather than in their own rooms. Joseph offers sympathy as well as interest, leavened by a good store of righteous indignation. He never judges students unless he thinks he can prod their own better judgments, never hands out punishments in anger, never fails to offer assistance, never finds a dilemma that does not have some element of humor in it. Fourth formers believe that Joseph can see through them. Fifth formers think him a fake. Sixth formers value his friendship. That year, four fourth formers told Joseph they were about to leave the school, so Joseph went to St. John, "precipitating the only crisis in my career. I said, 'You think *you* have problems! None of your problems is as bad as this.' " Joseph and St. John both talked to the boys, and they agreed to stay. Joseph grumbles: the boys aren't as good as they once were. Boys find it hard to find the time and inspiration to pursue the arts, music, and writing at Choate. If, by mistake, Choate hired a master as eccentric as Porter Caesar, "he would be fired at once."

In the course of the year, tensions build up in the dormitories. "We'd had a big go-around about water bombs," Malcolm Manson said. "Because they'd gone a little too far. At two on Sunday, I called the fellows in: *No more water bombs.* At two thirteen on Sunday: water bombs all over the place. So we had a big confrontation. Then Monday night, when I came back at eleven, there was a sheet hanging over the banister. Somebody had thrown a wastebasket down the stairs—bits of orange peel. It was so revolting! I was furious. I was in the mood to wake everybody up. The next day was to be a free day, but I wanted to give them all study hall."

"In the fall," said a new boy, a third former, "my first impression was that everybody was friendly, very nice. Toward the middle of the winter we started getting these cliques, bands of guys, and they're all tough nuts to crack. You couldn't get through to these groups."

"Look at us," said a friend of his. "We're as much of a clique as anybody else. My impression in the fall was that everybody was shocked, temperamental. Some of the guys looked weird. Then, in the winter, some people whom I didn't mind before I just did not like at all. You know that long time, the snow and slush. I got sort of sick of it. Now that spring has come, I think all the cliques have broken up. A clique is sort of a hibernation-type thing.

"The overfriendliness of some people," he went on, "can get on your nerves. There's one boy who gets obnoxious. I like to stay away from him. Once I went a little too far with kidding and he started crying. Everybody was so tensed up. I didn't do anything, but *I* was tensed up, and he started crying.

"Since spring vacation," the boy said, "guys are beginning to write their girls. One guy wrote a letter, you know, it was one of those things: 'Dear Ann, I guess you don't know what I look like.' (He had bought the girl's address off another boy.) 'I'm sort of a cross between Paul McCartney and Paul Newman.' (Unfortunately, he had a crew cut.) 'No pix right now' (you know: p-i-x, like you see in all the teeny-bopper magazines), signed 'l-u-v,' love."

The tensions work in subtle ways. Another new boy said, "I

was talking to a boy today about a problem I feel very deeply about. Automatically, you know, you're trying to explain how you feel about a girl, and then he fires back, 'Oh, I'm having the same problem.' And you don't really want to hear about the *other* guy. That attitude. You know: you sort of burn inside. You say, 'Yeah, well, anyway,' and he goes, 'Yeah, I know what you mean.'

"It's not so much one attitude that will drive you to hate somebody, but these attitudes slowly build up inside you and you might take it out on somebody who doesn't even bother you, you know? You won't jump on a guy for his attitude, but you'll jump on him for all attitudes everywhere. That happens with me quite a bit. I'm so tense at heart. Sometimes, I just have to let it all out at once and start all over again. It takes me about a week to accumulate all this stuff and then I just throw it out at somebody."

What would you say, I asked, to a new third former coming in?

"I'd tell him to come here expecting the very worst. Because if you come here expecting the very worst, you can never be let down. Come in here and expect little things like plastic wood on the walls. A bed with no springs. I came here expecting a big room, wallpaper, things like that, and the first day I almost tripped over my bed."

"What I say is," said another new boy, "come expecting yourself to be the lowest of the low. After all, we are."

"I would say," said the first boy, "if you're coming here, on the first night when you're lying in bed, you know, banging on the mattress to see if they're rocks in there or something: never judge a person on your first thoughts about him. Because I get the sense here that everybody at Choate is trying to put on an act of sophistication. If you *believe* this sophistication, you're gonna feel very belittled and very small in relation to other people because they like to run around with their nose in the air and they cut you down to size. In my day school, this wasn't true."

The other boy disagreed: "I think to some extent you have to put on an act. Because there aren't too many people around here you can be frank with."

"There are walls around the groups," the first new boy said. "For security. Everybody has to be secure. In a boarding school, where you have no other security than friends, you *must* form a clique. Or else you're lost, you don't have anybody to turn to. If you're having a feud with somebody, who can you go to? It's sort of a basic necessity at a boarding school to form a clique."

The boys are clever: they build their rooms into fortresses against the world of Choate. "One of the things which has irritated me," says Jon van Leuven, "is the degree to which these kids rely on record players. They use them in a therapeutic way." Walking anywhere through a Choate dormitory, one can hear Otis Redding, James Brown, Aretha Franklin, the Doors, and Ray Charles, who, with a flick of a glottal switch, soars to castrati heights. "They come up here," says Van Leuven, "just before lunch or just after chapel, any time they know they're going to be called on to do something, and they will turn on their record players full blast, *and then go into a room where there is no record player and talk.* So what they've done is provide a curtain of noise for the background. They don't care about listening to music. It's a drug. They don't care anything about the nature of rock 'n' roll. It's a wall between them and the school. Every student possesses a record player. It has become for me a kind of symbol of the student mentality. A symbol of trying to shield oneself from the processes of education. Perhaps demands made by parents —no, I think their parents were too permissive; they're not accustomed to having demands made on them. It's a reaction to people who are trying to tell them things."

The citadel that is a boy's room at Choate has always been open to assault. In my room I had a framed Van Gogh print, but—ha!—I cared nothing for that. On the *back* of the print was a picture of my best girl and me, snapped in a dance hall. Neither of us looked our best. When I felt romantic, I turned the picture over and then, of course, my housemaster walked in. He never knocked. "My," he said, "what a handsome rogue you are! Is that fat child your girlfriend?"

Even earlier, in 1920, George St. John raised the problem with one of his faculty. Then, as now, it was a problem that provoked considerable definition:

> In making your rounds, I wish you would report to me any room, with the names of the boy or boys who live in it, where there are pictures or other wall decorations that seem unsuitable and cheap: I mean pictures of girls in bathing suits, or chorus girl costume, pictures of ladies and gentlemen with goblets or cigarettes—just things that reflect poor taste on the part of any boy. I want in each case to see a boy who uses that kind of decoration and get him to change it, and I want to talk to the boy myself personally.
>
> Another rule of the School is that a boy may have in his room one banner and three pennants, or a second banner to take the place of the three pennants. This is all the pennants or banners the boys are allowed.

Nowadays, the regulations are even more complex. "No naked nipples" is the phrase used by the boys to sum matters up, but the *Master's Handbook* is more precise: "The regulations should be enforced not only at the beginning of the year, but periodically thereafter, to catch the sly boys who don't pin up their girls until after the first month." And the regulations continue:

> Wattage limited to 150 watts per boy.
> No coffee pots, toasters, sunlamps, only clocks, blankets & shavers.
> No fastening extension cords to walls with tacks.
> No nails, screws or staples on woodwork, walls or window shades.
> No scotch tape or thumbtacks on plaster.
> No writing on woodwork, walls or windowshades.
> No throwing knives against doors or walls or carving School property with knives.
> No removing mirrors from School bureaus.
> No loosening wainscoting to make a hiding place.

"One boy," says St. John with a chuckle, "built in a TV set behind the paneling in his room. It was discovered during spring vacation. Of course he had to pay for all the paneling and his TV set was confiscated for the infirmary. I asked him to come in and see me about it. He said, 'Well, you know, until I got working on that I just wasn't doing any academic work at all. I found things dull and boring, but once I got started on that, I'd work on it every night. I'd work on this paneling after lights. I got a *saw* and worked it all out, with a sliding panel, and my marks went up ten points. I could work the next day: I felt happy and gay."

The regulations continue:

> No leaving lights on when room is not in use.
> No opening windows when room is too warm instead of lowering heat.
> No bottles, food or other objects on outside window ledges.
> No dragging boxes or trunks downstairs without carrying them.
> No crowding books into study hall desks to such an extent that the hinges are strained when the lid is closed.
> No tampering with locks or possessing without authorization keys to School rooms or buildings.
> No throwing or letting objects fall or roll into roof gutters.

"I remember," says one sixth former, "in Logan Monroe House, the masters announced that there would be no more girlie pictures in the rooms. So everybody got together and handed in pictures of their sisters and mothers." He lives in a single room. Amid the general clutter, there is a cello in its case; a big color poster advertising the Italian Communist Party with Palmiro Togliatti looking like Clifton Fadiman; a gigantic photograph of a can of Shaefer beer; and a parody of a Walt Disney panorama, said to be drawn by an ex-Disney staffer, in which the Seven Dwarfs are peering down Snow White's bodice. Blankets cover every inch of the walls. The blankets—to be found in most Choate rooms—make the place seem more womblike. The trick is not to see a single square inch of school fabric.

"I'm generally quite liberal about the decorations I allow in my house," says Charles Pierce. "But I went upstairs the other day and I found in one room—the worst-looking room I ever saw—the walls covered with pictures of nude women. I simply went around and took down the pictures I found offensive. I took the pictures down to my room. I didn't destroy them. I didn't throw them out. I put them very carefully on a shelf in my closet. I didn't say a thing, and for two days I didn't hear a thing.

"Then one day a boy came down and said, 'Mr. Pierce, did you destroy my pictures?' And I replied, 'Why, no, I wouldn't do that, any more than I would go through your drawers. Those pictures are *your* property. They are here in my closet. You may do anything you wish with them, but not hang them on your walls.'

" 'Why not?'

" 'I find them in bad taste.'

" 'Why?'

"So we had a talk about bad taste. What *is* bad taste? The boy agreed—well, yes, he *accepted* my judgment."

The most glorious room in the entire school, from the point of view of decoration, serves two boys and measures 13 by 13, with a double bunk. The ceiling is about 10 feet high. On one wall there is a yellow poster with the Capricorn goat; geometrical figures covering the dates from December 22 to January 20; a NO SMOKING sign; a pink strip saying DILLY THE DRAGON; a placard stolen from an English pub saying BAR. W. H. BRECKSPEER & SONS, LTD.; antique photos from nineteenth-century magazines, including a harem lady in traditional pose. On the mirror there is a picture of many women smoking hookahs, and a DO NOT DISTURB sign. On the back of the door there is a poster advertising the Grateful Dead; there is a *B.C.* cartoon showing a turtle walking along; a big Peter Max poster; a sign saying SMOKE POT: POT IN A PIPE IS A GAS. A RARE BLEND OF MEXICAN WEEDS. HEADS BLASTED—THE BEST FOR YEARS.

On another wall there is a gigantic poster reading COME TO MIDDLE EARTH with Tolkien-type animals gamboling around it. There is a hockey stick; a broom; a WET PAINT sign; a hand-painted sign reading BOAT LORRIES UNLOADED; another *B.C.* cartoon; some very brightly painted pieces of cloth hanging all over the walls, forming psychedelic patterns; a Choate banner, and under the banner a picture of an atomic explosion with mushroom-cloud effect. There is a skull and crossbones, white on black; more colored paper hanging from an acoustically doctored ceiling. ALL BOSSES ARE SCHMUCKS, says a button pinned to the wall. A string net hangs down from the ceiling. An Art Nouveau poster exclaims: NOT ONLY TO BE LOVED, BUT TO BE TOLD THAT I AM LOVED. Another says: THE REALM OF SILENCE IS LARGE ENOUGH BEYOND THE GRAVE. There is a blank piece of paper with lovely calligraphy: "The Sound of the Lasting Mountain," and a beautiful color poster painted by one boy's sister illustrating all the imagery from "Lucy in the Sky with Diamonds." There is some psychedelic wrapping paper Scotch-taped to the ceiling; a big poster: ALICE'S TEA PARTY; some miscellaneous pictures: strips from an American flag showing one row of stars, one red and one white stripe. There is a sign: WORK IS THE CURSE OF THE DRINKING CLASS, and another: TO THE BABIES OF SAN FRANCISCO: BABIES MADE FOR $3. There is a cartoon of a football player entitled "The Living Legend"; more psychedelic posters; wine bottles; gallon jugs; an empty bottle of Beaujolais Brouilly; a Cornell poster; another reading PROTEST AGAINST THE RISING TIDE OF CONFORMITY; another reading BOOTH'S HOUSE OF LORDS; a "Peanuts" calendar; a strange photograph of a shapeless face dissolving, with a cigarette in its mouth; a Confederate banner; an Art Nouveau poster showing a smoking candle; a Pop Art poster; a Camp poster of a rough-looking man with a huge mustache saying, "Keep Smiling"; a framed color print of the little boy peeing into a pool; a button saying HELP, I'M A LONELY HETEROSEXUAL; another saying SEX BEFORE FINALS; a sign saying SAVE FOR A RAINY DAY—AT LEAST ENOUGH TO BUY A PAIR OF RUBBERS.

In January, the headmaster and Alex MacFarlane discussed

the problem with Student Council. "At what point is it sheer art and at what point is it just sheer?" St. John asked. MacFarlane admitted that he had once made a boy take down a picture of his mother. "Would anybody's mother be embarrassed by walking into your room?" St. John asked. "That would be enough to make it bad taste." It would also be enough to destroy the last-bastion quality the boys seek to give their rooms. Worrying about one's own mother is problem enough; worrying about *anybody's* mother leads to the asylum. MacFarlane refused to buy the idea that pictures of beer cans and cigarette packs are a kind of joke, a sarcastic acceptance of strict rules by which the boys must live. "It's a simple revolt," MacFarlane said, "that's all."

Unlike colleges and public schools, most preparatory schools offer no formal security, no system of tenure to their faculties. They cannot very well do so without changing their totally autocratic style of life. Tenure generally means that a teacher, having proven over a period of years his competence and compatibility, is told that he has a permanent position with the school as long as he desires it. The school says, in effect, we will give up our right to fire you because we believe in you, because we believe we will all profit if you are made totally free to say what you really think and act as you believe to be best. We don't want you to hold back, or quell your best thoughts through fear of administrative anger and retaliation. Tenure confers dignity on a teacher because it removes his fear of his employer, because it makes him without question a part of the fabric of the school. St. John tells his faculty that they are more important than the bricks and mortar in the school and he means it, and they believe it, and they *are*, but they are not safe.

In fact, there is a kind of tenure at Choate. "If a man stays with us five years," Gordon Stillman says, "he usually continues to stay with us and expects us to stay with him." Yet a number of masters who have been at Choate much longer than five years fear for their jobs, and, fearing, hold their peace. The headmaster is very fond of men who don't make waves: thus, the older, "devoted" men have tenure. One devoted man, whose blistering incompetence enraged both faculty and boys, knew perfectly well he would never be asked to leave, though the whole school was eagerly awaiting his retirement. A few others, like the acerbic director of athletics who antagonizes many masters, know that they can say, in the crudest possible language, whatever they want to St. John.

That they can do so fascinates faculty and boys alike, and spurs much talk of "Choate's Establishment." Jere Packard is probably correct in saying that there are *three* Choate establishments. First, there is an "establishment of longevity and connection." The director of athletics belongs to this one. The son of Choate's former chef of fifty years' service, Bill Pudvah "is a member of *the* Choate establishment in a way that no man who was hired here recently, no matter how bright he is, can ever be." The "devoted men" also belong to this establishment; most of them, huffing and puffing against the younger teachers and dozing through their classes, were hired by George St. John. Next, according to Packard, comes "an establishment of exact position." Gordon Stillman, Bill Sweeney (who directs the Studies Program), Alexander MacFarlane, and Mark Tuttle belong to this establishment, as do other members of the administration. Finally, says Packard, "there's an establishment which combines longevity and, in Seymour's light, supposed indispensability. In this category you would put Pauline Anderson and Jo van Straalen."

Pauline Anderson directs the Andrew Mellon Library at Choate. Both she and it are among the wonders of the world of preparatory schools. Pauline is a small, slim woman, with an acid sense of humor and strong opinions: "I hope they lock up Dr. Spock before he corrupts the minds of a whole generation." She is as able as anyone at Choate, and so she can afford to stay in the background, and, as the only woman at Choate with faculty rank—she is, in fact, the head of a department—she finds it politic to let the men do the blustering. Stillman occasionally forgets he has any women in his charge. Once he told alumni how he gets rid of female applicants: " 'You mean you don't take *any* ladies at all?' she asked me, and I said, 'No, I'm terribly sorry, we don't,' and she said, 'Well, I want to be the first one.' It was not easy to put her off." Pauline Anderson was not in the audience at the time, but had she been, she would have smiled and kept on knitting.

Pauline is generally thought to be the best director of libraries on the independent school scene. She has written a booklet on the subject, has traveled across the country, has talked to librarians representing 190 schools, and pulls down fancy fees for telling schools like Deerfield how to build libraries from scratch. Choate's library, endowed by a gift from Andrew Mellon, then the school's principal benefactor, was built in 1926. The day before Mellon arrived to see what he had wrought, two of Choate's more literary masters were rushed to New York, armed with two manila envelopes containing $500 in cash, to comb the secondhand bookstores on Fourth Avenue and bring back enough volumes to stock the library. When Pauline arrived in 1950, the library had 20,000 books. She threw out 8,000 of them, just to start, including 27 sets of the works of George Eliot. There was no regular librarian at the time—"only masters who couldn't coach sports"—but there was an annual budget of $200. "The library," Pauline says, "was supplied from old attics": there were bound volumes of old *New Yorker* covers, more volumes of boys' compositions and test papers, and ceiling-high stacks of back issues of the New York *Times*.

Libraries in schools across the nation are generally underprivileged, poor relations to the swimming pools that alumni are constantly providing, but this is not the case at Choate. The school provides an annual budget of $1,950 for the library; $2,100 more comes to the library from the annual giving program; and there are many special endowments: $5,000 annually for books in the humanities, for instance; $400 for foreign books; $40 for books on religion and $25 annually for books on Jewish subjects. The library also gets $700 to $1,000 each year from the sale of books no longer wanted. A few publishers send the library every book they publish; some departments at Choate give the library part of their budgets; there are separate funds available for books on Kennedy and Stevenson.

Pauline handles all this with a firm, no-nonsense approach. She has 25,000 books in the library now; 115 current issues and 1,800 back volumes of periodicals including *L'Express, China Today,* and *World Tennis;* pamphlets on 300 topics; collections of pictures in 200 subject areas; subscriptions to five English and three foreign-language newspapers; more than 2,000 musical and spoken-word records; the New York *Times* on microfilm from its beginning in 1851; the Aurora *General Advertiser* (Philadelphia) from 1790 to 1810; the New York *Herald* from 1835 to 1841; the New York *Tribune* from 1841 to 1852; the *Liberator* (Boston) from 1851 to 1865, and the Charleston *Daily Courier* from 1852 to 1873. The library sprawls over many rooms and alcoves: there is a subterranean archives division, and, in the main reading room, glass-topped library tables where something is always on display. That fall, to mark the fiftieth anniversary of the Russian Revolution, a life-size poster of Lenin was taped to the fireplace just under the portrait of Seymour St. John's mother. There stood Lenin, backlighted by the flames of 1917, under Cyrillic characters: LENIN LIVED: LENIN LIVES: LENIN WILL LIVE. Within a few days the poster was removed, "at the request of a faculty member."

Johannes van Straalen was brought to Choate in 1957, a month before the first Sputnik went up, "specifically for the purpose of introducing Russian" to the school. Now Van Straalen teaches Russian and Russian history, and directs a subdivision of the library: the Russian Studies Center for Secondary Schools. Van Straalen is forty-four, Dutch; he came to America in 1952 with his Swiss bride of two weeks to take a job as a credit investigator for the foreign department of the Manufacturers Trust. "I had never seen a bank from the inside," he says. "I think they hired me mainly because I knew Russian. In case business opened with the Soviet Union, they would be ready."

He quit to go to St. Louis to teach Russian. "It was the McCarthy period, the climate was very bad for teaching Russian. I came in class and on the blackboard somebody kiddingly would have written: *Johannes is a Communist.* The fact that you spoke Russian, there was something wrong with you. My program folded."

St. John, however, was very enthusiastic about teaching Russian—"He is a man with a certain vision," Van Straalen says—and by 1959 Choate had launched a Russian Studies Summer Program. Boys and girls from schools across the country would study Russian and Russian history for four weeks at Choate and then spend five weeks studying in the Soviet Union. The cost of the program is $2,000, and Choate now turns applicants away. Van Straalen spends much of his time chivying institutions into providing $13,000 of scholarship money. Seventy percent of the kids who went on the trip in 1967 received some kind of scholarship aid.

"Independent schools," Van Straalen says, "have no excuse for existence unless somehow or other they can make a contribution to education in general. They should not be ivory towers that just get people ready for the Ivy League." Choate, he says, has been lagging in such fields as computer development, and "the Choate school has to be tops in every single area that we possibly can." To be tops, Van Straalen had suggested a Russian Studies Center at Choate, a center so excellent that other schools would use it as a clearinghouse for their own programs. St. John jumped at the idea. "If he thinks that any master has a good idea," Van Straalen says, "he'll back him to the hilt. This is the great thing about working in this school, because you have room and—boy!—you really feel like you're working and you're living!"

The Russian Studies Center, which is a library containing about 1,500 volumes—"It could be three to four thousand volumes with more librarian help"—is run entirely by Van Straalen, with the part-time secretarial help of a faculty wife. The center is financially independent from the school. Parents, says Van

Straalen, do not believe in paying to help education in general; they want their sons to get a good education, the kind that will get them into a good college. Period. End. Finish. Van Straalen's center works on a school budget of about $2,500, collects books and papers on every conceivable aspect of Russian history and literature, and circulates them, free of charge, to any secondary school interested in using them. Van Straalen writes a news bulletin that he sends to 1,000 teachers across the nation in public, parochial, and secondary schools. He scrambles for foundation help. He began with a $10,000 grant from a small foundation, spread over three years, but that has now expired; now he must worry over minimal budgets, worry about how he can keep his center going. Grants as high as $160,000 are being given elsewhere, but not to Choate. "Maybe our function," Van Straalen says, "is to initiate, stimulate, and more or less to seed, and let other people go on from there." He pauses. "I've reached the limit of my physical and mental capability," he says. "Right now, I'm at the crucial point. Priorities, to me, are here." He pounds on the table in his center.

Van Straalen is a man of great charm and personality; his enthusiasm for what he does is contagious. He worries about the boys he has taught, where they go to college, and what they do with the foundation of Russian he has given them. "Harvard is terrible!" he exclaims. "Harvard stinks!" Van Straalen's boys are bright boys, and they can get into Harvard, but Harvard "stinks in the Russian Department!" Every single boy Van Straalen has sent to Harvard has stopped taking Russian; it is very discouraging. "This has been one of the most frustrating things for me. Harvard is the magic thing, so they go to Harvard and they drop Russian. It's a crime."

Van Straalen is so energetic that colleges have told him that what he is doing with Russian at Choate has influenced what *they* do in college. When alumni come to Choate, Van Straalen dances around them, coaxing them to learn how to say "Hello" in Russian—"the hardest word in the Russian language!"

"I hit the roof every single day," Van Straalen tells them,

meaning that he is *happy*. He folds one hand over the other as he looks out at all the faces propped over Brooks Brothers suits. "How many of you can say *that* in your jobs?" Van Straalen smiles at them; no offense intended. "I may not have the same bank account, but there is not a happier member of the faculty."

Playing the Game

> There are times when you'd like to get drunk and get naked privately.
>
> A FACULTY WIFE

> It's a hell of a life for wives.
>
> A BACHELOR MASTER

In the days of the Old Head, masters were not expected to drink hard liquor in their rooms. Today, Margaret St. John prefers not to serve anything stronger than sherry or wine at gatherings in the Lodge—"Boys might come in at any time with serious problems"—but she does not expect the faculty to follow her rigorous example. Even so, Malcolm Manson refused a drink from my bottle of unblended malt whisky until, with untainted breath, he had said good night to the boys in his house. It is simply a matter of discipline, of small sacrifices gladly made, and besides, the boys are everywhere and know everything. "As a matter of fact," Manson said, "the boys can probably hear this entire conversation, which is a part of the problem of Choate life. My wife and I discovered last year when we were in the Wood House that everything we said in our bedroom could be heard. Fortunately, we discovered it toward the end of the year, so it hadn't completely ruined our marriage."

Sooner or later every adult woman on the Choate campus wonders just how much of her private life belongs to the school. What, in fact, is she supposed to *be?* An independent woman, the equal of her husband, who dresses as she pleases and eats what she likes and makes her voice heard in community councils? Of course not. An imitation mummy to an endlessly changing procession of boys? Getting warmer. A school appliance, installed in each building, that no one pays for or ever needs repair, which produces, night and day, coffee from one spigot and comfort from the other? Oh, Westinghouse, where have you been? *That* is what she is.

The *Master's Handbook,* which defines everything else, defines her, too. She is a "lady of the faculty," which is not as ambiguous as it sounds because Choate's wives know what it means: it means that they are not a part of the faculty. It was months before Anne Longley, a faculty wife who took over a number of French classes on Howard Preble's death, was allowed to attend a faculty meeting. The other "ladies of the faculty" are expected to get out of the faculty room before the faculty meeting begins because, as I was told, women have idle tongues and would doubtless blather whatever they heard to the four points of the campus.

Still, if they are not informed of what goes on in the school, if they are not made a part of its decisions, wives are useful. There is work for them to do. "Wives are a vital part of the School," the *Handbook* intones. "It is hoped and urged that wives will attend meals and Chapel regularly." Wives are thought to be a civilizing influence on the table manners and conversation of Choate boys, but the children of these same wives obviously are not, and may never eat in the dining room with their parents. The wives are left to sort that problem out as best they can. In chapel, wives are allowed seats only in the balcony and, after the service, are expected to stand until the boys have filed out of the building. Few wives bother to go. They are urged to attend the school's plays, lectures, concerts, even its football games, and they are asked to visit boys who are sick in the infirmary although they know that, if they or their children fall sick, they will not be allowed care in that infirmary. Wives know that the school will pay for a faculty member's laundry, but not for his family's laundry, and that maid service and furnishings for his apartment are denied him once he is married. Wives know, too, that they must remember the birthdays of the boys living in their house that year, and they must give parties—"frequent but simple parties are preferred to infrequent and lavish affairs"—for which the school provides ice cream. The rest must come from the family budget. Wives are told what to wear: "sportsclothes, suits, sweaters and skirts, at meals, except for Saturday night and Sunday dinner, when more formal clothes are worn. Hats are worn for Sunday Chapel." Wives are required to pour tea and coffee when the school entertains, and write cheery letters to the mothers of new boys in their houses. All this helps "to break down a boy's shyness and loneliness and make him feel that he is an individual and not part of a mass. While wives are not empowered to give boys permission for anything, they can be of tremendous help in creating an atmosphere that is friendly and homelike simply by being around as much as possible and taking an interested and active part in the School."

So says the *Master's Handbook*.

Some wives say that the headmaster has told them they must put the interests of Choate boys ahead of those of their own children.

Margaret—or Peggy—St. John is, of course, the undisputed ruler of the domain of faculty wives. She sees that certain wives are paid to do certain work for the school: to wash linen for the chapel ($3 a week), to answer the telephones in the Lodge, and to write letters for her. Some say, too, that she has her own lines of information which are quite separate from those of her husband—faculty wives claim to know who among them passes information directly to her—lines which provide her with whatever she wants to know, or likes to hear, about the school. Certainly, when I went to see her in the spring, she knew more about my book than I did: "I hear very bad things about your book," she said, by way of opening our conversation, though she disapproves of "idle gossip."

I should, of course, have talked to her earlier, but Peggy St.

John is rarely seen at Choate. She has a history of ill health, keeps much to herself, and one hesitates to impose. Her withdrawal to the Lodge is, says one master, "nothing short of a tragedy. If only she were well, she would be able to do the things she ought to do." Others are less certain: "She *hates* Choate," says one faculty wife. "Who can blame her?" asks another. "She is married to a man who is married to the school. How could she like the place?" "She will not entertain," says the first. "She leaves parties at an embarrassingly early hour. She never goes to the dining room." It is true that her place at her husband's table is usually taken by Paul Juliff, one of the older faculty, who babbles amiably about masters he has known and meals he has eaten, talking nonstop in a mid-Atlantic accent that sounds for a while, at least, urbane. "The St. Johns do not entertain," the wife continues. "A little attention would go a long way. Even if Peggy had all the wives in for coffee once a year. She makes no attempt to call on new wives. It's a pity that she doesn't." "I've lived opposite the St. Johns for twenty years," says one master, "and I'd never dream of dropping by to pay a social call." But the way in which he says it implies: of-course-that's-the-way-it-ought-to-be.

Peggy St. John has difficulty feeling at home at Choate. The furniture from Williamsburg is hers, and the example is hers: her father, she says, "was a really great man, a dedicated doctor, and an even greater humanitarian." From the beginning, she has made heroic efforts. "When I first came," she says, "I was very young and very scared. It was not the thing for masters to be married." Like her husband, she has come to think of good things in broad, absolute terms, and, like him, she believes a little bit in change and a lot in loyalty. To be a young leader, she once told a young master, or to be a young *anything*, one has first of all to be loyal. She thinks about how to cope with everyday living: how to smile at an employee and pat him on the back, how to heal a bird with a broken wing, and how to visit the sick and make them cheerful, even if she can't remember their names. Some of the boys shudder: the lady they rarely see wafts into their rooms and wishes them good health, whoever they may be. "I can't possibly know all the boys," she says, but she goes to the infirmary every day.

From time to time, when Peggy St. John feels bad vibrations within the school, she offers a rebuke, often in the columns of the school newspaper, *The Choate News,* as she did in November, 1969:

IF YOU WERE HEADMASTER:

Would you first care so deeply about your School, its boys, its Masters, its employees, its parents, and its Alumni, that you would make every kind of personal sacrifice so that your School might be among the best?

Would you take exalted pride in the achievements of your boys and co-workers?

Would you suffer for others in trouble?

Would you discount idle gossip?

Would you have the patience in the midst of a hectic day to hear out all who want to talk, blow off steam, complain, and, happily, often tell you something good?

Would you have the magnanimity to look for good in people often where others had failed to find it?

Would you have the control to keep your balance under the avalanche of pettiness and egotism that sometimes inundates you?

Would you have the humor to chuckle at the foibles of others "and" yourself?

Would you have the wisdom to accept constructive criticism, to welcome new ideas, and the judgment to outweigh all factors before you make a final decision?

Would you have faith, in the most difficult times, that fundamentally boys are great?

Finally, when you spend your whole life working for your boys and are sniped at and hurt by the insecure to whom you have tried to give most, would you reach for the crying towel or would you face tomorrow with optimism, courage, and faith?

ANY TAKERS?

And in a footnote, Peggy St. John added: "Incidentally, if I were Headmaster, I would suggest to a certain few who spend so much time griping about the School and its Administration, they find a spot more to their liking!" "There is an unreasonable fear of criticism on the part of a great many of the powerful people in this community," the head of the Student Council replied.

But Peggy St. John knows, as clearly as her husband knows, what it is she likes about the school: "I found a very definite feeling of people caring for one another. When there is trouble or when there is celebration there is a great feeling of oneness—holding on to the best of the past and yet trying to move forward. I think there is a feeling that when anybody is in trouble, they can find help." She believes this: never mind if the boys are callous or indifferent. She has sat up many a night when a boy was under the knife.

"One thing we miss, of course," says her husband, "is girls. I think girls, to an extent, have more heart and compassion than you find in boys. At least it shows more on the surface. To get this in the way that all of us have some need for it, one almost has to turn to the female of the species. I happen to be incredibly fortunate in having a wife who feels the hurt of a boy in a very rare way. When she goes to the infirmary to see boys, as she does throughout the year, she feels their problems, she gives them a kind of solace and orange sherbet that makes a very great difference in their lives."

St. John tells the story of a boy who was hit in the face by a baseball bat. "Well, it was very scary. It took his nose away, it broke all the things in his jaw, his eye was involved, it just completely *mashed* him, and right first off we had no idea whether he had a killing brain injury, but Peggy took care of that one. His reaction to this was what I had hoped for—at its best—to the feeling of compassion and caring." St. John feels that this care becomes "part of the atmosphere that gets developed, that people breathe in, and they feel it. I would attribute a very real proportion of that to Peggy and to other women of the campus as well. Boys very often will turn without self-consciousness and with a feeling of ease to a woman in certain situations where they will not to a man."

Peggy St. John comes from a broken home. "You know," says her husband, "every year there are some boys whose parents get divorced, and some of them take it, apparently on the surface, in stride. Some are torn to shreds. What do you do for them? Peggy's family was divorced when she was young, and boy! she is good at that—ten times as good as I am. I just ask them if they wouldn't like to talk to her."

"My family was in a hell of a mess," said one boy who was kicked out of Choate for stealing. "My father left home and went to Florida with another woman in early January. Everything was kind of falling apart. My father was not paying the school bills. I was really finding the need to talk to somebody. St. John said I might find even more value in talking to Mrs. St. John because she had been through kind of the same thing with her parents.

"I did speak to her, and I never felt better in my life than when I walked out of that house. She was terrific. Absolutely terrific. She walked in. I felt it was going to be pretty damn awkward. How do you start talking to a woman you've never said three words to and tell her your most personal problems? She walked in and said, 'I hear you have problems.' I said, 'Yes, I do.' That was it—all the ice was broken. She did everything. I felt completely at home. She asked if I wanted a milkshake. If you come within ten feet of the house she asks you if you want a milkshake. And I did. You're just so comfortable. And I talked. I didn't hold anything back. She listened and then told me about her own problem. She didn't really give me any advice. We talked about what my mother could do after twenty years of marriage based on this man. What *can* she do? Can she build a new way of life? We sort of decided that it didn't really affect me much. It was *her* problem. And it became a question of what I could do to help her. Which was a hell of a big change for me. I feel that was really a turning point in my life as far as maturity went." This boy's brother took the hippie route—"totally frustrated, no goals, nothing to live for"—but he felt differently. "Up to that point," he says,

"I had been apathetic, but then I realized how much my mother needs help."

"She is always able to do something," St. John says. "I think it is her absolutely honest projection that she is concerned, that she cares, and that's enough. It doesn't matter what she says. It doesn't matter what else happens. That factor becomes a strength for the boys. Maybe it takes away some of the hurt. Whatever it is, it enables them to go back into the routine of life, to the normal day-to-day job, and *do* it, instead of feeling that they can't meet it, that too many other things are on their mind. Choate has always tried very hard for this."

More often, Peggy St. John is concerned with small matters, amenities to which she brings a grace and character which, in an institution as large as Choate, might easily be lost. She plans the Mothers' Day program, graduation, and the school dance, Festivities. The prize volumes given out each year are inscribed in her handwriting; it is she who arranges gifts for retiring employees and directs the distribution of 10,000 Christmas cards, of which she writes 2,000 herself. She writes notes to the mothers of girls invited to Festivities, assuring them that it is a proper invitation. She puts up visiting lecturers and boys who have been expelled but who have not yet left the campus. She takes charge of all decorations in the school, talks to boys who have been notified of a death in their families, decides what to do when divorced parents both insist on showing up for commencement. She moves in on faculty troubles, when she hears of a couple that is not getting along. In all these matters she is assisted by Marjorie Sa'adah, who serves as her aide-de-camp, and by Doris Fowler, a faculty widow, who sits at her typewriter clacking away as Peggy St. John sits in her study, by a flaking set of Tolstoy, counting off the things she has to do. "I came as a lazy Southerner," she says, remembering Tidewater, Virginia, "and I've been trained to work."

Of her husband she says: "He's an incurable optimist, thank God. How could we live if he weren't."

And she says: "For years we've been above criticism of any sort."

Anne Waters agrees with her husband that the faculty lacks wit. Not wit in the sense of intelligence or perspective, but the banter and joking that make prolonged association tolerable. "It is not the tone of the administration," she says, "nor of the senior faculty, so the general way one talks is not witty. I think a lot of the faculty is quite witty when it gets together, by itself, but it is not the style of the place."

Another wife goes further: "There isn't much intellectual stimulation within the faculty," she says. "The wives find that a large proportion of the faculty don't seem interested in discussing ideas. That's what a lot of people are in teaching *for,* that's what you come to a good school for. We want that intellectual exchange. When we came to this school the head of the English Department said that the masters would write papers on various topics, and they would be exchanged, and we would have discussions—English shoptalk—we would have an exchange of *ideas.* Not only has that not come about, there is just nothing. I've heard my husband try to talk to other English masters about anything from Pope to Hemingway and the answer is always a little smile. Maybe they don't care to talk at that moment. But the wives find it frustrating. They too want that kind of stimulation. They will find it in town, but they won't find it at Choate. The irony is that the townspeople think we are a hotbed of intellectual creativity."

But, says Anne Waters, the faculty rarely gets together. "It is just like living in a small town, perhaps isolated somewhere, where you pick your own friends. There doesn't seem to be any wives' get-together. I have my own personal friends, as I would anywhere. Some of the friends you pick you don't ever talk to about Shakespeare, but they're amusing for other reasons."

"The frustrations that mount up are not eased, and often not understood," says the other wife. "Part of the reason is that it *is* a boarding school. Everyone's here twenty-four hours a day; there isn't any professional and social division. One of the bywords of the wives is: Always do something in town to get away from Choate. In your first two or three years here you can become so involved in the school activities—there are many, and a lot of them are stimulating. Particularly new couples with no children, they take a lot of interest in the boys in the dormitory, which is natural and good, but if you stay within the school too much, I think, after a while the rut begins to tell on a person. It's not the school's fault. The person really has to make an effort to get out, into the community—the Y or a church or the League of Women Voters.

"Wallingford is good in that it's small enough for a wife to go into those organizations and be active. She isn't overwhelmed by a large urban organization in which she might be lost. Still, we aren't at Hotchkiss, which is out in the middle of nowhere, where there's no organization that you can join.

"Often what gets people down," she says, "is that you meet socially people who—if they are not now—may in another year or two be in a very subtle professional relationship with your husband. There cannot, therefore, be much freedom, even in social relationships. Unless you have one in town. My friends in town form not a large but an important part of my acquaintance. I feel that I can speak to those people much more freely. Wallingford *is* a dreary town, but you find many other people who find it dreary. They're awfully happy to find other people in the same boat."

A wife with young children wonders whether the faculty could not be stirred up more in the dining hall. "If getting kids to learn polite conversation were less stressed," she says, "perhaps the faculty would get to know each other more. It is tough to get to know the faculty when every man has his own table. I can't imagine any faculty member who would not like *not* to have his own table. Still, you get to know the boys—this is the whole purpose of the table."

But another has doubts: "There's a superficial sweetness among wives," she says, "that's awfully hard to cut through. There are certain people you go up to and know that they will always give you the professional, administration-supporting view of things. If they would just say *nothing*. It's hard to find the person underneath the image."

"The first two years we were here," says Polly Packard, "Jere and I felt the enormous lack of rapport between faculty members—partly because of the way the school is set up. Jere and I are used to calling people up at five and asking them for a drink. Now we've found out that it's practically obligatory to send out a written invitation." The Packards, who are just touching thirty, are listed in *The New York Social Register*. "If it weren't for the boys," Polly says, "I wouldn't be at Choate. For me, association with the Choate faculty would drive me up the wall. I'm antiestablishment. I won't give bridge parties. I won't give teas. I won't kowtow and attend. I run my own life—and this annoys the hell out of Jere—but I'm *me,* and I get along beautifully with the boys."

Polly's father thought she should have been a boy. He taught her boys' sports. Polly is short, but she can reach anything that comes over a tennis net, as I learned at some cost to my dignity. She had not touched a golf club for three years, but when she saw a boy practicing on her lawn, she took his club and chipped the ball 100 feet into a wastebasket. That fall, she played touch football and broke her finger—"It's going to cost me forty dollars to have my wedding and engagement rings enlarged to fit the enlarged knuckle that arthritis has given me at the age of thirty." She plays baseball, too. "The boys love it," she says. "They treat me so impersonally. I walk in anywhere and nobody gets up! They treat me as one of the guys. I'm flattered by this."

Grown-ups, however, are something else. "It's not a casual, informal, relaxed situation," Polly says. "Choate is just as full of gossip and bitchery as anywhere. There are many cats on campus, and many loud talkers like me. I had a knock-down, drag-out fight with a faculty member because he said I talked too much, was too critical." The faculty member was Polly's father-in-law, Hugh Packard, who teaches French, football, and wrestling. There had been an argument about why his son Jere had not been made head of the History Department. Finally, Hugh Packard turned to Polly and, as she tells it, said: "You want to know why? Because you're not an establishment wife. You do not give parties, you do not give teas, you do not give luncheons, *you do not play the game.*" Polly is, in fact, an excellent cook, but she saves her talent for her friends. "Still," she admits, "this guy's been here forty years. He knows Seymour. He knows the traditions."

A year and a half later, her husband was appointed head of the History Department. In the meantime, he took it all very casually. "If a visiting speaker comes to talk about history," he says, "Polly won't get dressed up, go to the speech, then to Gordon's or to the Lodge for a reception. She'd rather play Frisbee or shoot the crap with the boys."

"Your father feels I should give luncheons for all the important women on campus," Polly says. "Eugie Stillman, Marjorie Sa'adah, Peggy St. John."

"You should get credit for *asking* them," Jere Packard says, and then: "To my mind, this is phony horseshit."

"It's a boys' school!" Polly shouts. "It's not a social country club! I get along fine with the boys. And I *don't* feel inclined toward an artificial situation with the faculty."

"I'm sure Eugie Stillman resents what she has to do." Her husband sighs.

"We each do our thing," Polly says. "I think the boys appreciate that. I don't think any boy in this school wants every faculty wife to do everything for him. That's life, man! Let me tell you who the pro-establishment wives are," and she does.

"We can't invite them here anymore," Jere Packard says, "because if we do, we have to be so correct about everything we talk about."

"You can't talk frankly about the school to many wives," Polly says. "Jere and I feel the social conditions among the faculty are null and void, are so lacking in honest, informal, casual get-togethers. They're so cut and dried and lined out. One feels one must act ahead of time for everything."

How many faculty wives can you talk to easily? I ask.

"Our dogs get along better than we do," Polly says. "I'll tell you how many faculty wives I can talk to honestly: one. One. One!"

Why do you live here, then? I ask.

"One: we live in the country," Polly replies. "Two: we have better vacations. Three." She pauses for a long time. "Zero. No, not quite. One and two are quite poignant, when you think about it. That really is about as middle-class America as you can get. All right, now—three: I enjoy personally being around young people. Not my children, who drive me insane, but these boys. I enjoy them."

Would she be as happy at a girls' school?

"No," says her husband, "because Polly likes boys' sports."

"I like the kids," Polly says, ignoring him. "The kids are natural. They're to a large extent unsophisticated. They're completely natural in their reactions to most things. I feel very empathetic with their reactions, and the things they care about."

Can you control the extent of your involvement?

"No," she says, "no."

Does it overwhelm you?

"At times."

Pause. "Petty little things like our front lawn," her husband offers. "There are times when we'd like to sit out there and read without a Frisbee flying over our heads. The invasions of privacy are things that, yes, you can turn on and off, but at times it's difficult. For instance, I encourage boys to come in and watch television specials."

"We've said it's open house," Polly says, and the school says it is, too.

"Polly might have rather sat and watched this in her nightgown on the couch alone," her husband says, "but there were fourteen boys in here. She resents this."

"It doesn't bother me at all," Polly says. "Sometimes we ask them in to watch a show and there's some great inner joke going on, and they carry on in here, roughhousing over this private joke. I tell 'em to shut up or get out. But there are things that bother them, things that I can't handle because I can't respond, I can't understand them. The things that are really bugging them I have no answer for. My generation, my understanding, doesn't touch it. It's always about girls. They ask me things: 'Mrs. Packard, what would *you* do?' I tell them how I would react. There's a dead silence. I feel very inadequate. Like: 'I ask a girl to a dance and she says she has another date. Is this *real,* or is she putting me off?' I'm at a loss. They're very superficial questions, but they're very real questions that they're asking *me*. But I'm not in their generation and I can't interpret them."

"Naturally," says another wife, "the administration wants the education of the boys to be the best and they ask everybody to give, give, give all the time. They seem to think: 'Well, I know I'm going to get more than my money's worth out of you.' Well, naturally! I think if Seymour made the faculty feel that he cared about the twenty-five hours a day they devoted to the school, that he *knew* that faculty with little children needed more time with their families, and would *try* to do something—"

Her husband checks this flow: "You're implying he doesn't make the effort."

"I don't think he does," she says. "I think he's not aware of it."

David and Dino Rice are in their middle thirties. As we talk, a boy in the next room is working determinedly at the violin: Bach's First Violin Concerto. ("There," says Dino, "you would not hear that in any other house.") St. John knows that some day a school is going to ask David Rice to take over as headmaster and on that day Choate will lose the Rices. The boys think Rice wants to be headmaster of Choate. They recognize that he is firm but fair and think of him, in the school's spectrum, as a liberal. He defends the system, but he goes out of his way to support boys in trouble, or boys with unpopular causes. The boys know his opinion carries weight.

More than most faculty couples, the Rices work to expand the school's offerings: the boy on the violin is evidence of their most ambitious undertaking, the Telemann Society. "It was underground," Dino says, "but now it's official. It was underground because—" Well, because the school's music director is a fan of John Philip Sousa. "Nobody knows how sad the musical education of these guys who come for lessons is," Dino says. "They learn the technique of the instrument, and most of their education for the next three or four years is for what is necessary for the band or the orchestra." The school's orchestra, which plays at dinner on Saturday nights, favors popular music of the 1940's. "They are not being taught the literature of the instrument!" Dino says, upset even by the thought of oboes burping Cole Porter when the boys blowing them have never heard Bellini's oboe concerto. "No one suggested that something was lacking. In the English Department they do not read Agatha Christie and funny books all day long! But these boys don't hear great music. They don't study it. They don't know what they're missing."

They do now. For six months the Rices met with a few boys, some people from town, and one or two members of the New Haven Symphony Orchestra, on Friday evenings, the day the music director was away from school. Finally they brought it out in the open: St. John provided money for sheet music from his discretionary fund and the director was invited to come and conduct. He refused. A school club with *girls?* "He thought we were trying to undermine his authority," Dino says. "And horn in and steal his musicians," her husband adds. Pretty soon the Telemann Society gave a full-length concert with printed programs. Toward the end of the year, Rice began to work on an FM radio station for the boys.

The Rices did this on their own, with no encouragement until it was done. Dino believes such things could happen more often if, as she says, St. John tried to make wives more of a part of the school. "We're *very* good at baking cakes," she says sarcastically, "and providing birthday parties and sewing on buttons. We're very *needed*. Seymour has *said* he wished he could use us more effectively. That's what he said! *Use* us more effectively! Not a question of how he could help us develop more as people."

Anne Waters agrees: "A master's wife said to me the other day, 'Anything they get from me is completely extra because we're not paid a double salary.' The older wives, I assume, would be horrified at that statement—what it revealed. The woman who said it is not a selfish person; she does a lot for her house. But her attitude is different; for quite different reasons, she doesn't think she owes such service at all. She does it because she wants to."

Anne, too, does more than she need, because she enjoys making costumes for the plays or taking care of the chapel, but she has three very small children, and feels sometimes that her private life has slipped from her control. "It's partly due to St. John's feeling that the faculty are the servants," she says. "The boys sense this. They don't realize how little money we have. They will use you, a great deal if you let them, as a refrigerator, as a convenience. They're taught at Choate that a master is available to help them any time they need help academically, which I feel is all wrong. I'm sure boys are not attentive in class because they feel they can get it individually later on. The boys should learn that you don't take something for nothing in any field—in instant coffee, in studies, in affection."

The Waters live in one of the newer, smaller houses; even so, Anne must give seven birthday parties a year, and a Christmas party, and must pay for everything but the ice cream herself. "In one house," she says, "the faculty wife makes the kids contribute dimes to a jar for the coffee they drink. Not because she couldn't afford the coffee, but because she thought it was wrong for anyone to take, take, take."

Another wife believes that the demands made on wives become self-enforcing because the wives worry about their husbands' careers: "A lot of wives," she says, "pay attention to the formalities simply because they are afraid their husbands will be spoken to by the headmaster, who may say, 'Look, you don't have the boys in enough.' " Whether or not the headmaster actually would say such a crude thing to a master or his wife, some wives *believe* that he would and so redouble their efforts. "A lot depends on the boys in the house," she says. "Sometimes we'll have a group with whom we have a very easy relationship, another time they will be perfectly friendly but would rather stay by themselves. Their idea of a nice evening may *not* be to have you cook them a spaghetti dinner, but to go out by themselves."

"Seymour goes wrong here," Anne Waters says. "The boys you will get to know on the whole are the boys who are old enough to reach out for themselves. These boys don't need you —because they're interested in other people." But everyone gives parties, anyway.

"For us," says one wife, "in our first years here, it was not a burden. To the contrary, it was very pleasing. But after a while, when our own children came, and the students were there too, a wife may feel there is a hole she cannot fill. You'd like to give time to each, but you cannot. And pretty soon a wife feels guilt about what she is not giving here—or there."

"You are made here to feel *extreme* guilt," her husband says. "Unless you have an extremely resilient personality, your esprit de corps sinks because of the criticism that's heaped on. It always comes."

"It may be because the headmaster is so busy he cannot take the time to investigate fully," his wife says. "But he puts you in a position of defending yourself, which no true adult likes to do. If you do, you *sound* so defensive. If you say, 'Yessir, we *have* had the boys in,' it sounds like you're plugging the dike after the flood. The long hours a housemaster may spend with a boy in his dormitory, a boy who has problems, it's not an easy job to do always. It takes a tremendous amount of time. You don't want recognition, but then, the good job you've done appears, at least, to have gone unnoticed. Time after time after time."

"The problem around here," says one wife, "is that everybody is so busy. You hear when something's wrong. You hear when something dreadful happens, but no one ever takes the time to say, 'Thank you for doing a good job in your classes,' or, 'Thank you for being at your table—I appreciate the effort that you make.' "

Even the letters the masters receive at the end of the year, asking them to return and mentioning raises, if any, are said to contain paragraphs of criticism. A faculty wife mimicked one: "Although we are happy to have your devoted services, we also wish you could do this or that."

"And," said another, "the raises aren't very earthshaking. They barely cover the increase in size in your children's shoes. I think kind words go a long way. I'll bet you wouldn't have anywhere near so many gripes if more kind words were wasted around here."

The View from the Edges

Choate students aren't all that bright.

A FORMER TEACHER AT CHOATE

The alumni have helped kill off humanistic education in America by not insisting that it be kept alive. . . . The administrators bear special guilt—not for their apparently inescapable preoccupation with fund-raising and coordinating, but for their lack of intellectual acumen and moral passion in diagnosing the ills of their own institutions.

JAMES A. BILLINGTON,
"The Humanistic Heartbeat Has Failed"

1. *How to Get into Choate*

Once Charles Pierce rose to make a joke. "A clever admissions man," he said, "is careful what he admits and where he admits it." Quite funny, quite true. Pierce, like all the administration men who must constantly repeat the same speech to groups of alumni around the country, is an able speaker. He says "less" when he means "fewer," which is a liability for a man who deals in statistics, but Pierce is nonetheless liberal with those statistics. They vary somewhat each time he offers them, but they go like this:

For the 1967–68 year, Choate received about 2,000 inquiries from parents who wanted their sons considered for the 175 places Choate would have open for new boys. "Applications are down," Pierce says, "in some schools rather noticeably." Choate had, in fact, received 40 or 50 fewer applications this year than last; still, some schools were off by as much as 20 percent, and taking the long view, Choate's applications since 1959 had risen by 24 percent. One of the problems is that many independent day schools are extending their curriculum through the twelfth grade; another is rising costs. In spite of $165,000 Choate raised for scholarships that year, many families, particularly those with incomes of between $12,000 and $25,000—the heart of the upper middle class to which Choate has always appealed—were thinking carefully before committing themselves to Choate's $3,300 tuition, plus about $1,000 for clothes and travel. Another problem Choate faces is that, beginning in 1960, there was a decrease in the male birthrate. "That," says Pierce, "may hit us about 1973."

Nine hundred and fifty candidates and their families were interviewed at Choate, resulting in 755 final applications. For the preliminary application, parents simply send $10 with a form inquiring about church affiliation, bank, and personal references, but the final application is more complex. It requires a passport photograph (eliminating the need to ask about race) and asks for a report from the boy's previous school with statements about the candidate's integrity; conduct; manners; neatness; initiative and drive; concern for others; emotional stability; physical vigor; interest and proficiency in sports; willingness to work at tasks he dislikes; extent of need for supervision and prodding; persistence in the face of discouragement; and so on. To each person the parent suggests as a reference, the school sends another form, again asking about neatness, respect for authority, and manners and ending with a request for a rating on "the following continuous scale."

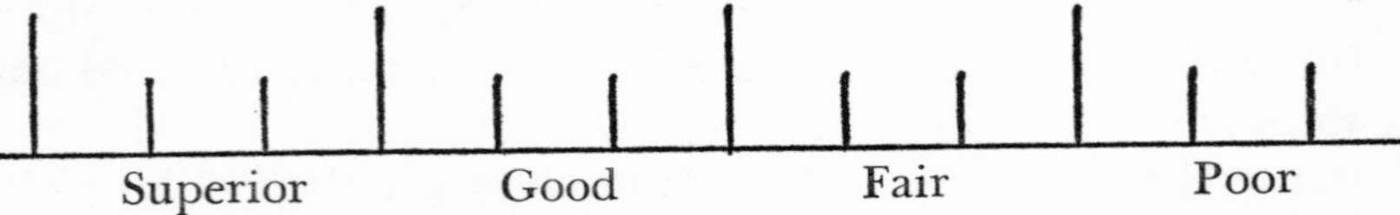

Meanwhile, the boy is interviewed at school. Pierce, or whoever talks to the boy, fills in yet another form with such questions as "Clue to life work?" and "Physical appearance?"

Beginning February 15, letters of acceptance were mailed to about 300 boys. About 62 percent accepted Choate: as the year began, there were, out of 578 boys enrolled in the school, 189 new boarding students and 10 new day students, but 1 old boy and 2 new boys withdrew before term began, leaving the school with 575. During any year, the school expects to lose about 25 boys. Almost all the new boys enter in either the third or the fourth form, and of those that did that year, 37 were sons of alumni. Only 4 sons of alumni were refused admission to Choate. "We feel very strongly toward applications of sons of alumni," Pierce tells the alumni. "We place fewer roadblocks in their way than for the unaffiliated. We feel we have been able to keep a happy situation here." One hundred and thirteen boys, or approximately 20 percent of Choate's students, are sons of alumni. Yale twits Choate about this, but Choate has countered by saying that Yale's sons-of-alumni percentage is the same.*

Of the new boys who entered in the fall of 1967, 59 percent came from independent schools, 41 percent from public schools. The next year, the percentage had changed: 55 percent from independent schools, 45 percent from public schools. Of third formers entering the school, 56 had fathers in business—the usual kind of business: heavy on investments, textiles, and shipping, but one father described himself as a "horse breeder" and another as in "Christmas Creations." Eighteen had doctors as fathers; 2 had fathers in the military; 2 in law; 2 in teaching and education; 1 each in architecture, diplomacy, and "retired." The occupation of 11 fathers was listed as "unknown." All told, the boys at Choate came from 37 states, the District of Columbia, Puerto Rico, and 16 foreign countries.

Asked whether Choate is looking for the best possible student or the student who best fits what Choate is equipped to do, Pierce replies: "I think we want a combination of both, don't we? I would think perhaps this is the ideal. Naturally, we want the best talent we can find. The competition for that talent is mighty keen. We have boys with academic problems, but we have certain obligations, like obligations to alumni." Pierce admits that the admission of alumni sons inevitably leads to "a

* Twenty percent of Yale's class of 1968 were alumni sons. Other figures: Harvard: 19 percent; Princeton: 19 percent; Dartmouth: 21 percent. Choate's policy in this regard, so often criticized, is clearly not out of line.

compromise with quality. We certainly have to work a little harder with these youngsters," he says, "but the faculty is willing to do it. We are much tougher on this than we were some years ago. We don't take a boy into the school that we feel is going to fall on his face. We don't." Pierce tells alumni that the qualities they look for in boys are: "ability, willingness to use it (motivation), curiosity, involvement—sports and other things—and every year we take into the school boys we think we can help."

This business of taking boys that the school can help poses a difficult problem. If Choate, more than any other school of its kind, is able to provide individual care, amounting almost to an affectionate concern for each boy, does it not then attract just those boys who must have such care, while more able, more independent boys go to larger, tougher schools like Exeter and Andover? "Conceivably," says St. John, but other masters insist it is true. "I don't think we want the really smart boys," Richard Hunter says. "What we have to do is build ruddy good citizens. I know we are going to have many boys who will get Phi Beta Kappas and will be research scientists, who will live in their little ivory towers. But the really important boys will be those who go to work for the Red Cross, the YMCA, leading this drive and that drive. I think if we can build a boy here who is very much aware of the other boys, the other *citizens,* who has a good sense of values, then I think we'll accomplish our purpose. I know a lot of boys here who have no values whatever. They're bright, and they're very often rich. But I don't think they're going to learn."

"By the nature of our setup," says Mounir Sa'adah, "we are bound to develop certain leaders. In my history class the other day, I went around the class to find out their backgrounds. I said, 'Let's see if you're class-conscious.' I discovered that the whole class was an affluent group. They were at least third-generation Americans. For at least two generations their families had been active in something significant in the life of the country. So naturally, I expect that these boys will drift into positions of responsibility, of leadership.

"Unfortunately," Sa'adah went on, "they are not aware of the existence of any other than their own class. They have had no contact with any other than their own class. They belong to the same clubs, they have gone to the same private schools. They are not aware of riots. They are not concerned. This is one of the things that worries me."

Jon van Leuven objects that the boys, backed up by the school, have "no sense of what the nonphysical is. No sensitivity to a world that is not dominated by externals. This is not an internalized world at all; it's an external world, full of noise and athletics. To get somebody who could sit in his room—this would be a tremendous test—to get somebody who could grapple with solitude. . . . I don't think they can. These kids, the kind of world they grew up in, which has given them objects to deal with—a preoccupation with *existentia,* or something—prevents them from concentrating on the *essentia.*

"You could never see a kid exhibiting enthusiasm over what another kid is doing with his life around here. At most there's a recognition of the humor of some common experience. It's a passive world in which things have come to them for so long that they feel programmed to it, they accept it. They don't know anything else—and yet they rebel against it. The teachers themselves are the same. They don't have a general educational philosophy, and if they did, I don't think it would deviate significantly from the general ideas of society as a whole. They're not spiritual people—this is definitely true. They're not poetic people. They're not profound people. The very fact that they have to coach athletics prevents them from being so."

The boys are equally convinced that Choate does not necessarily attract students of great ability. "They accept students that fit in with their approach," one third former said. "If they didn't, the whole school would be rebellious. You can't have a whole school full of boys who rise up saying, 'We shall overcome.' They accept boys who they think won't do this. And when they get guys like me who *will* do it, they hang their heads and say, 'Well, we blew it.' "

"Choate is overstuffed with 'go-alongers,' " said a fifth former.

"They make life dull and boring. I think the student best suited for Choate is the person who is on the near-verge of expulsion. Unfortunately, some 'go-along' administration officials keep many 'go-alone' students from entering the school. All I can say is that I wish I could tell them what they are doing wrong. Choate is doomed!" And a sixth former said, "I don't think I've ever met anybody at Choate who was really interesting. You know, we've had a few foreign exchange students, but even those—most of them are from England. Even those don't turn out so well."

In the spring, three third formers discussed what Choate was looking for, with particular reference to their own acceptances. "I get the impression that Choate's first thought in accepting a boy is not what he will later be," said the most articulate of the three, "but how he will affect the school. How he will *adapt* to the school. They see a boy who will not cause trouble, who is a pretty good student and who conforms easily, and they choose him over the boy who has the potential to be a great leader over tomorrow."

"I guess they pick the rich kids and the alumni kids," said another.

"I don't think they pick rich kids," said the first.

"Well," said the other, "then they try a few famous names, just to get them. They are concerned to get famous kids. They're so concerned about their image. I think that's what's holding back everything else: changing rules would damage their reputation of being an old-line private school."

"I also thought of going to Putney," said the third, "but my parents talked me out of that. They were kind of shocked, being older, to see all the kids with the long hair, looking like pictures of the Beatles—all of them. They heard that a lot of those kids are kind of alienated from society when they get out; it takes a couple of years for society to get them back."

"The other extreme from Choate," said the first.

"My parents thought if a lot of those kids were sick, alienated, I might not feel a part of it," said the third. "I'm not sure."

"This is more or less the best school," said the second. "Going from here back to high school would be ridiculous. It's that bad. My high school is considered good, but this is on a much higher level."

"I think the morals are important," said the first boy. "If you go to a public high school and you fall under the wrong influence and you don't have a strong character, you can be swayed. Which is true of so many people here! I think the reason parents send their children away is because so many people in the third form are so wishy-washy. If they stay in public high school, they could get swayed to the wrong side because their characters aren't strong enough. They might go on pot, or something like that. But if you're sent to a school with high morals, high spiritual values, no girls, little chance for corruption by drugs—of course parents will send them there. Choate does have high spiritual values. And parents are always fearing and dreading."

"We look for a sound balance of qualities," St. John wrote in a report in 1966, "not necessarily a balance in each boy, but a balance in the student body. . . . We work hard to bring to Choate boys of special ability and interests in some particular field. . . . We seek a wide geographical spread: boys can learn from each other and are good catalysts to the deprovincializing process which is one of our chief goals. We look for character: sound, balanced boys of integrity who have already heard something about contributing—in their families, on a newspaper route. . . ."

"I've really not thought much about it," says Charles Pierce when asked if social background has any effect on the admission of boys to Choate. "It's certainly not a conscious attempt on our part."

"It's terribly obvious," says Malcolm Manson. "I've felt the best thing to do is to ignore it. Which is what Eton does. I think it influences those boys who apply. I don't think it influences those you take in in the least—of the ones who apply. Sure, a great many parents bring their kids up here because they want social status. But even so, we're choosing between boys, not parents. I hope. But that would be impossible to determine. We have lots of great boys here and we just shake our heads over the parents. How can this fabulous child come from these awful parents? It's true that our parent body is a very, very rich group. Just unbelievable. And so are our alumni."

2. *The Money Problem*

Getting money from Choate's family into the school is an intriguing problem that occupies many in the administration. Choate is, as preparatory schools go, in excellent financial shape. The market value of its endowment is $14,080,650, which is a lot better than Taft's ($3,107,377 at that time), but nothing like as grand as Exeter's ($59,000,000), Andover's $50,-789,033), or St. Paul's ($36,251,504). Paul Mellon, '25, whose stated net worth, according to a survey *Fortune* made in 1957, is between $400,000,000 and $700,000,000, acts as angel to the school, as did his father, Andrew, before him. According to Stanley Trotman, vice-president of the board of trustees, the Mellons have given $7,000,000 to Choate.

When Choate's finances were tallied at the end of the 1967–68 fiscal year, there was a surplus of $6,714. Total income for board and tuition was $1,940,572, but after this was adjusted for scholarship grants and miscellaneous rental incomes, the figure was reduced to $1,857,422. Total expenses in the school amounted to $2,429,004—or a loss of $571,582. Income from investments and gifts for current use keep Choate barely in the black. Choate, in fact, gets only 4.24 percent on its investments. "I've talked with our board about this," St. John says. "We've had a rather conservative finance committee. I think they've done very well on capital gains, but some of the securities are, of course, in growth stocks"—which means little income. Choate's endowment grows, but there is not enough income from it to be of real help.

One of the problems Choate faces is that costs rise on an average of 5 percent a year, but tuition does not. Howard Jones, president of the Northfield Schools, was the first to propose that tuition at schools like his and Choate go up automatically 5 percent each year. In terms of purchasing power, tuition at Choate has gone down. "I always like to liken it to the loaves of bread," St. John says. "The loaves of bread you can buy today for $3,300 are many fewer than the loaves you could once buy for $1,700, which is what the tuition was when I came here."

Beyond its day-to-day expenses, Choate seeks increasing capital to meet three fundamental priorities: funds for endowed scholarships; funds for faculty salaries; funds for building. Scholarship money, which stood that year at $165,000, should, according to William St. John, be increased immediately to $225,000. Faculty salaries, according to Malcolm Manson, should be increased 10 percent immediately, and then 5 percent a year. Choate's salaries are, by most preparatory school standards, low. Groton's salaries were, that fall, 50 percent higher, Exeter's 25 percent higher, Kent, Lawrenceville, and other schools about 5 percent higher. St. John hopes to increase the number of endowed faculty chairs ($250,000 apiece, providing an income of not less than $10,000), and the faculty benefit program, which also lagged sharply behind that of many other schools.

The man whose principal responsibility it is to see that large amounts of money come into Choate is the man least understood by the faculty as a whole. His name is John Lupton. In 1964, Lupton was Barry Goldwater's campaign director in Connecticut; he is now the Republican state senator from the 26th District—Westport, Wilton, Weston, New Canaan, and Darien—a district which, if carved to suit his Stone Age philosophy of government, could not have been improved. Lupton can hold his job at Choate because the Connecticut state legislature meets only in alternate years. Even with so much free time, Lupton spends little time working for his constituents: he attended only 8 of 57 meetings of the committees to which he was assigned. Lupton has introduced two bills to fingerprint teachers in Connecticut—his colleagues on the faculty at Choate find this incredible—and is on record as saying that "Pollution is not a critical problem" and, "Public education is a privilege, not a prerequisite," which runs counter to one of the principal imperatives of any civilized society: that it educate its young.

It doesn't really matter: Lupton isn't working for public education at Choate. At Choate he can relax, as he does, and with a drink in his hand he will announce that he knows how to end the Vietnam War: "You tell Hanoi you'll drop an atom bomb in the demilitarized zone if they don't pull back. That'll stop 'em." What if it doesn't? "Then you drop it." Lupton, in 1968, was indignant that voters did not understand the essential *rightness* of Curtis LeMay's position on the war—"Only *intellectuals* are afraid of H-bombs," Lupton says. Lupton hates intellectuals; he hates "Hah-vuhd," as he calls it, and the New York *Times*—"the most slanted newspaper in the country"—and some of Choate's faculty are wondering just why this schoolman seems to hate ideas and the men who hold them. To be fair to Lupton, he stands for two good things: annual meetings of the legislature and the abolition of capital punishment (determinedly maintained by Connecticut), but it is not enough. One woman active in Democratic politics says: "The only way we'll get rid of Lupton is to wait for him to succumb to an attack of hubris—to run for national office." A year later, Lupton announced his candidacy for Thomas Dodd's seat in the Senate.

Few people know what Lupton does for Choate, but there is a general agreement that he must pull down a fancy salary. "I'm a salesman," Lupton will say when in his bully mood. "We have the best product in its field. It's always fun to sell the top of the line. The Choate family is a wonderful family. Well knit, loyal, and happy within itself." Lupton has met 500 of Choate's 5,000 to 6,000 alumni: he concentrates on those able to provide big gifts. He is also responsible for keeping track of what federal, state, and local governments have in mind for education and for evaluating the effect of government action on the future of independent schools like Choate.

"Over the years," says St. John, "independent education has been a bit naïve about its place in our society. We need to work with government, with the state, with communities and public education. We have always had government support in the sense of tax exemption to nonprofit foundations. We need more. All of us dislike giving up bits of our sovereignty, but when we live in a community, we find it our responsibility to do so."

Lupton also works for Choate at the Connecticut Foundation for Independent Schools, trying to solicit financial help from business corporations which can't give to individual schools. About 400 corporations, Lupton points out, will match employees' gifts to colleges, but only 170 of those include secondary schools: Lupton tries to persuade the corporations to be more open-minded. Finally, Lupton travels around the country trying to dig up grants, scholarships, endowments—any large sum for Choate. Here he encounters problems. "Regionalism," Lupton says, "is growing in our country. The 'hate the East' attitudes are no joke. Many alumni who have been out of school for twenty-five years haven't been east of the Mississippi since. Their wives have never heard of Choate, can't understand it. Their children have never considered coming east to school.

"I'm very much concerned with Choate's character," he says, "because my biggest job is to sell it. In order to sell it, you've first got to understand, and second, you've got to appreciate it. I think it's the easiest thing to sell that I've ever encountered." Lupton was originally a public relations man. "It's a good product. Wonderful product. I consider Choate to be the finest secondary school in the country, probably in the world. I think it's achieved great academic excellence. It has a method, a plan of operation that is very excellent and desirable. Its ability to personalize its ministrations to the boys is unusually ideal, I think . . . the dedication of its men . . . its leadership . . . the retention of the high-priority emphasis on character, leadership training instead of fact-filling"—which, presumably, produces intellectuals—"is most impressive. It's progressive in outlook and wise in its retention of methods and values which don't get out of date." Apparently, there are people around the country —in Choate clubs in Dallas and in Phoenix—who speak this kind of language. Lupton is tremendously successful at bringing in the money.

And, of course, it is fun. There is the Invisible Government aspect to it, the Choate Cabala, the password that opens, as Lupton says, the door of anyone of any importance in the country. St. John endorses the sentiment: "I do think it's magnificent," he says. "It isn't just in the United States; it's throughout the world. When I went around the world, I couldn't go to a spot where there weren't people who could open doors in any given society. The openings were there, and you could talk to anyone you wanted to. Of course, you hope that you don't ever impose, that you can give as much as you can get, but the openings are there."

3. *Can a Choate Boy Get into Yale?*

Getting boys into college, St. John insists, is not the main purpose of a school like Choate. Few parents believe it. That spring, a Very Important Executive, appalled by proof that his son, a fifth former, was a mediocre student, wrote to Choate's man in charge of college admissions:

> Dear Mr. Sweeney:
>
> William says he wants to go to Amherst. I would like him to go to Amherst in preference to Yale, Harvard, or Princeton; these three being all too close to major cities. I would much rather have the boy skiing in the hills of Massachusetts over the weekends during the winter months than to be "skiing" in the night clubs of Boston or New York where I know so many boys from Yale and Harvard spend their weekends.
>
> As I said to young William in my letter, he has a priceless character ingredient; namely, a beguiling personality and he can sell. If he could put that together with a drive for hard work, he could go far in business.
>
> I am grateful, indeed, to all the Masters at Choate for the great help they have given our boy. I'm delighted that he is going to Labrador this summer. It will give him an opportunity to see how the poverty bracket live.

At the same time, this executive wrote to his son:

> Dear Son:
>
> Attached herewith is a Xerox of a letter sent to me from William A. Sweeney, Director of Studies. You will note that your aptitude tests were verbal—524 and mathematical—641.
>
> You will note that on Page Two the median score for 1967 for boys entering Yale was verbal—697; mathematical—716 and that less than 1% of the freshman class in any of these colleges score below 500 in verbal aptitude. So you see, as far as colleges like Yale, the big three, etc. (I imagine Amherst comes within that category) on the verbal side, you are pretty close to elimination and I would assume that on the mathematical side you would be eliminated. Accordingly, you've got a good job to do in order to get yourself in good shape to get into Amherst where I would like to see you go and I think you want to go.
>
> You have a quality that is as important as the educational quality (meaning marks) and that is personality, ability to sell, etc. If you can get your verbal and mathematical grades up to around 700 and continued at that rate through hard work, nothing could stop you.

The father, apparently, had not caught on that the low grades for which he was upbraiding his son were aptitude grades, not achievement grades.

> You'd make a ton of money in the investment banking business [the father continued] but you are not going to be able to do it by merely being able to sell. It requires application and hard work; mostly concentration. You can teach yourself to do it by driving yourself. It will pay big dividends to you in future years. . . . A senior partner's job should be worth from $50,000 to $1,000,000 a year for each partner. Isn't that an objective to shoot at? You can have so darn much fun later in life if you attain that position.

Darn right.

"The college admissions picture," says William Sweeney, director of studies, "is not as rosy as it was ten years ago."

The competition for what the boys' parents believe to be the only good colleges is frenetic; in 1952 the median verbal score on the Scholastic Aptitude Tests for boys entering Yale was not 697, as it is today, but 579. Not only that, but nearly a quarter of Yale's class of 1970 had been class presidents and student council heads in their secondary schools; two-fifths had won varsity letters, a tenth had been captains of varsity teams, and nearly a third had been editors-in-chief of student publications in their schools. "Yale wants brains *and* evidence of other interests and achievements," a Yale alumni organization says, but it sounds as if only grim-jawed members of a master race will pass under the gate on which is carved: HE WAS BORN WITH A GIFT OF LAUGHTER AND A SENSE THAT THE WORLD WAS MAD.

Actually colleges want even more, as Sweeney explains to parents. Colleges look for strength of character, intellectual curiosity, dedication to something, demonstrated ability in a field, leadership potential, and concern for public good. Astonishingly, "they also seem to say: 'We are interested in people who demonstrate humility.' Many colleges today," Sweeney says with a small sigh, "offer educations as good as what only the most eminent offered ten years ago, but we find it hard to convince parents of that."

Virtually every Choate student goes to college. Choate is fiercely proud of its record in college placement, and rightly so: that year, 152 of 154 seniors went to 53 colleges. Sixty-nine students cared enough about Harvard to request interviews when the Havard recruiters came to school; 61 filed applications; 28 were accepted by Harvard—the greatest number ever—and 25 actually went there. Choate rejoiced; no other college came close to doing as well for Choate. At Princeton, 17 out of 30 were accepted; 13 went there in the fall. But Yale—well, Yale. Only 28 boys applied. Yale, with a fine flourish, rejected the senior with the highest academic record in his class, and accepted only 5 boys. Only 3 of those went to Yale that fall. "Up to two years ago," Bill Sweeney says, "if a boy was in the middle of his class and the son of a Yale alumnus,

Yale would take him." No longer. Yale, Sweeney thinks, is a little tired of bankers from the New York City area and is determined to reduce the percentage of preparatory school students it takes. Williams, too, has dropped its percentage of preparatory school students from 55 percent to 35 percent in recent years.

The Yale-Choate tension was acute that year. As long as it could, the administration insisted that *nothing* was amiss in its relation to Yale—if you read the figures correctly, you could see that—but then a Choate senior interviewed R. Inslee Clark, Yale's youthful director of admissions, and printed a mild article on the subject in the *Choate News*. St. John and the faculty roared with anger. Certainly, there was nothing in the article to provoke such outrage. What had happened was that Clark had questioned one of the sacred assumptions of the school; he had suggested that perhaps, just by being what it is, Choate *hinders* boys' getting into colleges. No one at Choate will even entertain such a thought. If it were to become commonly believed, Choate would wither and collapse because rich fathers, with Yale on their minds, would avoid Choate. The school's anger at Inslee Clark and the unfortunate senior who was such an enterprising journalist can be explained only if one understands that no one must even think such things as the boy reported, much less *say* them. Some masters grumbled that the boy had lent himself to a Communist plot (discredit the rich, the private schools, etc.), but by late spring, St. John and Stillman could explain that, with Harvard being so cooperative, it was clear that "*Yale,* not Choate, is out of step."

Indeed, something was going on. Only 38 percent of Yale's class of 1971, its freshman class, came from private schools; in 1952 the figure was 63 percent. Many people at Yale, let alone Choate, were worried about their new dean of admissions—"I'm a public school graduate," says Clark—and in 1967 a Yale alumni group reported: "The manner in which a few private schools were dealt with showed lack of tact."

Clark has strong opinions about Choate. "Is Choate doing its job?" he asked me. "This is a roundabout way of asking: What are they doing with the boys they take? What boys do they take?" Yale is proud of its new program of "beating the bushes" for talented kids. Financial aid has made it possible for them to "take anybody, regardless of need." Prep schools that want to get their boys into Yale, says Clark, should be tempted to get out and scratch for the best talents themselves. "A school like Choate, if it wants to be a truly national school, and wants to admit, say, one hundred new boys, might consider having two or three full-time men in the admissions department out beating the bushes throughout the fall term. Six to eight weeks' travel per man. The school has to decide what it wants to be. For example, is it going to be a school for the most talented boys in this country, in other words, a great national high school? That's one approach. The other approach is to say: 'We have a special kind of function as a boarding school—individual attention, special help, taking many of the sons of our alumni and helping them develop so they'll be better, stronger students than they would have been if they'd gone through public school. All of which may be justified. But this may not lead to great numbers getting into Yale.

"In the long run, what's going to pay off in college admissions is the capacity and the motivation and the performance and the talent of the individual—not just the training. I don't see any way, frankly, for Choate to get great numbers into Yale, if that's an objective, unless they go out and find the most talented boys in the country. Just training those that they've got will not do it."

Schools like Choate, Clark says, should be brave enough to experiment, to become lighthouses for other schools, for public schools. At the moment, Clark sees more experimentation in the really good public high schools—in Evanston and Montclair—where modular scheduling of classes has been tried. But, Clark admits, bringing a real diversity of boys into your school community can cause problems. "To what extent is Choate willing to let these people be free? And themselves? Supposing you go down to Philadelphia and pull into Choate the most brilliant potential biochemist. Granted he's only fourteen or fifteen, but he's got all the markings. Now this is the kind of boy who, in a public school system, literally locks himself in the labs after school, whether it's in the school or in his lab set at home. He works straight through the clock. He may be up till two at night on some project. Now to what extent is the prep school willing to tolerate, and indeed encourage, such individuality? And if it's not, then maybe it is better not to attract these kids to begin with. For a kid like that exceptions must be made, and then you have to multiply those exceptions by dozens and dozens of people you want to attract—and suddenly, you have a very flexible, freewheeling kind of place. It would be exciting, wouldn't it?"

Clark is not impressed by the academic record of Choate boys taken by Yale several years ago before Yale became more choosy. Nor was their discipline or "contribution" particularly "sparkling. Yale got what it bought. And Yale was not being as selective as today. The records on Choate boys now at Yale is a much healthier picture."

Sweeney begins talking to Choate boys about colleges in the fall of their junior year and hopes that by the summer they will be thinking in terms of twelve colleges. Then, he says, "you have to start all over again in September because after a summer at home their ideas have been inflated by their parents." When, each fall, the colleges send recruiters to look over Choate's livestock, Sweeney is armed with each boy's exact rank in class and his list of college preferences.

Some colleges play footsie with Sweeney: "He looks pretty good to us, possibly an A. Are we his first choice?" "No," says Sweeney, who feels obliged to tell. "Then we can only give him a B-plus." An A ranking, given to a boy in the fall of his senior year, guarantees admission to the college that gives it. Yale has abandoned the system, believing that it tends to promote the allotment of quotas to the schools. Harvard and other colleges vigorously deny that there is a quota system, but Sweeney knows there is, and needles them a bit. "They never give more than two more A's than they gave the year before," Sweeney says.

As the candidates are discussed, Sweeney can hear the recruiters whisper: "How many A's is *that?*"

"You gave four," one recruiter will say, "and he gave five."

"That leaves eight for the two of you," another says.

"Obviously," says Sweeney, "you have a quota."

"No, no, no," says Harvard.

Harvard, four men strong, arrived early in November. From Tuesday evening until Wednesday afternoon you could see nervous-looking boys perched on uncomfortable chairs in the basement of St. John Hall, waiting their turns to be interviewed, while hearing every word of the interview that goes before. This is Sweeney's hardest hour. He is forty-seven, a tall man with a pink face; meticulously courteous, he gives the impression of one who has for years deliberately kept himself under close control. Sweeney talks very coolly and in precise, measured words, with a flick of humor evident from time to time. He is very much aware that he holds tremendous power over the aspirations of both boys and parents; that he is playing a very delicate and formal game with recruiters from every college; that his chances of success are nil if he is not ruthlessly honest (which is often interpreted as "betraying the boys") ; and that, like the football coach, he must know all the players in the game if he is to come out a winner, all the movements they have ever made. He must be able to judge stress and character, bluffs and weaknesses.

The recruiters talk like horse traders; the horseflesh, at that moment, is not there to be pinched, so it must be described. "A fine, likable fellow," one says of the son of a Harvard alumnus. Of another, one says: "He seemed very nervous, uncertain, and to me appeared to be something of a black sheep. In talking about student marches, civil rights, he seemed intolerant of deviation." Sweeney groans inwardly at this kind of comment: it means the boy has tried to outsmart Harvard, and the boys are not going to do it. This kid figured that Harvard had had enough student trouble—hadn't every college? —so he put on a pious, conservative mask. Sweeney does not prepare the boys for their interviews; he does not think they *can* be prepared. Interviews can run for 40 minutes; the boys are often nervous; the interviewers are as highly trained as any CIA interrogation team and can do *anything* they want with an interview—let the boy run it or run it tightly themselves. The interviewers know exactly what they are getting from Choate: "The best boys are good cum laude boys," Harvard says, "the summas will come from places like Roxbury Latin." Still, some wise-guy Choate kids always think they can flummox Harvard.

As always, Harvard moves to adjourn leaving some boys' status open for later deliberation. Sweeney moves now. He once spent 45 minutes trying to get Harvard to raise a B-plus rating to an A and failed, and this evening, exercising the honesty he must to keep the trust of the colleges, he argues that a boy Harvard called "a great kid, warm, friendly; a strong candidate" merits no more than a strong B. "Another operator," Sweeney says. Then he insists that the deferred cases be decided *now.* "You never come back with an A," Sweeney tells them. "If you haven't got the conviction to give them an A now, you can't defend them before the committee. They will come back B's." Harvard sits down, takes out its papers, and resumes. When Harvard leaves, it leaves behind 16 A ratings and 4 "provisional" A ratings of which, says Sweeney, "only one will stick."

4. *The Product: Ever True to Gold and Blue*

"One of the most important things Choate does," says St. John, "is to produce a product that has an impact on the country." In a more reflective mood, he says, "I don't think it's easy to judge the ways that people contribute to our society." The contributions of some of Choate's alumni surprise the school: one man, for instance, writes elaborate erotica, struggling to find in words new ways to describe a universal human act; another, who was graduated at the bottom of his class—"On his account we made a new ruling," St. John says; "no boy could graduate that low again"—won the Silver Star in Vietnam. Nor is it easy to understand why Choate is pleased by some alumni and not by others. Emil Mosbacher, Jr., '39, a socialite with an engaging smile, won the America's Cup for the second time that fall, crushing Australia in what must be the most unequal competition in international sports. Choate could hardly contain its enthusiasm; the previous year it had awarded Mosbacher its Alumni Seal Prize, thereby elevating him over such alumni as Edward Albee, '46, Chester Bowles, '19, and Roger Stevens, '28.

The reactions of prominent alumni are almost predictably erratic, but then no one knows much about the alumni as a whole. Many hundreds stay in touch with the school, exchanging Christmas cards with the St. Johns and writing flattering letters about how they would never have become fine and distinguished people had they not been forced to go to chapel. But others simply fall away. "I met a Choate graduate at a party last summer," a master reports, "and asked him what he thought of his education here. He said, 'I don't remember anything about it. It's a chapter in my life that presents itself as a blank page. It was a time when I was not thinking and was never exhorted to think.' " Few would go so far. Edward Albee, who won first prize for Best Poem while at Choate, and honorable mention for Best Prose, returned to school in December, 1968, trailing, if not the Alumni Seal Prize, a Pulitzer Prize, five Tony Awards, and three Outer Circle Critics' Awards. Speaking of his education at Choate, he said: "I was encouraged to be as much of a pretentious fool as I could possibly be." But he added some kind words: Choate had taught him "the most important thing I think any educational institution can ever teach you: how to educate yourself."

In like manner, John F. Kennedy, '35, when asked what Choate had done for him, replied that it had not prevented him from becoming President. Although voted most likely to succeed in the 1935 class elections, Kennedy was generally known as "Rat Face" while at school. George St. John hastily explained that only the most popular boys acquired such derogatory nicknames, but Kennedy, making fun of the Old Head's favorite pejorative term, founded "The Muckers Club," which, it is said, was a rebellious and antiauthoritarian group. Kennedy also took part in dramatics because he had to choose between that and public speaking, and he hated public speaking. He was graduated sixty-fourth in a class of 112, and his football coach said, "Jack made up for what he lacked in athletic ability with fight."

Slightly more than half of the alumni contributed an average gift of $47.57 to Choate's annual fund-raising program that year, accounting for a record total of $139,762.42, a sum which made it possible for Choate to operate in the black. On Alumni Day, May 11, hundreds of alumni came back to the school, responding to a written invitation from Peggy St. John: "It's a time to renew old friendships. There's something for everyone from fun and conviviality: the reunion gatherings, the traditional Alumni party with two pianos churning the songs we use [sic] to hum—to the traditional: a full sports slate, Faculty, boys, meals in The Hall, the Alumni Seal Prize Award"—which, that year, finally went to Chester Bowles.

It was the fiftieth reunion year for the class of 1918, Adlai Stevenson's class. Stevenson had died three years earlier, but surviving him was the usual mix of professional and businessmen, as well as a charter member of a chapter of the Elks Club; a "semi-retired dealer in postage stamps"; Choate's oldest trustee; a retired dog food manufacturer who described his life as "utterly uneventful, no children, wandered about for last several years on extensive trips"; and another who said simply: "So—past fifty years the same as the preceding eighteen—get up, wash, work, go home, go to bed."

The Friday before Alumni Day, a select group of alumni who had been graduated in the fifties were invited to return with their wives for a briefing on the school. These briefings, called "Directions '68," are an attempt to keep prominent, rich and influential alumni in touch with the school. Some of those attending are aggressively coarse and as uninformed as they are conservative in their approach to education, but they are all very successful men, though few are over thirty-five. Among them are a race horse breeder, vice-presidents of oil and beer companies; presidents of golf ball, beauty products, and publishing companies. The school makes a great fuss over them.

They are of particular interest to me because I knew most of them at school and because one, a good friend, turns out to be working for the CIA. Every one of them wears a dark business suit and a conservative tie; most wear white shirts and all have very short haircuts. The race horse breeder smokes black cigars as long as, and thinner than, a pencil. "Their average income," said Malcolm Manson, "must be about fifty thousand dollars." They are certainly welcome at Choate, even the two most stupid who, Manson said, "were asked to Directions because they've got a lot of money. It's terribly important that they become involved with the school starting *now*. You have to make much worse compromises than those. I think I can persuade them that they are not specialists at education and that we *are*—we know what we are doing. *They* are specialists at making money, and we're lousy at that. But between us we can make a great school. I think I can persuade them of that."

Manson broods over Choate's failure to grasp as much money as it might from Choate's "family." "We've got a problem with the *trustees*," he says. "We have never yet got across to the trustees what other schools have: the responsibility of the trustees to support the school. With their checkbooks. At every other school the trustees are a major force in underwriting the school. That makes Choate very different."

Others at Choate are upset by the obvious priority that the search for money occupies at the school. It keeps the headmaster away from other essential concerns; it emphasizes the role of tradition in the school. Few rich alumni want to hear much about innovation or increasing liberalism. A school, if it is to produce men as successful as they, cannot afford to change much, certainly not so much as to produce *more* successful men. To heck with that. The best school is the old school where the alumni could still get away with the same pranks, preferably pranks played on the same teachers. So, when the alumni are asked to give their opinions of the school and St. John sits taking notes, glancing intently at the speakers over the rims of his glasses, he hears: "I'm not sure that change is all that good. I hope we stress this moderate evolution as opposed to something radical." St. John nods and smiles. "Most faculty feel that they will be most effective in a general continuation of the way they have always taught," he says. "We move as we can move."

This kind of reaction saddens John Lincoln, who quit teaching at Choate to teach black students in New Haven. "I know I sound so sure and pompous, but I feel that to worry about alienation is the wrong way to proceed in education. I think if, as educators, you believe in something—given your interest in young people—and you see a course of action to take, you ought to take it. If you don't survive, well, gee, it was a great voyage up to then and it doesn't really matter. It's too bad, but the ending was in context. You were right on course. I would hate to survive myself if I were on the wrong course. I don't see a school having as its primary aim the satisfying of alumni. One hopes the alumni are satisfied from time to time."

Most of the alumni, however, follow the conservative line. "I certainly agree Choate should be a progressive school," says one, "but it is a little bit scary to me." "I'm sorry I didn't see enough positive attitude in the boys," says another. "They aren't happy enough to be here. They don't recognize their extraordinary good fortune to be here." St. John nods and shows concern: "How can we make all of these boys feel a sense of participation, of fulfillment?" he asks. He thinks the Glee Club is an answer—which is extraordinary, since the boys have just told him that they want to feel a part of the problems of their times: they want to know more about the Vietnam War and the ghetto poor—and St. John offers the Glee Club.

"When you look back on life," says one of the older alumni, "the things you most appreciate are the things you were most regimented on." Nobody can cap that, but two or three of the young alumni show an extraordinarily acute perception of the school's problems. One praises the boys' "healthy skepticism and willingness to speak up"; another chides St. John for receiving boys' ideas with a "Well, that's interesting; we'll think about it." These men had listened to the boys and learned in hours what it takes many people a term or two to absorb. One of them,

Sherman (Chick) Chickering, '58, editor of a publishing company, spoke to the alumni the following day, causing his audience to hold its breath as he slipped into the mind and voice of an adolescent, explaining the world as teen-agers see it, knocking affluence and hypocrisy while reminding the alumni that "students feel no need to plug into the institutions of the establishment. The only way to be alive is to put their bodies on the line." Students, he said, belong to the powerless generation to whom no one talks or listens.

At lunch, the alumni, talking among themselves, spoke more freely.

"I don't think a damn thing has changed since I was here," said one, class of '54. "Except they've let their standards down. Can you imagine what George Steele would say if he saw kids with sideburns down to *here?*"

Another grumbled about the tiresome seriousness of these kids. "Not more'n five percent of us knew what we wanted to do in life when we got out of Choate," he said.

"We wanted a good time in college," said a third.

"Yeah, and avoid the draft," said a fourth, and everyone laughed.

"Dammit," said the wife of an alumnus, "whatever happened to ambition? I mean, these guys don't want to go into *private* business? The point is to get *ahead* of society!"

A boy who had been graduated the year before wrote to St. John from a school in England where he was taking an extra year. "To me the best thing about Winchester is the respect for the individual," he said. "There is very little conformity and no popularity game—in short, one can do what one pleases and not care about what others think. Unfortunately, this sort of attitude is peculiar to the English, and I doubt if it could exist in an American institution."

Another, who was graduated that spring, wrote to me in the fall: "I have only just begun to realize the enormity of Mr. St. John's influence on the school. I think it can be safely said that the school was him and his whole existence was the school. When the school was attacked as a prison, called intellectually provincial, etc., he felt that he was being attacked personally. That theory is simplistic, but it is what I think. Perhaps it is the utterly free atmosphere here that causes my amazement at all the rules at Choate. I suppose that the degree of freedom you give someone depends on the intelligence you think he has, and Mr. St. John was not willing to grant Choaties enough intelligence to dress properly, know when to go to sleep, what to eat, and how to behave off campus. . . . Often last year it seemed that Seymour's natural instinct told him to mash in the little whiners' heads just like papa would have. . . ."

Another, who had been out a little longer, wrote to Ted Ayres, the alumni director. "I believe that Choate can do more in relation to the civilization that we are creating," he said. "Two years ago I spent the better part of a year working in East Harlem. The experience caused me to question my total existence and to relate, in part, the meaning of Choate in relation to America. I discovered that I'd like to see Choate become a national high school ultimately. Instead of a steadfast service to the elegant, the wealthy, etc. . . . It would be a terribly poignant endeavor if Choate created scholarships in the name of John F. Kennedy and Adlai Stevenson to be utilized for worthy children from the "Other America" . . . I am appalled at the "Know Nothing" attitude of the majority of my dearest friends from Choate, and the indigenous disinterest in community affairs."

"What happens to Choate graduates?" St. John asks. "I don't see how I can conceivably answer that with any sureness of touch. What do you draw on for your reaction? Something as nebulous and indefinite as Alumni Day? I would say that of those alumni who come back—among them inevitably are some who perhaps were secure here and haven't been secure since. That's a possibility. We do give support in a way the world usually doesn't give support, and maybe there are people who still crave this. I'd say that was a very small minority. I think of some who just are excited and loyal and interested in what youth is doing, and just have a love of people and places, which is a *good* thing, a thing from the heart.

"Once in a while people say, I got my start on this from my years at Choate. Maybe most alumni could look back to *something* of which that was true. Maybe they couldn't, I don't know. You would have thought so. Or at least come to *life*—some seed would have sprung. The way you judge—well, people respond by letter; there is a lot of that. Perhaps the fact that a large majority seem to want to send their sons here.

"I would hope that we would provide our share of leadership. And if the establishment represents the best contribution that could be made to our society, I'd hope it would be in the establishment. If there came a time, for some reason or other, the establishment were bad for our society—in very general terms—then I'd hope that we would lead in another direction. I'd hope that it would be on the basis of thoughtful, responsible, mature judgment."

PART TWO

CRISIS

The Communication Gap

> What this school needs most is time for dialogue.
>
> AN ENGLISH TEACHER

> I've never, ever thought of going up to another master and asking him to have a talk about the school.
>
> ANOTHER ENGLISH TEACHER

No one knows just how the communication gap began, or why, after teetering so long on the brink, so many good people fell into it. At times it was tempting to believe that the hole was dug by outside agitators, or perhaps by little men who crept in at night to work with muffled chisels, hacking and chipping away until—boys could no longer talk to teachers, teachers could no longer talk to the headmaster, and the headmaster said nothing at all. During the fall, the faculty talked nervously about the fissure; by winter, everyone could see it: a gaping crater belching fumes of rhetoric and protocol. You could shout into it and not even hear the echo of your protest.

"We have very nearly a great school," says one master. "We have everything except a certain quality which rather disturbs me." He is worried about the school's *esprit de corps,* and about his own. There is an "oppressive atmosphere" at Choate, he says. "Many men have been in the darkest depths here. I'm not sure what can be done about it. Part of it lies in the increasingly tremendous centralized control from above and the appalling lack of communication between the administration and the faculty. There is no communication. Things do not get through."

The central problem of communication at Choate is that St. John is unable to get the best of his ideas on education and the Choate community across to his students, or even to a great many of his faculty. St. John's best ideas are not only liberal but noble, and when he talks about them to outsiders or in a relaxed forum such as a group of alumni can provide, his rhetoric changes. His words are more carefully chosen, his sentences hang together, an informed intelligence lends shape and vigor to his phrases. But the trouble is: he is talking to outsiders. Talking to groups of faculty within the school or, worse, to the students all together, he becomes blunter, more dogmatic; his thoughts fall before goal-oriented metaphors and the burden of the Protestant work ethic. "We do not always speak from where we stand," St. John said toward the end of the year, tossing off the remark so casually that it was impossible to tell whether he realized how important to him such an insight could prove.

Similarly, when St. John tells the boys "boys are great," he means it, even though everything in the school seems, to the boys at least, to be organized on the assumption that boys cannot be trusted. When St. John tells the boys that what some boys *do* is destructive, cruel, undermining, and so on, he means *that,* too. Probably, St. John deeply and truly believes that boys are (a) great, (b) untrustworthy, and (c) if left alone, destructive. As we have seen, his wife can, within the space of a few lines in the *Choate News,* reaffirm the belief "that fundamentally boys are great" and urge malcontents to pack their bags.

Burr Johnson, a teacher of English, believes this lack of communication has forced many talented teachers to leave Choate. He himself has often thought of leaving, and, by his own admission, the school has often thought of asking him to leave. Johnson is forty-three, a balding, intense man who chews his fingers, worries about his own poetry, cares passionately for the boys in school, and is, perhaps, the best-informed and most effective teacher in the English Department. Johnson carries everything Choate stands for to such extremes that he embarrasses the administration, which talks about the kind of commitment, passion, and intensity that Johnson dispenses every day, but which prefers to see a little more reserve, a little more dignity in its masters. Johnson makes some people nervous: there's always the fear that he may dump ashes on his head at any moment, or scratch his face with his nails. He *has* been seen, after a particularly fatuous faculty meeting, banging his head against the wall and shouting, "It's unbelievable!" when the point is that it *is* believable and Johnson has been there long enough to know it, though he will never be there long enough to accept it. This same intensity prompts Johnson to leap on his desk during class, to chew his necktie, and "do wild, wonderful things," as one of his students said, because Johnson believes "The Oven Bird" is one of the finest sonnets our country has produced and knows he *must* persuade the boys that it is—never mind the other English masters who haven't read enough American sonnets to know.

"You have to conform," another master says. "They say you don't. Maybe they mean it, but in general you have to conform around here or they'll break you." This teacher has been at Choate seven years, has done all that was required of him, but he feels out of touch. "The master is always the last person to know what is going on here," he says, "in disciplinary matters and in academic matters. Usually, if I want to know anything I have to go to a boy, or I will learn something because a boy has come to me and told me." This lack of information, particularly about disciplinary matters, bothers him. "There is often a time lag of two and three weeks before a dormitory master is advised of what action is being taken on a boy, and the boy has sat and *fried* without knowing whether he is in or out of the school. No matter what the error the boy has made, this is not justice. But it comes back to the fact that there is one person who has to make the decisions on everything in the school. This is just incredible. Not only does it wear the headmaster out, it leads to an autocratic funneling of everything—discipline, money raising, academic questions—toward this one person."

Burr Johnson regrets Choate's tendency to "hang on, not only to kids with emotional problems, but with real disciplinary problems." He feels the morale of the school would be raised if boys were let go after the first serious breach of discipline. "The headmaster has a conflict here," he says. "He's a devoted man. He's an Episcopal minister. He's also head of the school. I know it's Christian to forgive, but we live in an institution with over five hundred students and the boys have often admitted that they have gotten into trouble because they have seen others break rules and get away with it."

The year before, Johnson had discovered that one boy had in his room a shopping bag full of forged documents: a dozen driving licenses in perfect condition, about a dozen gun permits, thirty draft cards, and ten passports. Johnson turned the stuff in to the dean. Two weeks later, predictably, there was no action. Then, when Johnson was cleaning out the trunk room in his house, he picked up a rolled towel and an automatic pistol fell out at his feet. The gun matched one of the permits Johnson had found in the boy's room. Johnson reported this to Gordon Stillman. The boy protested that he was "a collector" and was allowed to withdraw from the school. Johnson is enraged that kids who take a puff on a cigarette are expelled, but this boy, a one-man Mafia, was allowed to withdraw.

"The administration," says another master, "is not perfectly honest with the masters and never has been. There are many things that have been carefully held from the faculty. Boys' records, for instance. It left me once at an extreme disadvantage. A boy had undergone psychoanalysis for an entire year because of extreme temper tantrums and other abnormalities. This was not let out. I faced that boy in an unpleasant situation, but didn't know his problem. You should be *alerted* to these things. In the last two years masters have asked four times in faculty meetings, 'Why weren't we told about the doctor's findings in these cases?' Two of the four times the headmaster looked at the masters and said nothing. You don't get an answer. Answers are scarce.

"There should be more communication between the headmaster and his faculty," he says, "between the headmaster and the various committees, and much more communication between the boys and the faculty." Like many masters, he feels the faculty is neglected. The headmaster, he feels, "should pay more attention to the *teaching* we do here and less to the outside programs—to the façade of the school, like building this new auditorium, though it is needed. What needs work is the selection of men who teach at Choate. We have a number of very weak masters here. They may be friends of mine, but in the English and history departments we have, not second- or third-rate men, but *fourth*-rate men.

"Many of the faculty," this master says, "have done extremely interesting things during the summer. They are never asked to give this information to the faculty, or in any way use it to enrich the school. They're never *acknowledged* in any way. Not that they want plaudits, but the average man who teaches here is given no support or hand in his way through Choate. I think Choate, or Exeter, or any school rises or falls in the way it teaches English, mathematics, history, languages, yet our weakness is in these courses." But he believes it is useless to talk to St. John about any of this: "All ideas and actions must come from the top."

Tom Colvin, who teaches history, does not agree. He thinks Choate's faculty won't try. "I think they're overtimid," says Colvin. "Because of it the faculty feels the administration is not understanding and will not support disagreement or criticism." Herbert Gutterson, head of the English Department and author of a novel about a death at a prep school, agrees that the fault may partly lie with the kind of men who teach at boarding schools: "There may be something lacking in us, you see. We have some dependency or need for this autocracy which makes us surrender or settle for certain drawbacks for a security of sorts."

But another master is appalled by what has happened to him, and to others, who have accepted their dependency on this autocracy. You may not get through to the headmaster, but he will get through to you when something goes wrong. "You get called before the headmaster," he says, "and all of a sudden he will lay you out for things that have occurred for the last four or five years—horrendous errors you have made, errors that were never brought to your attention at the time. You have practically no chance to defend yourself. I have seen faculty members practically walk out in the middle of the year. They were called in over something and then read the riot act. You are convicted of a crime before you have a chance to go before the jury. It really depresses a great many people. The headmaster accumulates these crimes, many of them by rumor." It is true that St. John will write a letter to a master, or call him to his office, to present extremely vague charges which, he says, have been made against the master by other faculty members whom he refuses to identify. "Speaking for my friends on the faculty," this master continues, "they're *afraid* of Seymour. They're scared for their jobs. A great institution like I'd like Choate to be cannot be based on fear. But masters don't trust him. I've never seen a master yet go into that office that he didn't worry."

Rod Furnald agrees. By December, he had the uncomfortable feeling that although nobody from the administration had even *talked* to him during the fall, St. John was forming opinions about Furnald, opinions that Furnald thought might be unjust, but which were brought to the headmaster by what might most kindly be called his informers. "If you do something wrong, you get called in," Furnald mused. "One master I know was called in by St. John, and now he doesn't trust *anybody* in this school anymore. He just won't talk to anybody. Students in the fourth-form public speaking class have to do an interview, but he won't let even *them* interview him; he refuses to let them tape what he says, because it seems to him that *everything* gets back to the chief. And I'm not so sure *I* trust people in the school now, either. I'm careful who I talk with. When I talk to students, or do this interview thing, I tell them to destroy the tape when they're finished."

"I've found it necessary to bring my wife with me the last couple of times I've seen Seymour," one master says, "because he has not told the truth. I brought her to check on myself. He does not tell the same story twice in a row. I am pretty well certain he doesn't do this on purpose. I hesitate to use the term 'lie,' but he can completely reverse his story. I was warned when I came here five years ago: 'For God's sake,' I was told, 'if he says anything to you, get it in writing because he'll switch his story on you.' I disregarded it. It's true."

This master's wife offers what is probably the correct explanation: "I think a lot of it is because he's so busy. He talks to so many people he doesn't quite remember what he says to you. And then he will talk to other people in the meantime and change his opinions. He feels he can manage his masters in much the same way as the boys. It's awfully hard to deal with a man like that, especially when he has such tremendous facility—the smile, the poise, the genuine niceness—a niceness which I am sure, when he's dead tired, he has to put on when he doesn't want to."

"Seymour is a terribly busy man," says Mounir Sa'adah, who once turned down a headmastership himself. "Consequently, no idea sticks in his mind after the next idea arrives. If you don't get action at that moment, it is likely—not because he is not interested in it—to be crowded out. This is the nature of his work."

Still, doubts survive. The head of the student Honor Committee worries too. "I always worry about the way the headmaster deals with things," he says. "In a way, he's a little bit set in his ideas, but he always speaks extremely well and he always convinces me of his ideas. But then, when I try to explain them to guys who ask me about them, I can't really convince them. I'm not sure—maybe he uses too broad generalities to pull the wool over our eyes. He'll come up with some generality that you can't say, no, that's not true, and you can't give him facts to prove that it's not true, so you feel it could easily be right, and when he says it, you agree with him. But you feel you can't really convince yourself he *is* right, and you feel he might *not* be right. The boys will ask me why we can't have more weekends in the fall, and I'll give them the reasons he gave, but they don't seem quite so strong anymore. It might be just that I can't speak as well as he can. I don't know. I sometimes wonder whether he's duping us." After a pause, the boy went on. "I trust the headmaster; I really do. I begin to wonder if I've been duped for the past four years. Yes, I do trust him."

"Seymour ought to take a year off," said one of the seniors, "and travel around the world and look at other schools and find out what's going on in the outside world."

"I asked him," said a Student Council member, "if he kept up with new ideas in education and he said, 'Yes,' and then he proceeded to tell me *his* ideas about education."

"His other deficiency," said the first senior, "is his feeling that he has to euphemize and beat around the bush. He can come into chapel one night and say, 'Well, we have a problem. We think it quite important—you might not—but we think some boy in a careless moment, not really intending to, not really thinking about it, blew up the Hillhouse.' Mr. Atmore says he *has* to be round and evasive to be a good headmaster. He can't really come out and commit himself."

"Seymour needs replacement," a faculty member says. "Or certainly a rest for three years. As much as I admire him. I would put another man in here who is academic and humanly interested in the core of the school. He can handle the board of trustees and the parents and the money raising *flawlessly*. But he handles the core of the school as if it were an annoying adjunct. There is a tremendous inequity in the work load here. I mean teaching *and* taking dormitories *and* coaching athletics." When he objected to coaching, he was criticized by the head of the Athletic Department. "And then I got laid out by the headmaster. 'How are we going to run this school? We can't give you a free season.' You burn yourself out here after ten years.

"If I were headmaster, I'd put through a crash program to improve communications between the administration and the working faculty. I'd quit barking at the working faculty, and treating them like dogs, and being rude to them. We are *human beings,* subject to failures and successes. And most of us work very hard for this school."

"In terms of people who complain," says David Rice, who also teaches English, "my observation is that either they're too young to know what they're talking about or they're the ones who think they're hired to do a particular job and this is *all* they do. This is the breadth of their interest." Rice says that, a year before, a questionnaire was circulated among the faculty about suggestions or ideas they might wish to have discussed before a panel of alumni. Out of eighty faculty, six replied. "The communication problem," says Rice, "if there *is* one, is two-way. There's a certain amount of apathy on the part of some faculty to really involve themselves in anything outside of their own department. My feeling is that *anybody,* anybody with a creative idea can put it across. It's about ninety-eight percent knowing how to proceed."

Robert Atmore, who teaches English and public speaking, and is co-director of Choate's excellent library, describes himself as "the greatest old suggestion maker in the world, and they all kid me about it, but I get what I want." He laughs at one master who quit in a huff, claiming he was not free to make suggestions. "I would guess," says Atmore, "that he did not make any suggestions. Or enough of them. And *then* he felt he was not free. I make my suggestions in writing and I *never* say, 'Seymour, the school ought to do this,' because he'll write back, 'All right, how do you do it?' I say, 'We ought to do this, and you can do it this way, and there's a man over there who can do it, and it will cost this much.' "

"There is a certain disappointment," says one of the older masters, "in Seymour, in the communication to him, a sense of being cut off from a power source you might have had that would go all the way from him through you to the student body. You have to decide whether you can exist, find a *raison d'être,* without that, and you find it in the work of the men you're with, whom you respect and like a good deal. Once you get by the feeling that you've got to convince the administration of your position, and realize that you probably can't, then you say, 'Well, is there anything else in this environment that I appreciate?' And I say, Yes. I appreciate these men that I work with, a wonderful bunch of people. They all work under certain shadows. Nobody is perfect. The thing that's going to keep these younger men here is basically an intellectual search and an environment that's fundamentally real, where they can be completely honest and open, where there's no bill of goods of any sort. They can be free in their own classrooms. A marvelous autonomy there—they can do what they please.

"We've all gotten so big. The building committees, the millions of dollars, the expansion, we don't know what is going on. But it's taking a lot of time from the very best minds. The result is a feeling that the academic side will somehow get done, but we may have to cancel some classes here and there—and somehow it wouldn't matter if we did. This bothers the masters, who feel there should be some priorities. The faculty does not feel it is in control of the school."

Which is why many faculty members do not talk much, if at all, in the faculty meeting. John Joseph, who has an authority of his own and little use for faculty meetings, openly reads *The New Republic* as the headmaster talks. "I don't stand up in faculty meetings," says Jere Packard, "because I've been inculcated in a certain way." "Inculcated" was a big word at Choate that year. Packard, like David Rice, is one of the younger men who is liked by the boys, who speaks articulately with blunt —often rough—common sense. "You can't sit through a faculty meeting and feel that the faculty has the meaningful rapport it should have with the administration," Packard says, but Packard doesn't really give a damn. "The institution, for better or for worse, is a hierarchical one. I, for one, don't want to sit in there and listen to cases of petty discipline argued over, or listen to people who couldn't run a laundry detail or supervise the handing out of jock straps standing up and saying how the goddamn school should be run. My time is valuable. There are other things that I can do for the school which are more valuable than this crap."

Others, through tiredness or fear, tend to talk less as they grow older. "The big thing," says Rod Furnald, "is that people see that talking doesn't get them anywhere. They have nothing to gain from airing their views, and quite a bit to lose if these views they express outside get back to the administration." At twenty-two, Furnald talked regularly in faculty meeting; at twenty-three, he kept his mouth shut. "For expediency's sake," says a member of St. John's administration, "I go along with many things the headmaster and the trustees do that I don't really approve of. I don't voice my dissent loudly enough, or at all, sometimes. I feel that my status might be threatened. I might lose what influence I have. Therefore, my other projects might not only be threatened, but thrown out."

"For years here we had a loyal minority," the older master said. "Men who would get up on occasion and thoroughly denounce an idea with no punches held. But slowly there began to be less and less discussion in the faculty room. More and more things were stated, but not argued. Where before many things were objected to openly, they now became objected to underground. You agreed on the surface, but then you went off and quietly circumvented it. Now whether this happened because men felt there was not an audience for their disagreements, or whether they would be thought disloyal if they spoke—because a few would get chopped now and then—well, I don't know.

"Perhaps we're overly tired, overly busy. There's hardly any entertaining now, hardly any sitting around in evenings to read a paper or get a good philosophical bull session going."

Some masters feel that their acquiescence, their silence, is imposed on them as the price of keeping their jobs, and they desperately need the low salaries they earn. "Pretty soon," said one teacher, "a man begins to feel that some of these financial benefits are what is keeping him here, when the actual core of what he is here *for*—the teaching—is almost the least of his reasons."

"I'll just have to keep my mouth shut from here on in," another said. "I have three children. The headmaster told me I was not as valuable as Jo van Straalen or Dick Whiteside. I had to beg to be kept on another year. The headmaster wants to get rid of me."

Another wept when he spoke of his fear: "You have to make a kind of separate peace to stay here," he said. "That peace is knowing you can go to the headmaster, but nothing will be done, nothing at all. You have to live simply because you respect what you are doing and the work of the other men around you, but knowing that you will get no help or notice from the administration.

"The income is so important, particularly when you have a child to educate. You get to the point where the extra five hundred dollars you might get as a raise is so important you will sell yourself for it. You will keep your mouth shut. If you have an independent income, you can say what you want. But I have to keep quiet. Even tenure wouldn't help: I need the raises.

"What does it profit a man to save the whole school if he lose his own job?"

This, then, was the silence of St. John: it was not a *real* silence, in spite of those masters who were too tired or too afraid to talk. It was, instead, a silence of inappropriate response. You could still talk to the headmaster in the same old way, and he would talk to you, and look you very steadily in the eye, but, as the year progressed, more and more masters and students felt that they had *new* things to say, even urgent questions and criticisms, and what came back from the administration was the same old pap, the fatigued rhetoric, the neat, round phrases that said nothing at all. It was as if the questions, the criticisms, were not even *heard.* Many people felt that St. John used hackneyed replies on purpose, deliberately refusing to listen to problems brought to him, and there was some reason to believe this was true. "When I talk to boys," St. John said to a group of alumni, "I try to go back to basic values. It's hard to argue about basic values."

Nor could the masters communicate easily with one another. "It's not a very close faculty," Rod Furnald observed after he had taught at Choate for three months. "Basically, nobody gives a damn about what's on the minds of other members of the faculty." "I wrote a letter to the studies office, about five pages long," said Jon van Leuven, "about the grading system and eliminating many examinations. I never heard anything at all. This fall I wrote an enormous analysis of the objectives of the Science Department, trying to get a scheme to amalgamate the Science Department with the Humanities Department under a framework of environmental studies, to lead to the possibility of new courses in the social sciences, like anthropology. My own department chairman didn't read it."

Both Furnald and Van Leuven would like to see the school run "democratically." "I would like to have masters with different views free to air them," Furnald says, "so that you could talk about what you feel about the school to anyone, including students. I think this makes for a dynamic and an honest situation." "I would really like to see a test of the democratic way of governing the school," says Van Leuven, who is interested in the theory of utopias. "In the sense of many more things—perhaps even everything—submitted to a faculty vote." Van Leuven's mentor, Mounir Sa'adah, prepared a report with a preamble: "We assume that a democratic society is the only form of human organization in which the individual can find personal and social fulfillment. . . . A democracy allows free, open and continuous discussion. . . . The Choate Community desires to evolve into a more perfect democracy." Of course, the Choate community desires nothing of the sort. The majority of the faculty and administration no longer smile at such presumption. One of the administration made its position very clear to a new master: "This is a business corporation and it is run like a business corporation. It may be a nonprofit business corporation, but it is like General Motors. *You* don't establish policy here any more than an employee at Ford can go to Arjay Miller and say, 'This is what should be done.' "

St. John believes that the coltish dissent of new, young masters can be turned into an asset for the school, but that the dissent must be "worked out" of these masters before they will become useful. St. John may ignore the *substance* of dissent, but not the *fact* of dissent: dissent is worrisome because it presents problems of morale. He knows, too, that boys of the age of Choate students may think they have a lot to say, and a lot to offer in the way of changes, but they have very little staying power. Boys in their early teens come on strong, but they wear out quickly. Sometimes . . . it just doesn't seem worth the trouble.

"Wilder and I went to the headmaster last year," said one senior. "We said we'd like to put up a student opinion bulletin board where students, so long as they signed their opinion, could put up a complaint or a suggestion, or just a thought. Seymour tried to bring out all kinds of little excuses not to have it, and every one he brought up we put down. He said, 'How about a person who goes around putting up dirty or useless signs?' We said a Student Council member could check it every day and take down things that weren't supposed to be there. He brought up four or five of these little things. It reminded me of that Steinberg cartoon of a guy sitting behind his desk and saying NO with all the writing inside the word. Finally, when we debunked his excuses, he said, 'Well, I won't stand in your way. You have to take it up with the Student Council now.' " The senior sighed. They were within sight of victory, but they were worn out. "There is just so much to do to get anything done that you just give up," he said.

In the spring, a frustrated junior wrote a burning editorial for the *Choate News:*

> I am speaking about the helplessness the individual feels in respect to making his argument heard and changing his school. It is exasperating when a student, responsible or negative or apathetic or whatever, who has a gripe or suggestion and truly wants to make an effort to help Choate, finds himself yelling in a vacuum. . . . It is very upsetting when he thinks that, no matter what he says or does, nobody gives a damn or will do anything about it.

The boy went on to complain that, when a suggestion was made to the Student Council, nothing happened. "Who knows what happens to it? . . . Does anyone know?" Suggestions taken to the headmaster fared no better:

> Mr. St. John has always said that we could come and talk to him anytime about anything. . . . But what if a student goes to Mr. St. John with a carefully thought-out gripe or suggestion? Perhaps the headmaster will agree and subsequently act (if it is truly he that has the power to do so). But what if the Head does not like the suggestion? I seriously doubt whether anyone else would ever hear about it, except perhaps a few angry friends of the student who spoke to him.

You could, the boy said, make your objections in the columns of the *News*, but then recriminations followed. He said he had criticized a master and was persecuted for doing so. He was

> denounced by at least one-fourth of the faculty, including my housemaster, as an immature, unintelligent troublemaker, who had no self-control and ought to have his head examined. This lasted, to my dismay, for close to two months, and in the process I lost not only much of my pride and self-respect, but also a great deal of that precious key to living at Choate, suck.

"Of course," the boy went on as he allowed irony to replace his anger,

> there is always the serious talk with a non-influential master, who promises to get something done about it, but more often than not, never does or simply cannot. . . . The point is, we are back where we started, and the student is as helpless as he was before. There is nothing left for him to do but yell at a wall or bang his head against a tree or curse the school and leave.

The editorial caused quite a stir: few faculty members could understand why such a thing was *allowed* to appear in the *News,* and so, instead of discussing the issues the boy raised, they discussed the feasibility of censoring the student newspaper.

Perhaps it was a part of the backlash against a new phenomenon that adults at Choate were only beginning to understand that year: that kids not only thought they had good ideas, but they insisted that adults listen to them. For thousands of years, of course, children and adolescents have talked among themselves, sorting matters out with their own contemporaries when they found adults unsympathetic. At the Lycée Louis le Grand, Camille Desmoulins and Robespierre met to talk about Rousseau, but it never occurred to them—as it never occurred to young Lenin and his hairy teen-age terrorists—to ask *adults* to pay attention to their views. "I don't give a damn what the teen-agers think of Vietnam," said one father, but the kids won't settle for that kind of intolerance any longer: they *insist* that grown-ups treat their opinions seriously. At Choate, the boys assume that if the headmaster doesn't act on what they say, he isn't listening to them, and if he doesn't listen to them, they aren't free to say what they want. It is a convoluted dialectic, but it is nonetheless the First Epistle from the Students to America, and that year, a few of the faculty—those who were not snorting in indignation—listened.

In the spring of 1969, a "want ad" appeared in a mimeographed edition of the student underground newspaper, the *Hard Core:* "NEEDED: A translator. Will somebody please translate just exactly what the Head says when he gives a formal speech? He talks around and around a point and never comes to say anything. Also, take away his Quotation books so that he can talk straight to us and not through the words of people in the past."

St. John, however, maintained his Gaullist calm. "One does not influence men," wrote Malraux about De Gaulle, "by knowing them, but by constraint, confidence, or love." St. John offered his pint-sized protesters constraint, confidence, and love:

"Dear Mr. St. John," one third former wrote:

Here are my suggestions:

1) New Haven. Day passes on Saturday afternoon for underformers. Boys can skip lunch but must return by Saturday dinner.

2) More modern concerts available to underformers as an alternative to the New Haven Symphony Orchestra.
3) More optional Sunday breakfasts.

Sincerely yours,

St. John replied:

Dear Mike:

Thanks for your three suggestions. One and two seem to me relatively similar, and involve underformers going off to New Haven on Saturday afternoons. Frankly, I don't see how we can open ourselves to a mass exodus to surrounding cities on the weekends without taking a great deal less responsibility than we try to take for our students. If there were some special event, I should feel quite differently about it. But just to go and wander around New Haven seems to me unconstructive. Because you have brought it up, I shall bring it to the attention of the faculty. But I doubt that it will get much support.

What I should like to see would be your own constructive ideas on ways to spend your time to advantage on the 800 acre campus with some pretty good facilities that you have the good fortune to have at your disposal. Perhaps that doesn't have a great deal of appeal for you; but I honestly think it should. Have you ever tried working in photography? In music or the arts? In astronomy or the sciences? Or just plain walking up in the woods? There's a tremendous amount to see, to be excited about, to learn, if you will keep your eyes open and make an effort, and those things lead to places that simply wandering around at loose ends do not lead. The latter can be left for your vacation, if that is the way you like to spend them. But again, and honestly, I think of it as neither very constructive nor grownup.

Now for a more optimistic look: your third point is one to which I can happily say YES! We'll have more optional Sunday breakfasts.

Yours sincerely,

Now that is a boy who is not going to write to St. John again in a hurry. St. John knows, however, that he can do even better when he talks to a boy in his office: "If I were going to flatter myself, I think I would flatter myself at this point. It is rare that I can't get on a very easy communicative basis with a boy when he comes in here. I think that's true. Every once in a while I miss. I remember feeling with one boy this year that I'd missed cold, and yet something happened, and he came around, and by golly, by the end of the year he was a completely different boy." The boy, of course, is the one who must change his stance. "I don't give myself the credit," St. John says, "but I just say somehow or other, things worked. I was, of course, only one of many who was working on it.

"Whenever you talk to a boy, of course, if you do it right, you listen a good deal more than you talk, to find out what he feels—what makes him tick, or what he *thinks* does." St. John is aware that many boys feel they can't talk to him because he has so little time, but it is true that boys who are called to his office are astonished at how perceptive and sympathetic he is—and at how they emerge from his office thinking what Seymour St. John thinks: about themselves.

"Quite often," St. John says, "you'll get something that looks absolutely clear, cut and dry, the image looks clear, and you talk to the boy and all of a sudden the image *changes*. That isn't the way you see him; there are other factors that come into it. So you say, 'Well, he *has* looked that way, but he doesn't *have* to look that way. He can look *another* way—with a little encouragement. Sometimes he can make almost an about-face."

St. John is particularly amused by a Texan boy who came into his office complaining he wasn't happy. St. John said: "Frankly, I don't care if you're happy. Don't mistake me—I am interested in *you,* but I'm more interested in what you'll be ten years from now than what you are today." St. John told him that perhaps Choate wasn't right for him. The student was startled, "but he thanked me for my candor."

When communication fails utterly, of course, the boy can be asked to leave. George St. John used to say: "Some of my best friends are men who, as boys, we had to ask to withdraw." Most adults at Choate believe in the salutary effects of expulsion. "He's not a bad boy," St. John will say of a student who is packing his bags, "he's just a boy that hasn't grown up. The best thing we could do educationally for him right now—it's always a guess, but we *think* the best thing we could do for him educationally—is to say: 'You've been tried and found wanting. Now you've got to start again.' More often than not, boys have written back to tell us we were right."

On another occasion, St. John admitted the existence of a communication gap. "I feel I can't get through to the students as well as I once could," he said. "I mean the students as a body. I can still get through to the individual at once. I don't tell him things. I just ask questions: What do you want? Where are you trying to go?"

Twice during the fall, St. John tackled major problems of the day and tried to explain them to the faculty and students. The first problem was the hippie problem, and it was already rather passé, but St. John made it the theme of his address at the Fathers' Day banquet. "Hippies," said St. John, "have lost the ability to be useful to their society, which is fatal both to their society and to themselves. At least some of our protesters are not for real; the vast majority of those who are left are sound, reliable, and capable of something great."

But, as St. John went on to talk about "major fashions among the phonies," and as the fathers nodded through the cigar smoke and their sons plucked at the unaccustomed tablecloths, *something* seemed to be wrong. St. John quoted Art Buchwald: "We've produced a generation of young windbags . . . youthful old gasbags whining through their guitar chords that not being true to yourself produced the atom bomb." Laughter from the fathers. Then St. John laid into youngsters whom he called "hippies." As it turned out, they were not hippies, but student leaders articulate enough to write for a national magazine—never mind. St. John blasted them for rejecting the wisdom of their fathers, which limited their effectiveness and created "a kind of stuttering society"; for "experimenting with values" because "the agnostics have never made great contributions to our society"; and for doing their own thing, which St. John says "the Greeks called hedonism, anarchy; we all want it from the day we are born, and, from our second year, we know we can't have it."

When he was finished, there was a smattering of applause from the fatter hands in the audience. Some of the boys were upset, but they didn't quite know why. It was a *good* speech; the headmaster is an accomplished speaker. But it may have worried them that he identified the more thoughtful young people in this country with hippies—and when St. John says "hippie" one thinks of hairy youngsters, stumbling half naked, their eyes blown wide on Turkish drugs. Perhaps the boys realized St. John had attacked the *vocabulary* of youthful dissent, thereby dismissing whatever might have been of value in the protest. Some may have thought that even real hippies oppose what Choate says it opposes. St. John, student radicals, and hippies object to the distortions and materialism our society imposes, but St. John does not see that: Choate and hippies, he believes, are antithetical, and the hippies are phonies. The irony is that Choate students dismiss St. John's ideas for precisely the same reason: angered by his tired vocabulary, they throw out his ideas as well.

"He's got a golden tongue," a senior said, "but his idea of hippies comes from *Newsweek* magazine. Seymour can't talk about anything outside the school with real conviction. He's been here twenty years and doesn't really step outside the Lodge. When was the last time *he* was in the East Village?" Still, this senior regrets that St. John is misunderstood simply because he chooses his line of attack so badly. "For a cynical seventeen-year-old," the senior said, "or someone who has heard people like him before—and there are a lot of people like him, take President Johnson—it is easy to degrade what he wants to say because of his method of saying it."

"I have difficulty staying awake," said one master as the speech ended. "The boys have heard this so many times it means nothing to them."

In December, St. John did step out of the Lodge: he went to Vietnam. Two years earlier, the *Choate News* had polled both the faculty and the boys about their attitudes toward Vietnam. According to the *Choate Newsletter,* a fund-raising pamphlet sent to alumni, "The study showed that the vast majority of the School is in favor of the present United States policy in Vietnam." An editorial in the same pamphlet said: "United States policy is being willfully or wishfully misunderstood and being labelled as a New McCarthyism, imperialism, or war-mongering. . . . How heart-warming that the Choate community is among that growing group of Americans who are willing to vociferate their support of policies based on principle rather than popularity."

Heartwarming it may have been, but many people had died in Vietnam since then. "There's no one in this school who questions the horror of Vietnam, including the headmaster," said one teacher, so the headmaster went out to see for himself. He might have felt that going as the guest of the U.S. Army, as a tourist to observe the efficiency of our military presence, being shown only what the Army wanted him to see, was not perhaps the best way to come to a *moral* conclusion about the justification of the war, but this did not bother St. John, who admires efficiency. The father of one of the students at Choate, General Robert Taber, Chief of Staff to General Westmoreland, asked him to come, and St. John accepted. He went "to spend a few days in Vietnam: to search and to learn." He had not, as far as I could discover, read any of the books by reporters who opposed the war—no book by Bernard Fall or David Halberstam or Robert Shaplen or William Fulbright or Mary McCarthy or Jonathan Schell or John Sack—but he had called a friend of his in the administration, Walt Rostow, who had told him what to read.

St. John left on November 30, arriving in Hong Kong on December 1. Three days later he was in Saigon. Four days after that he was in Bangkok, en route to New Delhi, Athens, London, and New York, which he reached on December 17.

"Seymour," said one of the seniors, "is starting a nine-month campaign as a new Republican dark horse. Circling around the world and hitting all the trouble spots. Even stopping off in Hong Kong to get a few suits to match his tasseled loafers." Certainly, a lot of boys thought he had already made up his mind when he went: Seymour, they said, was a hawk and can a hawk change its feathers?

But perhaps St. John's reaction was more complex. The next summer, he was still thinking about it. "Times do change, don't they?" he said. "Hardly a new thought. Yesterday I was looking something up in *Bartlett's Quotations,* and as always when I get into it, I started reading poetry of various times. I ran across a poem about the Empire days of England in China. A situation where two soldiers were caught by the Chinese when all the rest had withdrawn, and told to kowtow, to bow before the Chinese potentate. The first one did. And made all necessary obeisance. The second one said he would be damned before he would bow down before any Chinaman alive! Whereupon he was hit over the head and thrown on the dunghill. The poem was a tremendous eulogy of that man. *This* is the essence of England! The *real* England. The man who will stand up for pride and say he will never bow before any Chinaman!"

It is the essence of the worst of England, which St. John would probably admit if pressed on the point, but for the moment he was excited by this proud soldier who had become for him not just an unbending Britisher who, though he would kneel for Queen Victoria, would not bow to the Emperor Ho-Hum, but a man fit to join the Jews at Masadah, Thomas More before Henry VIII, Luther before the Diet of Worms. St. John is accustomed, when making a speech, to draw upon quotations which he rarely identifies, to make analogies, to look for the illustrative examples which will prove the truths he trots out before his students or alumni. Sometimes these analogies get him into trouble because he does not really think them through, does not weigh their implications or rummage through all the baggage that they carry with them.

"It *is* somewhat Kiplingesque," St. John said of his soldier, "but here was virtue. This was virtue in that day. And today, I'm afraid, we'd consider it provincial. In considering it provincial, of course, we lose a certain amount of nationalism, patriotism—if that's the right word. Like everything else that's an ideal, you make strange bedfellows. Hitler built on a feeling of patriotism, nationalism. In his early years, many things in Germany improved immeasurably. Certainly the spirit and strength of youth."

And so St. John went out to see what we were doing to today's "Chinamen," the men who were fighting for their country in Vietnam. He came back to tell the school about it, to tell a church in New York about it, and then to write a pamphlet about it. "Mr. St. John," wrote Malcolm Manson, "has been at great pains to present possible *guide lines* for decision rather than his own viewpoint—although his position is not difficult to deduce."

St. John had been with the American Army in Vietnam for four days.

He returned in January, to conduct the first chapel after Christmas vacation. The carillon banged out "Onward, Christian Soldiers," and Duncan Phyfe, on the organ, played the opening hymn: "Once to Every Man and Nation." "The singing of that first hymn," St. John remarked to the Student Council later that evening, "was the worst I ever heard. It just went dead." The hymn was certainly inappropriate to St. John's cause. As the boys sang such phrases as "By the light of burning martyrs. . . . Toiling up new Calvaries ever/With the Cross that turns not back. . . . Truth forever on the scaffold/Wrong forever on the throne," they *sounded* ragged and listless.

St. John talked briskly and for twice as long as usual; astonishingly, he had *become* an expert in the language spoken by the Americans in Vietnam. He talked about "slicks" and "choppers" and the "Yoos-Army," described "NDP"—Night Defensive Positions, and unrolled a map the kids couldn't see to point out: "It's IV Corps up to here and II Corps down to

Saigon," and then, with a stabbing motion of the finger, he fixed "the 14th ICC–Inventory Control Center." This is St. John, the naval planning officer, talking; he will end with moral feelings about the war, but nothing in his speech works toward that end—the moralizing is to be tacked on later, a necessary but almost gratuitous conclusion. The boys will sense this lack of development, of cohesiveness; St. John will lose them and know that he has. "I lost about a quarter of them," he said later. "That's a lot to lose, and I just don't know why I lost them." The boys probably didn't know *what* they wanted from St. John, but they certainly didn't want an itinerary, a glossary of war terms, or yet another report on the fighting. They suspected he would be a hawk and they weren't impressed by his arguments, but in this they were unjust to him, because as St. John waffled on about "amber, red, and green roads" and "the NDP on Route 13 held by the 3rd Battalion," they failed to see that he would conclude by being *tentative* about his position. Still, St. John failed to show why his trip had anything to do with the way a man might shape his opinion about the justice of the war, and his speech did not develop from observation to revelation.

"We took a helicopter over the battle area," St. John said—it was Bong Son where, right at that time, 200 people were being killed—"and sat there at 750 feet and watched as F-100's came in at 300 feet and first dropped bombs and then anti-personnel bombs and helicopters." He told the boys how he had seen a helicopter crash, and others come to pick it up and whisk it away: "It was the most astonishing operation you can imagine. And this is the kind of strange war we are waging." And so it must be, for a tourist hovering over the ignorant armies clashing. But if there were a moral issue involved in such voyeurism, it was never raised.

Then, at the end, St. John presented his conclusions. He began effectively: "The evidence of the war one has to balance for oneself. And I don't think anybody can make up anybody else's mind. If, for example, you believe that war is always more wrong than right—if you're truly a pacifist—then that's that."

This, of course, had alerted the students that St. John had brought out his scales again, in which he measures right and wrong and hopes to God they don't balance evenly because—what then? "If you believe," he went on, "as I have had to believe in my lifetime, that there are worse things than war, that Hitler was worse than war, that I had in conscience to fight against that, then you have to make up your mind whether this is a just and right war. What's more, you can't decide what you would have done two years ago. You have to decide where you are today. Then you have to take some pluses—and there *are* some pluses—and you have to take some minuses—and there sure are some minuses—and you have to weigh one against the other. . . .

"Because I can't vacillate," St. John said, "because I have to make up my mind, I find myself about sixty-forty in favor of holding on. Forever? you might say. No, not forever. With increasing forces? I hope not with increasing forces. . . . At the same time I don't see how conceivably we can leave flat millions of people when we have committed ourselves. And it's not only people in Vietnam. It's hard for us as Americans to recognize what the problem there is. We have done much more than fight a war in Vietnam. We have fought a saving battle for many nations. To me the evidence is still about sixty-forty in favor of going on."

Some of the boys could hardly believe what they had heard. This was a *decision?* The old 60–40 percentage? If the odds are only 60–40, how can one go on with such killing and destruction? When he got around to writing his pamphlet, St. John worked from his percentages—"There is a percentage of evil that will always be a part of warfare"—to a more literary and religious conclusion: "We have to base decisions on imperfect truth: on the percentage of evidence we can glean, pro and con. Having weighed the sacrifice and the commitment, having thought and listened to the roar of artillery and whine of shell through the dark hours of the night, one may only say: 'Here I stand, I can do no other.' "

The service ended with a prayer which seemed to dispense

with the doubt of questions and percentages: "Almighty God, who has created man in thine own image, grant us grace fearlessly to contend against evil and to make no peace with oppression." Christ, of course, had suggested doing good to those who persecute you. "And that we may reverently use our freedom," St. John concluded, "help us to employ it in the maintenance of justice among men and nations in the glory of thy holy name."

Later that evening, talking to his Student Council, St. John went off on a long digression about the wonders of warfare in Vietnam. "There are a lot of unpleasant things in Vietnam that you don't entirely like," he confessed, "but we're moving ahead. There's no question about that. Slowly. But we're in the driver's seat. We're moving." As he spoke, the boys reacted not at all. Their expressions were completely composed, much as they would have been had they been listening to a lecture on the national budget, except for one boy, who winced and frowned all evening. As always, St. John spoke with ease and an astonishing amount of hard information: he could shower statistics all over any question asked by any boy. But he never touched on the fundamentals, on the inhumanity of such slaughter, on the way our society at home was being corroded by the war. He profusely admires the military automaton—"One captain never let me out of his sight for four days—" and when he described the fighting, he grew very animated. After all, war is fun, and perhaps this is one of the percentages that must be added to that 60–40 balance.

"When you see it," said St. John, "you get so *excited* about it. A battle scene with a whole battalion of Viet Cong and two battalions of ARVN troops on each side and two of American troops on the two ends. And artillery lobbing in from the fire bases—I've got pictures of that—and planes coming over like this"—his hands swooping from high to low—"shooting their rockets." Boom. Zap. "It's *fabulously* exciting. And helicopters, gunships, following in! It's a *very* exciting thing. The doggone planes came in so fast I never did get a picture."

"Sir," said one of the boys, "did you get any shots of napalm?"

"No." St. John sighed. "I had one shot at it. But I missed it, because it's just a flash. I *did* see a couple of air strikes brought in by a reconnaissance plane. Reconnaissance planes fly in over all the areas, and, among other things, they have what's called 'people sniffers,' which is still classified, I think, but they're *fantastic.* They'll pick up ammonia fumes, and that, unpleasantly, is urine or B.O. A group of people, or a group of troops, they can pick it up very easily. When they find a place they drop a smoke bomb, which is what we saw first—a little plume coming up—and about a minute later we saw these F-4C's diving in at about 300 feet with 750-pound bombs in that area—bang, bang, bang!—followed in about thirty seconds by more F-4C's dropping napalm—great *big* flashes!—and then finally another plane, just one, with BTU: antipersonnel stuff. It explodes a certain distance over the ground, say thirty feet, and shoots balls—little round balls—which spread out in a very wide area, and when they hit the ground they explode and go out as shrapnel, so anybody that's not below ground in an area probably a hundred yards long and a hundred yards wide is just *blasted.* That looks like sparklers. You can see them coming in. I don't think I got a picture of them."

Sorry about that.

Being Black at Choate

> We are against all racial, religious and class prejudices and snobberies. We realize that they exist and that in some boys they are so ingrained that they cannot be removed by force. In such cases, pleasant discussion and gradual exposure to more civilized ways of behavior are more effective than angry denunciation.
>
> *The Choate Master's Handbook*

> For us, in the midst of honkiedom
> Is living in hell (everyday)
>
> A BLACK STUDENT AT CHOATE

Negroes are new to Choate. "I owe you an apology," George St. John wrote to the father of a student in 1916. "I supposed I was asking you to take two Kent boys to New Haven, and had no idea that the two members of the party which were left were a Negro and some other grown man, whose status with Kent even now I do not know."

Choate accepted its first black student in 1959. In the fall of 1967 ten were enrolled—which is more than can be found in the Wallingford public high school—but Deerfield claimed 11 black students, Andover 28, and Exeter 40. "I'm terrible at math," says Polly Packard, one of the younger faculty wives, "but it seems to me that if there are ten blacks out of five hundred and sixty kids, this is a kind of tokenism that Choate can't afford. If it's ever going to be the kind of school that many people would like it to be—I feel this strongly—they've *got* to go out and get more. Instead of sending a scouting party to look for potential Choate students around the swimming pool at the Sewickley Country Club in Pittsburgh, they ought to be looking at the busboys."

Polly does not believe that there is any conscious racism in Choate's admission policies—"It's a sin of omission rather than commission"—but she does feel that some of the white boys who are at Choate on scholarships are not as qualified for the work as are black boys who have come on the few scholarships reserved for the specifically "disadvantaged."

"I think Seymour feels he must be careful," says her husband, Jere Packard, a history teacher who works part-time in the admissions office. "He has got a going concern which, for over fifty years, has been successful in creating a secondary training program for the upper bourgeoisie of the Eastern establishment. This provides a useful service to America. Granting a certain responsibility to leaven the loaf, Seymour tries to do it by having foreigners in the faculty and student body—and of course foreign teachers cost less.

"I don't think Seymour would ever subscribe to Saltonstall's theory of a national high school," he says. "I think he is much more content to feel that there is still a place for Choate as it has been, catering to the upper middle class of the Eastern Seaboard."

Many members of that amorphous body Choate calls its "family" are ambiguous in their feelings about Negroes at Choate. "I *guess* I wish we had more black boys," says Malcolm Manson. "I *really* wish we had more middle-class boys here." A man high in the administration has serious doubts whether Choate is "performing a service for black students," whether the school doesn't create for them problems of adjustment to society that they should not, at their age, be asked to make, with the result that when they return to their own communities they feel at odds with their families and friends.

Charles Pierce, director of admissions, denies having heard such an argument. "That disturbs me," he says. "I have not discussed this in our meetings. It *has* been discussed by the SSAT board. If you have a big group of disadvantaged, would this defeat the purpose and advantage of their being here at the school? But certainly, there's no such feeling here on campus, at all. As I know the boys, the Negro boys, I don't see they've had any problems of adjustment, social adjustment. *Academic* adjustment, yes. We've certainly been much more tolerant. We ought to be. Have to be. I mean, bringing them back to summer school and giving them support in that way." Actually, only one black student has been brought back to summer school—"one that's not done so well since he's been here," Pierce says, "and how motivated he is, I don't know."

Many alumni are sympathetic with the black students' protest that "Choate's values are not ours" because they feel Choate has no business taking Negroes at all. Others oppose scholarships of *any* kind because for each bright, impecunious boy that Choate accepts one fewer of their well-heeled, dim-witted offspring can find a place. "Why should *I* support a school that takes a penniless Negro instead of my boy?" an alumnus asks as he blots his thousand-dollar check to Bob Jones University. Why indeed? Choate weighs his protest carefully.

Nearly half of Choate's students are opposed to any greater effort on the part of the school to recruit or accept more Negro applicants. Donald Bullitt, the conservative senior, speaks for many of them when he says: "Some teachers here profess very liberal ideas, but they have closed minds. You try to bring up a conservative viewpoint, they really knock it down. It's dangerous to have a teacher like that. Say Mr. Rice was teaching urban affairs. Mr. Rice is very much with the Negro cause, from the Negro's point of view."

David Rice is, in fact, white, a young faculty member devoted to developing some awareness of black consciousness at Choate. Once a boy asked for Rice's help in arranging a Negro roommate for the following year. "The boy's father," Rice said, "feels that not only do we not need Negroes, but that it was too bad the Nazis didn't finish off the Jews. Choate may be concerned with the welfare of both the student and the school, but it won't say, 'He rooms with a Negro.' The parents would jerk their kid out of school."

"If you went to Rice," Don says, "you'd get the Negro's

point of view. Especially now, these days, students are looking for an argument they can easily support—*then they'll close their minds to the other side.* That's why I don't think the school should support teaching social concern. Nobody should give you books like this to read"—he flourishes a copy of the Kerner report on urban disorders—"because this is a biased book, too. It's from one point of view, the point of view of riot conditions. Now you can teach this book from a very unbiased viewpoint, or you can teach it from the Negro's point of view."

"We can be accused of tokenism," says William St. John, the school's director of scholarship funds. Bill St. John is a cousin of the headmaster and, perhaps more than anyone else at the school, exemplifies its professed concern of care, even love, for the boys who come there. He is always confessing frustration and failure: "We take but a handful compared to what we could take if we had the money." That year Choate spent $167,500 helping 84 boys of whom "only thirteen or fourteen could be described as disadvantaged." The rest come from middle-class families—Choate's vertebrae—who could not afford the tariff, but it is these families, the families with incomes of $20,000 to $25,000, who will find it hardest to get scholarship aid in the future as the trend in scholarships goes more and more toward helping the very poor. No one at Choate wants to lose the sons of these families, but the school is committed to doing *something* to help American Indians, Puerto Ricans, and Negroes who, in urban public schools throughout the nation, come out of the twelfth grade more than three years behind white students in verbal achievement and more than five years behind them in mathematical development. Bill St. John aims at a scholarship fund of $250,000, but even that, when obtained, will not be enough because tuition will have gone up, and of course, black ghetto students require *more* scholarship money than the mildly poor offspring of the middle class. That year eleven Choate boys received more than $3,000 apiece in scholarships; because Choate has always aimed at giving larger grants to fewer boys, its percentage of boys on scholarship funds does not compare favorably with many schools.

"The frustrations," Bill St. John sighed as he tried to explain to a gathering of Choate mothers what the scholarship program is all about. "The almost certain knowledge that our token effort can never have enough ripple effect to be truly significant. The glimpse, too, that maybe Choate isn't even an answer. We thought so, six years ago. We thought: sure, take a boy out of his environment, give him our brand of education, pass him on to college, and part of his problem is solved. But what if that boy on vacation has to take the abuse of his black buddies because he is an Uncle Tom? Are we, as one Dartmouth black suggested, creating schizophrenic people who conform one way at Choate and another way on 125th Street? Is it then fair to admit them?"

Five years earlier, Bill St. John, together with representatives from thirty other independent schools, met at Andover to set up a talent search program designed to find black students in the ghettos who could cope with the level of education taught at preparatory schools. The program is called A Better Chance, or ABC. St. John and his colleagues hired a Negro from the Harvard School of Education to help them find the boys, and wangled $2,000,000 from the federal government through the Office of Economic Opportunity.

Each summer, candidates for places at preparatory schools are brought to the campus at Williams or Dartmouth for an indoctrination program. The boys have all taken the SSAT test, the same test every applicant to Choate must take, and invariably they do extremely badly with it. Choate regularly turns down white applicants who score in the 90's on this test and feels that a boy who scores lower than 65 in the verbal part cannot cope with the work he will encounter at the school. For its ABC boys, however—and there were four at Choate that year—the school considers a grade of 30 the cutoff point. Boys who score lower than 30 don't get into Choate. Some schools are more adventurous in accepting risky students, but Choate is proud that it has not yet failed with any of its ghetto boys, though it has come very close to failure.

During the summer, the boys are trained in basic learning skills. Their dossiers are submitted to the member schools. Each dossier contains test scores, notes on family background, a school guidance counseling recommendation, and a note from some kind of sponsor—usually a settlement house officer, a minister, or a policeman. The dossier also contains an essay the boy has written in answer to the question: "Who is the man who has most influenced you in your life?" That man is almost always a settlement house officer, a minister, or a policeman. Schools can reject the dossiers they see, and others will be submitted. Invariably, boys are accepted because they impress the schools with their character, their motivation, their *durability*. One boy, accepted that year at Choate, came from a Trenton slum. His father, nearly blind, hasn't worked since 1957; nor can his mother work. There are nine other children in the family. This boy shined shoes and worked a paper route to earn the money to buy clothes to go to school; his studies suffered because he had to keep dropping out to earn more money. He was fourteen years old, and when he got to Choate he was unable to do a single pull-up in the physical exam. He found it hard to believe that for the first term in five courses he would be given sixteen books; in his Trenton school he was lent five books which had to last the entire year.

That year the federal government, pleading economy, dropped its support of the ABC program. Bill St. John hopes private corporations can be found to take up the slack.

Black families from slum areas do, of course, apply directly to Choate for scholarship aid. "As a parent who has tried to consider all aspects of her son's development," one mother wrote,

> I have many questions. First I must state that we are Negro; we are financially deficient though, to the best of my knowledge, not culturally deprived; and we are a part of the American divorce

> statistics. In view of these facts, attendance at Choate may seem a rather lofty ambition. However, my son is bright and has a potential which I feel could not be developed in New York City's public schools.

As he always does, Bill St. John wrote back with grace and encouragement. "The warmth of your letter of December 29th," replied the mother, "started our new year with the brightest conceivable beginning." Many letters followed, as St. John brought the boy's case forward, toward that crucial meeting in spring when all scholarships are decided. As the day drew near, the mother wrote again:

> Given this opportunity, I have no doubt that John will make a positive and significant contribution to his society, and perhaps humanity itself. I am wonderfully blessed to have a child like John. He is bright and loving, and his assets heavily outweigh his liabilities.
>
> If a mother's faith can influence your committee, then tell them that this mother's faith is limitless, and not without justification.

How could the son of such a mother be rejected? When she received notice of his acceptance, the mother wrote: "John feels he's leaving home to join friends in a marvelous adventure in growth and devleopment." This mother understands Choate's language.

Sometimes such boys must be turned away. One, who came from the slums of Rochester, New York, was "according to the criteria we have set up, undoubtedly very close to the line," but if the boy was a bit weak, the mother was not. "Tom must understand," Bill St. John wrote in February, "that I still have faith in him; he must also realize that the race is a swift one, the competition excessively keen. But I hope you can sense my particular disappointment." Tom's mother replied:

> Thank you so much for your kind letter of non-acceptance. It was a blessing and an opportunity for you to grant us an interview last fall otherwise we never would have had the wonderful visit

and experience we gained. Tom preferred you and your school but I explained to him that sometimes one doesn't do well on a single test and he shouldn't become discouraged.

He received the scores from the SSAT and he was shocked. I told him he could take it again next year. He is so eager and conscientious and I told him he would make it even though we aren't financially able. He does quite well in music so I told him maybe an opportunity might open up for him. I pointed out that character and attitude was more important than marks in the 90's and to keep his hopes high.

May God bless you as much as he blesses us.

"The lovely thing about this job," Bill St. John replied, "is that I associate with superior people of understanding, patience, and wisdom. You are one of them." The mother took this cue to write back assuring Choate that Tom would curb whatever immaturity he might have if he could get into the school, that the family would repay Choate later, and that Tom's older brother had offered to quit school and go to work to help pay for it.

Bill St. John tried to persuade ABC to take Tom in its program. ABC declined, but St. John persisted until they did take him. In that way, Tom got to Choate. "God knows my heart," his mother wrote, "but all I can utter is heartfelt thanks." Then she wrote Bill St. John five letters in seven days—"The cardinal was sitting in a tree and his song was full of praise and Thanksgiving—or is it I? That reminds me of Tom's expression, 'I'm going there and be a radiant light bulb.' "

"I think I'd make the same choice again," says Joe Rigney, a senior who is the unofficial leader of the black students at Choate. "I made a lot of sacrifices coming here, but now, especially in my senior year, I feel they have been worth it."

Joe is discreet almost to the point of wariness, but some of his fellow black students make it clear, to the few who care to listen, what some of the sacrifices are:

- Listening to white Choate students say, "Shine my shoes, boy."

• Listening to the headmaster invite students who are not happy at Choate, who do not approve of what the school stands for, to leave on the next train. "It's okay for him to say we should leave if we're not happy—*but we have no choice!*" Except, of course, to go back to the ghetto.

• Listening to an administration that reminds them that, by virtue of accepting scholarships, they have limited, if not completely abdicated, their right to complain. "It seems to me," one black student said, "that once we have the scholarship, we ought to be equal with everyone else."

• Listening to their friends in the ghetto at home kid them about their establishment manners, their WASP-y way of talking. "We *have* changed," one told me. "We *do* talk differently. Our friends say: 'Hey, Unc! Is your name *Thomas?*' Sure, they accuse us of selling out to Whitey—and we think we have, too. We don't want to be actors at home. We want to reassimilate ourselves, but we don't have time."

By spring, three of Choate's black students were seriously thinking of not returning to Choate in the fall.

Joe Rigney, though, has made it. He will go to Harvard next year, and that is a long way from the slums of Youngstown, Ohio, where he attended public schools until a group of black businessmen sent him to a private school. "A lot of people have a tough decision whether to continue in public school or to come to prep school," Joe says, "but in my case it was made a little easier because I'd never have gone on to anything if I hadn't come here. My high school has probably sent one person to Harvard in twenty-five years."

Joe is slender, more articulate, more mature than most Choate boys. His expression is a calm study—a careful blend of impassive courtesy and alert intelligence—but his hands are long and delicate and move quickly, nervously; he pays them no attention. On the walls of his room hang large pictures of Malcolm X and H. Rap Brown and a poster: PENETRATE PENN.

"Choate has given me a better understanding of white society," Joe says. He, and all of Choate's other blacks, are ruefully aware that the experience has not been reciprocal. Choate, they know, stands for assimilation, a chance for blacks to learn something, as much as they are capable of learning, about being white. Choate, at least as a whole, has no interest in learning about being black, and many teachers and students feel that it is a waste of time for black kids, given a chance to learn about, and be treated like, Whitey, to spend precious hours studying negritude, or whatever—the kind of stuff they could hardly help learning in the slums they came from. Some Choate teachers couldn't understand why the black students didn't, for heaven's sake, *forget* they were black while they were at Choate, a place where they would be treated the same as if they were white. Some people, of course, having had a lot of trouble in their lives, just go right on making problems for themselves, and though it wouldn't do to say so (we might be misunderstood), this black business is boring at best and something of a, well, threat at worst.

"I'm not entirely sure that a white man is capable of learning how a Negro feels," Joe says. Carmichael, Hamilton, Cleaver—most other black militants—would agree with him, and with some justice: we know what *you* are, buddy, because we have had to live in your society, but you've never looked at us; you haven't a clue. "I don't feel that I have any very close white friends," says Joe, "that I can really talk about anything with. I don't say that it's an impossibility, but I still don't have any. I know the seniors in this house"—they are white—"pretty well, probably as well as I've known anybody here. We talk over different things in bull sessions—Vietnam, for example, or black power. He may *think* his point of view is the same as mine, but I think my being black has in a way hindered my ability to communicate with him, the white boys here. I still have a few close friends at home that I can just relax with and talk about things that I could never discuss here, they just wouldn't understand.

"I can almost forget the race business in a few things. For example, in classes, when we're talking about literature and abstract ideas—these apply to just about everybody. It may not be *my* literature, but I don't feel that it has nothing to do with me. I feel it *is* literature and it helps me to know about it, but it has no specific relation to me." In fact, Joe has been reading books by black authors in his spare time and suggesting that they be included in Choate's curriculum: Stokeley Carmichael's *Black Power, The Autobiography of Malcolm X,* Lerone Bennett's *Before the Mayflower.*

"It's not so much forgetting race, it's the attitude toward it," Joe says. "The answer to the race problem is not to forget that I'm black; it's to *realize* that I'm black, but that I'm not necessarily unequal in intelligence or sports ability or anything else. There have been a few minor incidents here, but I think the main thing is a lack of understanding. The race problem is *passed over.* Kids here would rather make friends with me and forget that I'm black—as if I'm a white student with a black skin. They think by doing this that we can be closer friends, and this will impress me into forgetting the race problem.

"To *be* a Negro has changed in the past few years. And this is a peculiar place to be while becoming aware of that change. Ever since I've been at Choate I've missed being at home, and feelings of black identity. I've felt misplaced here. I was always hoping that it was going to work out that the sacrifices I was making would be outweighed by the benefits. A lot of times I was pretty doubtful about it. Last year a man from the ABC program asked me a lot of questions and I gave him some pretty vague answers because I wasn't sure myself."

But that fall Joe went down to look at Columbia, one of his two top college choices. He met a Choate graduate who had become a member of the militant black student movement at Columbia; the alumnus spent a lot of time talking to Joe, and an idea began to form in the back of Joe's mind. "He had changed so much since he had been here," Joe said. "He felt he didn't see anything here. It was almost as if he had been brainwashed; his social consciousness was *asleep;* he just didn't realize things he believes he realizes now. He's done a tremendous amount of reading, and discussions with other students there, and is a member of the Afro-American Society. This is what got me interested in doing such things here. He made me feel that *I* hadn't seen much before, and that *I* had a lot to learn about American society and racism and race relations. He said he thought it would be a good idea if we had some discussions up here."

In this way black power came to Choate. For a long time many white students, and some masters, would be confused, wondering just what *had* happened, and why. Student Council members reported to a concerned headmaster rumors that the blacks had threatened mass retaliation against any Choate boy who picked on them or made racial slurs again. Then, just before Joe went to Columbia, somebody put up a sign on a bulletin board saying that there would be a meeting of the ABC students at Choate. Few people knew what ABC meant and, among all the other bulletins of obscure intent and even ominous purpose, this one might have gone unnoticed, but someone figured out that ABC stood for Advancement of Black Choaties and reported the matter to Peter Tower, in whose dormitory the sign had appeared. Tower took it down. "Naturally," says Joe, "he thought this was pretty serious. Next morning he spoke to me about it for about half an hour. This especially helped me realize that we should get together to discuss things among ourselves."

Joe read some of the books suggested to him by the alumnus at Columbia, then called the other black students together for a series of meetings. Pete Tower told Joe that he thought this was a bad idea. "He said that the black power movement had no meaning at Choate. Everyone had equal opportunity here. I don't think," Joe says, "that he realized there was a need for us to discuss what black identity *was*."

The old "Who am I?" question sidles across the horizon of every adolescent. Some feel the question must be stormed, shaken, and kicked until a provisional answer has been gouged from it. Others, a large majority, turn away from it, perhaps with the only metaphysical shudder they will ever feel. Neither approach is particularly satisfactory, but there is a kind of moral aggression to the former that one might think schools would encourage, and they *do*, in a rather general and gentlemanly way, but there are proper forms to be filed for every crisis, and few schools are prepared for boys like Joe Rigney who bandy the question about in a way that attracts public notice. "Who am I?" may be an essential question, but it is also just the least bit vulgar. It is the kind of thing one asks in a closet or under the blankets after lights are out. To make one's interest in the problem a matter of public record is like shouting "I want to be like Jesus" in church, or like being caught examining one's genitals in a mirror. Others, embarrassed for you, will find an explanation. All through that year Choate's black students would patiently explain that they met to discuss black *identity,* not black power, that they met to talk black and think black and laugh black for an hour or two, in a way they could not ordinarily do at Choate, where black students make up one-fifty-sixth of the student population, and all through the year, they were told that black *power* had no place at Choate.

Tower told Joe that there might be a need for such meetings in the ghetto, where Negroes needed to acquire pride, but not at Choate. "He gave me all the reasons why it would be a bad idea," Joe says, "bad for the school and bad for us: Choate runs on public relations, and no matter *what* we did, bad connotations would go out—black power. Southern parents, even if their children weren't necessarily prejudiced, *they* would be, and wouldn't look on this too well. We might hurt ourselves by limiting the number of black students that would be accepted in the future. He mentioned *that.* And a few other things. There's so much tradition locked up here that people are very reluctant to change anything. It seems even more at Choate than at other prep schools. Mr. Tower felt he was best equipped, being my public affairs teacher, to know about the problem since he felt he knew more about the black community than most people here."

Tower told Joe to take up the matter with the headmaster. Joe believes that Tower assumed the headmaster would respond from the gut—his wife is from Virginia—but such assumptions are dangerous. The headmaster can stun the students with a conservative reaction, but it is usually not his first reaction; he is quite willing to let his kids try things out, make mistakes.

"This is where Seymour is a genius," says Robert Atmore, one of the most astute headmaster-watchers on the faculty. "He'll take risks on the Student Council. He's a mile ahead of anybody else in progressive thinking, in liberalism. The problem for him is that if he shows it too much, everyone will get all in a fuss. He's got to lead very carefully." In the case of Choate's Afro-American Society, St. John made what may have been his best decision of the year: he told Joe to go ahead.

The reaction in school was mixed, ranging from total opposition to confusion. "I've never felt that there's been much prejudice here," said the head of the student Honor Committee. "I've heard guys telling race jokes, but I've never seen a direct insult to a colored boy. I think Joe feels a little self-conscious. He seems self-conscious all the time; it might just be the way he is. Maybe quite a few of them are. I don't see any reason for them meeting as a group." That was the typical liberal argument, freighted with unconscious racism. A more ingenious attack, advanced by "moderates" who really wanted to stop the society, held that all groups, clubs, and societies at Choate were required to be open to any interested student and so the Afro-American Society should be outlawed—not only because it is exclusive, but because it is clearly racist. That argument nearly prevailed in the fall of 1968 when, after a bitter debate, the faculty approved the society's charter. Shortly thereafter, a small advertisement, apparently written by a student of the words and thoughts of the late Dr. Goebbels, appeared in the *Choate News:*

IF IT BE BIGOTRY THEY WANT,
THEN IT SHALL BE BIGOTRY THEY GET

The Afro-American Society has gotten its charter approved by the Student Council and the Faculty, despite the fact that the society is excluding white students from membership. Since the school seems to be condoning bigotry and segregation, we announce the formation of an Anglo-American Society. It will publicly promote White power, and privately promote race SOLIDARITY. We are not bigots. We merely wish to emulate the example set by the Afro-Americans, who seem to have concluded that segregation really is best. We trust that the Anglo-American will be welcomed by those liberals and Negroes who backed the Afro-American Society.

[signed] Choate's Enlightened Liberals.

In fact, the Anglo-American Society had had an abortive birth the preceding spring. As usual, Don Bullitt, the conservative senior, had a great deal to say about what the blacks were doing. "I think this school is not set up to represent any minority point of view," he said, forgetting that there is no minority as small as rich and well-connected reactionaries. "When a minority bands together and excludes the majority, then there's something wrong, basically, in their attitude in a free academic society. We're not here to represent the Negro population; we're here to learn. What's the Afro-American Society going to do? It's going to tear this school apart. In an academic community, and I think Mr. St. John would agree with me, we're here to treat each other as individuals and learn what we can from individuals, not from masses. That's what I feel like every time I talk to a Negro boy in the school now—that I'm talking to them all at once. It scares me."

To restore his courage, Don proposed an Anglo-American Society. "It was a way to express my dissatisfaction with a minority group seeking club status," Don says. "We would have discussed problems of civil rights, but we would have excluded blacks. I wasn't very serious about the idea. I just wanted to make my point—how would *they* like it?"

"We learn," Joe Rigney says. "We get to see exactly why white people feel the way they do. We get a firsthand view of the white establishment. This will help later on. We're getting more angry and more militant all the time."

Partly in response to questions from white students who wanted to know what "went on" in their secret meetings, Choate's black students, late in April, held an open meeting of their society. The lecture room in St. John Hall was packed to overflowing—perhaps 120 boys and masters had squeezed in. Some

Southerners sat in the back and talked among themselves. One boy waved a fist sheathed in a white glove. Choate's ten Negroes faced this scene from the podium, wearing expressions of varying concern. Some were impassive and silent, others smiled and joked, one sat with an anguished look, straining to communicate without words. Joe Rigney presided, flashing his long and nervous hands.

Don Bullitt began by reading an interminable speech. For a while it looked as if, once again, the blacks were going to do the listening, the whites the talking. Don pleaded for the plight of "the lower-middle-class white man" and denounced the blacks for "stooping to violence."

Negro student: Do you think America would be a so-called free nation if it weren't for the violence of the Revolutionary War?

Then the exchanges came, between the blacks and the whites:

Negro student: We've been denied an education.

White student: Isn't it also true that many of you people dropped out of school because you couldn't do the work? (Hoots of anger from crowd—"Don't dignify that with a reply"—more hoots.)

Negro (heatedly) : *This* is the way the Negro in America is now being treated! (He pauses, embarrassed.) *So-called* Negro, excuse me. (Raucous laughter, particularly from Southerners in back.)

Negro: There's a theory in America that Afro-Americans have to be controlled.

White: After Watts, wouldn't *you* say it was a good idea to keep an eye on things?

Negro: Watts is not an effect. . . .

White (cutting him off) : Newark? *Detroit?*

Negro: Watts was spontaneous.

White: They were *all* spontaneous?

Negro: Yes. We don't have plots like white men have. (Laughter.)

White: I think a Negro should put himself in the shoes of the white man to see what *his* problems look like.

Negro: We can't afford those shoes. (Laughter, applause.)

Another Negro: If you're Italian, and your name is Mariano, and you don't like it, you can change your name to Jackson. You can walk down Broadway and another white man will see you only as a white man. But a Negro walking down Broadway, we have what is called high visibility.

White: Change your name to Mariano. (Laughter from the back.)

Negro (angry now): That's not what we need in America! People standing around making useless remarks. (Louder laughter, whistles.)

Another Negro: No other minority in America went through anything comparable to slavery!

White: The American Indian.

Negro: Yeah, and see how many there are left.

One white boy asked about racism at Choate. "We'd rather not go into that," said Joe Rigney, but the audience cried "Go into it!" so one of the black students answered.

"Well, first of all, the students. Look at 'soul men.' You know what soul is. Well, we seem to have a collection of soul men of the white variety among us. Who, when they see one of us, they say, 'Hey, man, I'm a soul man,' and we're supposed to be impressed. If you're going to accept our music, accept us. These soul men will listen to our music in their homes, but they won't associate with 'niggers.'

"I'll go into another specific. During football season I was in the locker room, the only black person in the locker room. The boys were discussing Stokeley Carmichael, Rap Brown, and so-called Cassius Clay, and one guy, when he heard about Carmichael, he said verbatim: 'Why, those dirty, no-good, black nig—' and then he saw me, and he choked on the word 'nigger.' And right after practice, he came back into the locker room, turned on the radio to someone singing 'I'm a Soul Man.' "

Another Negro said: "Notice during third period all those white boys lying out there in the sun. They're getting *brown,* that nice brown color."

"Coming back on the train," said another, "I heard one of

the boys explain to one of us: 'Get to the back of the bus, black nigger.' "

"At a student dance at Greenwich Academy," another said, "I was the only Negro there, and every time I tried to dance with an attractive-looking white girl, certain members of the Choate School cut in as soon as they could, to save her from my presence, or possibly my evilness. Or maybe she'd get *infected.*"

This was too much for Don Bullitt, who was on his feet. "I was at a girls' school dance and there was this boy from Exeter, who was colored, asked, 'Where is my date?' Well, there were no colored girls at the dance, so one girl who was there said, 'I'll be glad to be his date'—just to be kind to him."

Negro: To be *kind* to him? (Uproar, laughter.)

Don: Hold it! Stop laughing!

Negro: What do you *mean,* to be *kind* to him?

Don: They hadn't planned on him being there. She was kind enough to be his date. What do you think he did?

Negro: What *did* he do? You were there. You tell me.

Don: I'll tell you what he did. He was arrogant the whole night long. Just like you, when you look at us or talk to us, or when we try to show you some understanding. (Derisive laughter.) Now the girl obviously came from a family where it was very hard for her to dance with a Negro. You have to accept this. He *forced* himself on that girl. We have to be careful with things like this. You can't expect people—

Negro (jeering): He *pushed* himself on that girl, yet she decided to give herself!

Joe Rigney changed the subject. Throughout the evening he had kept matters very cool, squashing his own men and showing no emotion, no emotion to all, to anything said by the whites. "We want to be part of a better American society," Joe concluded. "That's our hope."

After two hours, David Rice broke up the meeting—it was everybody's bedtime. "I suggest," he called loudly as the students filed out, "that everybody read every conceivable book by a Negro author they can get their hands on."

"Once a teacher, always a teacher," said a white boy.

That spring a course in the history of minority groups in America was announced for the fall. Ten boys were needed, but only four signed up for it and it was not given. The following year, however, the black students were angrier and more militant. In February, 1969, the *Choate News* ran a centerfold spread of scraps of prose and poetry, most of it by the thirteen black students at Choate that year. "Don't shoot until you see the eyes of the whites," said the most succinct of the maxims. Others, as Choate students do so often, tried poetry:

If not now, soon.
It will come.
Be patient.
We've waited four hundred years
To see you burn.
Be patient.
It will come.

Eenie meenie, minie mo
Catch a honkie by the throat
If he hollers nigger . . . cut it.

The light of Truth and Freedom
Now Shines bright in the rising
flames Of your Cremation.

This was too much for the headmaster, who had just recently announced a plan to establish an Afro-American Studies Center at Choate, similar to the Russian Studies Center. St. John "took a chapel evening," as he likes to say, on the subject: "As you intended," he told the black students, "you have given us pause. The naked hostility of some of your phrases is deeply disturbing. Do not mistake me; we are not intimidated." There are, St. John continued, greater values to lose than buildings and lives; what he feared was that blacks would alienate the whites altogether. "We too feel," St. John said. "Our greatest need is to feel together." Once again, he came to the theme he has sounded so often: "Our common values are universal, human values. . . . In *every* student there are not only human weaknesses, but qualities of fineness, elements of greatness. We must count on these qualities in you—qualities far deeper than race or creed to help us all toward a goal that is bigger than any of us. We believe the balance in you and in us is on the side of that goal. If we are right, we shall indeed overcome." He then asked that the boys rise to sing "America the Beautiful."

"A philosophy of racial harmony that dates back to the Civil Rights Movement," grumbled the *Choate News* as it peered deep into history for its editorial reply. "Overly vague. . . . Refusing to address himself to those he was obviously speaking to." It was indeed a tired speech. Once again, St. John extolled individualism while denying the legitimacy of diversity. No one can quite understand just how he does this; no one can grasp how a man of such limitless good will invariably falls upon arguments that antagonize those who have offended him.

"Put it over there," said a faculty wife, smiling at two black students struggling with a bulletin board. When they had left, she sighed. "They're really very nice," she said, "but they *are* shiftless! I mean, irresponsible, won't ever do more than they have to. Still, they're very quiet. They could cause so much trouble if they wanted to. We're very lucky."

Choate Goes to Pot

> That's policy for you. Policy is what the kingpins want. What the others want is juvenile delinquency.
>
> JOHN UPDIKE, "A&P"

"I was told in the morning," Jack Deal, a senior, said. "Bill Hart was on my floor. There were several boys not in class, Student Council members, but nobody knew there was a Student Council meeting." The day was Friday, October 9, less than three weeks after classes had begun. "I took a shower early in the morning," Jack said, "and took a shave, and a boy came into the bathroom and said, 'Is it really true that Bill Hart is being kicked out for marijuana?' And I said, 'What's this? I haven't heard a thing about this.' " Jack smokes pot regularly at Choate. "And he said, *'Is it true?'* and I said, 'I don't know,' so I went to talk to Bill and he said he wasn't allowed to say. I got enough out of him to know it wasn't drinking or smoking, so it had to be the other. We got down to it, and he said, 'Well, nobody is supposed to know.' "

"Two weeks ago," the headmaster told the trustees when they met for their regular fall conference on October 20, "we had our first brush with marijuana. We've been lucky up to this point, I think."

But one of the faculty insists: "I told the headmaster last spring about boys smoking pot on campus. I had conclusive evidence. He didn't pay any attention. He didn't want to know."

"This is the first time," the headmaster told the trustees,

"that, knowingly at least, we've had any marijuana within the school."

The best estimate given by boys smoking marijuana at Choate is that pot came to the campus three years ago. Last spring, about fifteen boys were smoking it regularly, if discreetly, in their rooms.

Three boys were involved in the October scandal, all of them fifth formers. Bill, who lives in Mexico City, had paid 80 cents for a vial of what he was told was marijuana—enough for 20 or 30 joints—which he brought back to Choate. Bill told Jack Deal that he had never smoked marijuana in his life—"What's it all about, Jack?"—but added that he had been accosted in a Mexican park by a pot pimp or something, had bought the stuff because he had a friend at Choate who bragged about his pot-smoking prowess, and gave it to him in what Jack calls "a sort of an effort to be one of the cool guys." Bill didn't try it himself, but his friend, and his friend's roommate, rolled the pot (or whatever it really was) into cigarettes and smoked them. Because marijuana gives off a sweet-smelling smoke, the boys confused the scent by burning a little incense in their room. For some time masters had wondered why some boys became interested in incense burning, for heaven's sake, and now that they know, they have made a rule against it.

Just about then, another friend, attracted by the smell of incense, walked in and caught them at it. Unhappily, this boy was part of the school establishment, a member of the Honor Committee, so he had no choice: turn yourselves in to the dean, he said, or I will have to report you myself. That was on Saturday evening, October 3.

By Wednesday, nothing had happened. The Honor Committee boy, grappling with his conscience, spent two hours with David Rice, the faculty member most trusted by the boys to provide an opinion which is not only just but uncontaminated by establishment ethics. The boy then went to the three offenders and presented his ultimatum: report to the dean by Thursday noon, or be reported. The boys yielded. On Friday morning the Student Council met; by 10 A.M. it had agreed to expel the boys.

There was, however, the legal problem. "This had overtones, of course, of illegality," St. John told the trustees, "since it is illegal." Usually boys are expelled from Choate for offenses like smoking or cheating that are not illegal, but are against the school's rules. If a boy is caught stealing, restitution is made so quickly that the discipline is rarely severe. The father of one of the pot smokers was a lawyer and asked a sticky question: "Have you tested this out? Do you know it *was* marijuana?" "Well, no," said St. John, "we don't. All we know is that the boys thought it was." Six days had intervened since the boys had been caught; understandably, they had disposed of the evidence. But it didn't matter: smoking of any kind is illegal at Choate, so the boys were expelled for smoking.

Still, the more Choate thought about the problem, the more complex it became. What, the Student Council asked, should the school do? Call the cops? The FBI? They decided to call Yale's attorney instead. Call the cops, said Yale's attorney; that's what Yale did, and the cops don't move unless somebody is selling the stuff. So Choate called Wallingford's police chief, who was out of town.

By this time the school grapevine was smoldering from overwork. The boy who rings the chapel bells rang the secret, but traditional, death knell for expelled students—a long peal of discordant notes—three times.

By Saturday morning the three had left the campus and St. John decided to convene the school "to discuss the whole situation, because obviously there was a lot of rumor about it and I wanted to lay it on the line." He did. He talked about responsibility, about compromising future careers—could these boys now be employed by the Foreign Service?—and generally kept it cool, naming names and stressing that the boys had behaved foolishly.

"Obviously," St. John told the trustees, "I'm no medico, but I see a leader problem, which is a very real one. Where a boy may go up for a year in jail in Connecticut, where he might lose out in admission to the bar, to a commission in the Army, where he might lose out in any government position. This is a critical situation. There are people who come back with the fact that the law is wrong anyway. This to me is absolutely untenable. The law is the law, and if it should be changed, that's somebody's business, but in the meanwhile we should uphold it every way we can."

Most of the students took it calmly, even apathetically. So what? was the general reaction. One boy wrote a poem about it for his English class:

> We all knew a boy who loved to talk quite a lot;
> Thought he was perfect, he talked only to God.
> Then came the day he was caught with some pot.
> He hemmed and he hawed, a bad verdict to rout,
> But to no avail, for St. John kicked him out.
> And now of him no vestige is left,
> But I do not think that we are bereft.
> And we know that his life is a horrible mess,
> But it matters not; we've our happiness.

The boy who suffered most was the informer. He was the *friend* of the pot smokers, boys kept telling him. How could he have done it? The head of the Honor Committee, a sixth former and in some ways the most outstanding boy in the school, supported his colleague's action. "The pot problem," he said, "was potentially a pretty big problem. It did a lot to scare off guys. I think the way it was handled was good. Seymour's feeling was if you have to smoke marijuana, don't do it here. Lots of times I think a guy needs to be made an example of. Sometimes we give them too many chances. I think I would have reported them; they should have been kicked out. I haven't quite made up my mind. It's this problem whether a kid should get a second chance, or whether he'd just fall back. Would he be thankful for a warning, respect what I said, and not do it again? I don't know. If I see a boy with marijuana now, I don't think I have the option not to turn him in."

But the boy who forced the issue could not make peace with himself. In times of anguish that year, many boys wrote poems, and this is the poem the informer wrote:

Me the big detective.
    "I think you better come with us."
Me, another James Cagney.
Arresting Bill.
I could have warned him.
    Said I couldn't find him,
    Gotten rid of the evidence.
No, kind old me turned him in . . .
He wasn't bitter.
He knew it was my job.
My duty to Bill.
    He helped me.
    I really "helped" him. . . .
"You owe it to the 'community'."
    Damn the "Public."
What about Bill?
He's gone, dead.
    I did it.
    I did it when I owed him me!
I killed him! I killed him!

"I think the honor system works," said the head of the Honor Committee. "I think I should be a part of it; I don't really think it's a dirty job."

"We called the police on Saturday," St. John told the trustees. "On Wednesday, however, the Police Department came up in some irritation and said they understood that there was marijuana at Choate and they hadn't been notified and were in a very embarrassing position. Well, we told them the story, but we didn't give them names and they didn't insist on them. We reached an agreement with the police which we were ready for long before they came: to keep them informed on anything in connection with drugs that came up in school. I hope we never come to the point of turning a boy over to the authorities. That's something we'll have to play by ear. Of course, with every boy in school knowing the situation, this has been general talk in many places. A newspaper mentioned that three boys had been expelled from a school attended by the late President."

Two days after the boys were expelled, Dr. Dana Farnsworth, director of University Health Services at Harvard, came to Choate to talk about the problem of drugs. The boys didn't believe it, but Farnsworth's trip was not a cause-and-effect reaction; it had been planned for six months. He spoke to the younger boys in the afternoon, to the older boys in the evening. Before he arrived, the boys were busy setting up a microphone in the Speech Room under the chapel. One boy tested the acoustics: "LSD is not good for your body, and besides, the Food and Drug Administration doesn't like it. LSD stands for 'Lousy Stinking Drug.' " He popped his bubble gum.

"Drugs," said Farnsworth, are "something spreading all over the United States." Before he got to drugs, however, he offered other observations: "Boys and girls seem to be good for one another," and "Hippies—a synonym for drug takers." The boys watched him in glassy silence. Farnsworth plunged ahead: "Marijuana produces temporary psychotic episodes. People who take it begin to lose their judgment while feeling they have gained new insights. . . . Marijuana is a harmful drug. . . . A person who willingly ingests an unknown substance into his body is a seriously disturbed person." Marijuana, he went on, produced psychosis; take it long enough and you become "psychologically estranged." Possibly, there is physical damage as well. People who take marijuana become "punch-drunk boxers," nice guys who can't handle their jobs; they lose motivation and ambition. Glue-sniffing is the same: it destroys brain cells and causes mental retardation. "Why don't they take Drano?" Farnsworth asked, waving his hand at the students. "That will give them something to think about." A boy asked, politely, if Dr.

Farnsworth had had direct experience of marijuana. Dr. Farnsworth replied: "I'd as soon take marijuana as jump six hundred feet into a six-foot bucket of water." During the question period, St. John took notes. The boys thought he took notes of the names of those who seemed interested in drugs. Everyone left the auditorium much edified.

"He was tired," St. John told the trustees. "It was a tough day for him. It's interesting what the boys will accept and what they won't accept. They'll accept very direct word; they'll accept facts, but nothing of moralizing—of any sort. They'll just back right away from it. It gets their backs up and they get mad about it and they want to argue the other side of the case. So communication in that area is very tricky indeed. Fascinating. Absolutely fascinating."

Nobody thought much of Farnsworth's tirade. "It scared off the boys who wouldn't smoke it anyway," Jack Deal said. "The rest of us know better." "Marijuana is pleasurable," said one of the younger masters who smokes it from time to time. "The school should confront this when warning the boys against it."

That fall, as marijuana was driven underground at Choate, the commissioner of the United States Food and Drug Administration announced that he would rather have his daughter take pot than alcohol and teen-agers from all over the country flocked to Iowa armed with special maps of the marijuana harvest. At the Hun preparatory school in New Jersey fourteen boys were dismissed for using marijuana, and at the Masters School in Dobbs Ferry, New York, three girls were arrested and charged with "possession of a dangerous drug," meaning marijuana, and released in $1,000 bail. Meanwhile, the Gallup polls taken in colleges revealed that only 6 percent of the students had tried marijuana. Mounir Sa'adah wrote an article for a magazine describing drugs as "covers for frustrations," as "substitutes for the expression of real virility and adulthood" that "induce a state of infantilism which carries one back to the preconscious days when such care and longings did not exist." Some of the

Choate students, had they read it, would have agreed: "It's just a matter of doing something for the sake of doing something," one said.

"The head has slowed the problem down by kicking those three boys out," Jack Deal told me. "A lot of boys got rid of their pot. But he hasn't conquered the problem, because boys aren't afraid of him." Jack smoked pot all year at Choate and took my interest in it seriously. In the spring, after things had loosened up a bit, he made a survey of his friends and came up with the following figures: 33 boys at Choate were smoking pot on campus. Four of them were fifth formers, one a fourth former; the rest were seniors. Pot was being sold on campus and boys were looking forward to turning on during the big spring dance, hopefully with their dates. Jack's figures were supported by the student poll in which 110 Choate students, answering anonymously, admitted to smoking pot at home, and 24 at school. Only 8 confessed to smoking it "more than ten times" at Choate, but 6 students, known to be pot smokers, told the president of the *Choate News,* who conducted the poll, that they had ignored the question. Half of the school expressed a willingness to smoke marijuana "in a certain situation," whatever that meant, and 32 boys admitted they would take LSD as well.

Jack believes some boys take speed, of which he disapproves. "You can take speed in pills, you can smoke it, you can eat it in peanut butter cookies," Jack said. But he is not surprised that no boy was ever caught with speed. He himself has screened the seeds from marijuana in his room at Choate and never worries: "Masters never know what they are looking at." He and his friends make jokes about being stoned in movies, about being discovered lying on the floor—stoned again—when masters walk into their rooms. The school doctor was unaware that when he handed out Darvan, a pain-killer, to boys with "injured muscles," the boys would cut it up to extract the white powder inside, which they would then mix with marijuana for an extra high. They used Soma, a tranquilizer, for "a four- or five-hour trip"; even Elixir Terpenhydrate, Jack assures me, "is good for a short trip if you drink a lot."

"Now from the easy one," said St. John to his trustees, "I'll give you the hard one. About three days later a boy who was asked to write a report, who had a free season for creative writing, handed in a complete play-by-play account of having taken a tablet of LSD. The boy was obviously overwrought and felt he had to get this off his chest."

"The way it started originally," said Jack Deal, "was that Tom's housemaster went to Seymour and told him, 'There's a very weird kid on this floor.' He's the least weird kid I've ever known," Jack said with a sigh. Jack is a large boy, but unexpectedly mild in his speech and in his actions. Inside, he is wound up so tightly you can almost hear the sinews creak and, on occasion, snap, like a violin string turned just a bit too far. Jack rarely has a harsh word for anyone, but speaks of wanting to love other people, and of finding love and simplicity very difficult at Choate. Life's little formalities—like tucking in a shirttail or getting into a good college—baffle Jack, who wants only to live without thinking of any of this crap. "A boy of some unusual ability," wrote Seymour St. John in a report, "but in my opinion not yet in touch with the hard realities of life." Actually, Jack has not only touched these realities, he's had his fingers bashed by them. Jack senses he's on his way to becoming a loser, but he won't admit that the condition is real. In a little more than a year, he will be dead.

"Anyway," said Jack, "the housemaster said Tom was 'doing very weird things. He has flowers in his room and he likes colored lights.' " Jack shook his head in disbelief. "I heard him telling Count Stillman this, too. He said Tom didn't participate, had a negative attitude. He didn't come out and *say* he was an acid head."

This particular master bugs Jack. He has a dog who pees in the corridor, and in class he once taunted a boy who had argued that marijuana was not habit-forming. "If you can quit smoking pot for a week, let me know," the master said. That shook the boy, who does smoke it. The same master has charged Jack with smoking pot. Jack thinks he's bluffing, but is fearful there may be a leak.

Word that Tom Liddell was "weird" reached the headmaster, so when Tom's English teacher came in to say he had a report of an LSD trip "written in confidence," the headmaster could ask quickly, "Was it Tom Liddell?" which astonished the teacher, who swallowed and said yes.

Jack was with Tom when he was on his trip. Tom took the pill at the midmorning break between classes. Nobody noticed any change in his behavior. "The most shocking thing to me is that I didn't know he was up," says Jack. "He went through the day very pleasantly. It was such a nice, quiet trip that nobody noticed it, not even me, and I was his best friend."

After lunch Tom seemed moody—a common enough condition for anyone in Jack's circle of friends—so they went walking in the woods behind the infirmary. "Toward four o'clock," Jack says, "he really started going up high, very, very high, to the point where he was getting lost. We had some pot and we were smoking that." Sometimes pot helps control the fluctuations of an LSD trip—or so the boys believe. "It helps bring you down," Jack says, "instead of all of a sudden dropping and having a terrible crash you can get high enough on pot and come down gradually. You have a pot letdown instead of an LSD letdown."

But at that time Jack didn't know Tom was bouncing along beside him, lost in his secret trip. Then Tom started to "go up" alarmingly and Jack said: "You seem to be very strange!"

"Haven't you noticed?" Tom asked happily. "I took some."

"What?" Jack asked.

"I took some of the acid."

"God," said Jack, "you didn't tell me. I didn't notice. What on earth did you do something like that for?"

Tom said, "Well, I had it and I wanted to try it. It was a nice day and I just took it."

Jack was worried. "Let's taper off on the pot," he said.

"We were having beautiful sights," Jack told me later. "And

every once in a while terrible things would happen to Tom. He'd get lost looking at a leaf or something. I would coax him down, like a child—in that tone, you know—being very nice to him."

But walking back toward school, Tom "got lost in a certain tree. He thought the tree was trying to kill him. It was a large evergreen, about half dead. We had been looking at plants in the nurseries and Tom was reading them, telling me what they spelled. Some pretty fantastic stuff, something about war. Then he jumped over a hedge, and right over the hedge there was the tree that kind of bothered him extremely. I said, 'Tom? Tom?' and he said, 'Look at it! It's going to kill me!' So we got away from there and I assured him I had killed the tree. That bothered him a little, that I had killed it. We got talking about the fact that there are good trees and evil trees and this was one of the very, very evil trees."

They went back to school for chapel and dinner because attendance is taken at both places and Tom, with his brains blowing fuses in his skull, could hardly afford to have people looking for him. "We got through with that as soon as possible," Jack says. "Then we walked around for a while. He was still further up than he should have been. And still pretty freaked out. Pretty scared. Dinner is a bad place at Choate, dinner and chapel, after you've been up. They're extremely scary and you get very paranoiac."

Then Jack conceived a lunatic plan: take Tom to see his best friend on the faculty, John Joseph. Joseph is as astute and observant as any master at Choate. Many boys find talking to masters as difficult as sailing through Antarctic waters: ice is always forming over every surface and has to be painstakingly chipped away. Joseph senses this. He talks to boys as if they are interesting human beings and really listens to what they say. But he enjoys putting boys a bit off balance, too, and because of this he may not have been aware of just how scrambled Tom's wits were at the moment.

"Tom?" Joseph asked, as soon as he was introduced. "What's your favorite color?"

There was an anguished silence while Tom tried to think of a color, any color. "Blue," he said.

"Who's your favorite poet?"

A long pause, followed by uh's. "Uh. Uh. Dylan Thomas."

"This kind of mixed Tom up," Jack said, but Joseph took mercy and brewed some tea. "We drank tea and Tom got very confused sitting on the couch," Jack said. "Mr. Joseph is a very wonderful person and under most circumstances it would have been fine. I was trying to hold up the conversation and answer for Tom, but it was difficult, and when he nudged me, I knew it was time to go."

Tom woke the next morning in an "almost suicidal" frame of mind. He called his parents and asked to be withdrawn; they refused, pointing out that they had paid for the entire term. But the next day, Tom was cheerful again. He had had a beautiful trip, he told Jack: there were "a lot of doors" that had opened. Tom had enough LSD for seven more trips, so he, Jack, and another boy debated whether they should all try it. Finally, Tom decided he would not take it again, "so we went and flushed the rest down the toilet in sort of a little ceremony."

That would have ended it, Tom having survived at least a dozen attendance checks without anyone's suspecting his condition, except that Tom decided he wanted to write his experience down and give it to an English teacher whom he trusted. Jack advised him against it, but he did it anyway, and the teacher, aware that faculty are charged with the health of their students, decided that Tom had to have a medical examination at once and went to the headmaster. St. John called Tom in and Tom confessed.

"How did it go?" Jack asked him when he came out.

Tom looked away from him: "I can't tell you now."

"Is it what we thought?" Jack asked.

"The worst of what we thought," Tom replied. Later, when they met again in Tom's room, Tom said, "I'm going home right now. Keep it very quiet. He hasn't decided yet; I don't know whether I'm in or out."

At the trustees' meeting, St. John asked for advice. Tom's

psychiatrist, he said, had called to say that Tom had needed treatment for a long time and that, "getting no help, he looked for self-help and thought perhaps this might be an answer. The psychiatrist said the entire experience had been a highly beneficial one. He now felt that the boy could function normally and would be far better off than he was before."

Still, there was the problem of precedent. Two boys knew about it, and if Tom "comes back, they know. You have to presume then that a large, large number know," St. John said, "because rumor is rife." The boy's father, he went on, had argued that Tom's case was one of illness, not misdemeanor, that rather than committing a crime against the school, he had not had the help he needed. "We knew him just as a quiet boy," St. John said. Most of the trustees thought the boy should be expelled because of the danger of precedent. "He may be in better shape now," said one, "but why shouldn't other boys say, 'I'm in bad shape; I'd be better for it'?" The Reverend Edward Miller, one of the most articulate and liberal of the group, was for keeping Tom: "A sense of justice is very important to this community," he said. "No adult would be convicted for such an offense." A long debate about summary justice at Choate followed, some wondering whether it would not be both fair and educational to have boys represented by "counsel" when they appeared before the Student Council, which, St. John admitted, acted as "both defense and prosecution. Perhaps we are a little simple and direct in the way we handle things. These boys rankle at injustice more than anything else in the world." But he cannot remember ever expelling a boy who had not confessed to his crime.

Most of the trustees wanted to tell Tom he couldn't return, but they left the decision to St. John, who told Tom he couldn't return. St. John was mistaken, however, about the number of boys who knew about the affair: no one ever knew anything about it. "I've decided to keep it this way," Jack Deal says. "I just figured the less they know, the better it is, and to hell with everybody else. My standard reply is that Tom didn't like Choate, that he got fed up, and that he was on the verge of a mental breakdown. As soon as you say somebody got kicked out for LSD, then obviously he's an evil person." Nor was any master ever told of it, either, by the administration—perhaps the first time a boy has been expelled from Choate without a general discussion of the affair. Tom Liddell took LSD and disappeared. Pretty soon he became an unperson and no one even thought to ask about him.

"I've learned a lot," St. John says. "I'm not disconcerted at all about it. I don't think the kids are any different at all from what they were. Not one iota. The boys who got into this were not bad boys; they weren't motivated by any evil design or any motivation that kids weren't always motivated by, which is the desire to be one of the boys, to be one of the group, a desire for status and excitement, to try something new, and the only difference in quality is that this is a more hazardous area than most of the areas that we have been confronted with in the way of status symbols in the past.

"The thing to remember is that when we're scared to death of this drug explosion, these kids are kids, and have to be dealt with summarily, but who are still kids like all the rest of the kids. It could happen to a lot of people."

Bad Times

> To exact of young men a proper silence in the presence of their elders. . . . To lay down laws on such matters would, I think, be foolish.
>
> *Republic,* 136

> You can defend a boy from everything but himself in a school like Choate. . . . The ways in which man can victimize himself are astoundingly many.
>
> HAROLD TINKER, CHOATE ENGLISH MASTER EMERITUS, speaking to his class

Trouble of a more public sort, of the kind that cannot be quashed in conferences with doctors and trustees, is bound to occur in a closed community like Choate, and it usually begins as the weather turns for the worse. One Saturday evening in October, two third formers walking back from the Winter Exercise Building were mugged by townies. "It's almost a game," said Jack Deal. "It's not anything where they hate us. Nothing to do on a Saturday night, let's go get drunk and kill some Choaties." Even so, Choate was shocked, and the next day cops appeared on the campus. Over Thanksgiving, townies stole two rifles and what one master called "incredible thousands of rounds of .22 ammunition" from the rifle range; an anonymous phone call led to the recovery of the rifles, but the bullets were never found.

By winter, there is always something of a discipline problem; rebellious spirits abound. "There's a certain tediousness, a certain boredom, particularly in the winter months, that's built into a boarding school existence," says R. Inslee Clark, dean of admissions at Yale. "It's okay for the first month in the fall when the leaves are on the trees and the air is crisp, and all right in April, but between mid-October and mid-March there can be a deadly quality to the routine which almost stifles, I think, exciting imaginations, and doing things differently, and going in ten different directions at once. I guess the thing that scares me most is that a boy can't escape. He can't be lonely, he can't be isolated enough. Everything he does is known. If he has a funny little habit, everybody knows about it. If he has a weakness, he can't get away with it. I think a kid ought to be allowed to be himself. It's very difficult in a boarding school, if not impossible."

Everyone goes indoors. It is a time to write, to paint, or to compose music, but very little is done. "The school is not geared to creativity," one of the older masters says. "There is very little creativity going on. Among five hundred and sixty boys, there ought to be at least fifty of the brilliant variety, but if you ask me at this moment if I know any brilliant or creative boys, I would say no." "We have found rather few talents of that sort," says another. "We don't seem to breed it." A third believes it is hard for the boys to find time and inspiration to pursue the arts, but then, he says, "the boys aren't as good as they used to be."

There is some creative work being done: two boys took a term off from athletics to write "folk" songs. Their voices are just adequate, and everything they have written so far is in 4/4 time, which gets dull enough, but they have an imaginative use of dissonance.

Telling funny stories Sunday morning
  Near the yellow apple tree;
Playing chuckle belly Sunday morning
  Near the yellow apple tree.

"We got the first stanza," one boy said, "but we didn't know what it meant. So we said, 'Let's put something about the church in it.' "

Jesus, he was born in another land;
  Jesus, he died in another land;
Making lovely music in a bush behind
  The yellow apple tree.

Eating all the fruit that I can pick
  From the yellow apple tree;
Jesus, he was born across the sea,
  But Jesus: he *was* the yellow apple tree.

"We write our songs on weekends and vacations away from Choate," the other boy said. "We can make our arrangements here, but you can't get ideas here. This isn't a good environment for creating."

The worst begins in January. The long vacation is over, and there is nothing but slush, college boards, and a brutal term ahead. The windows are shut; pools of mud and melted snow stand in the corridors; the steam rises, and tweed and flannel, too long removed from the cleaners, acquire a smell of their own. The closeness, the breathlessness, is most evident in the room below the chapel where films are shown on Saturdays. The boys guzzle soft drinks by the quart and candy by the three-pack; popcorn is scattered down the aisle, followed by cellophane and cardboard. "Siddown!" the voices shout as the frames flicker at an odd angle across the screen. The sound does not come on. In fact, that is the sound being *shown* at the right of the picture. A girl undresses. "Focus!" a cracked voice cries, and then there is silence, a tense quiet broken, when the scene shifts, by an audible discharge of breath. An actor vomits a moment later and a laugh goes up. "Taste good?" a boy cries. All is back to normal.

"A lot of guys really gross out," a senior says. "In winter, you see N.A. at its worst." "N.A." is short for Negative Attitude, a cliché which, like "conspiracy" in our criminal courts, seems to mean the crime with which a man is charged when nothing specific can be determined. Since N.A. is clearly opposed to "constructive," "supportive," "contributive," and all of St. John's other favorite adjectives, the boys have long embraced it.

"We're always accusing each other of having N.A.," the senior says, "and we're not putting people down by it. We say, 'So-and-So has a healthy N.A.' We like to see that."

Low spirits, however, are never amusing for long. One boy, feeling very depressed, stood in the basement of Steele Hall next to a tray of pies about to be sent upstairs to a room where favored guests were dining. Another boy, working as a waiter and very happy, whistling with happiness, came bouncing down the stairs. The gloomy boy hit the happy boy in the face with a pie. MacFarlane restricted the offender to the campus for two weeks. An emergency arose in his home, the boy said, but MacFarlane wouldn't let the boy leave; the boy grew gloomier than ever.

"I feel so depressed," said Jack Deal later in the winter. Jack didn't like the colleges he had chosen, knew he couldn't get into better ones. "In fact, I've felt literally close to going insane. I don't know what to do. I think I'm pretty mature, but I'm just not ready to go to college. I need a year off to go and hide. I won't go in the Army, but the question is how to avoid it. There's nobody here to talk to, not my parents, and the masters—are masters.

"It's been pretty bad recently. I feel you should love people, but nobody here, the kids, want to get to know you."

Problems of student discipline and morale are discussed by the Student Council. The council meets every Friday evening, often to discuss trivialities, and in closed session to advise the headmaster on whether a serious breach of discipline merits expulsion. Councils of this sort have an honorable history. George Washington and the French democrats of the Revolutionary era thought that in a true community, as Choate tries to be, people would put the welfare of the community above their own interests. Therefore, faction and conflict were wrong. In time, people discovered that, except for concerns with foreign communities, there is no such thing as community welfare, but rather a collection of interests. A community, therefore, should be a balance of interests. In many academic communities, students, faculty, and administration have met to represent their own positions in a kind of triangular confrontation which recognizes that, after all, interests *do* differ, that perhaps it is best they do, and that communities within a community should represent themselves, hoping, of course, to work harmoniously, and to avoid such alienation as is seen on campuses where students speak of themselves as *labor* and everyone else as *management.*

Choate's Student Council, however, is told that it represents *both* students and the school. The council is, the headmaster tells the boys when they meet in the fall, "simply leaders of the best, representative of what you honestly think is best for the outfit rather than being representative of group wants or selfish wants, but also representative of individuals." The boys, new to their awesome duty, do not protest, do not quite see how their teeth have been extracted, how, in fact, they will spend too much of their time representing the school to the students, or how the headmaster believes that the council is a useful tool to teach these boys lessons in leadership. Members are elected to the council by the boys, on a popularity basis, which will be helpful when the administration wants to channel its ideas to the boys through the boys. "They're just finks," said one senior. "It has good representation," said another. "There's a captain or a letter winner from just about every team."

In fact, the headmaster runs the council meetings very closely, and almost without seeming to do so; he is here, as in faculty meetings, operating at the peak of his performance. The council formally convenes at 8:00, but the boys are invited to come down to the Bamboo Room, which opens into the headmaster's Lodge, at 7:30 to bat the breeze, gossip, and decide what, if anything, they want to bring up. Alexander MacFarlane comes in first, at about 7:55; he is the dean of students, the school disciplinarian, and—some boys believe—St. John's professional no-man. MacFarlane has an infallible memory for the school's rules, when the headmaster forgets or finds it convenient to forget them. MacFarlane can be relied upon to say why something cannot be allowed when the headmaster shows some sympathy for the suggestion. Boys who have noticed this yes-and-no syndrome are divided in their opinion: Is this just the way they are—St. John tending toward liberality and MacFarlane locked in conservatism? Or has St. John hired MacFarlane specifically for this purpose—"I must look liberal, and be the good guy; but we need a bad guy: you're it."

"MacFarlane will defend everything in the school," says the head of Choate's Honor Committee, who, by tradition, sits with the Student Council. "His immediate reaction is to say, 'Well, no, you can't change anything.' Right away, he'll jump on you. Like we didn't have any fall weekend free until this year. Last year, he jumped on the idea, listing reasons, past cases, and going right after it, but this year we *have* the weekend, so now he defends it as strongly as he attacked it last year. Because it's part of the school now. Once we talked about optional attendance at Sunday breakfasts and MacFarlane said, 'Ah, we've saved three boys' lives by taking attendance at Sunday breakfast.' "

MacFarlane comes in and asks the boys what is on their minds: slowly the issues are getting weaker through overexposure: "We've got that problem again, sir, like teachers in history giving the same test to the first and fifth period class; kids talk between," and MacFarlane, with his little hammers, softens them up a bit, like the comic who works over the audience before Johnny Carson steps on stage, and then St. John comes in. By tradition, the boys speak their minds first. Then MacFarlane: "Mr. Nuzzo is concerned with the obscenities that are written on john walls, toilet stalls. What concerns us is that it exists at all."

St. John (hedging) : I think we should get definite word on where this takes place before we ask the Student Council to take over. In the past, when we've run into this, and it has been chronic and constant, it has usually been in the Memorial House—younger groups, and perhaps more frustrated. It's usually just fighting it, you know. Hard to find another outlet.

Head of the council: It's a hard thing to pin down. You know: stop.

St. John: It is. I will take a chapel evening on it next week. It doesn't mean you stop it, but at least maybe you can make a few people think about it. I'm sure everybody is basically on the same side.

A general discussion follows on how hard it is to catch kids doing it. St. John, who may have been surprised by the introduction of the topic, has now seen that his council is compliant, is looking very much as if none of *them* uses obscenity, and now has no need to hedge. He opens up: "I don't know how to talk about it except in broad terms of what makes people what they are. And the fact that this passage in the Bible that says what comes into you can never hurt you; it's what goes out that hurts. If it goes out in the form of vulgar language, vulgarity with a pencil, or vulgarity in any other way, this is part of you that *shows.* I think that at a thinking age people will be reasonable. The ones who won't be reasonable are those who can't yet think enough or those too frustrated or too unhappy to care." It is really quite a good recovery, and it stops the discussion.

St. John looks around. "I have half a dozen things I want to touch on, if we've covered the rest. Joe?" he looks at the Student Council head.

"Yessir, I think so."

"First of all, start of term, winter term, is always our difficult one. I felt that a bit in chapel tonight. I noticed it particularly in the singing of the first hymn, which was the worst I've ever heard. It just went dead. Understandable, to some degree, but if you're dead, and you allow yourself to be dead, you can go from bad to worse instead of picking it up. One of these days I'll touch on that in chapel. In fact, I think we'll have a practice singing session. It's *good* to sing, you know; it's just a plus." Singing, or the lack of it, St. John went on, is "a symptom" of the mental health of the community. Sports, too, help relieve anxieties about girls, and other tendencies boys may have to turn in upon themselves in winter: "Of course, if you're in a varsity sport, most people are in that enough so that they get pulled out of themselves. But some don't get pulled out of themselves *very much* for a while."

"I think the council accomplishes things," one of its members said. "There are areas where you can make progress. You can make authority change a little bit. What it really takes is for the students to keep *driving* at it, keep going every week and come back again, driving at it. I haven't done that. I should have. Should have kept hammering. But the school has worked pretty well, even though they are against changes, generally."

St. John presides over the faculty meeting, too. This occurs on Monday, after dinner and after coffee with masters' wives in the faculty room beneath the library. There is, in the dining room, a large and ugly painting of the death of King Arthur bearing the title *The Old Order Changeth*. It should hang in the faculty room, but there, carved over the mantel in large letters, is a single word: AEQUANIMITAS, and indeed, most of the faculty meetings are conducted with calm and composure. The faculty address each other by their last names, with a "Mister" attached, a formality St. John enjoys: "I guess it originally evolved from mutual respect. That we were there on a professional basis, and not just for chitchat." Each man takes the same seat every week, with the more conservatively inclined masters—most of them from the science and mathematics departments—generally sitting at St. John's right hand, and the liberal masters—from the history and English departments—sitting on his left. This division of sentiment makes it easier to hurl charges across the full length of the room, or for the conservatives to mutter in unison and stamp their feet without anyone being sure just who is saying what.

St. John conducts the meetings quite strictly according to a mental agenda from which he deviates only with reluctance. In a brisk and orderly fashion, he calls on masters for reports or opinions. He delivers brief lectures, recognizes other masters who wish to speak, but is capable of cutting them off or turning away from them—no one can be blind to the changes in his expression—when he wishes they would stop. No one interrupts the headmaster; few venture to inject levity unless St. John himself begins it. When discussing a problem, St. John will often say, "I was wrong on that one," but some of the faculty believe he uses such admissions to avoid taking corrective action. "When Seymour says he has made a mistake," Malcolm Manson observed, "it does not necessarily mean he has changed his mind." Nor is anything that occurs in the school too trivial for detailed discussion before these eighty masters who have been drawn from their families, work, and house responsibilities to hear that:

- "Twelve dozen towels have disappeared. Will masters please make a thorough check when towels are changed. We have to run a housekeeping outfit as well as an educational outfit."
- "Fifty unidentified toll calls are coming in each month. We need all the help we can get on this."
- "When I go through Common Rooms with guests I notice boys not standing up. Manners is one of the things they're learning."
- Crackers and milk will be served in a new location.
- A pianist who composes music to express the Greek revolution will give a concert at school.
- "Most of the people here would think it fair to give between one half of one percent and one percent of their salaries" to the Wallingford United Fund. "It's a matter for individual conscience," of course, but what masters give will be put on record at the bursar's office and if masters have not yet sent in their pledges, "will you please get busy."

All of this, the masters say, could be handled by notices put on the bulletin board, or by announcements distributed to mailboxes, but St. John clearly relishes what he calls "housekeeping items." Still, it is in faculty meetings that the major ills of the school are discussed at excruciating length, and that winter, the ills came quickly and in force.

"It has been a busy week," MacFarlane reported on February 12. A boy was suspended for smoking. Another boy without friends "just left." Three boys were put on probation for using false telephone credit cards. Two boys broke into the Tuck Shop—a soda fountain on campus—took candy, and stole $400; another boy, on a dare, broke in and stole two bags of potato chips, which he put on the bed of the boy who dared him. Finally, three boys had been "forced to confess" their guilt in the Chapel Alarm Clock Incident.

It was not, in fact, an alarm clock, but "a buzzer device" which was set off the night after St. John had "taken one of his chapel evenings" to reprove the boys about Negative Attitude. There had been, the faculty agreed, too much talking in chapel, too much climbing over pews, too much slouching into chapel with hands thrust deep in pockets, too much reading of newspapers in the dining room during grace at breakfast. The headmaster, at the faculty's request, had lectured the boys, and the next night, as Riess Potterveld, the school's new chaplain, was delivering a prayer—"In our silence we pray," he was saying—the infernal device went off. The boys laughed. No one could do anything because the boys involved had screwed the device behind the heating system in one of the chapel walls. Potterveld, a pale young man, blushed and pushed his way through to the end of the service, and the alarm kept ringing. "It was a prank," the headmaster told the boys the next morning, "but can we allow disorder in our community, in a place sacred to the vast majority of us?" He took away a free day that had been declared in honor of a Choate boy, then at Yale, who had been awarded a Rhodes scholarship. "I think," said Stephen Longley later, "that if boys will go to that extent to disrupt what is being said in chapel, we should not be asking what is wrong with the boys, but what is wrong with what is said in chapel."

St. John, however, was intrigued by what was wrong with the boys. "They turned out to be boys of iffy balance," he told the faculty on February 19. "*Interesting* boys. I think Ralph is an interesting boy. He talked to me for three-quarters of an hour on philosophy while I was trying to talk to him about setting off the bell in chapel. I didn't get a word in edgewise. Very clever, very bright, and we were talking about a hundred other things, but not on that point at all. He did lie, as did the others."

St. John explained to the faculty why he had made such a stormy issue of the incident, and yet gave the culprits only restrictions to campus and work crew details, whereas those guilty of less ingenious crimes were being punished harshly. "I made the issue," he said, "because in pranks we know perfectly well that if one lets them go, each one tries to outdo the other. This is Standard Operating Procedure. Unless you make a point, an issue of something that is as devastating to our regime, our continuum, our—the *dignity* of our chapel service—unless you make the issue at *that* point, you are almost bound to be in for more serious things at a later time."

Also, as St. John observed, he was considering more serious crimes at the time, and it "seemed well to make a clear distinction." The stealing from the Tuck Shop "was clear-cut." One boy was expelled. "The boy has a psychological problem," St. John said, "there's no doubt about that in my mind. He didn't keep his room very well, but he had no striking aberrations. But now that we have learned this about him, we learn there were worse things underneath. He stole things from the chapel. He perhaps had—and now I'm on hearsay rather than fact—a .22 pistol in his possession. He was somewhat sadistic and close to psychopathic. I feel very badly that communication in these matters was so slow." The boy, in fact, had stolen Christmas candles and the hands from the clock of the chapel; he was, as MacFarlane said the previous week, "a very sick boy."

Then there was Dick Tully, a senior suspended from school for smoking. The students have long tried to understand why Choate cares so deeply about smoking—the more medical evidence there is why one should not smoke, the sillier it seems to compel people to refrain from smoking—but they *cannot* make sense of it, no one can, so they explain it by myth. "You can't smoke at Choate," says one senior, "because Paul Mellon says you can't. Paul Mellon has given money to the school on the stipulation that smoking isn't permitted at Choate. It's a rumor, yes, but I believe it could be true. I probably believe it *is* true." It is all false, of course, but no one thinks rationally about smoking at Choate. Malcolm Manson, his voice rising several decibles, says, "If anyone *ever* suggested that a boy in my house smoked, I'd hit him in the face. I'd just *hit* him."

The headmaster resorts to philosophy: "I feel the rule has done us a lot of good," he says. "My father used to say that it is essential for people to have some sacrifice to make. This was a good one, and if we didn't have this, we'd have to replace it with some other one." Nor does the headmaster like the butt rooms he has seen in other schools, "the least constructive areas in the schools." Still, for St. John the plan behind the No Smoking rule is even yet more elevated: "You've got the problem of keeping idealism on a high level and developing that kind of atmosphere that makes for idealism and the best you can get from the boys. This is difficult enough to work out without making it harder for them and for the school. The one thing to be gained by allowing smoking is to give the boys the opportunity to decide on it for themselves. It *is* good for them to have certain amounts of opportunity to decide, for better or for worse, on their own. But I think this is heavily overbalanced by the losses.

"When you try to balance pragmatism against idealism, pragmatism is always going to lose, and rightly so."

At the beginning of the year, nobody had an accurate idea of how many students smoked at Choate. The boys guessed about 50 percent had tried cigarettes on campus; a boy who had been expelled the previous year told me "nine-tenths of the students smoke." The faculty, as the year began, probably would have guessed 10 percent, but the true figure is closer to 20 percent. The student poll revealed that 98 students have smoked at school (67 have drunk at Choate); 43 students have smoked "over ten times" and may therefore be presumed to flout the rule regularly. Slightly more than half the students object to the smoking rule, but many were astonished that Dick Tully should have been suspended, whereas the boys who stole from the phone company were only put on probation for a term.

J. P. Cosnard asked at the faculty meeting on February 12: "Why expel a boy for smoking, but put him on pro for stealing from a phone company? It makes no sense. The boys are upset about it." Cosnard was wrong; Dick was, in fact, the first boy in twenty years caught smoking and *not* expelled. Still, the scale of punishments was clearly out of joint. Gordon Stillman, who presided over that particular meeting, tried to show how charity worked: "We are an educational institution rather than a punitive one. The boys who stole from the phone company are fortunate enough to learn a lesson from it without terminating their education here."

Bill Maillet, one of the few dissidents who sits at the headmaster's right, got angry: "We are dealing with moral issues on a monetary basis!"

Stillman demurred: "We deal with all these on an *individual* basis, taking into account the deed, the boys, and their attitudes. The boys volunteered to pay for what was stolen." Even so, Stillman said, the Honor Committee had wanted an easier punishment.

Maillet was adamant: the boys should have been expelled. "We throw out a boy for stealing from the Tuck Shop," he said, "because we know the man who runs it. We don't know the phone company. There's a feeling in our society that it is okay to rob from a corporation, but not from an individual."

No one had an answer to that, nor to the charge that suspending a boy for smoking while putting thieves on probation was moral chaos. In private, it was said that a member of the Student Council had been caught smoking with Dick Tully; those who knew the Student Council member agreed it was most likely. "Probation for smoking," Stillman explained, "was tried in the 1930's and found ineffectual. There is no moral or legal reason for firing a boy for smoking; it is purely a pragmatic answer to a problem."

Maillet rose to his feet and sputtered. "We're *never* allowed to discuss this. Let's have an open hearing!"

MacFarlane said, "No smoking is a *condition* for living in this community."

"Isn't no stealing a condition for this community?" Maillet

asked. "What can we *tell* the boys when they ask us about this discrepancy?"

The following week, St. John was back and explained what was in his mind: "Smoking," he said, "is a rule. And, of course, anybody can cavil, as all of us have to some extent, for many years. We recognize that smoking is not immoral in the wide world. It is a school regulation, and boys are asked not to come to Choate if they want to smoke. The rule is clear. My feeling is that the student body feels that Dick Tully did not get a bad deal; he got a square deal."

But this was in the future. While the Student Council deliberated Dick's fate, Dick was sequestered in the infirmary, forbidden to talk to other students. He spent a day writing eighteen poems about the Choate experience. "The channels by which discipline goes at Choate," said one master on February 12, "leave individual masters little to say. We have given too much strength to the Honor Committee and the Student Council. The men who *teach* here: *their* voice should be heard! Not the word of the boys! I don't care how good they are!"

Stillman let the conversation run on; probably St. John would have cut it off at an early point. "We're supposed to be teaching morality here, too!" Maillet yelled, and Stephen Hawkins, who is rarely heard from, said, "I think the boys are laughing in our faces. Honor Committee restriction means nothing to them."

"Many boys," said Stillman, "see nothing wrong in having a fraudulent identification card and using it to *deceive,* not to steal. We have a tremendous job trying to educate the boys and convince them that our standards are right for them. Can we allow them to set their own values?" In fact, one of the Honor Committee boys was extremely upset by such intransigence. He felt the thieves should be pardoned, that many boys cheated the phone company in small ways—by jamming the coin return box, for instance—and that the faculty should be mature enough to admit it made a mistake. "Students are grown-up enough," he said, "to respect the faculty for changing punishment."

The arguments wore on. "The boys are restive," Stillman

admitted, "as they always are after a quick succession of problems of this sort." But some masters thought this did not begin to express the crisis that was developing. "There is tension in the school," Herbert Gutterson said, "a temporary loss of student confidence in morale, in the school." "There is a general lack of manners," said Mark Tuttle, "worse than anything I have seen in thirteen years." Sa'adah rose to give the kind of speech that only he and Jon van Leuven can deliver extemporaneously, a speech like those heard in the faculty room in the School of Athens: the framework of our society here must be redefined, he said; we must discuss how to readjust the framework in an orderly way. "We cannot deal with people arbitrarily. We must learn how to reconstruct the boy." It is amazing how little patience the faculty, particularly the mathematicians and scientists, have for this kind of talk. Stillman sighed. "You cannot in five minutes or even in an hour and a half revise an institution," he said.

"What we really want to do is to take the rose-colored glasses off the headmaster," Gutterson said. He may have meant it as a private aside, but the room, for once, was quiet and everyone heard and laughed.

The next day a sign hung by the boys' mailboxes in Steele Hall: ROSE-COLORED SPECTACLES FOR SALE, said the Art Nouveau lettering: APPLY TO S. ST. JOHN.

A week later matters had deteriorated further. Choate's Political Union took a poll. "Do you approve of the recent disciplinary actions of the school?" Yes, said 77 boys; no, said 315. Ninety-one boys said there were flaws in the structure of the honor system; 118 thought there were "flaws in the present Honor Committee." "I didn't think it was a very effective poll," St. John said. "I thought it was meaningless. It didn't give any constructive answers."

The score at the end of the week was:

1 boy expelled for theft from Tuck Shop;
1 boy suspended for the same offense; would return next year;

1 boy suspended for smoking; would return for exams at year's end;
3 boys on probation for stealing from the phone company;
2 boys on Honor Committee restriction for the buzzer incident.

Nobody was happy. When St. John returned to conduct the next week's faculty meeting, he was unhappy because the faculty had resolved to conduct a meeting of the newly formed General Committee right after the faculty meeting ended. The General Committee, to be run by David Waters, would debate such issues as student unrest, school policy toward discipline and infraction of major rules, and how the faculty—particularly those who know each boy best—might become involved in disciplinary decisions. St. John would listen to the meeting: he would be there as an observer, to learn. Some people predicted St. John would never allow the General Committee to meet, and, that night, he did not. Firmly holding the chair himself, he let the faculty talk itself past the point of exhaustion. Men kept rising to suggest that, after all, what the faculty was discussing was the province of the General Committee, and wouldn't St. John *please* adjourn the faculty meeting? "I want to," said St. John, "when the whole faculty is ready." There was always someone else who had a grievance or fatuity to offer, and as the evening wore on, Waters sat there, shaking his head incredulously. By the evening's end, he looked as if he had aged ten years.

It was the year's stormiest meeting. Few masters understood the punishments meted out; fewer still agreed they had been wisely arrived at. The decision to put the telephone thieves on probation, it seemed, was not announced to the faculty for three days, leaving the masters to face the boys' questions by saying, "I don't know," and, in effect, "I'm not consulted around here." "I am admonished by you," said St. John to his faculty, "which I like, because I respect you. Your major object is to help, not hurt. Sometimes a boy may be best helped by expelling him; sometimes, not. Then you have to think about the needs of society. I think we are a stronger institution for considering different punishments for different boys."

But still, the faculty argued that it was powerless in making decisions. "The reason we don't take up each disciplinary matter with you is simply time," St. John said. "Time."

"Shouldn't *we* be the ones who decide if we have the time?" Jean Pierre Cosnard asked. "We care so much, and we must discuss it later with the boys. We are trying not to confuse smoking, which is not a moralistic issue, and stealing, which *is.*"

Robert Clements, chairman of the mathematics department, rose to speak in a voice choked with emotion: The third and fourth formers in his house, he said, "are nice guys. But I'm worried about the changes that occur to them here as the years pass. What is going to happen to them in the next two years? We're not doing our job. *I'm* not doing the job. You"—and he pointed at St. John—"must ask, why aren't we doing it? Can't we do it? Haven't we the men to do it? I can't do what I used to do. I know I should stop boys talking in chapel. But I don't. Recently, I've felt it was sort of futile."

David Vietor, twenty-six, one of the new men, protested that responsibility was withheld from the faculty everywhere—even in the classroom.

St. John crossed his arms over his chest and walked quickly over to Vietor: "I couldn't disagree with you more." Vietor quailed. "We've been working on these things for twenty years now without undermining the faculty! I don't want to argue with you," St. John went on, "but we should sit down and have a long talk some time without taking more time here." Vietor left school at the end of the year.

Other young masters took a pounding, too, that night. The older, conservative faculty—the devoted men—could not understand why, when faced with a rebellion from the troops, the faculty did not close ranks. Why should the younger men join the students in dissent? Jon van Leuven, twenty-five, rose to say he did not want to listen to older masters haranguing younger masters: "We need not listen to a debate on the school's discipline," he said. Van Leuven is gaunt, wears owlish glasses; there is something proletarian about his wrists and his corduroy jacket, and something intimidating about the logic and austerity of his arguments. "No committee should be formulated for the purpose of having older masters tell younger masters what the philosophy of education is." Now the older masters were muttering. "Shut up! Sit down!" they suggested. Van Leuven pushed on: "We should discuss the goals of education, the needs of society, and why young masters get disillusioned and leave Choate."

No one could remember hearing such a thing before, not in the faculty room, not to St. John's face, not from a stringy kid who—they say—hangs a picture of Trotsky over his bed. Owen Morgan, sixty-three years old and an amiably gruff conservative, rose trembling from his seat. His voice and his finger wavered as he took aim at Van Leuven. "Some of us," he rumbled, "have lived here long enough, and put enough of our lives into this school, to have something to say!" His voice cracked; Morgan was crying. The conservatives applauded. "And I think"—Morgan was bellowing now—"we ought to get down to basic facts! Maybe we can go off into clouds later on. But right now we're faced with a difficult situation. We better clarify our own standpoint on that!" He paused; Van Leuven nodded politely. "All right then," said Morgan, "let's shut up about the cloudy things and talk about the thing we *need* to talk about! Then maybe we can be philosophical afterwards!" Morgan collapsed then, and stumbled from the room amid applause, table banging, and shouts of "Bravo!"

"I think, once again," said St. John, covering Morgan's exit, "that our problems, where they lie, lie in the realm of communications. And I think our communication with good will, with strength of standards, and with understanding for each other and with each other can bring us to the goal which we are all individually and collectively after."

But one particular communication had upset St. John deeply. Tom Dorland, a bright dissenting senior, had written a long piece in the *News* protesting Dick Tully's suspension for smoking. It was a moderate essay. Tom had urged the school to act "firmly but rationally" in future cases and pointed out that Dick was a superior student who had made a mistake. By teaching him his lesson "the hard way," Choate may have left the boy bitter and cynical—"the lesson learned will be one which he must pay for for the rest of his life . . . I just don't think it's right."

"This is irresponsible," St. John insisted in faculty meeting. St. John wrote a long letter to Tom Dorland in reply, and sent copies around to his administration, but he would not release his letter for publication in the *News*. Now St. John wanted the *News* censored. Tom Colvin, twenty-eight, made a simple, moving defense of a free exchange of views in the *News*. The student paper, he said, should reflect student opinion and not be a propaganda sheet designed to bolster student morale. "This is risky," said St. John, who thought, too, of the rich alumni who get subscriptions to the *News* and don't want to hear about trouble at school, don't want to be offended by smart-aleck kids speaking out. "It takes courage to allow your kind of responsibility to the *News*," St. John told Colvin. "I'm not sure we can afford it. The chance for education with such freedom is strong. The chance for hurt is also strong—too horrible, perhaps."

The masters, generally, were not in favor of freedom of speech in the paper. "It hurts the third and fourth formers," one master said, "who believe everything they read." Colvin said he would resign from his duty as faculty adviser to the paper before he would censor it. St. John said he was "disturbed by the immature, irresponsible boys who do the speaking out" in school.

All this palaver was, for John Lupton, who rarely attends faculty meetings, a sign of weakness. "I've talked to many men who've been expelled from Choate," he said. "I find them leaders all over the country." Lupton has a way of isolating his sentences so that his audience has no idea if more is to come; nothing he says necessarily depends on what went before, nor does anything ever seem to require further elaboration. This time, however, there was more: "Major discipline," he said, "is traumatic. It should not be democratically arrived at. It needs to be handled quickly and discreetly." The student, perhaps, should kneel, his head thrust down, and the Luger, which is placed two inches from the epidermis on his neck, may be discharged into the socket that connects the brain stem to the spine. Quick, discreet, and admirably undemocratic, but the problem is: one fewer Choate boy expelled to leadership in America. Lupton does not care for Choate's "ultrapermissiveness. It makes a bad impression," he told the faculty that night, "on Choate's wealthy alumni. Particularly the general broadcast of irresponsible student opinion."

Lupton had not noticed that, for the first time that year, John Joseph was on his feet, speaking very softly. "What do you mean," he asked, "by 'discreetly'? What makes you think *we* cannot act discreetly?"

Lupton ducked: "The punishment was swift and severe, as it should have been. Everyone feels it was wise and fair."

Joseph later said: "I often feel the urge to speak in faculty meeting, but I almost always manage to suppress it. It does no good at all."

Three hours after the meeting began, St. John still held the chair. Waters looked on in dazed disbelief. Everyone had said pretty much what he would have said in General Committee, but St. John had controlled the entire proceedings. It was the neatest parliamentary trick Waters had ever seen. "I fear," he said, "that we have talked ourselves out."

"I'm glad," said Bill Maillet, "that after seven years we have a chance to open up this kind of communication."

"I would have thought," said St. John, "you always had."

"Excuse me, sir, but no."

"News to me," said St. John and smiled as he turned away.

"Minor infractions," one master had said that night, "are eating away at our foundation," so the next day, at lunch, St. John announced that the school would assemble in chapel for a few minutes "after lunch." Some of the masters smiled knowingly—"At last!"—and boys who had their ears to the ground knew exactly what was coming: "It's about minor discipline," they told their ignorant colleagues.

The balcony of the chapel was crowded with extra masters.

The organ played moodily. St. John strode in. Shuffle, shuffle, everyone up, and then sits down again.

"Our meeting is held today at the request of the faculty to put before you our shared convictions, about which we feel deeply and strongly, about which we are certain you feel basically equally strongly." Later St. John would issue a printed version of his speech, sprucing up the syntax a bit, but this is what he said then:

"We believe in our school. We care tremendously about it. We're proud of its heritage and determined to hold high its standards and values which have been passed down to us. We believe that the vast majority of the student body want to be members of an outstanding school and are willing to subscribe to the personal disciplines that are an inevitable part of greatness.

"It's been noticeable that recently we have slipped in some areas. Small areas, usually. It is essential for all of us together to realize this and to take strong and immediate action—primarily within ourselves—to get back on the track. There are a number of areas that we have discussed together in faculty meeting, and which I will put before you now. Clearly, I can't touch on everything:

"Courtesy. Choate is known throughout the world—mentioned from Hong Kong to London—for courtesy to its visitors. Miss Moore, who deals with hundreds of students in England and America, said to me in December, 'Choate is the most sophisticated school in the world today, because its boys are the most courteous and gentlemanly.' "

The boys sat there stunned. The most important thing about Choate is that its boys are polite? "Don't you think Choate boys are more polite?" a mother later asked a rebellious senior who replied, "Maybe they are, but they are not made polite at Choate. They come from families that made them polite." Nor had the students seen a letter that an executive of a ball bearing company wrote St. John in 1952—the kind of letter St. John saves: "This is written to commend the boys of Choate School, and you, for their continued courteous and gentlemanly conduct on the New Haven trains. Their quiet and generous behavior has caused much favorable comment and perhaps it would be appropriate to let them know. It is a pleasure to so advise you." And now all this was threatened.

"This is important to you," St. John told the boys, "and to every Choate boy, past and present." St. John went on to tick off areas where boys were slipping: not standing up when ladies pass before them; not offering food at the table first to faculty, guests, and wives; not being courteous to athletes from rival schools, particularly Taft; not being neat—"You know, the little things: ties pulled up, shoes clean, hair neat, reasonably cut" —and, worst of all, not being neat about litter on the campus. "I still find it awfully hard to believe," said St. John (though he cut it from the printed version of his rebuke), "that you can go down to the Speech Room after a movie and find litter all over the floor. To me, it's really incredible. This is just my background, and all of you don't share it. But it is to me absolutely incredible that you can eat a piece of candy and throw the wrapper on the floor; it's unbelievable! Because you know darn well somebody else has to pick it up! It's to me the essence of self-centeredness, and I just don't understand it." Then there was language. "Only you and a very few others know what kind of language you use most of the time. But your language, like dress, has a marked effect on the tone and morale of all of us together." And there was posture in chapel. "In courtesy, we shall never put our head down as though sleeping when someone is speaking to us. This is the essence of rudeness. Obviously, we don't chew gum in chapel." The night before, St. John had said, "If I saw gum-chewing in chapel, I'd go right after it from the front of the chapel. It's untenable."

And so it went until St. John approached his peroration: "We're here to do a job," he said, "to train ourselves toward sharp minds, strength of character, moral fiber. These are not gained by looking for the easy way. There are much easier paths, but they don't lead to the goals we seek; so those who prefer them must follow them elsewhere." He closed by saying that 85 percent of the students "were fine"; only 15 percent "made trouble for the group. I don't like to think that there is such a fifteen percent here at Choate. Although I know that perhaps each of us has in us a little of that fifteen percent. Our aim, then, is to wash out that weakness and lead with strength. I have confidence, as always, that through being faithful to small things we shall be faithful to large principles and *the* large principles that can make for all—you and I—are determined our school shall be."

St. John then excused the school, to solemn organ music, and asked that the sixth form stay on for further exhortation. "We need your help and your support," he told them, warning them that their increased privileges meant increased responsibilities. "A third former the other day said with real hurt, 'Why don't the sixth formers care?' He cared very much about you." You must lead by example, he said, "example of word and of deed. We're here to get to know ourselves, and one of the ways we do that is to have responsibility. You are asked to be leaders, to live up to the highest standards. Most of the time in small things, of course, but, as I said, small things add up to big things. They make the difference between mediocrity and greatness."

"Fascist drivel," said one senior as the boys filed out, and another said, "I don't think the sixth form does care. He says we do, but I think he's wrong. We should and we don't. The little kids look up to you, they want to know you because it makes them feel good, and you don't want to snub them, but you don't care about them, either."

Later that afternoon, some seniors met in a bull session. No one had anything favorable to say of the headmaster's speech, recognizing that he had missed the point, and wondering why he hadn't seen that he had.

"It seems like he's trying to solve the problems of the school by trying to tighten it up, get it shipshape," said Tom Dorland. "I think he knows, everybody knows, that the recent disciplinary decisions have been absurd. They're unwilling to face the fact that something needs to be done here, so they're trying to correct it by getting a big moral revolution: everyone get haircuts." Small things, most boys at Choate believe, do *not* add up to big things. They are apples and oranges. "You can criticize the little things, sure," said Tom, "but it's ridiculous when there are other things that should be made big deals out of."

Jack Deal said, "What they're trying to do now is force respect for the school. They're going to get you to cover your disrespect up. The actual fracture of rules—smoking, drinking, or gambling—is not going to be corrected by any of that."

Both Tom and Jack were upset by the decision to suspend Dick Tully. Dick, everyone knew, had smoked often before. "I had some friends last year," said Jack, "who *learned* to smoke at school. There are even social pressures to smoke here. People say, if you don't smoke, you're a coward."

"It's true," Tom said. "In the Student Council, which is composed of nine boys, five have smoked at Choate. At least five. That's five that I'm sure of. In St. Andrew's—the chapel society—eight out of sixteen. I have *definite* proof. The school should be able to recognize these things. They should be able to do something besides just wait until somebody else breaks the the rule and then pounce on him. The school has to adjust, sometimes, too."

The phone business was just as bad. "Just from this floor and the one over in Hall Two," said Jack Deal, "I know of half a dozen boys who use false telephone credit cards. Most of them have little tricks like putting in pennies and jamming the thing. Constantly robbing the phone company."

"The phone company gets you for so much money anyway," Tom said, "it's like playing Robin Hood."

"Gambling is another thing," said Jack. "In the Clinton Knight House and the Cook House, go down there any Saturday on the second floor and there'll be two tables in the middle with chips. They're *all* gambling. If you look under the table, that's where they keep the paper that shows how much you owe."

"In the past two days," said Tom, "I've been losing up at the game on Hill Three. There's nothing wrong with gambling. We usually play gut poker. It's usually a nickel a chip and you have to double the pot each time."

"They've got a twenty-four-hour running thing in Hall Two," Jack said. "They've got professional chips and three or four decks of cards. So many people are breaking the rules that I think it's unfair to jump on Tully for smoking, which is not even against the law. If you're caught by the Student Council and warned, and the faculty doesn't know about it, you are allowed to smoke that one time, but if you're caught by a master, then you're kicked out. What's the difference?"

"With Tully's case," said Tom, "they didn't give him a second chance. They acknowledge the fact that this is a time when you're growing up and making a lot of mistakes, and you're changing and everything, but then, you make mistakes, and then you've sinned and must be taught a lesson."

"What bothers me," said Jack after he had explained how to fill a Micrin bottle with gin or vodka and shoot blue coloring into it, "is that we don't care. I don't care. I should care. I just don't know the boys younger than me."

Not all the boys were unmoved by St. John's speech. "I think Seymour should have spoken to us six months ago," Hal Steadman said. Hal admires St. John—"He knows more than anyone knows, but chooses to ignore it"—and taps St. John's pipeline. "I've built up a grapevine," Hal says, "the only one going. I've come to know some masters and some secretaries. I could write a book about this school, using the inside information I've obtained from my grapevine, and blow the school apart." Hal has some keys to Steele Hall offices, and knows how to comb through administration wastebaskets just before the trash man picks them up. When I told Hal I couldn't get a copy of the *Master's Handbook* from the administration, he said, "No problem," and produced one from his files. For all his flippant boasting, Hal approached the school's problems that February with intelligence. "The problem is not only in the student body," he said, "but in the faculty, too. It's a pity Seymour didn't say, 'This job is not only yours, but the faculty's. It will have to hold up its job too.' He couldn't say that, I suppose, not in chapel.

"I don't think there's anything basically wrong here. Except, perhaps that new masters think about their image with the boys when they should be thinking about what they can do with the boys."

At the next faculty meeting, on February 26, St. John announced: "We now have a high tone of discipline in the school," which spiked any further discussion from the start, but it was almost true. The fact is, you could tell the difference. The boys for a brief while responded to St. John's admonitions, and now the question was: Can the faculty admit its mistake and allow Peter Landman back in school? Peter was the boy who sneaked into the Tuck Shop on a dare from an older boy, a boy who now, it seems, was responsible for the theft of a trombone from Duke Ellington's band. He had hung the trombone from his dormitory window by a string, thus revealing, as one master said, "his diabolical side." Peter had been mesmerized by this boy—"this selfish, sick, almost evil person," as one master called him in faculty meeting, where such words are rarely heard.

In fact, St. John asked—or *implied* that he was asking—the faculty to let Peter back in school. "I'm sorry," said David Rice, "that it wasn't possible for the school to protect Peter," a new boy, cheerful and sincere if not good academically, "whose problem was he didn't know how to say no." A big discussion followed. At first, there seemed to be a tide in favor of Peter's return, then there was a reaction. "Once we make up our minds," one of the teachers at St. John's right declared, "we should stick with it. The fifteen percent that make trouble should be expelled, then everyone else would be grand! We need firm ground to stand on. What about the morale of the school if we take him back? Is the school strong enough? Do we need now a show of love—or a show of *strength?* Will the cancerous worm destroy what we have built?"

Rice said, "One of the signs of greatness is a degree of humility in the face of a mistake." Right at that moment, it was obvious Rice had blown his chances. The faculty was nearly ready to readmit Peter, but not to admit its own mistake. As the uproar grew, Rice went on: "I think it would be too bad if we have a chance to rectify a mistake and don't rectify it with grace."

Another master rose and shouted: "The boy lied! He stole! And he broke into the Tuck Shop! I don't think we made a mistake!"

Suddenly there was a voice from the conservative right, from Don Hickman, the art teacher, who never speaks. "We have," he said, "potentially all the charity and compassion in the world if we want to direct it to individual offenders. For certain practical reasons, we don't do so."

"I am voting to consider a change," said Stillman. "I do not feel we made a mistake." Here Stillman showed his mastery of faculty politics: we do not do wrong, we do better. "This is an educational institution," he said, "and we may be able to help this boy."

Rice sank into his seat. A vote was taken. Twelve faculty members voted to readmit Peter, sixty to keep him out.

David Waters, at this point, was still hopeful that the faculty meeting would be adjourned early, or rather dissolved into the meeting of the General Committee, with St. John doing the listening, that had been promised for the week before. No luck. There was other business: a father had written St. John to say: "My son isn't doing well on exams. What are you doing about it?" "I wanted," said St. John, "to tell him *he* should have done something about it seventeen years ago. The boy is not bright, but the father assumes he has 'a psychological block' against exams. It isn't a good thing for a boy to be here if he doesn't really want to be here. It is tremendously important for him to know that he doesn't *have* to be here. There are no bars on the windows. In fact, if he hasn't got something to offer the school, we should cut him off."

Waters now thought his General Committee could take over, but there was not a chance. Vincent Nuzzo, the business manager of the school, rose to say that "two hundred towels have been lost. Please check your boys' rooms. We won't have towels for Festivities."

"I don't know," said St. John, "that we'll ever come to the point where talk of discipline and housekeeping details will be separated from our talk of new ideas," and, because the hour was late, he adjourned the meeting. Waters looked stunned again.

"I can't believe it," said one master, who, like most of the faculty had waited to see what the General Committee would do if ever it convened. "He'll kill it yet. You have to admire his audacity."

St. John said, "I see us now in another period of rethinking. Ferment may not be too strong a word, considering what comes out of it. We'll try to get together all our best ideas and see that something useful comes of it." The General Committee, he said, "is a good idea. We'll set up an agenda ahead of time." But no one had asked him to be involved with agendas. "The means for the faculty to give us their constructive thoughts," St. John purred on. "I think it's a very important thing."

Dangerous Times

> "Then do you think," I asked, "that in our city the brass-smiths or these true guardians will be in a majority?"
> "The brass-smiths," he said, "easily."
>
> *Republic,* 141

> *Elector:* If I were Dey of Tunis,
> I certainly would sound alarm at once
> At such ambiguous proceedings. I would put
> A silken cord upon my desk,
> Would barricade the gates and draw up cannon
> And howitzers before the palace walls.
>
> HEINRICH VON KLEIST, *The Prince of Homburg*

> What they were doing was not constructive.
>
> JULIE NIXON, commenting on the young people clubbed by the cops in Chicago, August, 1968

"I think there is a searching for directions here right now," said Tom Colvin one dark February afternoon, before things got really bad. Colvin is twenty-eight, a man so sparely built he looks almost frail. His head and hands are prominent, his speech softened by a haze from North Carolina. "When I talk to masters now," he said, "there is a feeling of pervasive uneasiness. People recognize that the school is in a transitional period. I feel that the school is not sick, but is being born again. While there is a great deal of criticism to be uncovered, and I'm very critical myself, I think this is a very healthy sign, born of a sense that the school is about to move."

The previous summer Robert Atmore had said, "I think it's

very healthy for a school to have one great moral crisis a year," but few faculty cared for the size and shape of the crisis which, as winter yielded to spring, was clearly unavoidable. One or two like Mounir Sa'adah doubted that the boys would be involved —"The present generation have almost despaired of the world," he said. "What they want is security, a good income, not to be *bothered*"—but the boys were ready to burst. There were four principal causes of student dissent:

• There is not enough *time,* the boys said. Our lives are over-organized at Choate. With every moment of the day taken up, often in trivial details, we cannot stop to think, to find out who we are.

• We do not have enough *information,* they said, about what is going on in the world. Choate is a closed community, unwilling to let us hear from the people who are really making things happen. (In fact, Robert Atmore, the man usually responsible for obtaining guest lecturers, was on a leave of absence; Gordon Stillman, who took over the task, admitted he didn't have time to do it properly.)

• There is not enough *excitement* in the school, the boys said. No signs of life in class. Instead, the atmosphere is repressive.

• There is almost no *communication* between students and faculty, between students and administration. Their education, as they saw it, had been entrusted to a pack of leather-covered trolls, a group of graying elders who dozed through classes, one sleepy eye on the clock, repeating by rote the lessons they had prepared a generation earlier.

Later, some of the most astute of the dissident students would add a fifth complaint:

• We ourselves do not care enough. We protest our own apathy.

But it was not time for that yet. Although 80 percent of the students felt Choate had placed too many restrictions on them, 53 percent said they would come to Choate again. Angry dissent was still, if only barely, limited to a minority of students, but that minority could express itself with vigor.

In February, some influential alumni were invited to attend lectures on developments at Choate. Someone had the bright idea that these solid alumni ("We love the establishment, all of us," one had said in a discussion) should be allowed to talk to a handpicked group of "articulate critics of the School." The "critics" would be drawn from the sixth form and would be told that "development of personal responsibility" would be the perspective from which they should talk. They were supposed to follow a printed agenda—the school was, that year, queer for agendas—which contained such questions as: "Can there really be an 'individual' at Choate?"

The boys spoke bluntly. "I don't think you *can* be an individual at Choate," said one to the startled alumni and their wives.

"I don't think that's true for a second, ha, ha," said a wife to the boy. "And I don't think *you* believe it either."

"I think you can," said another boy. "Simply by reacting *against* Choate."

"I think you have to fight to be an individual," said another. "Individuality of thought is certainly lessened in a place like this. Very few people are allowed to pursue what really interests them."

"Why," asked the wife of an alumnus, "is it so important to get college-type freedom *now?* You're going to get it later."

"Freedom *to* is what we're talking about," replied one student. "Not just freedom *from.*"

The grown-ups retired in some disarray. "You'll come to appreciate it," they said. "In fifteen years all this will make sense to you." The fact is that fifteen years ago, in Eisenhower's Silver Age, dissent and troublemaking at Choate were the prerogatives of the duller boys and misfits. The bright boys—who did well in classes and led in extracurricular activities—rarely challenged the school on any issue at all. The school wishes this balance could be maintained; often it insists that the balance *is* maintained, that only troublemakers are heard at Choate these days, but the balance has been irrevocably reversed. Choate's bright boys, including those who edit and write for Choate's publications, are almost unanimous in dissent. For the first time in the school's history, a boy known for his cogent and articulate criticisms of the school was, for the academic year 1969–70, elected head of the Student Council. Today it is the duller boys, St. John's silent majority, who don't make waves.

Choate's alumni have not quite figured this out yet. One wife reported to St. John that one of the "articulate critics" had struck her as being "mentally unbalanced." St. John, discussing the incident with his faculty, said, "We have let one boy down." He thought the faculty might look over the list of "articulate critics" to figure out who the boy was. There were several objections. Mounir Sa'adah said, "These boys were *volunteers*. We cannot, like the Chinese, say, 'Let a Hundred Flowers Bloom,' and then, when one blooms, cut off its head." St. John, however, insisted he did not have punishment in mind: "It is an opportunity to give the boy some more education." The faculty persuaded him: Drop the idea.

Fortunately for the alumni attending the conference, a meeting with the school leaders—the Student Council and the Honor Committee—was scheduled to counterbalance the articulate criticism. Again, no faculty was present, and surprise! The leaders, the boys who had made it in Choate's terms and were presumably happy with the place, were just as critical. "The school," said one boy, "isn't bringing in the outside world. We want outspoken speeches on Vietnam." "Not many people are excited here," said another. "We need more excitement in the student-master relationship."

The alumni were confused. So much criticism! "In our day," grumbled one, "most boys were able to talk freely with most masters."

"But the older masters are ultraconservative," said an Honor Committee boy. "Their ideas are really set."

"More and more students learned that the most significant aspects of education take place outside of the classroom," said another, "and in this respect Choate is pretty restrictive." He complained about the requirements of sports and homework which kept kids from getting involved in other projects.

"Choate," he concluded, "is too much involved in getting kids into college and not enough in turning out a well-rounded individual."

What did the boys want? Time off, they said. Time to go to a concert in New Haven, for instance.

"You won't have any time in life to go to *concerts!*" one alumnus said, his voice rising.

"That's why we need it now," the boy replied.

The alumni shook their heads and smiled wisely. As they left, one boy whispered, "They all seem exactly the same. Maybe all Choate graduates are the same."

"If we can just get some more information coming into the school," said the head of the Student Council. St. John, too, was concerned: "I hope we can make something useful out of this ferment," he said early in April. "Frankly, I've been too busy so far to do much about it." Everyone meant well, but, clearly, the "articulate critic" business could not be repeated at the next gathering of alumni. Once again, the kids tried writing:

Perched upon ancient thrones
Wrought from decaying foundations,
The antique people survey
What is Theirs: A
Corroded dead castle
Stuffed full of coffins and
Cherished mementos to remind them
Of life.
Their minds out-maneuvered,
Bewildered by change, they
Stumble back snidely
To sacred clichés—once catchy
Now worthless. Their wisdom is
Wasted, petrified by tradition
And tied down by stays.
Gasping for breath in a world
That's not theirs, they
Butcher young futures
To prolong their own past.

But the stormclouds are massing
On the ancients' horizon, as the
New children muster
With time on their side. And
Screaming doves of the
Once peaceful past crash
Through failing truths
As rocks shatter glass.
With progress behind them and
A World left to save, the
New Children push the dead
Back to their graves.

The poem was called "Time Is on Our Side," and it is clear enough. The trouble was that almost no one saw the poem. It was privately mimeographed and distributed to a handful of masters and boys. The senior who, as president of the *Choate Literary Magazine,* ran that publication by himself, would not have printed it. "Controversial material usually doesn't come our way," he said, "and if it did, it would probably be censored by Mr. Manson or by our adviser, Mr. Gutterson. We're given free reign. On the other hand, *I* wouldn't want—our editorial *staff* wouldn't want—something in the magazine that would degrade its editorial quality: outright, unnecessary criticism of the school or anything like that." The *Lit* is very thin, but marvelously glossy, with photographs of trains disappearing into the mist, and a few "very serious pieces," as the *Lit*'s president calls them. "We have the usual boy-girl relationship, the love-affair-type thing. Death, murder—things like that are emphasized. We're subsidized. We don't have to worry."

The *Choate News* is subsidized, too, and it had to worry all year. In my day, the *News* was fat and glossy and uncontroversial. I wrote editorials about showing the proper spirit for Fathers' Day, and the business manager paid his way through college (so it was said) by the revenue he collected from cigarette advertising. Now the *News* allows no cigarette advertising and commonly runs to eight tabloid-size pages. Its editors are fierce, outspoken boys, and its faculty adviser, Tom Colvin, is a man who speaks softly, knows the value of silence, and only rarely makes suggestions. The administration, however, knowing that the *News* is sent free to influential and wealthy alumni is alternately nervous and outraged. Hal Steadman writes a piece comparing the athletic department to the Communist Party, and a master, acting for himself, tries to seize every copy of the paper as it is distributed. Tom Dorland, objecting to the severity of the February punishments, writes a piece only to be refuted at length—and privately—by the headmaster. The editorial chairman takes the trouble to interview Yale's dean of admissions on Choate's recent problems getting kids into Yale, and he is denounced—by the faculty and by the headmaster—for "irresponsible and inaccurate" reporting.*

None of this activity seems as exciting as the discovery, three years earlier, that the opening letters of each paragraph in a certain *News* editorial would, if read vertically, spell FUCK CHOATE. Nobody noticed, so the boy, miffed, had to talk it up a little around the campus, whereupon he was suspended for his vulgarity. Malcolm Manson seized all the copies of that issue he could find, but there are still a few circulating around the school at black-market prices, perhaps reminding the boys of what "irresponsible" journalism used to be like.

In the spring, a new editorial board took over the paper and pronounced a policy. "The new *News* is a response to the academic provincialism, the intellectual smugness, and the spiritual poverty prevalent at Choate," wrote the new editorial chairman. "Choate students have too long kept their disillusionments to the bull sessions; they have too long refused to actively contribute to the school; they have too long hidden behind the mask of cynicism." It was a strong beginning. Like so much of what Choate students wanted to say that year, it was, perhaps, no more than a bold flourish of a trumpet announcing a parley, a reasonable discourse to follow. "I want to make it clear," the author continued, "that the sole aim of the new *News* will be to help and aid an institution which is already

* This article, to which the headmaster continually referred, is printed in full in Appendix D.

a leader in almost every way." Unfortunately, the author was too late with his qualifications, with his reasonableness. St. John, angered by the opening sentences and by another tedious piece which talked of life at the Toache Correctional Institution, banned that issue of the *News*. Later, the paper was published, but without the offending articles.

This kind of thing shakes the boys up. St. John censors the *News*, but he has the good sense to censor it only sporadically. The boys never know when he will be offended, or by what. St. John tells them they must use good taste and restraint, and above all they must be *constructive*. Constructive is the opposite of critical. The boys are, in effect, bullied by vague terms and occasional seizures into self-censorship and the fear of saying what they want because they fear possible recrimination. The strong stuff, after a while, does not get written at all.

St. John worries about censoring the paper. "We have to maintain a balance," he says. "Some people think the balance has switched too far to one side." He does not say *who* is offended, or why, but his hands are extended in the form of a scale, and his left hand drops. "We may be losing our stability," he says. A suggestion is made that from Heraclitus onward philosophers had agreed that stability was, in fact, expressed in flux, that the *News* may only be redressing a balance that had already gone awry, but this is not the kind of argument that St. John cares for, and he turns away.

Other members of the administration see no need to worry about censoring student opinion. "There are some standards you simply must not let crumble," says Charles Pierce, and Malcolm Manson adds, "This is one of my *big* things. As a school, we are *much* too careful to give rationalizations for our authoritativeness. *I* think we should say: 'No! You don't write that in the *News* because we say you don't! When you're old enough to write like that, we'll tell you!' It irritates the heck out of me."

So the students, whose protests to the alumni were criticized and whose protests in the paper were suppressed, had to find another way to say what was on their mind. They decided to speak through silence. This was the great crisis the school had anticipated.

On Friday morning, April 26, National Student Protest Day and, as it happened, the day girls would arrive for Festivities, the annual weekend of dances, a group of boys met before breakfast to stand in a silent circle in front of the chapel. At breakfast, six students handed out a mimeographed broadside:

> A number of students are congregating in front of the Chapel from 7:15 A.M.–12:30 P.M. this morning. We are conducting a silent vigil in conjunction with National Student Protest Day. Our aim is to create concern for the problems confronting the United States in this time of national peril and to offer a forum for individual thought.
>
> We wish to emphasize that our class boycott this morning is not a last resort but, we sincerely hope, a first step to consider these problems as an integral part of our daily lives and education. This is not a symbol of protest but a gesture of promise—a promise that we will devote as much thought to the problems of the country as they deserve.
>
> Recognizing that as Choate graduates we will be leaving this environment to be faced with oppressive moral and social problems, we hope that the school will join the students in re-evaluating its aim of total education so as to equip the Choate graduate with the means and desire to deal with social ills.
>
> We urge all who are in agreement with our position to stand silently with us. We understand that the administration must take action, and all who join us must be willing to accept hours [punishment] for each class missed. In addition we propose to devote our spring day to a social work project.

The faculty could not credit what it saw. There, as the mists rose off the grass, stood a score or more of boys in a kind of Druid circle. Virtually every student leader in the school was there, all of them flagrantly cutting breakfast. Plot, undermine, subversion: how had the headmaster *allowed* it to happen? The fact was, the headmaster didn't know anything about it. Pale and shaken, St. John advanced to the microphone behind his table in the dining hall and asked for the boys' attention.

Two days before, at lunch, Bill Harnoncourt, a disaffected senior, had approached Tom Colvin to say that he and his friends were planning a protest. Would Colvin help? "I couldn't give an immediate answer," Colvin replied. "I told him I'd have to think about it." Like most Choate masters, Colvin has served as faculty adviser to many projects. Protests were something else, of course; still, if the boys were going to stage a demonstration—and it soon became clear that they would do so—Colvin could help the school and dull the blow by insisting that the boys act maturely, with some thought toward the consequences of their actions. The experience would be part of the boys' education. On the other hand, if he was to do that much for the school, he would need to be trusted by the boys, and to be trusted by the boys, he could not betray them. It was, indeed, a hornet's nest. Wednesday night, Colvin told Harnoncourt he would "talk with them" that evening in the room occupied by Riess Potterveld, the chaplain.

"All along," Colvin says, "my attitude was that I personally don't approve of my own participation in a boycott or a demonstration of this sort. This is not my style." In fact, Colvin told the boys that they must *not* ask the faculty to participate: masters had too much to lose; it was too much to ask of them; and anyway, masters had pride: they would do nothing which would compare them to public school teachers who do go out on strikes.

Steve Wilder, a senior, remembers that Bill Harnoncourt dragged him into it on Wednesday, too. "We want you to help with this," Bill said—Steve was chairman of the Debate Council, and a bright, witty, articulate dissenter—"We aren't sure what we're going to do. Everyone's going to cut classes Friday to protest the war, the draft, and civil rights." At the Wednesday night meeting, with all the school's leaders attending, it became clear they could do nothing political. Many of the boys they had to have with them were political conservatives. "I wanted it to be an antiwar protest," Steve said, "but that couldn't happen. Kids here aren't interested in the war." Bill said, "We don't *know* anything about the war." Steve said, "Any protest is better than none." Bill very wisely said he didn't want it to be an antiadministration rally.

Steve had wanted speeches, too, but everyone agreed that boys would be bored after an hour of speeches—and their protest was to last all morning. Steve suggested, "How about a silent vigil?" There were cries of "No, no, we want speeches." Steve said, "We'll have hecklers, and how are we going to keep out people who just want to cut classes?"

Colvin didn't interrupt them. He said at the beginning, "I'm simply going to alert you to the problems you may face from students and faculty." From time to time he spoke, always slowly and softly, reminding them that the faculty's reaction would be stronger than they anticipated. He also tried to help them define exactly what they were doing. Were they protesting against the school? the administration? things in general? Gently, he led them to the idea that the administration would have to counter with disciplinary action. The school had no choice. Therefore, the boys should tell the school in its manifesto that they were *not* attacking the school, or the administration, and that they would welcome the school's disciplinary response.

The boys agreed: accept punishment and a silent vigil. "If you're silent," Steve told them, "that immediately sets you apart from everybody else. And standing involves some willpower. These two things make you different from the crowd, which is the basic axiom for nonviolent protest. Either you're a member of our group, or you're not."

By lunch on Thursday, John Olson, the boy who had been in so much trouble over his *News* article on Yale, had prepared a rough draft of the manifesto. They agreed to meet that night in Colvin's quarters, bringing as many boys as they could. "It had to be a fairly large group," Steve said. "Six people, like Wednesday, would be ridiculous."

"Okay," said Bill Harnoncourt at the meeting, "this is going to be an antiapathy thing." There were 25 boys there and still a lot of doubt whether the protest would go off at all. Everyone who joined the circle, the boys agreed, would have to sign a statement, so that no boy could join irresponsibly, without fear of the reprisal that was sure to follow.

Colvin again calmed them down. The wording of the manifesto was carefully combed. "Some of the critical words are mine," Colvin admits. "I didn't write it"—John Olson wrote it—"but I intruded every now and then." Colvin got them to associate their dissent with National Student Protest Day—this proved to be an error. On Saturday, angry masters were seen all over the campus slapping their New York *Times* which reported the Choate protest *in the same article* as a protest held by students in Prague or Warsaw or some such Commie place. Is *Colvin* a Commie? He teaches American history, so, no, he isn't, but *will you look at this!* Colvin also wrote the penultimate sentence: "We understand that the administration must take action. . . ."

There was only one more matter to discuss. Do we tell St. John in advance? Why not? Well, you *know* why not. "He'd just say, 'Why don't we talk,' " Steve Wilder explained. " 'Why don't we talk?' He could have *stopped* it." "We couldn't have announced it beforehand," said another senior, "because one thing we didn't want to do was to sit down over tea with the headmaster and talk about it." "He would have brought out every weapon in his arsenal to stop us," Steve said. Also, until the last minute, they had few supporters. St. John could quickly have quelled a demonstration announced by half a dozen boys.

"Instead," said Steve, "the whole thing just came off *beautifully!*"

At the beginning of breakfast, St. John held the microphone in one hand and the mimeographed manifesto in the other. The boys had put it on top of the pile of breakfast plates at his place, on top of a letter from the organizing boys, containing all their signatures. St. John did not see the letter. When he got to the microphone, St. John said, "I do *not* approve of demonstrations, of boycotts, of shirking responsibilities or obligations. I would like anyone who wants to talk about this, I would like the boys involved"—he still did not know who they were—"to come to my office."

Already, the boys knew something was not working. Later, the headmaster would ask them: How can you do this to your parents? "He means by this," a third former explained, "that apparently we came to Choate because we are supposed to learn and we're not learning by doing this." But at this moment, some of the leaders were upset. The head of the Student Council, who had backed the protest, lost his nerve. "I signed this," he said, "and I signed it just before breakfast, but I'm fearful that it is becoming a stand against the administration." Those in the circle knew it was not a stand against the administration, but some thought St. John would lose no time in making it one. *That* he could cope with.

Colvin was worried. Right after St. John spoke, he went up and said, "I have a great deal of background on this and will make myself available to talk with you at any time." They went to the headmaster's office in Steele Hall. "It was very brief," Colvin recollects. "I told him my role. His response was that I had betrayed the school. I was very upset. I don't think he would say that now." Colvin was talking on the afternoon of the protest; he didn't then know what the headmaster had in mind. Colvin went over the manifesto with St. John, making sure he understood exactly what it meant. "Another point I made," Colvin said, "was that by virtue of this statement, the situation was still kind of *neutral*. Not positive or negative. Certainly, the boys cut classes, but they didn't attack anything, really. The situation is still sort of undefined. The school's reaction is what will give it definition. If the school responds negatively, then it becomes negative." But there was a hope that the protest might open a ventilator so that new ideas might be considered.

St. John told Colvin: "You're responsible, because you didn't absolutely say no to it."

St. John was not alone. Ed Berry, one of the Old Guard, came to Colvin and asked, "Are *you* responsible for this?"

"Well . . . ," began Colvin.

"This is the worst thing you could possibly do," said Berry. "You are absolutely ruining the school. It's dreadful."

Malcolm Manson told Colvin he should be fired. "My first thought," he said, "was that it was a very ill-mannered slap in the face of the faculty. In Europe there is very much a team thing among masters. We don't pay anything like as much lip service to the idea of boys and masters working together toward a common goal. We tell 'em what the goal is going to be. And," he added, "we listen with great care and courtesy to their *suggestions.*"

Nobody—not anyone—asked Colvin what *he* thought he had done.

Throughout breakfast, as Colvin talked to St. John, boys popped into the headmaster's office. The head of the Student Council tried to disassociate himself from the demonstration. The head of the Honor Committee said simply, "This is a legitimate and proper demonstration and I support it. Period." One of the boys involved in the telephone theft came in to say, "Sir, I want you to know I think this is *terrible.* I don't agree," and St. John thanked him profusely. Another boy, who had come in at the same time, said, "Sir, I want you to know I agree with it." St. John stared at him in silence, then dismissed him. "What do *you* think?" St. John asked a third boy, the last to come to his office. "I don't know," the boy replied. "I just want to be up on the facts and I don't want to get anything garbled. I want to be where the action is."

St. John called a faculty meeting after breakfast. He brought in four of the student leaders, but Hugh Packard rose to say, "Some of us have classes in five minutes." St. John said to the boys, "Okay, you have three minutes. That's more than you gave me." The head of the Student Council took thirty seconds to mumble that the protest was not directed against St. John, but was "a rethinking of our personal selves. A lot of us have guilty consciences that we've been too apathetic. We hope good, important things will come of it. It's really been directed more against ourselves than anyone else."

It was the truth, but it was not impressive. Some faculty members strode out to their classes. The other boys spoke briefly, and the meeting broke up.

At the start, there were 25 boys in the circle. By 10:30, there were 95, 39 of them seniors. Later still, the number rose above 100. The boys reported that some masters had allowed or even urged the boys to participate. One or two canceled their classes. Mounir Sa'adah and Riess Potterveld joined the boys briefly, but they were the only faculty to approach the group. Other masters were vehement in their wrath. One, asked in class if he would punish the boys for cutting that class, replied: "They're lucky if I don't flunk them for the course."

"I think it's a pain in the ass," Richard Hunter said. He gestured vaguely toward a round man hung with cameras. "This man is from the papers," Hunter said as the man tried to curtsy. "He was going to take a photograph and now he's not going to do it." Hunter glared at the man, who beamed back. "It's unnecessary publicity," Hunter said. "You get a camera down there and *every* boy would be down there."

"They think they're doing the right thing," the photographer said.

"An *awful* thing," Hunter replied.

"They listen to all this stuff," the photographer went on. "We're all concerned about Veet-nam and world situations. We gotta get the *Democrats* outta there, that's all." He giggled.

"I could get out a bigger protest over food," Hunter said.

"My wife," said the photographer, "is the best cook in the world, but a lotta times I don't like the food she puts out. You gotta eat scraps once in a while. You can't waste it. Leftovers."

Every twenty minutes or so, on a signal, the boys would silently sit down, then, twenty minutes later stand again. Up the slope, on the steps of Hillhouse, twenty or thirty boys surveyed the scene. Hugh Dale, a perpetually sullen senior, debated Dick Whiteside, the school's director of development. Dale felt bad. Like many students, he thought the vigil was ridiculous. He had been in on the protest at the beginning and had dropped out, just as, a year before, he had been elected to the Student Council by boys who hoped he would voice their criticisms, but he had not said anything since.

Dale: One of the things they're protesting is *student* apathy.

Whiteside (incredulous): They're protesting their *own* apathy? Why don't they, instead of standing around silently, decide that they will be interested and be enthusiastic?

Dale: A lot of people come here with a lot of interest in the outside world and then, after four years here, end up apathetic. Toward Choate. Toward life around us. Once you get out of here, you realize things have been happening. You have to get adjusted to a different life. A *real* life. Not this stuff. This is a *sham!*

Whiteside: Do you think it's different in public schools?

Another student: Yeah, they get home nights.

Another: They're daily deserters.

Dale: They're exposed to ideas. They're exposed to feelings. Here, we're all sort of one person. One basic environment. Like a cushion around the school.

Whiteside: Would you say what you think if you could say it?

Dale: We're afraid if we say anything people will listen, say yes, and do nothing.

Whiteside: What you're saying is that you don't get the kind of reaction to what you say that you want to get.

Dale: Sir, are you *arguing* that this place isn't apathetic? The point is, no one *listens*. So often, on the Student Council, we've talked to Mr. St. John, and he'll sit there and nod, nod, nod. After four years, we're all sort of idly lulled to sleep. If you say what you think, you're branded: NEGATIVE. I heard some master this morning saying, "Well, if you don't like it here, get out!" What's *wrong* with criticism? Really? Choate isn't perfect. It's a long way from it, but most masters are laboring under this incredible idea that Choate is *the* perfect place.

Another student: There are pressures on you not to speak out, and when you can't speak out, you get cynical. You do speak out and you get branded: NEGATIVE. It keeps you out of college. Mr. Sweeney writes on his report: "This boy is negative."

Dale: Don't you feel this place is cut off? We're educated almost at an *angle*. You think of education as sort of going upward, you know? We're educated at an angle—you sort of learn these nebulous facts which may or may not help you. You don't get any grasp of *people* or of situations. They say, "Learn! Do your biology!" You know, it's ridiculous! All you learn is how to be cynical and hate school.

Whiteside: Maybe you're growing up and out, and maybe that's your job. After all, Choate serves a certain structure.

Dale: What structure?

Whiteside: Maybe you should have gone somewhere else. You say Choate is not the real world, well, then, *go* to the real world.

Dale: Maybe the people who make the decisions around here should stop and ask, "Are we absolutely sure that what we've done is right?"

Whiteside: No one can ever be sure of that.

Dale: This is boring. Let's go play softball.

The irony of a silent protest launched by boys who felt thoroughly discouraged from voicing any protest was not lost on all the faculty. "This is what it's all about it, isn't it?" one of the older faculty said in an undertone. "More and more students and faculty know that we cannot communicate with the headmaster. The General Committee didn't work because too many of the Old Guard here have lost their spark. There's a credibility gap here, just like with LBJ, because Seymour tells the boys they can dissent, but dissent in a constructive way, which means the school's way. I remember one friend of mine on the faculty," said the older master, "who five years ago wrote an extremely frank letter to Seymour, but the reception his note got was so violent it turned him off as a teacher. He will never again venture an opinion on anything. He stays out of everything." It is true; the man is never heard to speak in faculty meeting. "That's what I'm afraid of: Seymour hearing only what he wants to hear."

He looked down at the circle. There were only forty-five minutes to go, and at that point one boy stood apart to announce the time and to say the last minutes should be used by everyone to think about why *he* was dissenting and what he would tell the other students who, in a few minutes, would tell them they had made damned fools of themselves.

"This school could be the greatest damn school in the country," said the older master. "If only the man who ran it moved among the boys, not to make a show, but because that was where his heart lay. But he's too busy, you see. It's a problem the trustees should understand, but they won't. They're handpicked men who are pretty much sold on Seymour because Seymour is a dynamic speaker, he sells them on his ideas. He can communicate with *them,* but not with the boys. That's the irony; how *can* the trustees understand it?"

Suddenly the master looked very old indeed. "It's a dangerous situation," he said. "It's like an abscess. It's working up the pus to a bigger and bigger head until finally—POUM!—it's got to go. It'll go Monday night in faculty meeting. That'll be a show. Some of the sanest heads on this faculty feel that there's got to be a facing-up to the headmaster pretty soon. We're just going to have to say, 'Mr. St. John, I hate to say it, but you simply are not doing this school any good.' I don't know how else to put it.

"Half of me," he said, "wants to be down there"—he pointed to the circle—"because I sympathize with them. Half of me feels this is not the way to do it. It's painful for a man to work in a society like this. He must be loyal because, after all, if you're paid a salary here you must do the job and, as an adult, you can't run with the kids and draw your money. On the other hand, you have an obligation as a human being not to desert your kids, *not* to play it safe and be a hypocrite. Still, some of these older guys, about twenty of them, are foaming at the mouth over this. They think it's ungrateful, they think it's a personal slap at the Head. Since the Head doesn't deserve it, they want to be punitive to the *n*th degree. They've lost their cool completely. But they have a compelling argument: that they must be responsible. A man gets up in the morning, he has to go to work, he has to look after kids, he has to put up with colds, with pain, with agonies of various sorts—that's living. These kids, a lot of them don't want to put up with any of this. They're self-indulgent; they launch spectacular demonstrations for what they want. You see, that's what a lot of the faculty feels: that these kids are hitting below the belt. There's a great division now among us. Some of our best men are going to be very alienated, some may be lost.

"What am I to *do*? Should I get up and leave Choate? Because I don't agree with the Old Guard? I don't think I should do that. But what am I being paid for, really? I am *asking* these questions. Is my salary for stamping everything that comes through me with a rubber stamp? Or is it for doing what *I* sincerely believe to be right for Choate? Even if that means changing its leader? How do you answer *that* one?

"I'm having a hell of a time, really. I feel very torn up. I don't feel angry with the students; I *can't* feel angry. I don't think anger is the right solution. Besides, I need my salary, everything I can get. If Seymour finds out that I've been anti-Seymour, there's no doubt about it: when it comes time for my little personal concerns. . . ."

His voice trails off. "I feel I *should* be down there," he says. "No, I don't know. I guess I haven't got the *guts* to go down there."

"I don't know how I am," St. John says, replying to the routine inquiry. "I don't know how to evaluate this. I am probably back in the Dark Ages of the Sermon on the Mount: when people want to pray or think deeply, they go to their rooms and don't make a show in the open." It is 12:15. The spring birds are calling frantically, and St. John has had a bad morning; in calmer times he would not have banished the most successful outdoor speech in history to the privacy of Galilean bedrooms. "Perhaps good can come out of this," St. John says; "I think that remains to be seen. The question is whether this has turned out constructively. I guess one of the ways you earn the right to protest is by making high contributions to a community."

"The right to protest" is one of St. John's favorite phrases; it apparently is not a right we acquire as we enter the world, protesting the slap that starts us breathing. Only after an apprenticeship, a long period of doing things Choate's way and having one's work recognized and approved, can one file for a protest permit, and even then it may not be granted: the protest, when it finally comes, must be "constructive," and, of course, being constructive means that it will be tamer, more easily dealt with than criticism from those not yet numbed by the system. "He's got to earn his right to dissent around here," St. John once snapped. He was speaking of Rod Furnald, whose first year at Choate this was. One could hear George III yelling at Thomas Jefferson: "You're too *young* to protest! How *dare* you tell the Mother of Parliaments what it must do?"

"When you have given the community the very best you have," St. John continues, "*then* you have the right to protest." The boys have heard this so often they have come to believe it, though one, defending the vigil, said that the purpose of the protest was to involve those who had not yet earned the right to dissent, who had been too apathetic even to be aware of problems.

Now St. John stands by the library steps, looking down at the vigil, feeling more cut off from his school than he ever has, feeling that good boys acting badly have slapped at the school and perhaps—as one master unkindly suggested—they have slapped at him, too, because he *is* the school. As he talks, it seems that he is still not listening, not to what these silent boys are saying; he is instead trying to figure out what he should say to them. Communication is still one-way.

Would he consider standing with the boys for five minutes?

"I have, of course, considered this very seriously. If I could go and talk with them in ways that seem to me would bring a constructive result, I'd go instantly." Steve Wilder had foreseen that contingency: be silent, he said, then no one can talk at us; they are either with us, standing silently, or against us. "To go and be silent," St. John says, "which would be saying blatantly, 'I think this is the way to do it'—that I can't help having reservations about."

It might, he is told, look like a gesture of good will, of continuing desire to be in direct communication with the boys. It might show sympathy and concern for their sincerity and recognition of changing forms of communication. Besides, it would astonish the boys and make talking with them afterward much easier.

"I asked my wife if she would like to go down with me," St. John says, "and she feels so deeply and so strongly, and has talked so strongly to boys who feel deeply on the other side, that she said she just didn't *want* to participate."

"On the other hand," says one master, "if these kids are going to form a recalcitrant faction in the community, it might not be a bad idea on your part to go down and show that far from being a danger to you, you sympathize with them."

"I sympathize *completely* with them," St. John says, "and much more with the larger body of the school who meet a situation constructively. I don't know that I could stand in the ring. It says a lot of things, doesn't it? Some of which are things you want to say and some of which are not things you want to say. Have you undermined all those loyal men who take this as apartness—*apartheid*—if you join the *apartheid* group?"

You would, he is told, anger some of your faculty and perplex some of the boys, but the witness of continuing communication would be very effective.

"If that were the meaning of it," St. John continues, "I couldn't agree with you more. It is an appealing point. If I could do that, if I could *talk,* and make my position honest and forthright, I'd like to do it."

He did do it, finally, but he botched it. He walked first to a tall, bronze man, *genus alumnus influentius,* whom nobody knew, wrung his hand, and propelled him into the group of boys. They entered the most crowded section of the circle, stood for 150 seconds, and then walked together, chatting calmly, toward the chapel.

"Look at that!" said Hugh Dale. "Look at who's finally going down for two and a half minutes of solid vigil. Aren't you *impressed?*"

"Sixty-forty," said a master, weighing his hands like scales.

"It's so beautiful! We've actually *done* something!" shouted a boy, but Tom Colvin was not so sure. Over the weekend, events took an ugly turn. "You've betrayed my trust," Malcolm Manson told Steve Wilder, but later he relented. "I told Colvin I would have fired him right off," he said. "But it's Mr. St. John's problem. If he can accept it, I guess we can, too. After all, it was a blow at *him.*" Still, there was a growing movement to sack Colvin. On Saturday, St. John met with a few faculty, including Colvin, and admitted that his first thought had been "to fire Mr. Colvin." Another master volunteered that his first thought had been the same. St John announced that his chief concern "is to unify the faculty," which was clearly impossible, and probably undesirable. No one asked Colvin to say a word. Colvin said later that he was "afraid my scalp may be nailed to the wall at the faculty meeting Monday," that the main issues the vigil raised would be bypassed in favor of finding a solution favorable to faculty harmony. "All he cares about is law and order," Colvin said. "The school can only survive as long as every regulation is maintained intact. I've never felt so awful inside in all my life."

Sunday night, the leaders of the vigil met in Colvin's room to discuss strategy for a forthcoming confrontation with a hand-picked group of faculty. How could they even talk to the Old Guard? Many, like Bill Harnoncourt, were bitter: "You wouldn't believe the amount of prejudice here!" he exclaimed.

"Far more than in regular society. Oh, sure," he said, "more than *half* of Choate doesn't like the word 'nigger.' "

The boys argued. "What you have to do is raise a doubt in St. John's mind. We can't say: We're a bunch of kids and we're right and you're wrong."

"Don't make it personal."

"We could say, and I believe it, that for the first time I felt a *part* of the student body."

"We didn't talk about smoking rules, weekends, and dances anymore. We were trying to change the world, not the school."

"How can we help him with his dissident faculty?"

"Did you know what words are carved on his chair in the dining hall? *Integritas et Fidelitas!*"

The next day, the head of the Honor Committee reported that there was absolutely no communication between the boys and the headmaster who met them with his conservative faculty drawn about the table. "On any other campus," the boy said, "you'd have to kill ten guys to get the reaction we got here."

That same evening, April 29, the faculty met to discuss the vigil. St. John began talking. He talked for a very long time, telling the whole story as he saw it. "Frankly," he said months later, "I was trying to do two things: to clarify the situation and to protect Tom from a very strong antipathy that had come from the people who felt that for a master to *connive*—their feeling, and not a wrong feeling—in boys' using extralegal means to present their case was disloyal to them, to the faculty as a body. I feel that way. I still feel that way. I think Tom made a vast error. It was a time of high intensity."

At no time did St. John ask Colvin or Riess Potterveld to talk. He might have said, "Tom has been carefully working to keep these boys in line; he has told me a great deal of what happened, which I think you should hear from him," but he did not; he did not even look at Colvin. Colvin had been preparing a statement for three days, but he never gave it, determined, he said later, that he would rather look wrong than impose his views on the faculty and thus risk widening the breach. Nor did it occur to anyone else to ask Colvin to speak. "There was a strong feeling," St. John said later, "that Tom shouldn't remain a member of the faculty. That could easily have blown up had Tom talked, and I wouldn't be surprised, frankly, if we might not have been forced to an action we would have regretted. He was right to keep silent."

"We respect and commend the boys' concern," St. John said that night, "with the great issues of the day. That goes without saying. We support idealism and we want to work with them toward their goals in regard to the rights and wrong of Vietnam and so forth. But we must make it clear that we have a *structured* society." The boys must learn how to communicate through English, how to sharpen their minds through mathematics, he said, and how to understand the past so that they will not repeat its errors. "For these reasons we have set up a structure. This is the essence of our school life. We cannot and will not allow it to be undercut. They *did* undercut it by themselves cutting classes and by asking for a schoolwide boycott. It was a difficult position for us to be in. And the work that we give our best to do was, of course, to that extent undermined.

"There is a principle involved here, a principle of regulations—the laws of the school which we cannot give over to the boys under any circumstances. And this we feel we must hold to, and for this reason the boys involved will be disciplined. If there is an expansion of this kind of undercutting of our structure we should have to take, obviously, prompt and extremely strong action.

"I felt badly that I had not won enough confidence of some of the boys. I just don't know them that well. The boys were afraid that they would be, they said, talked out of what they wanted to do, so they were not willing to take that chance. The result, of course, was that we did not have that opportunity for communication with them."

St. John went on, in measured terms, to say that Colvin and Potterveld had erred—"with right motives and I think with wrong judgment"—and told the faculty it must in the future "stick with me, stick with us, stick together, that we form a united front—never *against* the boys, of course, but basically *for* the whole unit, the whole structure which supports the boys individually." If, he said, there were masters who couldn't submerge themselves into the team, "then I would have to feel that we didn't have a future together.

"This is," he said, "in no way a threat. It's just the opposite; it's a plea for understanding." Then St. John did something curious. He referred to a German play he had read at Yale; though he did not name it, it was Heinrich von Kleist's *The Prince of Homburg*. "It concerned a young lieutenant," he said, "who led his battalion to the battlefield and was told by his superior to stand—not to move—until he was given a signal. He watched the battle going on around him for some time, and finally he saw a crucial moment and he felt that if he moved in fast and hard with his battalion, he would wipe out the enemy. He did so and he won the battle." St. John paused for a moment. "Later he was brought to trial for disobeying orders and was sentenced to death." St. John paused again. The silence in the faculty room was absolute. "I didn't care for the play when I read it," St. John said very softly, "but there is perhaps some relevance in it to our experience here." Colvin, sitting against the wall, looked very much like a man about to be executed. What St. John did not say, and what no one else in the room knew, was that the point of Von Kleist's play is that the young lieutenant is pardoned.

St. John went on to speak of "constructive, continued constructive thought. And making our efforts more than ever worthwhile. Are there any questions?"

Jean Pierre Cosnard said he wanted the boys to apologize to the faculty, "to keep that courtesy which makes Choate pleasant. They were desperately anxious to make martyrs of themselves. If we do punish them, we are putting a halo around them."

Paul Juliff said, "This may sound like a bully speech, but my first reaction is that I doubted if there's a headmaster that's worked as hard and sincerely as you have keeping open the lines of communication with the boys."

St. John replied, "I appreciate that. I have felt that I have not been as close as I would like."

Cosnard blamed the faculty: "Obviously, you cannot be the only line of communication with five hundred and seventy boys. The clog must be with us."

"Where have we missed," St. John asked, "with boys like Steve Wilder and John Olson?"* As for the heads of the Student Council, and the Honor Committee, "they came to me with tears in their eyes."

At that point Jon van Leuven rose. There was a groan from St. John's right even before he spoke. "I think," Malcolm Manson would say later, "that there is a limit to the number of Van Leuvens a school like Choate can manage," but when Van Leuven got up everyone knew that, for the first time that evening, the opposition would speak. "I think some things have been oversimplified," Van Leuven said. "We should ask whether students should not substitute any other kind of activity for classes. We should ask if there is not in fact a lack of communication which aggravates the issue."

"Oh, sit down!" a master shouted.

"A protest," said Van Leuven, "gives the boys a rest from academic activity and rejuvenates them."

"No!" said another master. "There are lots of things we replace classes with—on a *structured* basis. It is *our* decision, not a *student* decision. This is the way it has always been."

St. John tried to change the subject: "To accept from a boy derogatory statements about another master is in very poor taste. He is one of our teammates. We must not accept that. We should say to the boy: Will you go and say that to the master concerned? If we accept clandestine word from boys about other masters, we undermine each other."

Van Leuven, who probably suspected that the headmaster was

* As this book goes to press in the spring of 1970, John Olson, a sophomore in college, is being considered for election to Choate's board of trustees. "Mr. Olson was especially active in school publications," said the official pamphlet which announced his candidacy. "[The] leader in numerous *ad hoc* student projects, Mr. Olson was one of the significant influences in the School. . . ."

criticizing him, said simply, "I think we must ask ourselves how far we are willing to *hear* criticism, rather than question the boys' right to voice that criticism."

St. John sneered. "That's a fair philosophical question," he said. "Philosophical" is for him, in times of stress, a pejorative term.

As if on cue, the school's other philosopher arose. "There is a certain poverty in our insulated lives," Mounir Sa'adah said. He spoke of Martin Luther King's murder and of the boy who had said to him, "The only thing I regret is that it wasn't Bobby Kennedy." Now the demonstrators, Sa'adah continued, were concerned with correcting error, yet they made two errors: "One. They were not democratic. They confronted me with a decision, they did not ask me to participate in one. Two." By now St. John was staring at the floor. Other masters were muttering to themselves. "Two. They interfered with the area of our deeper concern. We stand by your side," Sa'adah said, and St. John looked up, "even in your mistakes. I would like for *us* to share in the punishment given these boys. I want to share in their failure, as we share in their victories."

"You may share in their Sunday work crews whenever you have the time," St. John snapped.

For a while, the liberals were quashed. Richard Hunter rose next. For the rest of the term, masters and boys would argue about what he said. "You've been more than fair," Hunter began, "and understanding in dealing with the faculty concerned." Colvin sat behind Hunter, who never turned; Colvin's expression never changed. "I don't know why you *don't* make some threats." Hunter paused. "I guess we can blame this on Doctor Spock.

"You say you won't allow anyone to speak ill of anyone else," Hunter said, "but indirectly, these kids are yelling at you when they won't even come to see you. You can speak ill of someone by saying or not saying something. You have sins of omission and commission, and as far as I'm concerned, this is a very definite sin of omission."

"I agree with you, Dick," said St. John, who uses first names in faculty meeting when it seems advantageous. "I've said this loud and clear," St. John went on. "There is no misunderstanding between us."

"As long as it's definite that this *is* a threat," said Hunter. There was laughter, but not from Hunter.

"It's a stand that we must stand by," St. John replied.

Hunter paused. St. John looked at him. Hunter smiled. "I can go on," he said.

"Go right ahead. We're all ears." More laughter. "You've been good so far," St. John added, and there was more laughter.

"I am very worried about this whole protest," Hunter confessed. "Directly after the damage, Friday night, I went back to my house and turned on my television and watched Channel 5. It just happened to be Joe Pyne. On the Joe Pyne Show that date—now I realize I am going to make some people unhappy—they had a member of the Student, uh, Democratic Action."

"SDS," said St. John.

"SDS," said Hunter. At that moment, members of the SDS and some black militant students had occupied several administration buildings at Columbia for three days. "And also," said Hunter, "a member of the FBI, who had been an undercover agent in their activity. And the member of the FBI made me realize a lot of things that were going on. He said one thing the Communist student front—this front—does is work on the ten percent idealists in the student body. Work on them. Get about a group of ten percent of students in one place at one time and then they call up all the media, Walter Cronkite and so on."

In fact, some boy had called the local press.

"And get in there," Hunter said, "and photograph. I'm very worried—not that they're behind our thing, but that in a misguided way we're contributing to Communist activity in this country. I talked to a reporter from the Meriden *Record.* He had an anonymous phone call that morning. Come down to Choate for the protest. This is the way they work. Maybe *we're* working for them, when some of our misguided idealists call up Walter Cronkite. I'm really very worried. This is permissive. It is not constructive. It's against the organization, against the institution."

St. John listened, leaning against a table, never moving.

"The *Choate News,*" Hunter went on, "is against the institution." He spoke of John Olson's article on the admissions problem at Yale. "This is the most damaging article we've sent out," Hunter said. "Our philosophy is *attacked. You*'re attacked." St. John needs no help in identifying himself with the school. "*Everyone* is attacked. And yet, it just comes out. The boy wants to say something without guidance—or with guidance, which would be more frightening—and this article comes out."

There it was. Hunter had made it clear that Colvin was behind all expressions of dissent. Colvin didn't blink.

"All I can say is," Hunter went on, "*please* threaten. Threaten the faculty. Threaten the student body. Then maybe we'll get back to normal, where we belong. But don't show all our dirty laundry and say, God, here we're *democratic! Look at my underwear!*"

Hunter had finished and there was loud applause. Herb Gutterson rose: "Maybe this doesn't have to be said, but I think what the headmaster said tonight and said well was *his* prerogative. But there is a question whether Mr. Hunter should cast the first stone. I do not honestly feel that the credentials of Mr. Potterveld and Mr. Colvin as gentlemen and teachers are under question."

It was all the defense anyone offered. A few days later, St. John said of Hunter's speech: "It was a man saying, 'Look, we believe in the school. We are loyal to it. We want to pull it up, not knock it down.' " St. John was still incensed over John Olson's article on Yale. "Some of our men," he said then, "feel a little less proud of their work here than they once did, and articles like Olson's make them feel that way." He paused. "What," he asked, "can you do when you find a new attitude in your school, which threatens to undermine what you have established? No: *undermine* is not too strong a word."

In the faculty meeting that night, however, the bloodletting was not over. Dave Vietor, who had recently been smashed for suggesting that the faculty were stifled even in their classrooms, rose to make a wandering speech. "I think one can get too carried away with this," he said, and he waffled on for a while about students asking questions until he settled into the meat of his argument: "Students feel," he said, "that the biggest thing today is the fact that the institutions as we know them have begun to crumble, and we are watching them begin to crumble" —Vietor apparently was not watching St. John's face—"by the war in Vietnam and the domestic situation," and so on for a while until he ran out of steam.

St. John said coldly, "You have raised more things than we could ever take up in a meeting. But if a master is doing his job, and he does it up to the hilt, I think he has every right to suggest what our weaknesses are." St. John has his knife out now; only Vietor cannot see it. "Were *you* here over the weekend?"

Vietor (shaken) : Yuh, I was.

St. John: I understood that you were not!

Vietor: I was here Friday afternoon, Saturday, and, uh, yesterday.

St. John (absolutely icy now, words cutting like blades) : *Not* Saturday night. Not over the weekend when you could have been helping with the house.

Vietor: I was in the house Saturday night for a while, yuh.

St. John: Oh, David!

Vietor (frightened) : I was! I drove out here Saturday evening!

St. John: Well, maybe. *Perhaps.* (He moves slowly down to Vietor, and stresses his words carefully.) Let me tell you that the structure you see that is built here is built by the blood, sweat, and tears of a lot of men who are working like dogs here, day in and day out. And if others are not willing to pull their weight in the boat, there's a strong feeling that they don't have quite the same vote and quite the voice in affairs as the men who are working within the basic structure—so that *others* can have the luxury of criticizing and changing.

Vietor: I'm not suggesting changes. All I'm asking is moderation.

St. John (has him now, pauses, and then): Well, *I* think we have moderation. Don't *you?*

Vietor (destroyed): I admit there are a lot of things I could have done much better and with more strength than I have. And I don't mean to put myself on a negative course. I'll be quiet. I didn't mean to bring up anything that could be construed in this way. I apologize—to the faculty as a whole.

Malcolm Manson took pity on him, and as Vietor sat down, said, "I think we're on a side issue, sir . . . fundamental questions . . . tremendous need for concern . . . for tightening discipline . . . I don't think we need say, 'On the one hand,' " etc., for quite a while. "I didn't say a thing," Manson said later, "but I thought I should do something. Seymour was *angry*." It worked. Colin McDougall rose to ramble over petty lapses in discipline—"behavior in chapel . . . it's very hard to walk across and deal with someone else's pew"—and then David Rice poured oil over everything, reminding everyone of the seniors' concern with problems outside of the school, with the tutoring program in New Haven ghettos, proposing that "our school involvement—not the curriculum, I don't suggest modifications there," be opened to areas of national and international concern, and so on, with phrases like: "To summarize, I think this is a very important part of the boys' lives" and "Dialogue is going on!"

It was the ideal speech to present to the headmaster. Rice made his point. He talked so long that tempers could only cool. He turned the meeting to unexpected but unexceptionable praise of Choate. "Thank you, Dave," said St. John. "I've been waiting for our questions to be over"—no one asked what *questions* had been offered—"and I could bring up the constructive side of things which will be continuing," and so on for a while. "I want to close," St. John said, "on a note of very deep faith in our faculty and in our student body as well. I think a reassessment of ourselves individually and our relationship to the boys in our charge, and our reactions to their thoughts and hopes and ideas—often, if not entirely maturely expressed—is always in order. I have no doubts of the sincerity and desire of our outstanding boys to come to the conclusions that will make us steadily stronger." He said the last two words with a slight upward inflection which seemed to make them well thought out, and therefore particularly convincing. "I thank you very much."

Afterward, Don Beaton, a mathematics teacher and a friend of Colvin's, was asked: Why didn't anyone stand up and support Tom?

"Well," said Beaton, "no one ever does.

"This is a benevolent dictatorship," Beaton said. "It is not a democracy . And if we don't like it, we can go somewhere else. We can only hope that the dictatorship *is* benevolent. All we can do is hope."

A few hours after the faculty meeting ended, Grayson Kirk sent the New York police in to break up the student demonstrations at Columbia.

At their own request, the boys who were punished for the vigil worked off their time at the Stonegate School for the mentally retarded in Durham, Connecticut. Eight groups of twelve boys each cut a nature trail, planted shrubbery, leveled a rocky athletic field, and built a small bridge crossing a small creek.

"What I fear," said one senior on the day of the vigil, when its leaders were acclaiming their success, "is that it will become Seymourified."

"All in all," said Gordon Stillman, speaking two weeks later to a gathering at Alumni Day, "we handled this very well. The vigil is proof that Choate is a vital place in which to live and learn. The boys put questions to us and we must answer."

The following fall, one of the trustees who knew no more about the vigil than what he had been told, rose before another group of alumni to say: "We should be grateful to Mr. St. John for making something good come out of this. It was a very dangerous situation."

The next problem was the poll. John Olson and two other boys had, for one course, done nothing in the spring term but prepare an exhaustive questionnaire containing 138 questions, many of them complex in the extreme, to determine Choate students' opinions on virtually everything. The boys worked with several faculty advisers and with a professional sociologist at Yale. They persuaded the English Department to give Choate students a free period on May 3 to reply to the questions. Eventually, 536 boys completed the form under conditions which assured that no boy's identity could be revealed. What was revealed was that:

• 110 students, or 20 percent of Choate, had tried marijuana.

• More than half of the students believed their families ranked in the top quarter of all American families.

• Nearly three-fourths of the students came to Choate because they thought it was the best way to prepare for college.

• Nearly half of the boys who had smoked at home had smoked at Choate.

• A quarter of the boys admitted they exaggerated their experiences with drink and sex.

• Half the boys admitted to taking "a cynical outlook" on life.

• Half the boys felt they could not talk freely to more than two members of the faculty, and 360 replied that they were "hesitant to discuss their true feelings about Choate with the headmaster."

• 23.2 percent felt that "My parents' expectations of me at Choate are too high"; half felt obliged to fulfill those expectations, but most admitted they were not working to capacity in sports or studies.

• 83 percent believed that there was a "mold of the stereotyped Choate graduate."

• Nearly a quarter of the boys believed they were leaders

in their form, and nearly two-thirds thought they were more popular than the average boy.

• One-third did not believe they had "a moral commitment to people less fortunate" than they.

• 80 percent thought that Choate placed too many restrictions on them.

These responses were bad enough, but there was worse to come. Fifteen percent of the students admitted to cheating more than five times; fewer than half said they had never cheated, but a rousing 68.5 percent believed the Honor Committee was doing a good job. Masters discussed that revelation for months. "If you have cheated," the poll asked, "does anyone else know about it?" Yes, said 41.5 percent. A third of the students said they had *seen* more than five boys cheating; only one-quarter said they had seen no cheating at all.

That kind of information came as a surprise to most of the faculty, and they were upset by it. The statistics revealing the boys' overwhelming apathy toward chapel services annoyed some of the masters, but hardly surprised them. The cool figures on how many boys smoked at Choate (98), drank at Choate (67), and took pot at Choate (24, with six boys later confessing they had ducked that one) were higher than anyone expected, but at least it seemed reasonable to ask such questions. What enraged St. John and many of the faculty were the questions about the boys' experiences with sex. "Have you ever had sexual intercourse?" the pollsters asked. Yes, said 22.8 percent. "Have you ever been to a prostitute?" Yes, said 6.1 percent. "Would you ever go to a prostitute?" Yes! shouted 40 percent. And 82.7 percent said they would have premarital sexual intercourse with a girl they intended to marry, up 5 percent from those who said they would with girls they "had no intention of marrying." These figures were made somehow worse by the pollsters' diligence in breaking them down by forms. Thus it was revealed that ten third formers—boys of about fifteen—claimed not to be virgins and four claimed to have been to prostitutes.

No one had ever known so much about the life-styles and attitudes of boys in a preparatory school before. The three boys who conducted the poll were proud and delighted. Nearly every student had taken it and, it seemed, had taken it seriously. Trick questions designed to check consistency and honesty showed no alarming variances, nor did any boy return the poll with grossly distorted figures or sarcastic comments. Boys might lie a little, and exaggerate, and probably they did, but still, there was no getting around it: this was what was going on. A computer was set to work cross-tabbing the results which would then, it was said, be published in the *News*.

It did not work out that way. The faculty was fuming over the poll. St. John was incensed by "questions of bad taste, the weighting of questions calculated to appeal to the weakest, the softest, the least-disciplined in us all." The results, he said in a speech before the entire school, "will never be published." Later, he relented. Clearly, the poll could not be all bad—three of the most able boys in the school had worked on it, supported by the faculty and by a professional—but, because figures "can be used falsely," the poll would be copyrighted when it appeared and, of course, it would be rigorously censored. Through a mix-up, no copyright was applied for and the laundered poll did appear in June, with no mention of the questions on cheating, sex, smoking, and drinking.

The president of the *News,* who had worked on the poll for a term, looked grim. "I've tried to do three things which I thought were constructive in this school," he said. "One was the vigil, one was the poll, one was my work on the *News.* Each one of these has been singled out as not only fantastically ill-advised, but irresponsible and unconstructive."

A few days later, on May 9, St. John announced at breakfast that all fifth-period classes would be canceled and he would address the entire school in the Remsen Arena.

"I have brought you here this morning," he said, "to tell you about the straw that broke the camel's back. Yesterday afternoon a boy walked into my office and said, 'There's a great deal of dissatisfaction in our group.' That's all, but that did it." Then St. John changed to high gear: "I am so *fed up* with human beings who expect to be happy without working for it—the sniveling, self-pitying, noncontributing crybabies—that I can't keep it to myself any longer."

There was a tangible tension in the arena, which is a huge place, with louvers open to the warm spring air—boys would later refer to the speech as "The Gunfight at the OK Corral." No one had ever before heard St. John so angry. His imperturbability irritates the boys, but now he was no longer nodding and saying, "Yes, but be constructive"; he was slamming it in to the boys, his voice loud, his language as strong as he would ever allow it—and very carefully chosen. There was nothing spontaneous about this speech: St. John read it to the boys.

"I refer to a few chronic gripers who have been given everything, for whom men and women at this school and elsewhere have worked their hearts out; carpers who have never in their lives had to worry about whether they would get an education, or where the next meal was coming from. They know that classes will always be held for their benefit. They know the kitchen staff will always be up at five A.M. so that their breakfast will be ready. But they're 'dissatisfied.' They are too young and too spoiled to realize that satisfaction and happiness cannot be served up on a silver platter; that these are by-products, hard won through effort and contribution to the lives of others."

The boys were stunned. The force of the speech, of St. John's emotion, got to them in a way the words did not. Few boys—or faculty—noticed what a curious speech it was: St. John condemning boys for their youth (if they are too young to realize something, why chide them for it?) and for their good fortune (it is not their fault they need not worry about getting an education). Working for happiness is, of course, good, sound Protestant ethic, but it ignores the teachings of the New Testament which suggests that happiness—joy—is already within us; it is free and we need only to open ourselves to it. There is a clear message to what St. John is saying: it is not enough to hate the sin; one must hate the sinner, too. The boys rather like it. St. John is clear for once, and direct; it is all quite different from the administration's usually bland and weary response to dissent.

"Let me tell you something about gripers," St. John said. "They are parasites—and that's not a pretty word—parasites that feed on the effort and good will, on the blood, sweat, and tears of others. They are doubtless right at times about what is wrong. But they are dreadfully wrong about what is *right.*

"I don't refer to those who suggest constructive change. They can be helpful (although frankly the faculty—yes, the old men! —are as a rule well ahead of them in their thinking). My target today, and I take careful aim, is a small handful—I could name a few—who spread a poisonous virus of discontent. They haven't an inkling of what is meant by appreciation or magnanimity, not a shred of gratitude for lives that are spent on their behalf. And frankly I have become sick of them—to the point where we are not going to put up with it any longer. We are not going to have a potentially *great* year ruined by a few ingrates.

"One of our wonderful boys—typical of those who joyously give of themselves in the classroom, on the athletic field, with the Glee Club, wherever; his kind are the reason men go into the teaching profession—this boy asked me the other day what was the matter with these gripers. He cited among other things the number of boys who had made Ivy League colleges—over half the class—the fact that every boy in the sixth form was in college; and he said, 'What do they want?'

"I'll tell you some of the things they want. They want to *live* at the expense of what others *give.* They want the luxury of criticizing those who spend their lives on their behalf without giving an iota in return. And it just won't work.

"No one believes college admission is the major aim of education. But listen to this. A boy said a month ago that if he didn't get into the college of his choice he'd walk out of school—if you can imagine such an attitude. Well, through our joint efforts he did get in. And do you know what he then criticized? The fact that Choate is too concerned with college admission—that college admission really isn't that important—that he wishes he'd gone to a school where less emphasis was put on academic work and more on something else. How can you win? Our need is for a solid phalanx of boys who give as well as take, who help lift tone and morale and joy in our school instead of dragging it down.

"Let me cite another example or two: boys who air their gripes in public—and not for constructive reasons. If they wanted to be constructive, they could come to me or a faculty member or the Student Council, have their say, and see what we could do about it. They prefer to make a big splash, to be cool, to gain applause by criticizing—in the *News* or on the bulletin board, sometimes in the most cowardly of ways, anonymously. One article recently struck at the heart of men who have served brilliantly on our faculty and in the admissions office."

The article, which bothered St. John all term, was John Olson's piece, "Why Yale Turned Cool on Choate." St. John usually tries to impress upon the boys that criticism which offends anyone, or runs counter to anyone's beliefs, is illegitimate, or, as he would say, "nonsupportive," but he hasn't persuaded the boys yet. "I wouldn't send that kind of an article to a dog, let alone my friends!" St. John then thundered, but edited that remark out of the written version of his speech, as he edited out most of his derogatory remarks about the poll ("Imagine asking third formers whether they have been to prostitutes!"). John Olson, the target of these attacks, was away from school that day and simply shrugged his shoulders when he heard what had been said in his absence. Olson knew the headmaster liked him, understood that the headmaster needed to make a sacrifice of him, knew that if the headmaster needed this, he was strong enough to bear it. Later that day one master said: "I think we had come to the point where the Head needed to sacrifice John. It's too bad, but when you write a piece like that you have to assume all the responsibility for it. And that responsibility includes what the faculty will think." Nevertheless, it was a strange scene: everyone at Choate had heard St. John denounce boys who had, knowingly, done ill to the school, but no one could remember St. John denouncing a boy who had tried to behave, who had thought he *had* behaved, responsibly.

St. John proceeded to what must be the most curious definition ever offered of the freedom of the press (a freedom defined in fewer words by our First Amendment): "We talk of freedom of the press. Freedom carries responsibility—and when the bounds of justice, truth, kindness, and loyalty are overstepped, at that point freedom ceases. It's well to recognize this now, for history is full of examples of freedom killed in just such ways."

St. John went on to the poll—it would be "useful and relevant just insofar as it leads us through high standards and values to a more imaginative, more challenging, more effective education and school"—and to the alumni who would, in two days, return for Alumni Day. "This brings me to my final point. I don't want one boy left on the campus day after tomorrow who cannot feel that kind of appreciation and gratitude. I can only hope that if after careful thought there is such a boy, he will have the courage to tell me, and to pack up and go. Too many people are working too hard toward great goals for us to allow them to be undercut. There is no place left for the disgruntled. . . . The cynic, the underminer, the weak complainer, we cannot abide. Like Nehemiah rebuilding the walls of Jerusalem, we are doing a great work and we cannot come down—to the pettiness of those who simply want more jam on their bread before they have earned even the bread.

"We live in difficult times—times when education and learning can be terribly hurt by a few. I can promise you that we will never yield to individuals or to pressure groups, no matter what their motivations, that use illegalities to force their will on others. There are other schools, and anyone who chooses may attend them. We shall keep our school moving forward in strength and dignity, with good will toward all who wish to work with us toward great ends: our action based to the best of our ability on law and order, on reason and love.

"I close by saying that there is not one boy here at school

whom I do not care deeply about, for whom I won't work my head off, who cannot have my full support. But that is a two-way street. If there is a boy who does not wish to give this school—the men and boys who make it—*his* full support and loyalty, then he must go. It is not right for him nor for us that he remain. It's awkward to leave school at this time of year. But it's better, more manly, and more educational than to stay if one is opposed to it.

"I shall be in my office from three to five this afternoon to see any boy who cares to talk with me about these matters—from any point of view. And by tonight I expect to have a *clean* school—a school made up of those who have thought things through and who *want* to be here not because we are perfect, but because of what the school can give them and of what they are ready to give in appreciation and loyalty in return. Then we can meet our alumni this weekend—meet *you* on future alumni weekends—and say honestly with joy in our hearts, 'We are also of the Tenth Legion.' " He was done.

"The Tenth Legion," Ralph Symonds explained later, "was Caesar's favorite and most effective, known for their loyalty—their *blind fidelity*—if *that's* clear enough for you." Two days after the speech, Mounir Sa'adah, one of the few faculty members who had heard St. John's words as well as his emotion, looked genuinely stricken. "I feel the atmosphere is now repressive, and how can you work in that?" he asked. "The faculty can be united and dead, or divided and free."

But when St. John finished, there were few dissenters. He had never spoken so effectively. He had unleashed the dynamism, the rhetoric, the sentiment and know-nothing belligerence that many of the faculty and boys had wanted to hear all year. He had divided the school into the good guys and the bad guys, and he had told the bad guys, the black hats, to be out of town by sundown. Almost before he had finished, Jean Pierre Cosnard, in the front row, leaped to his feet applauding, and, slowly, the school followed. "A good speech," said Don Beaton. "That's the way this school has *got* to be run." Peter Tower said, "We've let this dissent go on too long; we had to put a stop to it," and even Tom Colvin, faculty adviser to the vigil, the *News,* and the poll, said, "I thought it was a fine speech."

The dissenters, however, were not about to take up the headmaster on his offer to clear out. After all, their parents had $3,300 invested in a year they would have to repeat if they left now, in the final month. St. John didn't talk about *that.* "I should be in his office right now, talking," said one boy, "but that would be committing suicide." "I'm not losing any sleep," said another. "After June twelfth"—Commencement Day—"they can drop a bomb on this place for all I care."

The following week, Malcolm Manson explained why the speech was necessary—not so much for the school, perhaps, as for St. John himself. "Seymour," he said, "is one of the few great optimists left in the world, but because this is such an autocratic institution, the institution depends on his confidence in himself. Take the last masters' meeting. We had the vigil and the *tremendous* gut business—you know, D. H. Lawrence would have thought it was a fabulous occasion—and the institution lay bleeding. And Seymour had this big thing: he realized that he had not been as close to the boys and the faculty as he should have been. He said—and I have not contradicted him—that he spent too much time in development and fund raising, but *those* people are dancing up and down because he doesn't spend enough time with them! It was at this stage that I felt he ought to retire. Because he'd allowed himself to be distracted from everything.

"Anyway, we had the Gunfight at the OK Corral, and I was really excited about that; that's the sort of occasion that really involves me. Fabulous! I thought: Yay, team! This was really what we wanted. *Because we need the feeling that we are part of a system that knows where the hell it's going.* I run my house better because of that. So here he was, really mad, and I was very excited. I thought: Here we go; now we can really do something. And then, at the last masters' meeting he was just as awful as he's ever been! It was an atrocity! He spent five minutes saying he wasn't going to tell us about the Mellon wedding, which we're not interested in anyway. I think that after the Gunfight we had an occasion to make up for all the disturbances, worries, and so on—and he muffed it. He really did."

"The greatest criticism," said St. John, "that I got out of the May ninth talk—I've learned to call it that because everyone else calls it that to me—was that it hadn't been done earlier. I think there's truth in that, too. The only difficulty is that I don't find I can put on an act of that sort. I have to feel it right down to the bottom of my soul. And that comes slowly because I try to weigh and understand all the thousand factors that come into a situation. It takes time to be sure that the balance is that heavy in one direction. As I said at the time, this one came out of a straw. It was just a thing that finally tipped the scales."

Pulling Out

> There is a peculiar agony in the case of the young adults, particularly those close enough to the boys in age and taste to share many of their dreams while being at the same time restrained by all the terrible bonds of the establishment.
>
> One of Choate's older masters

> You can't be informal with a man who can fire you.
>
> One of Choate's younger masters

In February, as the turmoil over discipline began, a small group of masters—the oldest was twenty-eight—met privately and late at night to discuss the school's problems. At first there were half a dozen—two or three more joined them later—who would convene after the regular masters' meeting Monday nights to hunker over a case of beer and argue until two in the morning. The headmaster heard of it, as he hears of everything, and didn't like it, but he didn't stop it. Other masters muttered darkly of "subversion" and "treason," but these young masters had heard all that before, they were used to being told they were troublemakers. In time, the administration would recognize the extraordinary skills of two of them and absorb them into its ranks; the others would leave or be fired.

The young masters asked questions: Why is life at Choate so very *busy?* Why is the structure so rigid? Who do so many boys have little—some said no—intense interest in any area of school life? Why are there so many factions operating within the faculty? Should the third and fourth forms be eliminated altogether? Some thought that four years at Choate was a deadening experience, that the ninth and tenth grades were years of rapid social growth, but that Choate boys, lacking opportunity for social contacts, do not grow as they should. "Ninety percent of the boys I know are incapable of creating or developing an idea," one master said. What *was* the problem? Is it, as the chaplain suggested, "Ex cathedra," meaning that the boys have never suffered, or is it "Ex cafeteria," meaning that they have never hungered?

In the second meeting, there was little agreement but much aggrievedness; like Jonson's humors, the masters repeated themes peculiar to themselves. Rod Furnald said, "The kind of school *I* want to work in is the school which will accept me and listen to *me.*" Adrian Bullock, an Englishman who wears orange neckties, said that the faculty was prejudiced against Englishmen who wear orange neckties. Jon van Leuven bridled against "the headmaster's synthetic maljudgment" and advocated a "teachers' socialism. Some school is going to have to make a start away from headmasters' rule and toward faculty rule." Tom Colvin announced that he had opened a lot of lines of communication, "and I don't want to jeopardize them. I've got people listening to me who really oughtn't to listen to one who's been here only four years. I'm in a precarious position and maybe shouldn't be affiliated with this group." Adrian Bullock, accusing Colvin of working through the structure "to become a future establishment man," asked whether that was not "what we are trying to get rid of. You're *condoning* the system. You'll be just another faction in the faculty in twenty years' time."

Later, the masters tried to define the nature of education. "Education is the search for self-identity," Furnald said. "Education is the drawing out of the student his best *abilities,*" Bullock countered. "*Educare* means to lead out." "Intellectual development can only take place if they consider values that have no bearing on their positions now," Riess Potterveld suggested, and Jon van Leuven agreed: "If you cannot empathize with dead men and dead issues, this will be reflected in an inability to empathize with the living."

Furnald was having none of this. He did most of the talking: Creativity, he said, must be stressed in education. Let discipline come later, maybe in college. "Find a guy who wants to write poetry and let him write poetry. *Then* tell him he's got to learn the discipline."

Bullock needled Furnald all evening: "That's putting the cart before the horse. You're trying to create a *bon bourgeois* through education."

"Part of our obligation," said Colvin, "is letting these kids sample as many different dishes as possible."

"It's like saying get into my car and have as many crashes as you like," Bullock said to Furnald, "and *then* I'll tell you what you do wrong."

"Creativity in itself is worth nothing," Potterveld said. "Creativity can be chaos. Many great scholars work from *synthesis,* not creativity."

"I'm all for creativity," Bullock said, "but I'm for discipline first. What about a kid who wants to thumb through color pictures of football stars from bubble-gum packs?" Apparently, some kid had dropped out of Choate—because all he cared for was farm machinery. "You're not even disciplining his mind; you're letting it run rampage through his creativity!"

"The only discipline that's important is self-discipline," Furnald insisted. "The big problem here is that discipline is being imposed from *outside.*"

"You tend to forget," said Bullock, "that you're a product of the educational system you want to abolish. And yet *you*'re creative enough, and so is everyone in this room."

"The logical result of what you're saying," Stephen Longley told Furnald, "is To Hell with Schools. Rousseau must be your idol. You must worship him every night. There is no such person as Émile, who can be given freedom and use it without discipline."

"I'm not advocating Rousseau," Furnald interrupted. "I'm advocating a *direction.*"

"How can you direct without structure?" Longley asked.

"Okay," said Furnald, "a *fluid* structure."

"How can you direct with a *fluid* structure?" Longley demanded. "It's a contradiction in terms. Parents don't spend more than three thousand dollars a year to send a kid here unless we have a system in which they have some confidence. Provided the system is based on the right priorities, then I think we can justify it."

The meetings of this group of younger faculty continued throughout February. Longley, a latecomer to the group, proved much the clearest thinker of the lot, and though Furnald tended to direct the meetings, Longley gave Furnald considerable opposition. Longley supported the system that Choate had developed, and he supported St. John. "I admire St. John," Longley said, "because he is an extremely able headmaster. He's a darn good headmaster for Choate." Longley thought him an able administrator and tactician. "I think he honestly believes that he is trying to do something, and I honestly believe that what he is trying to do is *right*. But I think he has got out of touch. He doesn't *see* anymore. The administration doesn't see what we see: that too many kids are negative in their classes and outside of them. The headmaster kids himself that the system is working positively."

So the question became: How can we make the headmaster really *hear* us? The young masters were sure no one would listen to *them*. Furnald wanted to write some more of his lengthy position papers which he delivered, from time to time, to St. John, but the joke going around was that as Furnald hauled his manifestos through the front door of St. John's office, the janitor appeared to wheel them out the back.

"All this writing down ideas is crap," Longley said. "This is divide and rule! This is the way every administration hopes that it can keep everybody happy. 'Okay, if you have an idea, write it down, put it on paper; I'll be very interested to read it.' Fooey!" Nor would random speeches at faculty meetings help: "We can talk our heads off—we can talk through our ass—and still not impress them that there must be some action following upon talk.

"If one intends to change something," Longley said, "it is

done through people organizing themselves in a faculty meeting. One guy says something, another backs him up. This is Bolshevism. This is the way the Communist Party gains control. When someone outside our group wants to add something, let him. If he goes the wrong way—according to our lights—someone else from our group steps in to bring it back to the right issue. *You keep on the issue all the time.*"

"You're assuming that we are in agreement as a group," Furnald said. "You're assuming that we understand each other. You're assuming that we're going to be *able* to conduct the kind of dialogue we want in a faculty meeting."

"You may not agree," Longley said, "but if we were good Bolsheviks we would agree on a manifesto. You can back somebody up differently—and it is still a vote of no confidence for the administration. No one in any administration can tolerate any expression of no confidence. Ideally, good Bolsheviks begin talking with their second most important man. You always reserve your big gun for last. You get another man ready to step in after the first, to give another instance of what you are trying to get across. And then you get your minions coming in after. Coordination! You must agree on what topic everyone brings up. This is where Lenin was so masterful. I'm not being facetious. I think it *is* possible to effect change in a system of divide and rule. The confidence that when one gets up to speak one is not going to be left out on a limb. This is the basic thing."

"My trouble," said Dave Vietor, "is no sooner do I begin to think than all of a sudden all sorts of fuzzy phrases from Hegel start floating through my head. I like to get abstract."

But could Longley's system *work?* St. John's skill as a parliamentarian is awe-inspiring. "The only way to beat St. John's parliamentary techniques is to rattle the chair," Vietor said. Rattle *St. John?* Vietor and Longley thought it could be done. "If you really concentrate," said Vietor, "you can confuse him. You can speak in abstracts and lead him around to cross himself up."

No, you can't.

The Bolshevik attack never got off the ground, nor, perhaps, did the attempt to define the course that the education should take at Choate, but the ideas exchanged in those late February evenings were the first proof that the dissent developing in the school would probably prove more healthy than harmful. The young masters, even those so far out of step with the school that they would leave, cared enough about what was happening at Choate to spend a lot of time discussing what should, or could, be done.

In December, for instance, Rod Furnald decided that Choate needed girls. A lot of people thought so. There is no problem of homosexuality at Choate, which sets it apart from the English public schools. Malcolm Manson, who is English, thinks that possibly the English fagging system leads to homosexuality: "Boys required to perform a number of services for their elders may find themselves obliged to perform others," and he thinks it may be a problem in England because "education there at that level is so grim," with far more restraints than are found in any comparable American school. In any event, if there is any homosexuality at Choate, no one hears about it. There was no talk of it in the years I spent at the school, nor any talk of it when I came back to ask questions. A few of the boys and a few of the masters' wives speculate cruelly on the "tendencies" of the single masters, but there has never been any scandal, no case anyone remembers of discipline being taken in such a matter.

After living in a dormitory with a score or more of fifteen-year-old boys, however, Furnald decided girls were a necessary part of the educational process. The all-male school, he protested, is based on the Anglo-Saxon ideal of the stiff upper lip—no emotions showing. Furnald didn't like that. Nor did Furnald like all the goosing and ass-grabbing, the flying fingers and fertile language spontaneously generated in any situation where men must live together without adequate safeguards for privacy. One of the things boys this age have to learn is what being a man, even being a male, entails. Educated apart from girls, boys tend to think of them as sex objects or status symbols: the only girls they see are impeccably turned out in suits from Saks and hair from Mr. Kenneth. The only challenges such girls present are The Territorial Imperative (Only My Hands Can Touch This Property) and The Physical Imperialistic (How Much of That Saks Suit Will She Take Off?). They learn nothing about a girl as she really *is:* puffy and a bit stale at breakfast, with melted butter on her chin; sharp and argumentative in class, with her assignments done two weeks ahead. Seeing girls like that, Furnald believes, would help boys understand them, and without understanding girls, they cannot really understand men either. That was what really got to Furnald: the false fabric of masculinity that boarding schools develop. Boys, he told St. John in one of his memoranda, need to make moral decisions. "Females would introduce difficult ethical situations," but Choate is structured to relieve boys of the need for making such decisions—"Almost every decision is made for them."

St. John, too, was working in the same direction. Girls, he felt, could be integrated into a few Choate activities: in drama ("the most obvious and noncontroversial of these things"), in the Glee Club, and then (perhaps a bit later) "into the arts, into areas of literature and psychology, of religion and philosophy." Girls could be used to beef up enrollment in some of Choate's showcase courses—the computer and Arabic and Chinese courses—but on the whole, girls would be applied only sparingly. Coeducation was out, or at least for the foreseeable future. Coeducation, he said, might be "shock change," meaning, perhaps, that it would alienate alumni; instead, he favored coordinate education, a sort of separate but equal arrangement of separate faculties and administrations, with a girls' school being built from scratch somewhere within a five-minute walk of Choate—probably in Choate's nurseries. "One of the problems," St. John said that June, "is that if we go into this we'll probably go out for a fund-raising campaign of twenty-odd million dollars. More or less immediately." It would be Choate's responsibility to build the physical plant for a girls' school, an existing girls' school which would then sell its property, give the money to Choate, and move in. It would not be a financially profitable move for Choate because girls' preparatory schools are notoriously underendowed: their alumnae marry men who support boys' schools and colleges. St. John polled his faculty on how it felt about a girls' school. Six expressed indecision; two voted strongly against; fifty were very enthusiastic. The *Choate News* ran an article on "Coordinate Education," featuring a picture of St. John titled "Broad-Minded." St. John was not amused.

On September 26, 1968, Choate announced that in 1971 it would merge with Rosemary Hall, one of the oldest and most fashionable of girls' preparatory schools, and a school which had once stood on the Choate campus. Rosemary Farm, where the school began in 1890, was part of the estate of Judge William G. Choate. In 1900 somebody gave Rosemary a large piece of pasture in Greenwich, Connecticut, and thus began Rosemary's seventy years in the diaspora. Miss Alice E. McBee, Rosemary's headmistress, made the announcement with St. John and said that separation of the sexes in private education was a result of feminism, and "Now feminism has fortunately died." The New York *Times* ran a very nice story on the affair and released it one day early among a tangle of advertisements for plays and concerts on its entertainment page.

Rosemary is a far smaller school than Choate. It has only 250 students, half of whom are day students. Sale of its Greenwich campus will bring no more than $2,000,000 to $3,000,000; rebuilding Rosemary at Choate will cost at least $6,000,000. It might have come cheaper had not Rosemary insisted on its own chapel and its own *library*. The thought of Choate's fine library strengthened by Rosemary's resources, and the whole system incorporated in the present Andrew Mellon Library building where it would neatly fit, all run by Pauline Anderson, is irresistible, but it will not be. "Festina Lente," warned a 28-page pamphlet that Choate and Rosemary released together in July, 1969. The pamphlet was designed to calm the fears of alumni, and it contained some of the worst writing and most egregious thinking that Choate has ever mustered in its behalf. There is the usual stuff about "loyalties" and about being "a giver rather than a taker"; there is an admission that perhaps 2 percent of "the mixed group . . . will become interested in a boy-girl relationship in an excessively time-and-mind-consuming way," but that may be reduced by the seven-minute walk to Rosemary. "In this separation," the pamphlet coos, "lies Mother Nature's tacit approval of the terms of the affiliation"; maybe so, but because of the new buildings there will be a lot less of Mother Nature in the area to do the approving. Coeducational classes, the pamphlet says, will be limited to "honors and advanced sections of Sixth Form courses, where the maturity and ability of the students are well established." "Few girls elect to study physics," the pamphlet continues, "few boys choose to study the history of art or music. . . . If the study of history to a boy tends to emphasize wars and exploration, it means something very different to a girl, who sees and hears quite other sights and sounds in what she reads." If Choate and Rosemary really believe this kind of nonsense or, worse, *approve* of it, as the pamphlet seems to, coordinate education may be in for some rocky days.

"Young people," the pamphlet concluded, "have always needed leadership. Today's young people need it more than any previous generation." Again, as always, a pessimistic view of youth, but somehow, it didn't matter so much. Coordinate education, even the most cynical of Choate's critics admitted, was a very important, very necessary step toward genuine improvement.

In the second week of May, with warm and light-green weather settling in for good, and the headmaster's final spate of fury in the "Gunfight" speech receding from memory, the atmosphere at Choate improved. St. John announced the formation of faculty-student committees—the idea seems to have come from Mounir Sa'adah—to study "various means of achieving our goals more effectively." Some people complained that mossback masters were given control of the committees, but they worked surprisingly well.

One committee, charged with discussing changes in the structure of the school's rules and regulations, came up with recommendations (only the headmaster makes *decisions*) that boys be allowed unlimited access to Wallingford, that sweaters be allowed under jackets in chapel, and so on—Mickey Mouse stuff, but the accumulation of petty rules at Choate had depressed the boys for years. This committee, a kind of housecleaning committee, did useful work. An indirect result was that the *Master's Handbook* was retired permanently and that, for 1969–70, the *Student's Handbook* was rewritten by Tom Colvin. Colvin was not, as so many in the administration wanted, fired from Choate; he was promoted to the administration. Having been abused all year for his handling of the *News,* he was made director of publications. (Colvin first resigned from his post as adviser to the *News;* that post was then awarded to the man who had attacked him, Richard Hunter. Everyone anticipated a year of reactionary drivel from the *News,* but instead the *News* became more volatile, more outspoken than ever.) Colvin's version of the *Handbook* showed, for the first time, the fun and excitement of being a student at Choate; it came out clearly for a humane approach to regulations and made clear Colvin's own conviction that boys have dignity.

Another committee produced a complex report on the nature of sixth-form responsibilities and privileges and the duties that the oldest boys are expected to perform in their houses. A third committee, devoted to internal-external affairs, discussed ways in which boys might become more actively involved in social work—such as the tutoring program in New Haven's ghetto run by a few Choate boys—and in cultural activities at Choate. A curriculum committee urged that fifth and sixth formers be given more latitude in choosing their courses, a broadening of elective courses, and a small beginning toward the abandonment of exact grades in favor of a pass-fail system. An honor committee devised a new honor constitution which, it hoped, would reduce the terrifying statistics on cheating that the poll had revealed the previous month.

Mounir Sa'adah took charge of the most difficult problem: the committee on communications. Communication was, after all, what the troubles at Choate had been about. Sa'adah had plans to reorganize student government entirely, basing it on the houses. It was a rather extraordinary attempt at democracy for Choate: recognizing that faculty wives are residents in the houses, it gave them votes; it proposed that delegates from the houses attend an assembly which would in effect be the school government, that its meetings would be open, and its members given "total immunity for all that they say." Sa'adah's committee proposed an ombudsman to mediate among students, faculty, and headmaster; it urged that the *News* be "totally autonomous and free," though subject to a few restraints; and it began with a preamble advocating Sa'adah's philosophy that Choate should be a democracy.

Sa'adah's recommendations were hotly debated among the faculty. "I think we're going to divide, subdivide, and committee this school to death," Herbert Gutterson said. "The boys have got to expect some censorship; they just aren't equipped." Someone else challenged Sa'adah: "Do we *want* to be a democracy? If you mean equal votes for boys and masters, I think not. We'd get outvoted every time." Gordon Stillman said, "It does not provide for one vote for each man, a grave error that our Supreme Court has accepted," and *everybody* was confused. Was Stillman joking? St. John opposed the phrase "total immunity" for the *News,* urging "freedom with good judgment" instead. Hugh Packard said, "The ideals are fine," but the proposals just added more structure to a school with too much structure that wasn't working properly, and Burr Johnson added, "I gave away my idealism about eleven years ago." "The faculty," said Stillman, "is united in its belief in communication and improving it," which, said one master, "is a vote for motherhood, but no suggestion of *how* we can improve."

Slowly but surely, the faculty voted down the suggestions made by Sa'adah's committee. The Assembly of House Delegates proposal fell before a 26–16 vote. As others fell, Stillman said, "We have not closed a single door by any vote today." Jon van Leuven challenged this. "We have voted down most of the proposals made by most of the committees," he said, but the faculty disputed that. "Half of this report has been voted down with no telling criticism," Van Leuven protested. "There's no question in my mind that a basic revising of our channels is needed, but the faculty is so divided that there's no possibility of arriving at a reasonable conclusion." For that day, at least, it was true. Van Leuven rose to report that of forty-three proposals made by the six committees, only eight had been accepted by the faculty.

One of the older masters felt that student pressure would force these questions to remain open; students *had,* after all, a majority voice in arriving at them. "I fear mounting disorders in the years to come," he said in an aside. "Some of these masters are pathologically afraid of change. They feel that the school is not what it once was. It isn't, and it never will be."

"How do you weigh these things?" St. John asked, moving his hands in the scale gesture. A boy had just been caught smoking—from examining the burns in the lid of a cookie jar the faculty tried to determine how *many* cigarettes he had smoked—and Sa'adah was urging a relaxation of the expulsion rule. St. John then offered a parody of Sa'adah: "I would suspend him for the duration of the summer school and then require him to come to summer school to work off the suspension."

Sa'adah, showing no emotion, looked at St. John: "Is *that* the way I sound?"

"Our committees," said St. John as the meeting concluded, "have contributed more to our school life than we can swallow in a couple of days." Indeed. The school year had ended, and nothing had been discussed thoroughly. There was no time. But a start had been made, and as the more thoughtful faculty had foreseen, the discussions continued the following fall amid an even greater tide of discontent. "The students," said one of the radical younger teachers in the summer of 1969, "have taken the initiative away from the faculty, who are running scared." A year earlier, the thought would have pleased him, but not now. "Things are abolished," he said, "but nothing takes their place. New attitudes must be developed. And new internal disciplines."

And an older, more conservative master, who had packed up his family and fled the school for good, reported St. John as saying: "This is no longer fun. I used to enjoy being headmaster, but what is the point if all you do is fight with the faculty and with the students?"

Departures

> And hath that early hope been blessed with truth?
> Hath he fulfilled the promise of his youth?
> And borne unscathed through danger's stormy field
> Honour's white wreath and virtue's stainless shield?
>
> A prize poem written at Harrow in the nineteenth century and quoted in *Eric, or, Little by Little*

There is still talk at Choate of the new master who arrived and, on his first day, asked if all the seats in Memorial Study Hall would be filled. He was told yes, and so, appalled by the number of new students, he packed his bags and left. A few years earlier, John Lincoln, then head of the English Department, quit to work with black students. He speaks kindly of Choate, though he has doubts about it: "I think if you look at the daily structure, day after day," he says, "a lot that matters in education doesn't happen. And a lot that is harmful in education does happen. It's lock step. The boys are right: it *is* a prison. I didn't notice it at the time, and I was one of the best jailors, I suppose, because I was at my post when I was expected to be. It's highly systematized. Except in intellectual ways—say, in a class, where's there give and take—gee, there seems to be so much stereotyping, such reinforcement of only one or two views, and a premium put on things that are less important than real things. Like punctuality. I can understand the need to teach dependability, but you have to see the dean if you're late. You don't have to see the dean if you've been a bigot, or if, intellectually, you've been a dullard."

Rod Furnald left less gracefully. It is impossible to overestimate the rancor that accompanied his departure in the spring of 1969. Furnald, some of the masters said, simply could not be trusted: he was charged with passing on to the boys what was said in confidence in faculty meetings. Furnald continued to write letters, memoranda, and articles critical of Choate—"because it was a matter of personal integrity and conscience and because I thought I was in a freer position to speak out than most students and faculty, although I was partly disgusted and partly sorry for the cowardice on the part of much of the faculty"—but, somehow, these criticisms began to irritate the faculty more than they had once done. Matters reached the point where Furnald was once warned not to enter the faculty room "because there was a master inside who was ready to cut my head off."

Furnald had thought everyone understood that his second year at Choate would be his last, but in February, 1969, St. John wrote Furnald a letter to the effect that, after long and hard thought, he had come to the reluctant conclusion that Furnald would be better advised to inflict his ideals on another school. Furnald shrugged. It was, perhaps, all he could expect after the furor St. John had stirred up over an article Furnald had written for the *News* just the month before.

At first, the article was called "Challenging the Choate Experience." It was a fairly long piece, containing the criticism of Choate's brand of education that everyone who knew Furnald had heard him say, or seen him write, before. Richard Hunter, the *News'* adviser, intercepted it and sent the manuscript to St. John, who called Furnald at eleven thirty one January night. "He told me, 'This is the kind of thing that can't wait,' " Furnald recalls, "and when I got to the Lodge, he said that Mrs. St. John had been in tears and that 'this cuts deep, Rod, very deep.' He said I was saying evil, destructive things, that I was in conspiracy with Inslee Clark to destroy the school, that I was a sick, sick person and had no love in me."

The result of this was that St. John refused to allow publication of the piece. That news caused a flurry around the campus, and was deplored in the *Hard Core,* a mimeographed underground newspaper that had appeared on the campus that year. Finally, St. John went to a lot of trouble to edit Furnald's article, and the edited version, bearing the title "A Time for Examination," was published. Furnald keeps the original manuscript with the headmaster's crossings-out and pencilings-in because, better than anything else, the manuscript reveals what St. John means when he talks about "constructive criticism." Constructive criticism is, at Choate, a code phrase meaning, roughly, if I agree with you, it's constructive; if I don't, it isn't. It helps, too, for constructive criticism to be limited to peripheral details. As one master defined it for me: "Constructive criticism means that although there is always room for improvement here, Choate is just about perfect now."

In any event, Furnald's original manuscript provides a unique opportunity to see how the headmaster thinks one should write about his school. A few passages, necessarily taken out of context, show what happens when destructive (or, as St. John would say, "disloyal") criticism is turned into constructive criticism:

What Furnald Wrote:	*As St. John Rewrote It:*
We assume too readily, I fear, that the quality of education (both in approach and content) and that the environment here at Choate are basically sound.	Because many aspects of education are handled with excellence, there is risk of taking it for granted that the quality of education [etc.].
We are kept so busy and are so bogged down in the details . . .	We are kept so busy and are so caught up in the details . . .
There was a lot of life up there in the beginning. Diversity, positiveness, excitement, and some creativity. What happened was that so much of what was good became crushed.	And then it seemed to me that as learning and discipline grew, much of what was good became crushed.

What Furnald wrote:	*As St. John Rewrote It:*
Order and conformity were imposed.	Order and a measure of conformity were required.
Hope turned to resignation. . . . Meanwhile, other boys on the floor simply submitted and kept quiet about it. They went through the motions and counted the days to the next vacation. And all this was called "education" and "maturity."	A certain amount of spontaneity turned to resignation. Meanwhile, other boys on the floor simply submitted and kept quiet about it. They went through the motions and counted the days to the next vacation. And all this was called "education" and "maturity." Why? Is the assumption essential in the competition for knowledge and academic success? Must one trade enthusiasm for disciplined thought and action?
. . . the perceptive and intelligent few who do see the realities.	. . . the perceptive and intelligent few who understand the situation—who can take the best and slough off the rest.
Masters are so busy keeping the students busy and in line . . .	Masters are so busy teaching and helping their students . . .
Barlow . . . doesn't have the most expensive school organ on the East Coast . . .	. . . doesn't have a great organ . . .
Barlow has its problems too. But maybe Choate ought to look harder . . .	Barlow has its problems too. Its students are not so efficiently trained, nor do they have anything like Choate's college admission record. But maybe we could look harder . . .
Big things are worked out at other schools where the little things aren't fussed about and don't get in the way.	Is it possible that big things are worked out at schools where the little things don't get in the way? Might there lie here an answer to

What Furnald wrote:	*As St. John Rewrote It:*
	the problems inherent in structures and disciplines?
Choate has got to justify the old man's forking out thousands of dollars beyond what he's already paying in taxes to public education.	Choate has got to justify more than ever the high cost of independent education.
The School eventually (and there are signs already) will have to face the realities of 1969.	The School is beginning to face the realities of 1969.
A few weeks ago, two former Choate students from Harvard came back to talk. . . . But something happened to them when they walked into the Bamboo Room that night. One student in the room called it fear. And there are many people at school who know this feeling. Fear is an important factor in maintaining discipline, obedience, inhibition, and automatic respect for age. But those two graduates had something they wanted to say. I think I know what they wanted to say. . . . I've been at Choate long enough to know why they couldn't really say it. The atmosphere is not really conducive to openness. How do they tell the Headmaster, the Assistant Headmaster, the Dean of Students, with years and years of their lives wrapped up in this environment, all three sitting with their eyes on them,	A few weeks ago, two former Choate students from Harvard came back to talk. . . . Those two graduates had something they wanted to say and somehow never managed to communicate it. Why? Is there something in the atmosphere that is not conducive to openness? Perhaps some of the communication gap comes from each generation; and we need to work hard to fill it in, to make contact.

that something basically is not right with the environment here? That they feel it and came all the way down here to express their concern? Where do you begin? Predictably, the discussion quickly got bogged down in the traditional trivia and then there were donuts and milk. Soon after, that which never began was all over.

The sparring between St. John and Furnald continued until the end of the year. In April, 1969, St. John wrote Furnald, urging humility upon him. Efforts toward perfection, St. John said, can undermine the good things we don't recognize. He quoted Barrie's *Peter Pan* to the effect that every time a person says he does not believe in fairies, a fairy dies, and he went on to point out that people who act negatively become parasites on those who do the constructive work at the school. In May, Furnald wrote a long, angry letter to St. John, protesting what he felt to be an attempt to malign his efforts to work with students toward a new definition of education, and to make him a scapegoat. "The hope," Furnald wrote, "does not lie in the present faculty. Nor does the future. It is the student body which will cause the death of the old scheme. The Vigil of 1968 set the precedent. Milkshakes, meal cuts and personal intimidation will no longer win the day." St. John wrote back, accusing Furnald of virulence and meanness, of arrogance and intolerance, of inaccuracy and disloyalty, and of a divisiveness which resulted from his need for popularity.

Mrs. St. John wrote too, telling Furnald that he was more than disloyal, that he had turned traitor to the man who was trying to help him, that he was a phony and a small man who should grow up, that she feared she might feel hatred for him, but prayed that he would learn his lesson the hard way. She, too, urged humility. Furnald steamed. He did not feel he could reply to Mrs. St. John. He was particularly hurt that a number of people in the school felt him to be a traitor, a conscious agent of evil. He may have made mistakes, he may have been rude and immature, but he was trying to do the best he could. Why could not the St. Johns appreciate *that?*

One of Furnald's students wrote the Choate brand of free-form poetry to lament his departure:

He, unlike others in their sameness,
Struck out after different paths,
And soon became known for his
"Difficult and disturbing" beliefs.
His goal was simple:
Bring the Society around him
Into the Twentieth Century. . . .
He will be gone within two weeks,
But the revolution he started will continue.
Change is demanded.

At the same time, St. John had to cope with Jon van Leuven's departure. Van Leuven had completed a manuscript of poetry, had worked on productions of his plays at New England colleges, had shelved his book on economics, and was brooding about his novel. He had saved enough money to bum around Europe for a while. He resigned from Choate in January, 1969, his letter crossing St. John's letter firing him.

Van Leuven's letter, typewritten and single-spaced, ran to twenty pages. He began by admitting that St. John thought him "less than an optimally reliable observer," but then he lit into the school, writing with the kind of Thomist logic and Byzantine rhetoric he had used to zap the Yahoos in faculty meetings ("The amount of administrational reform that would daily prove itself exigent"), but also with wit, with insight, and with a perspective that must have made St. John peculiarly uncomfortable. Van Leuven, after all, was supposed to be the school *Communist,* but here he was using a kind of humility in his arguments ("Having had very little critical supervision in either teaching or advisory capacities since my arrival, I cannot but think it sheer luck if, once having hired me, the school has benefitted from my presence"); a Christian frame of reference ("I am a good Christian, and in Christian ethics good never exonerates bad"); and finally, as a karate chop, he insisted he was a *conservative:* "In addition to producing many graduates who reject secrecy and autocracy as principles of government or adult-youth discourse, Choate is producing more wild-eyed radicals than I would like to see as future American leaders."

Van Leuven attacked the faculty: for its "profound fear of being fired"; for its ignorance: "There are mathematics teachers here who have an impossibly vague command of subjects they have taught for years. . . . There are in all departments men who freely admit they have not read a book outside of their course reading in years, as well as men who admit their commitment to academics to be secondary to that for athletics. It is never said publicly," Van Leuven continued, "that our faculty contains a proportion of sadists and psychological incompetents."

But the bulk of his letter was an attack on St. John and his administration. "The school has no stated purposes. It has, instead, stated ideals or goals for the student, which place the burden and initiation of proof on him, rather than on those who teach him . . . the tolerance of incompetent teachers necessarily prevents the attainment of such goals by the students. . . . All collective activities within the school are regarded as having administrative implications, and all opinions on the conduct of such activities are regarded as recommendations, even when these opinions are unanimous, as they sometimes have been." Van Leuven charged St. John with encouraging faculty dissent because "it conveys a sense of democratic participation by the faculty in school policy, while exposing the impracticality of democratic school administration." He criticized "the divide-and-rule tactics of our Administration." Students, faculty, alumni, and trustees, Van Leuven said, are given different information about school affairs "and hence have widely differing concepts of the nature of our community." He charged St. John with rejecting "the principle of accountability" because neither his nor his trustees' decisions could be criticized by faculty or students. "The school," he wrote, "contains no structural means of assuring [students] that they will get a fair shake of any kind."

Please, Van Leuven asked, stop insisting "that Masters and students be at least 75% for the school. . . . None of us attaches numbers to the quantity and importance of our enthusiasms. . . . Since the school is so slow in tackling the more than 25% of its affairs which retard its education, and indeed tends to use the other portion to applaud the status quo, it is 100% in the wrong as regards its obligation to those who enter its doors." It was a neat kind of medieval humorous sally, a scholastic parody that probably missed its mark.

"Our assumptions differ," Van Leuven concluded. "You seem to think that where a way to conform exists, a will exists; that intellectual regimentation will lead to intellectual motivation; that social discipline will lead to communal cheer and good citizenship; that material resources and opportunities will create their own demand; that the withholding of information will stifle the demand for it; that authority commands respect; and that ignored problems, like diluted promises, will go away. Reverse all these notions, and you have what I think." He urged St. John to worry about the young masters who leave Choate—"Whatever you personally think of such men in retrospect, the fact remains that they were once thought worth hiring"—and, with a reference to the forthcoming merger with Rosemary Hall, he urged him to reconsider his problems "and, like Cadmus, attempt to raise Thebes before the cows of Greenwich come home."

But Van Leuven himself would not be there to see if, as he believed, St. John's problems multiplied. "I cannot teach in an atmosphere where so many spirited but bewildered boys are distracted from educational pursuits and must heap invective on their mentors to retain a vestige of self-expression. For a while I was able to persuade myself not only that their gripes were superficial, but that such tension has an instructive value by exposing the factors on which good community life depends. I no longer subscribe to pedagogy by negative example, or to the principle of noblesse oblige to the naïve. These lessons are my own reward."

St. John never replied. "I understand," Van Leuven said later, "that he never got past the first page."

"Enthusiasm for Choate . . . and what Choate has done for him. . . . Has he any negative qualities? . . . Not a strong or balanced boy; he has a lot of growing up to do. . . ." At the end of May the faculty convenes in the first of two meetings in which the achievements and shortcomings of many of the students will be discussed. The first meeting is to award prizes. Choate loves prizes; there were twenty-three handed out at graduation, but most of them were for special fields—Latin translation; achievement on the cello; best poetry in the *Lit,* and so on—and are matters to be handled by the departments involved. This meeting is concerned with two particular prizes: the first, the prize for earnest and persistent effort, and the second, the School Seal Prize.

Everyone likes these meetings. Feeling runs high. For days before and after, there is a lively debate as to whether St. John tries to railroad the prizes through or whether they are, in fact, awards made by the faculty as a whole. The Earnest and Persistent Effort Award is for the dull plodder who overcomes handicaps to do an adequate job in his studies and to impress the school that he is a decent, hardworking guy. The boy who wins it may be the boy who has been accepted by a small college *after* he spends a summer at the college's summer school. Nominations are made; the candidates' housemasters speak about them; then the masters of each class each boy has had speak—it is all very thorough—and then St. John, as he says, "summarizes" the evidence: "Perhaps you've taken your own notes, but this is clear," and he ticks off two boys who "have nothing but pluses going for them" and three more "with strong pluses and some reservations." A vote is taken, the winner announced, and everyone feels good.

Candidates for the School Seal Prize—"the boy who has made

an outstanding contribution during his sixth form year"—are subject to much livelier debate, this year more than most because virtually all of the school's leaders had been involved with the silent vigil outside the chapel. "I don't see how people leading the vigil can possibly be considered," said one of the masters from England. "They have done the school no good at all." If so, said Van Leuven, they would have difficulty finding a candidate for the prize. "We are making a mockery of this prize," the Englishman insisted, "if we nominate boys who make trouble for the school." "Sometimes," said Herb Gutterson, "the thorn in the flesh does some good, like the sand in the oyster."

St. John proved magnanimous and ready to forget past injuries: "I have long since forgiven the part that was wrong for the school," he said, "and accepted their expiation and their punishment. I look to the good that motivated it."

And so the boys were considered. One boy, said St. John, was "entirely on the side of the angels, a boy entirely on the side of the school." Another boy "doesn't have the same kind of *give*." The masters expressed interest in the "conviction and honesty" of the boys nominated, particularly in one who was said to be "honest, straightforward, kind, and sincere," but they worried that the class had, in fact, produced no strong leaders who strongly supported the school. One of the strongest candidates was described as "most like a loyal faculty member"; one of the weakest was said to have "listened to his friends, and his friends were not always the strongest."

Slowly, as the debate developed, some of the masters grew irritated. "I feel that this prize should not be for a *safe* boy, but for a *distinguished* boy," Stephen Longley insisted. How could anyone seriously admire a boy who was like a loyal faculty member? But, as Mounir Sa'adah pointed out, the prize is not intended for the school's most outstanding boy. It was never meant to recognize excellence. It represents a contribution to the school—whatever the school may think a contribution is. "There are many different types of contributions," St. John said. He thought Jack Olson's had been "spectacular," but he was more inclined to go with the more patient, less interesting leaders of the student government.

"We're perpetuating the status quo!" said Don Hickman. "Jack Olson," he said, "has perceived, wrestled with, and tried to resolve some of the tensions in the school which we ourselves, as mature men, haven't settled."

It was the best speech of the evening, but that didn't matter. The prize went to the head of the Honor Committee.

The other meeting, commonly called "the body count," is much more impressive. It is the last faculty meeting held in the year. It begins at nine in the morning and may extend to dinner or beyond because, at this meeting, the faculty discusses the school's problem boys, not only those who will be dropped, but those who will be allowed to return for another year in hopes that the school can still prove right for them. Masters let St. John know before the meeting which boys must be discussed; during the meeting Bill Sweeney sits behind a box containing the boys' entire records at school. The debate flourishes, but it is quiet and orderly.

"I have an idea," St. John says, "I could be wrong, that Jeff is going to come along next year and be quite a boy for us." Jeff had a 65 average that year; he had failed Spanish and had no grade above 70.

"I feel he could do the work," his Spanish teacher says, "but just won't."

"I can't figure the boy out," his housemaster says. "I can't communicate with him."

"I think," says another, "that we gave this boy the chance he wanted and now we are stymied."

"Perhaps," says St. John, "we are not the right answer for this boy at this time." St. John often wonders whether "you are really doing the boy a favor" by keeping him in school. This became clear in the case of another boy, whom the school did ask to leave that June. Looking through his file, one can see the pains to which St. John and his faculty went to keep him in the school, though they were in doubt about him for more than a year.

In his fourth-form year, Will Hamblin had seen the school psychiatrist about his "withdrawal tendencies." The psychiatrist had presented an optimistic report to St. John, who told the faculty meeting: "I said to the boy, 'I had a nice talk with Dr. Isay and he said you were great.' Then Will just stopped smiling. He didn't want to talk about that at all." So St. John wrote a letter to Will's parents:

> As far as next year is concerned, we should be glad to have Will back at Choate on the following basis: that both you and he, separately, choose it as his best course of action. Second, that Will continue treatment as seems necessary with some psychiatrist; and finally, that if we should get into another sort of situation of the past year, we should have to agree that we had lost this particular bout, and we would have to help Will find another course.

Will's father wrote back expressing his belief in Choate and his hope that with a little more maturity and assistance Will would be able to contribute more to the school—and to himself. He concluded with thanks to St. John and the entire faculty for taking care of Will when, undoubtedly, many more qualified boys who would be more of an asset and less of a burden to the school were waiting to take his place. Sometimes, Mr. Hamblin said, boys like Will turn out to be great men and sometimes not. How can you tell when the boy is sixteen?

The trouble with Will Hamblin was that he was a violent boy. He taunted smaller boys, twisting their arms behind their backs until they screamed in pain. "There is no question," said his housemaster, "that boys are scared to death of him. Most boys wonder how they can avoid him."

In his fifth-form year, Will took his SAT tests and proved an indifferent scholar: Verbal score: 606; Math score: 545. "Will's performance," wrote a teacher of his work in English, "was a disappointment." Furnald thought him an interesting student capable of honors work, but "due to his undisciplined nature and lack of effort, Will produced only the minimum required." By the end of the winter term, the teacher took a dimmer view: "He is often a disruptive influence in class." Will's German teacher agreed: "Will's work did not improve this term. He lacks concentration." Will dropped an optional course in engineering. "Will does not take a serious approach to history," another teacher wrote, and of his work in math, his teacher said: "Will's disastrous handling of the comprehensive examination was a shock to us both."

His housemaster was required to write a broader kind of report to the parents. "Each year in June," he said, "the Faculty carefully considers all prospective sixth formers in regard to maturity, enthusiasm and leadership potential. Will and I both realize that the possibility of his name arising is likely."

At the same time, St. John wrote the Hamblins:

> We are struggling along, and Will has made some gains. At the same time, in all honesty he has not yet shown the kind of maturity and self-discipline that would make us happy. . . .
>
> I think you know that I have always had a particular kind of fondness for Will. But in his own interests I have to admit that the time has come when he has got to prove something. And that something is whether he is mature enough as a member of the community, as well as academically mature enough to be faced with some real challenges in the Sixth Form. . . . We have handled Will with kid gloves for some time; and now we must take off the gloves and work side by side toward a common goal. If this does not pan out, then we should make a mistake in continuing together next year.

Mr. Hamblin replied that he would hate to see the boy's entire future drastically altered because of the few difficult years he was having just plain growing up, at a time so crucial to his academic career. He had to see the light some day and if it wasn't turned on now, he must face the consequences. He asked St. John for a conference. St. John replied:

> I told Will that I was available to you and to him at all times. I must confess that at this moment I feel we are somewhat talked out. Will knows the situation clearly. . . . I told Will that from

my point of view he was the boy who was now carrying the ball; and if he were successful, we should all be happy. If he is not successful, we'll do our best to support him.

"This was no springtime fun," one master said in the June meeting. "It was at night, and the rope was tight." Will, it seemed, had tied a third former to a tree and left him. Two hours later the little boy was released by another student. Will had then written a note to St. John: "I would appreciate any ideas you might have that would make me more responsible."

"He states two class officers and others were involved," St. John said, "but how much can you afford to help one boy if that help hurts others? One of the things we care for is the character, the spirit of the community. How do you weigh that?"

"We have expended on this one boy more than his share of our compassion," a master said.

"He wrote an obscene composition for me," another said. "He knows no limits."

Another reported "a grossly insensitive remark in front of black students shortly after King's death"—what Will had said was that Martin Luther King's killer could be charged only with "shooting coon out of season."

One of Will's coaches announced that Will was an "utterly incompetent hockey and soccer player who backs away from rough play but 'talks big.' "

"He put his fist through a plate-glass dormitory window," another master said. "He just stood there and could think of no reason. He had a big cut on his hand."

And still another: "He's a neurotic. He once wrote, 'I can't stand between twenty percent and one hundred percent of every person I've ever met.' "

"I see very little point in voting a boy out of the school because none of us want to work with him," Jon van Leuven said. "I think he is completely sane. I will take him on my floor as my sixth former."

But the faculty did vote, 37–7, to expel Will. St. John wrote again to the Hamblins:

Will has simply not grown to self-control in the way we had hoped by the end of this year; and we have very grave concern about considering him for a position in the Sixth Form where boys take on a specific and high responsibility for younger members of the School. Just before the end of the year, Will was reported to me for bullying, including tying a younger boy to a tree at night where he was left alone.* Will wrote me a note about this saying that he was only one of a group who were concerned, and that it was all in good fun. Unfortunately, there are a number of previous instances where Will seemed to lead in a rough approach toward younger boys. The best I can make out of this is a propensity in Will for working out his own problems by taking them out on others. . . .

We have worked long enough with Will so that it hurts me very much to think of not continuing to a conclusion. . . .

Please know that I shall miss Will personally; and that we shall continue to think of him as part of Choate.

Mr. Hamblin replied that he had dreaded receiving just such a letter from St. John, that seeing the verdict in writing left him and his wife speechless with grief. He had, he said, read an article in *Life* about why people behave cruelly to others, that he had worried endlessly about why Will did such things to others and himself. Still, though he hated telling Will what Choate had decided, he felt that Choate had done what it could. He had his son back now, but he thanked the school, St. John, and all who had been part of this difficult decision.

* To protect the boy involved, details of the case have been changed, necessitating the alteration of eleven words in St. John's original letter.

St. John for Himself

> We are grateful for your magnificence. . . .
>
> It is my privilige [sic] to be able to say that I am a Choateman.
> Letters to the headmaster

He has been headmaster for twenty-one years and looks forward to nine more, although he sometimes admits that this past year has been the worst, the most unsettling he has known. "That's all right, too. We have enough basic stability, I think, to take care of the problems." A pilot himself—he was nearly killed fifteen years ago when he fell from a pontoon into the propeller of his plane—he likes to think in terms of flying when he talks of the troubles he is having. A pilot, he says, will tell us to keep our seat belts fastened in case of unexpected turbulence. "I have the feeling we all will be keeping our seat belts fastened in the weeks ahead, in the year ahead. There is unexpected turbulence around us, just about in every way." Toward the end of that year and the beginning of the next, he often told a joke about a pilot who asked for his passengers' attention and announced that he had two bits of news to give them. "One bad news, one good news. The captain said that their gyro compass had gone out and they had no idea where they were going, but the good news was that they had an excellent tail wind and they were going there at seven hundred miles an hour."

Once, in response to a boy's request, he took notes during a typical day at school so that he could say just what it is a headmaster does all day. His memorandum went like this:

After breakfast—about 7:45—go through desk mail (my sweet wife gets all mail addressed to "Mr. and Mrs."). 23 letters in early morning, about half of which are shuttled to different Department Heads for replies. Of the remaining dozen, six can be answered immediately and six have to be sent out to Faculty or Staff members for background information prior to a reply. 4 of the letters also demand personal conferences with Faculty and boys. Of the letters that can be answered at once, these matters are touched on: a possible program for the National Association of Independent Schools, in regard to the Draft for boys who are 18 years old and want to take a year abroad before college; a gift to the School from the parent of an alumnus; request by a fellow headmaster for a conference on football policy; letter from an alumnus' father telling of his son's Phi Beta Kappa; letter notifying us of the death of an alumnus' mother; memorandum from Faculty member concerning plans for groups of boys visiting Chase Bank, United Nations, Time, Incorporated, Lincoln Center, etc., at start of spring vacation. 8:00 A.M.—Secretary arrives and we go over appointments and calls for the day:

1. Call from boy's father about an appointment at 1:30.
2. Call regarding boy's spending the summer in Spain.
3. Call from Treasurer of Board regarding disposition of a gift.
4. Call from FBI regarding an alumnus applying for "a sensitive position."
5. Arrangements for appointments with 5 boys after lunch.
6. Appointments with 2 Masters during late morning.

8:30—Meetings or telephone conversations with Faculty and Staff members:

a) Alumni Director regarding Hockey game in Madison Square Garden.
b) School Postal Director regarding plans for Post Office in new Administration Building.
c) Athletic Director regarding (1) plans for Hockey Arena; (2) plans for next year's Football schedule.
d) Director of Dramatics regarding a special Christmas Chapel Service.

e) Chaplain regarding (1) boy on verge of problems; (2) a key workman who has died.
f) A Housemaster regarding a boy who needs special support.
g) Library Director concerning schedule for Theodore Sorensen, who will be speaking to the school in the evening.
h) Another Housemaster in connection with a boy and House situation.
i) Director of Rooming Committee regarding possible change of 1 boy.
j) Director of Studies regarding a schedule change for a boy.
k) College Guidance Director regarding a boy who is discouraged.
l) Head of Mathematics Department regarding personnel for next year.

Noon. Late morning correspondence:

1. Letter from Honor Committee re matter of plagiarism.
2. Letter concerning another school on whose Board this Headmaster serves.
3. Letter from a former Master regarding Alumni Bulletin.
4. Letter regarding Foreign Summer Programs.
5. Official notification regarding Civil Defense and Fall-Out Shelters.
6. Request for a newspaper interview.

Arrange for evening party at home for Mr. Sorensen: fill decanters and order Benedictine (this is quite unnecessary, since there are loads of other people to do it, but makes for a pleasant interlude!).

Time to write 3 Term Reports on new boys (out of 170) before lunch.

1:05—Lunch with 8 boys and a set of parents and applicant student from Chicago.

Immediately after lunch:

1. Father and boy who are interested in a German school for next year.
2. Boy regarding lost coat (after normal channels are exhausted).
3. 3 boys regarding problems in academic work.
4. Alumnus in Admissions Office of RPI regarding a scholarship program in upper New York State.

5. Start for School Hockey game but never make it.
6. Call regarding Friday's Chapel Service for those who have served at Choate 25 years and more.
7. Rebuild the fire for evening party (and then forgot to light it!).

5:00—Time for fast shower, dress, welcoming evening speaker, and writing 2 more reports.
6:00—Chapel Service.
6:30—Dinner with speaker and 10 boys.
7:30—Faculty Meeting covering a multitude of minutiae, some thoughtful philosophy.
8:30—Introduction of Mr. Sorensen to the School at evening lecture.
9:45—Party for History Department—24 people—at home.
Cable from daughter in France asking for immediate telephone call.
11:00—Plans for early morning—and bed, with alarm set for 6:45.*

St. John is also the treasurer of the National Association of Independent Schools, a past president of the New England Association of Colleges and Secondary Schools, a past treasurer of the Connecticut Association of Independent Schools, a member of the Executive Committee of the Headmasters' Association, a trustee of the Barlow School in Amenia, New York, and of Athens College in Greece, and a past trustee of the Independent Day School in Middlefield, Connecticut.

This gives him no time to teach. He regrets the loss—"I love teaching"—but he does not feel it necessary for a headmaster to teach, "to keep his hand in," as some of his faculty urge. "To teach, and to teach well," he says, "I would have to spend a lot of time. It all comes down to time. I hire people that are just plain better than I am at teaching."

He gives, in addition to his numerous speeches within the school, about ten speeches each year away from Choate: sermons at other schools, talks to educational organizations and alumni groups throughout the country and, this year, some speeches to Rotary clubs about Vietnam. He keeps six speeches fermenting

* Peggy St. John says her husband rarely stops work before one.

at once and scatters notes for them about his small office on the third floor of the Lodge, a pleasantly disordered room which, in the summer, contains a large bulletin board with pictures of every new boy entering school next fall. "Here they are," he says, riffling through sheaves of loose paper, "notes for my opening sermon; the Fathers' Day talk; the opening masters' meeting. By August I have usually planned talks through Fathers' Day, never farther than that."

St. John also spends a great deal of time studying the reports masters write about boys. These reports, he believes, tell him a great deal about the masters as well as the students. "They keep us in touch with the parents," St. John says. "They make us put our finger on where the boy really stands and what we think about him, and put the finger on ourselves to say what the problem is and what we're going to do about it." He goes through every report himself, adding a personal sentence to many; sometimes he adds a full letter. At the end of the first term, there are reports on 175 new boys which he must check to see if the boys are correctly placed in their classes, are adjusting to the school's atmosphere; at the end of the second term, there are reports on all old boys who are not sixth formers; at the end of the third term, there are reports on all sixth formers. These reports keep St. John in touch with his faculty when specific problems with boys arise, and they help him to judge the new teachers: "I find out how they write, what their reactions are, and how well they diagnose boys' problems." This may be very difficult because the masters are not, in these reports, being entirely candid with the headmaster; they are writing judgments specifically phrased to be sent home to parents. "They *are* carefully worded," St. John admits.

Outsiders cannot appreciate how much praise the headmaster receives. "For years we've been above criticism of any sort," Peggy St. John says, and it is virtually true. The school floats on a chorus of praise for its headmaster. Much of it is quite spontaneous and sincere; many of the faculty, for instance, have lived and worked at Choate for so long that the school's successes are *their* successes and praise directed toward the head of the school, even if it comes from their own ranks, is partly praise directed at them. Some of the praise, however, is directed by necessity. This is not to say that it is hypocritical. It may indeed be sincere. But the fact is, the school and its headmaster must have that praise if the school is to operate efficiently. Malcolm Manson correctly observed that the school would suffer greatly if the headmaster's self-confidence were severely damaged. Many of the faculty sense this; a few realize that if the headmaster is in trouble, *they* are in trouble. Understandably, they want to avoid doubts of their own, the fear that lurks in some of them that they have wasted their lives, and so they bolster St. John in his certainties.

St. John quickly admits he wants criticism of a sort. "The best safeguard," he says, "when you stay a long time in one position, is to be wide open to needles. Maybe sometimes they have to be sharper and longer than you anticipated." But everyone who knows him knows that in fact he does not welcome much criticism. Few people do. St. John's seemingly repressive attitude toward criticism, however, does not stem from any particularly morbid fear of being criticized himself; it stems from his recognition that, in his kind of closed community where much of the strength and cohesion comes from him, criticism of him is much more dangerous than it would be elsewhere. "All these people who have spent their lives building up the school," he said to Rod Furnald after he had read Furnald's article criticizing the school, "their tenderness will be destroyed!" For this reason St. John spends a great deal of time stressing "constructive" criticism—the kind that is perhaps not really criticism at all—and loyalty—which is to be preferred to criticism—and for this reason the most influential trustee was summoned at the end of the year to warn me that only minor criticism of the school would be tolerated in the book I was about to write.

Finally, there is another kind of praise for the headmaster which is born of necessity. The school, as one master observed, lives on public relations. Parents and alumni must be kept happy; the way to keep them happy is to remind them that the school remains substantially unchanged, and the quickest way to do that is to remind them of the virtues of St. John. "A Tenth Century Anglo-Saxon in his regard for loyalty, integrity and courage," burbles the *Alumni Bulletin.* "In his enjoyment of outrageous double meanings he would have been completely at home in the Seventeenth Century. Had he been born an Elizabethan, he would have stowed away with Cabot or Drake. Already he has secretly put his name down for that first rocket trip to Mars! . . . From Toynbee, he has the theory of challenge and response . . . the Headmaster's mind is agile and quick," and so on.

The school must convince the alumni that Choate is basically unchanged if it is to get their money, but the alumni must believe it, too, if Choate is to remain for them a pocket of emotional stability to think on with fondness when an unstable, changing world makes too many demands on them. "Just because the hippies have sideburns, we must make our boys cut their hair," an alumnus told me. "Just because there is change everywhere else, we must make sure nothing changes here." Audio-visual aids, language labs—those are okay because they are no more than frosting—but *do not change the core!* "It's a very reassuring thing after one has been out in the world for a few years," wrote one alumnus to St. John, "to return to one of the places that *counts for most* and find that the same basic truths are still being sought for. As an alumnus, it makes one stop and take stock of oneself to see if one is still measuring up—the way the boys are so obviously measuring up at school. That friendliness and willingness to help which has always been a Choate hallmark is more evident than ever in masters and boys alike."

"I feel without a doubt," wrote another alumnus, "that you are and will continue to be the finest educator in this country. Time will prove my point. I remember your great Father so well and have always asked myself who can replace a man like him. But you have Seymour and it's wonderful for America to know men like you are carrying on. As long as we have men like you America will be strong for you are molding the leaders of our country. This is from my heart dear Seymour."

Anyone would like to receive such praise. St. John keeps letters like that in a file he calls his "Special File."

"My image is a very varied one," says St. John and then corrects it: "My own image of my job. It centers around boys and faculty here at school. In a way, that's a little ironical because that was the very spot this year that was most jumped on. And rightly, probably, because when you take three weeks out, as I did in Vietnam, at a critical time of year, and when you give as much thought as I did to that aspect of life, it just plain takes away from other things you're doing.

"Staying always at the school," he says, "does enable you to stick closer, to know better every iota of what's going on, and to direct. It also runs the hazard of developing provincialism.

"It's hard living in a closed community like this, where you never get out. It takes a lot more patience and tolerance and understanding than when you can leave your place of business and go to your suburban home. It's demanding. Highly demanding. All of us are rising above weaknesses in ourselves, we hope, and in others—absolutely."

St. John thinks of what he calls constants—"You keep a certain core of your absolutes, your primary values, and with the rest you play a little bit"—and he thinks often of why these constants no longer appeal as much as they did—or as we remember they did—to young people. "You go back to the old hackneyed thoughts of a farm where everybody had to pitch in because they were part of a family," St. John says. "Everyone had to be part of it to make the place go, and that was part of their daily living, their daily bread—they really earned it. Today a large percentage of people just plain don't do much earning until they get a lot older. I think this has been one of the problems. And in filling in the gap with education we have too long—and I blame this on education as well as everybody else—we have too long stressed that young people learn and learn and learn, take, in, take in, take in. We haven't given them opportunities to put out. All of us get our main rewards from putting out. That's the *fun*. When we're just taking in for ourselves, acquisitively, it's okay for a while and it has to be done, and I guess it has some reward, but the real rewards are spending. Spending ourselves. What we have accumulated. Never to have that opportunity, I think, has been the major cause of dissatisfaction of children in schools, the major cause for dropouts in college. They haven't been able to give."

Looking back at the beginning of his career as a headmaster, St. John regrets only that it was never possible to fulfill the request he made facetiously to the trustees: "They asked me what I'd like and I said I really didn't feel any immediate need other than twenty-five million dollars so we wouldn't have to charge tuition. To be at the point where you're forced to consider the economics when dealing with a boy is a very scary situation. When your school's life's blood is its money, it takes real guts to stand aside with principle and disregard the economics. I'd love not to have to charge tuition."

Looking ahead to education in the seventies, St. John addressed some alumni on the day after his "Gunfight at the OK Corral" speech. The contrast in tones and the emphasis on liberality were astonishing. The "Gunfight" was St. John at his worst; the next day he was at his best, at his most perceptive. His sentences were well phrased, and he showed an understanding of what was troubling the boys that, for some reason, he was not willing to reveal to the boys themselves.

St. John ticked off three fundamental aspects of education: (1) the traditional concern with helping students acquire the skills, the knowledge, and hopefully the enthusiasm which would carry them further into education; (2) the experience of working with others that education provides, including both the students' work "in the large social claims of the day" like civil rights and the imminence of a girls' school on the campus; (3) "the motivation of the individual in his own ways to develop a responsible independence of thought and action." St. John then acknowledged "the growing impatience for an understanding of the immediate," the tendency toward "self-determination as opposed to determination by others." He recognized that some traditional courses, particularly in history and literature, would yield to new courses in psychology and sociology, that "courses will search for new data" and that "abstract and open-ended problems will replace the neat and packaged unit. Emphasis," he said, "will be placed on discovery rather than absorption." The teacher, St. John said, will become more of a "coordinator and guide than an informant and stimulant to passive minds." There would be more independent study, and more of that taking place out of the classroom; students would in the future spend more time in specialized areas of their own interest. "People become bored more quickly," St. John said, in part because of the revolution made by television, "and they are less ready to accept presentations that do not satisfy eye and ear together."

Such challenges, particularly that of the students' growing insistence on developing their own values, would, said St. John, "involve a risk, and there will inevitably be some who lose by it. It involves an increased motivation and self-reliance, and I should expect that the gains would outweigh the loss. It involves a delicacy of relationship between faculty and student that puts our sensitivity and wisdom to a far greater test than ever before."

Such challenges also bring St. John home to the heart of the school, to the words which will reassure any alumnus who might have been made uncomfortable by all the talk of change that went before. "Our stabilities," he said, "will reside first in the religious faith on which the school was founded. . . . And secondly, we shall find stability in the law, which we hold to be a necessity if we are not to fall before the forces of anarchy and resultant dictatorships. The structure of school life will to an extent give way to greater freedom in the use of time. Freedom to make mistakes, to choose courses and goals in accordance with interest and talent, to have exceptions made for the exceptional, but the basic disciplines will be firmly upheld. The basis of our actions will reside to the best of our ability in reason and in love."

"I suppose," St. John wrote to Leopold Stokowski seven and half years earlier, "the great question is whether a nation so spoiled by the material things of life can hold on to the disciplines and the faith that underlie not only greatness but continuing existence. In a way one can be optimistic in the belief that those groups which are disciplined and have a true faith will continue. But one can't help wanting also to fight for one's own."

And in a letter to me he wrote: "In these times of change, sometimes change to the point where it is hopelessly uncertain what one is changing *to,* we do need to hold fast also to the proven good. I don't believe one has to be a stick-in-the-mud to do that; but it takes balance, soul searching, a lot of listening and a lot of reviewing—and, as usual, faith, hope and love. The hope has to be relegated to the area of being 51% right and only 49% wrong!"

On the back of a printed copy of one of his speeches he has scribbled notes for another:

"What can we do?

"Understand and hold standards.

"Never fear to stand up for what you believe."

APPENDIXES

Appendix A

Masters at Choate Referred to by Name in This Book

Seymour St. John	Headmaster
Miss Pauline Anderson	Librarian
Edward B. Ayres	Alumni Director
Donald J. Beaton	Mathematics
Peter C. Benson	Chemistry, Physics
Edward B. Berry	French, Administration
Harold E. Brown	Head of Science Department
Adrian Bullock	French
C. Robert Clements	Head of Mathematics Department
C. Clifton Clerke	Head of German Department; also, French and Spanish
Thomas B. Colvin	History
Jean Pierre Cosnard des Closets	French, Art
Rodman A. Furnald	English
Herbert L. Gutterson, Jr.	Head of English Department
Stephen Hawkins	History
Donald F. Hickman	Art
Richard E. T. Hunter	English
A. Burr Johnson	English
John F. Joseph	Etymology, Greek, Latin
Paul Juliff	Chemistry, Physics
Stephen R. Longley	History
John M. Lupton	Development
Alexander M. MacFarlane, Jr.	Dean of Students
William A. Maillet	English
Malcolm H. Manson	Greek, Director of Publications

Colin D. McDougall	English
Konthath K. Menon	English
Owen H. Morgan	Latin
Vincent Nuzzo	Business Manager
Hubert S. Packard	French
H. Jeremy Packard	History
Duncan Phyfe	Organ and Choral, Music
Charles V. Pierce	Director of Admissions
J. Lawrence Pond	Science
Riess Potterveld	Chaplain
Howard B. Preble	French
William A. Pudvah	Director of Athletics
Donald A. Reed	Chemistry, Physics
David Rice	English
Mounir R. Sa'adah	Head of History Department, Arabic
William H. C. St. John	Director of Scholarship Aid
James A. Spencer	Chemistry
P. Gordon B. Stillman	Assistant Headmaster, Dean of Faculty
William A. Sweeney	Director of Studies and College Admissions
Ralph Symonds	Speech and Drama
Peter P. Tower	History and Current Affairs
Mark Tuttle	Dean for Third Form, Mathematics
Charles P. Twichell	Head of Classics Department
Jon C. van Leuven	Science
Johannes van Straalen	Head of Russian Department, History
David B. Vietor	German, Russian, Spanish
T. David Waters	English
Richard H. Whiteside	Development Director
Robert H. Williams	Football coach, Mathematics
Thomas A. Yankus	English

NOTE: This list does not include masters who appear in this book, or who are quoted in it, but not by name; it does not include former masters; it does not include faculty wives.

Appendix B

Choate's Official Songs, Prayer, Etc.

The School Song

To our School upon the hillside come and sing a rousing song,
Till the echoes clear send back our cheer in accents loud and strong.
Then ever true to Gold and Blue shall be our loyal throng,
So we'll hail our Alma Mater, 'tis to her our hearts belong.
Cheer then for Choate! All hail her bright name!
Far through the land her sons shall bear her great fame.
Forever down through the ages renowned shall she be.
Fairest in all the land, ever thy name shall stand!
Ever thy sons sing to thee!

The School Hymn

Thy name will we sing, thy praise ever telling,
Thou who in youth keepest watch o'er us all.
In life's gladsome morn, thy spirit compelling,
Thy sons, ever faithful, respond to thy call.

The Chapel Hymn (by Paul Mellon, '25)

From dreams and visions, heaven-sent,
From simple faith and Godly trust,
Great empires, yea, each continent,
Has risen from the dust.

To those who saw this spire arise,
  This composition out of nought
Is like a light from Christ's own eyes,
  A glimpse of Christ's own thought.

And through these doors, continual youth,
  Our sons shall pass in after years,
To hear the beauty of His truth,
  To live His hopes and fears.

The School Prayer

O God, who art the fountain of all wisdom and source of all grace, be present always, we beseech Thee, with this School to direct and bless it. Established in faith in Thee and endowed for the service of truth, may it ever rest under Thy gracious benediction. We pray Thee to use the School for the glory of Christ and to make it a pure fountain of sound knowledge, holy principles, and Godly learning. We beseech Thee to give those who teach here wisdom, patience, discretion and zeal for God and truth; and to those who are taught give manliness and aptness to learn. Make us studious, truthful, pure and temperate in all things, so that by Thy grace the same mind may be in us which is in Christ, that our character may be formed in His Holy likeness. Prosper Thou, O Lord, our labors, and may the good name and influence of this School be handed down from generation to generation for the comfort of this nation and for Thy glory. Amen.

Goals for Each Graduate of Choate

That he be equipped with the skills, techniques and fundamental knowledge necessary for future study.

That he be intellectually alive and concerned to attain wisdom and understanding through continuing study of the arts and sciences.

That he be courageously and responsibly independent, joyous in his commitment to life, honorable in all his dealings, and courteous to all men.

That, aware of his advantages, he be trained and eager to serve his family, his community, his country, and the world to the full extent of his talents and opportunities.

That he be physically fit as well as practiced in good sportsmanship and some athletic skills.

That, looking beyond the merely transitory, fashionable, or superficial, he lead his life in accordance with enduring values.

That reverence towards God and respect for others' religious convictions move him to search out his own spiritual faith and to be true to it.

Appendix C

Courses Offered at Choate

In the spring of 1968, Choate announced the following major courses would be offered in the academic year 1968–1969:

English
Latin
Arabic
French
German
*German 4
*Greek I & II (half courses)
Russian
*Russian 4
Spanish
History 3 (Ancient)
History 4 (Modern)
History 4X (European & American)
History 56 (American)
History 5X (American & European)
*History 7A (Arabic & Islamic)
*History 7R (Russian)
History 8 (Public Affairs)

Mathematics
Biology
Biology II
Chemistry
Chemistry II
Geology
Physics
Physics II
Science 3
*Architectural Drafting
*Engineering Drafting
Art Major
Drama Major

*Applicant must cite alternate in case course is not offered

and the following minor courses:

Art (all forms)

Developmental Reading (extra charge)

Chinese I & II (half courses)
Computer Programming (no credit)
Film Minor (half)
Latin VX (half)
Music Theory
Typewriting (all forms, extra charge, one half year)
Drama Minor (half course)
Etymology
General Design I & II (half courses)
Mechanical Drawing (half)
Sight Singing
Voice Lessons (extra charge)

In addition, fifth and sixth formers are required to attend lecture courses on art, music and religion.

Lessons are offered in piano, organ, violin, cello.

Other new courses were offered provided enough students signed up for them:

Introduction to Economics
Introduction to Philosophy
Introduction to 18th Century Russian Literature
Study of American Minority Groups
American Diplomacy Since World War II
Psychology of Human Development

Appendix D

The article which so incensed the headmaster, written by a boy I have called "John Olson," appeared in the April 27, 1968, issue of the *Choate News:*

WHY YALE TURNED COOL ON CHOATE

If one were to ask the typical prep school student what justifies the existence of a prep school, he would probably answer that the prep school gives him a better chance to gain admissions to the college of his choice. But when this becomes the sole use of a prep school, the educational content of that four year experience suffers and, ironically, so does the college admissions success.

It was a curious phenomenon to see last week that only five students were accepted at Yale University. It particularly puzzled me, and I had a chance to talk to R. Inslee Clark, the Director of Admissions at Yale, about Choate-Yale relations. Undoubtedly, they have cooled in the last ten years to the extent where relatively few boys, perhaps 25 or 30, even apply to Yale.

Mr. Clark offered two reasons for this trend. He said first of all that you can't accept talent if it isn't yours to accept, meaning that Choate's most qualified students usually turn to the other top Ivy League colleges before Yale. More importantly, however, he said that you can't accept talent if it isn't there.

He went on to explain that there are so many qualified students throughout the country that it would be foolish as well as unfair to dote too heavily on Choate. Of the 25,000 secondary schools in the country, Mr. Clark and his admissions staff maintain consistent contact with 8,000 of these schools. Of these 8,000 schools they can only visit personally 1,500 schools. It struck me that so much of the intellectual resources in those 25,000 schools still remained unexplored.

To use an example, he told me that of the 900 members of a senior class down at The Bronx School of Science in New York City, there are about 200 boys whom they should be interested in. So Yale sends two admissions men down to Bronx School of Science at the same time as they send two men up to Choate to talk to thirty applicants.

Most significantly, he tried to explain why, in his mind, the talent just doesn't exist at Choate. He first put his finger on the Choate Admissions Department. Much too much emphasis is placed on the admission of alumni sons, he thinks. This will weaken the content of the student body to begin with; for if you have a loose foundation in the freshman and sophomore years, how can one hope to build anything on it?

In discussing school policy, Mr. Clark had three major suggestions to make. From his experience he said that Choate always seemed to take the defensive whenever a new idea came forth. So first Choate has to stop being defensive in the idea that we have a great school—let's pat ourselves on the back and salute our famous alumni. Secondly, Choate must be experimental; there should be no end to the new ideas that should be tried. Mr. Clark said that he had a mountainous stack of letters from schools around the country, predominantly high schools, asking his opinion on some innovations they want to try. Lastly, Choate must be a "lighthouse" in secondary school education. The high schools have taken over in being the first to offer a new trend. Choate and most prep schools have followed dilatorily behind.

The consequences of being defensive, maintaining the status-quo, and following are disastrous. Enthusiasm, so keenly expressed upon entrance to Choate has been snuffed out by pettiness in the life of the intangible Choate experience. Mr. Clark explained that the idea of a Choate experience or a Yale experience was ridiculous; that if a boy was interested in the problems of the New Haven ghetto, then maybe he should live in the ghetto.

Talking to Mr. Clark and in light of the student expression of interest in national affairs which are more meaningful than the Georgian calm and gentile greenery of the Choate campus, it dawned on me that perhaps Choate graduates are so well-rounded that they simply roll through life without catching any of it.

I would propose that we call in Mr. Clark and other forward-looking educators like him to discuss future possibilities and vowing to ourselves that we won't be defensive. It's not what we can't do but rather what we might do that counts.

Notes

12 The lines from Martin Duberman appear in an essay called "An Experiment in Education," in *The Uncompleted Past* (Random House, 1969), p. 263.

13 "What is real and what is not?": *Mary Poppins Comes Back,* by P. L. Travers (Harcourt, Brace), p. 182.

21 The lines from Cyril Connolly appeared in "Off the Playing Fields," an article in the *Sunday Times* (London), October 6, 1968.

23 "Dating from 1760": *The Handbook of Private Schools* (Boston, 1966), p. 232.

23 "In 1851": *Forty Years at School,* by George St. John (Holt, 1959), p. 64.

24 "Who can say": *Dreamers of the American Dream,* by Stewart H. Holbrook (Doubleday, 1957), p. 19.

24 "Were convicted of witchcraft": *Wallingford Community Guide 1967–1968,* by the Wallingford Jaycees, p. 7.

26 The book Mrs. Rush had just finished is *Who Rules America?* by G. William Domhoff (Prentice-Hall, 1967), p. 17: "The most prestigious of the private schools for boys are probably Groton, St. Paul's, and St. Mark's, but Choate, Hotchkiss, and St. Andrew's are not far behind." Also, *ibid.,* p. 34: "A person is considered to be a member of the upper class if he has attended any one of the private preparatory schools listed below"—a list which includes Choate, but not Exeter and Andover "because of their large minority of scholarship students."

26 "A letter in *Life*": *Life,* October 27, 1967.

46 William Golding's article "Headmasters" appears in *The Hot Gates and Other Occasional Pieces* (Harcourt, Brace & World, 1966).

47 "For cold was generally the result": *Vittorino da Feltre and Other Humanist Educators,* by William Harrison Woodward (Cambridge University Press, 1897; reprinted by Teachers College, Columbia University, 1963), p. 34.

The other information about Vittorino in this paragraph is also drawn from that source.

48 "That word, *gloom*": "Rugby Chapel," by Matthew Arnold (1857).

48 "Used to attack offences": William Golding quotes Clough in *op. cit.*, p. 119.

49 John F. Kennedy's speech at Choate, from which I have quoted excerpts, appears in its entirety in the *Choate Alumni Bulletin*, November, 1946.

53 "To be a schoolmaster": quoted in a memorial written by Roger Burlingame for *The Century Association Yearbook 1967*.

64 "A study of private schools": Third draft of a prospectus, dated October 20, 1967, of "A Study of the American Independent School."

65 Lee A. Du Bridge: *The National Association of Independent Schools Bulletin*, January, 1965.

67 Domhoff, *op. cit.*, p. 17.

81 "A Jesuit priest": Reverend Francis X. Moan, S.J.: "The School in Action: A Visitor's View," in St. Paul's alumni magazine, *Horae*, Summer, 1967.

102 Connolly, *op. cit.*

105 "I walk with him": George St. John, *op. cit.*, p. 151.

139 Father Moan, *op. cit.*

189 "Twenty percent of Yale's class of 1968": *Alumni Board of Yale University Report*, October, 1967.

205 "Yale wants brains" and the figures in this paragraph: *ibid.*

206 The material on John F. Kennedy at Choate, from "Rat Face" to the end of the paragraph, comes from *Triumph and Tragedy: The Story of the Kennedys*, by the Writers, Photographers and Editors of the Associated Press (Morrow, 1968), p. 58.

268 "Covers for frustrations": Mounir Sa'adah in *The National Association of Independent Schools Bulletin*, Vol. 27, No. 2., p. 38.

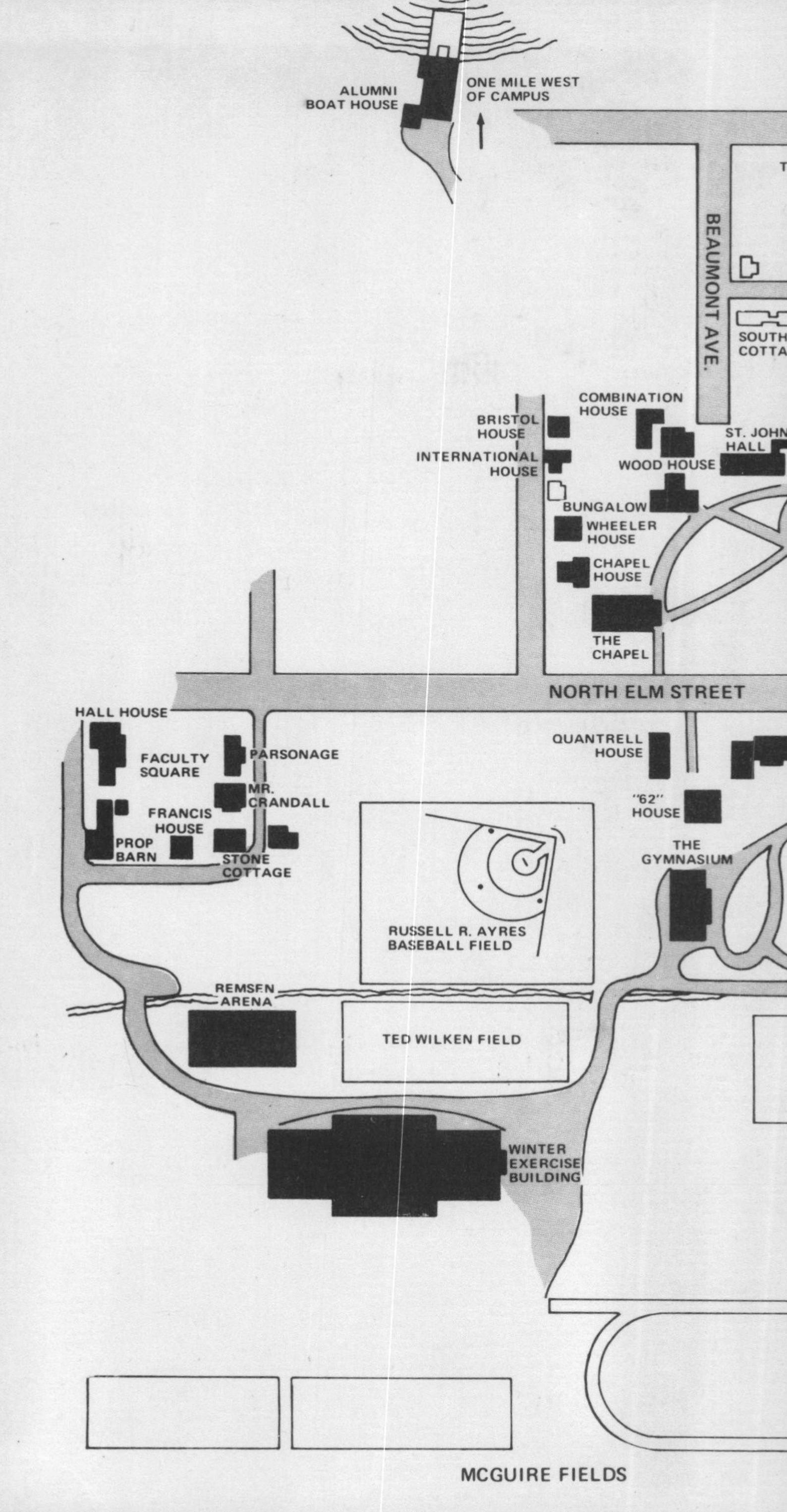

ALUMNI BOAT HOUSE
ONE MILE WEST OF CAMPUS
BEAUMONT AVE.
SOUTH COTTA
COMBINATION HOUSE
BRISTOL HOUSE
INTERNATIONAL HOUSE
ST. JOHN HALL
WOOD HOUSE
BUNGALOW
WHEELER HOUSE
CHAPEL HOUSE
THE CHAPEL
NORTH ELM STREET
HALL HOUSE
FACULTY SQUARE
PARSONAGE
MR. CRANDALL
FRANCIS HOUSE
PROP BARN
STONE COTTAGE
QUANTRELL HOUSE
"62" HOUSE
THE GYMNASIUM
RUSSELL R. AYRES BASEBALL FIELD
REMSEN ARENA
TED WILKEN FIELD
WINTER EXERCISE BUILDING
MCGUIRE FIELDS